The Chinese Love Story from the
Tenth to the Fourteenth Century

SUNY series in Chinese Philosophy and Culture
———————
Roger T. Ames, editor

The Chinese Love Story from the Tenth to the Fourteenth Century

Alister D. Inglis

Cover credit: Fragrant Mouth at Midnight While Watching over the Spirit, from the album Illustrations to the Plum in the Golden Vase (Jinpingmei) (detail). Chinese, 18th century, Qing Dynasty (1644–1911). Album leaf, ink, and color on silk, 15½ × 12½ inches (39.4 × 31.8 cm). The Nelson-Atkins Museum of Art, Kansas City, Missouri. Purchase: William Rockhill Nelson Trust through the George H. and Elizabeth O. Davis Fund, 2006.18.12. Photo: John Lamberton, Nelson Gallery Foundation.

Published by State University of New York Press, Albany

© 2023 State University of New York

All rights reserved

Printed in the United States of America

No part of this book may be used or reproduced in any manner without written permission. No part of this book may be stored in a retrieval system or transmitted in any form or by any means including electronic, electrostatic, magnetic tape, mechanical, photocopying, recording, or otherwise without the prior permission in writing of the publisher.

For information, contact State University of New York Press, Albany, NY
www.sunypress.edu

Library of Congress Cataloging-in-Publication Data

Name: Inglis, Alister David, 1963– author.
Title: The Chinese love story from the tenth to the fourteenth century / Alister D. Inglis.
Description: Albany : State University of New York Press, [2023] | Series: SUNY series in Chinese philosophy and culture | Includes bibliographical references and index.
Identifiers: LCCN 2022032830 | ISBN 9781438492544 (hardcover : alk. paper) | ISBN 9781438492568 (ebook) | ISBN 9781438492551 (pbk. : alk. paper)
Subjects: LCSH: Romance fiction, Chinese—History and criticism. | Love in literature. | Chinese literature—History and criticism. | LCGFT: Literary criticism.
Classification: LCC PL2419.L68 I54 2023 | DDC 895.13/0850904—dc23/eng/20220922
LC record available at https://lccn.loc.gov/2022032830

10 9 8 7 6 5 4 3 2 1

Dedicated with gratitude to Professor David L. Holm

The course of true love never did run smooth.

—Shakespeare

Contents

List of Illustrations	xi
Acknowledgments	xiii
Introduction	1
Chapter 1 The Mid- and Late Tang Dynasty	29
Chapter 2 The Northern Song Dynasty (960–1127)	95
Chapter 3 The Southern Song Dynasty (1127–1279)	161
Chapter 4 The Yuan Dynasty (1279–1368)	209
Conclusion	257
Notes	273
Chinese Character Glossary	303
Works Cited	307
Index	319

Illustrations

Figure 1.1	A Tang dynasty style oxcart.	48
Figure 1.2	Goddess of the Luo River.	82
Figure 1.3	Liu and Ruan meet the immortal women of Mount Tiantai.	83
Figure 2.1	Busy city street scene in the Northern Song capital, Bianliang (Kaifeng).	96
Figure 2.2	Goddess of the Xiang River.	146
Figure 2.3	West Lake, Hangzhou.	148
Figure 3.1	The female Gaze.	182
Figure 4.1	Houses facing a canal in Suzhou.	253

Acknowledgments

This book has been a long time in the making, during which my sabbatical year spent in Taiwan was particularly fruitful. I therefore first wish to thank the Research Institute for the Humanities and Social Sciences, administered by Taiwan's Ministry of Science and Technology, for accepting me as a research fellow. I am particularly grateful to National Taiwan University for accepting me as a visiting scholar. Their facilities, particularly the library system, was essential to my research. Thanks to Professor Lee Long-Shien, then chair of the University's Department of Chinese literature, for making this happen. All this would not have been possible were it not for the Taiwan Fellowship I received from Taiwan's Ministry of Foreign Affairs. I am also very grateful to my readers at SUNY Press, especially Professor James Hargett for his exceptionally thorough reading and excellent suggestions. I would also like to thank my editors at SUNY Press, especially James Peltz. Thanks also to Ms. Jennifer Berry, Rights and Reproductions coordinator at the Freer Gallery of Art and Arthur M. Sackler Gallery, Washington, DC, for permission to reproduce art work from their collection. I am also grateful to the Metropolitan Museum of Art, New York, and the National Palace Museum, Taipei, for making available other artwork in their collections through open access. Last, but not least, I am ever grateful to my wife, Emily, for her sustained domestic support and intellectual companionship without which this book could not have been written.

Introduction

I shall now tell of another woman by the name of Zhu Yingtai, who was a native of Yixing in Changzhou. From an early age, she was given to the pursuit of learning. When she heard that Yuhuang was where civil arts flourished the most, she expressed her wish to pursue her lessons there. But her brother and sister-in-law objected: "In the old days, upon reaching the age of seven, boys and girls were no longer allowed to share the same seat and the same dining table. How preposterous for a sixteen-year-old like you to travel around and get mixed up with men!" (*Point well taken.*)

Yingtai replied: "I have a better idea." Putting a cap on her head and a belt around her waist, she dressed herself up as a man. Even her brother and sister-in-law failed to recognize her when she walked up to them in her new attire.

It was the beginning of summer when Yingtai was ready to set out on her journey. She plucked a branch of blooming pomegranate flowers and, planting them in a flowerbed, prayed to heaven in the words: "As I, Zhu Yingtai, am about to go on a journey for the pursuit of my studies, I pray that this branch will take root and grow leaves every year as long as my good name and chastity remain unsullied. Should anything dishonorable happen to tarnish the family reputation, may this branch wither and die." With this prayer, she crossed the threshold and went on her way, calling herself Master Zhu the Ninth.

She came to cultivate a friendship with a man by the name of Liang Shanbo, a native of Suzhou. The two studied at the same school and, out of a mutual affection and respect, swore an oath of brotherhood. For three years thereafter, they ate together during the day and slept in the same bed at night, without Zhu Yingtai's ever taking off her clothes. There were several times when the puzzled Shanbo asked her a few questions, but each time she got by with evasive answers. Their studies completed by the end of three years, they took leave of each other and went their separate ways, but not before Yingtai made Liang Shanbo promise to visit her in two months' time.

As it was again the beginning of summer upon her return, the pomegranate branch in the flower bed was heavy with flowers and foliage, which convinced her brother and sister-in-law of her unbesmirched purity. An immensely rich man named Ma in the Village of Peace and Happiness heard about the virtues of the ninth daughter of the Zhu family and asked a matchmaker to approach Yingtai's brother, who readily gave his consent. The preliminaries were completed and the wedding ceremony was scheduled for the second month of the following year. The truth of the matter was that Yingtai was in love with Shanbo and was biding her time until his visit to reveal her plans. Little did she know that Shanbo was detained by some business at home. She did not presume to suggest postponement of the wedding, for fear that her brother and sister-in-law would suspect her motives.

It was not until the tenth month that Shanbo set out on his journey, six months late. Upon his arrival at the Zhu manor, he was told by a tenant upon his inquiry about Master Zhu the Ninth that there was no one by that name in the manor unless he meant Zhu the Ninth Daughter, Suspecting that something was amiss, Shanbo submitted his visiting card whereupon a maid appeared and led him into the main hall, where whom did Shanbo see but Zhu Yingtai herself in full womanly attire. Shanbo was astounded. Only then did he realize that Yingtai was a woman who had been disguised all along. He reproached himself for not having been discerning enough to guess the truth. After an exchange of conventional amenities, he raised the subject of marriage. Yingtai declined, saying she had already been betrothed to Mr. Ma by her brother and sister-in-law. Bitter remorse swept over Shanbo for having arrived too late.

After Shanbo returned home, he pined away until he died in his sickbed as the year drew to a close. His parents buried him at the intersection leading to the Village of Peace and Happiness, as he had requested. The following year, as Yingtai's wedding procession approached that intersection on its way to the Ma residence, there sprang up a savage blast of wind that darkened the sky, preventing the procession from moving on. As Yingtai raised her eyes, there wafted up into her view Liang Shanbo himself, saying, "I died of lovesickness for you and I am buried at this very spot. For old times' sake, please step out of the sedan chair and take a look." As Yingtai did so, the ground split open with a loud bang, leaving a ten-feet wide [sic] gap, into which she threw herself. Her clothes, which followers in the procession tried to grab, flew off in pieces, like skin sloughed off by a cicada. The next moment, the sky cleared. The crack in the ground was found to be no wider than a thread, and the sedan chair was seen resting right by Liang Shanbo's tomb. Now the realization came that the two sworn brothers in life were now husband and wife in death. Eyes then turned to the floating pieces of Yingtai's clothing, which changed into a pair of colorful butterflies. As the legend has it, it was the spirits of the couple that had changed into butterflies, the red one being Liang Shanbo, the black one being Zhu Yingtai. The species multiplied and spread throughout the land and are, to this day, still called Liang Shanbo and Zhu Yingtai. A later poet left behind these words of praise:

> For three years they shared their days and nights;
> Their marriage bond was fulfilled only after death.
> Blame not Shanbo for overlooking the truth;
> Praise Yingtai instead for her unflinching virtue.[1]

Given the paranormal event at the story's conclusion, the two lovers are commonly referred to as the "Butterfly Lovers." This charming story is perhaps the most famous of all Chinese love stories. It was adapted for numerous traditional operas, songs, ballads and, as recently as 1963, the Shaw brothers of Hong Kong produced a cinematic version. Such has been its enduring popularity that, in 2006, six Chinese cities collaboratively applied to the United Nations Educational, Scientific and Cultural Organization for the story to be recognized as a Masterpiece of the Oral and Intangible Heritage of Humanity.[2]

The "Butterfly Lovers" is part of a prolific literary tradition known as the scholar-beauty genre, popular throughout the seventeenth, eighteenth and nineteenth centuries.[3] Such stories typically recount romantic affairs between educated young men and beautiful young women. While the "Butterfly Lovers" concluded tragically, many featured happy endings. Detailed plot development and frequent inclusion of the lover's poetry made for relatively lengthy narratives not unlike novellas in the West. To be sure, when one thinks of love stories in the Chinese cultural context, these scholar-beauty romances may immediately come to mind.

Although their heyday spanned the closing centuries of late imperial China, scholar-beauty romances owe an enormous debt to the short stories of a much earlier period, the Tang dynasty (618–906), when many of China's most famous and endearing love stories were written. Almost always taking young men as their chief protagonists, these stories narrate men's fleeting affairs with various types of women, including courtesans, concubines, inn keepers, fox-fairies, daughters, and palace ladies. Love stories of this period were considerably shorter than those of the scholar-beauty genre and their plots less formulaic. In fact, the mid-Tang dynasty (late eighth to early ninth centuries)[4] was a golden age in regard to several literary genres, during which time the short story attained an unprecedented level of sophistication. Throughout the centuries following the fall of the Tang, love stories continued to be produced. Besides oral renditions, written versions filled many short story collections while some anthologies focused exclusively on romantic love.

While both Tang dynasty short stories and the late imperial scholar-beauty romances have attracted extensive scholarly attention, love stories of the intervening era—some five hundred years—have been comparatively neglected. So as to help bridge this considerable gap, this book aims to trace the development of the short, classical language (as opposed to vernacular) love story throughout the period—that is, the Song (960–1279) and Yuan (1279–1368) dynasties. Contextualizing selected, individual stories in a continuum between the Tang and late imperial periods will afford an overview from which this important literary corpus may be compared and evaluated. My primary focus is the love story's dynamic nature over time. Questions I would like to address include: What are the major reoccurring themes, motifs, and plot devices? How did the love story as a literary corpus thematically develop throughout this period? Can new themes be attributable to a particular time period and, if so, how might this reflect contemporary social, political, and intellectual trends? How can thematic change help evaluate the status of the period's love stories vis-à-vis Chinese literary history? Answering these questions will not only enhance our understanding of the love story's development but also that of the short story in general. It will also complement existing research focused on both Tang and late imperial narrative literature. As Richard Wang has observed, "Only by revealing the influence that earlier stories had on Ming fiction and drama can we understand the real significance of, and the new ideas in, Ming fiction and drama."[5] Daniel Hsieh makes a similar point when addressing the importance of the Tang dynasty love story vis-à-vis Chinese literary history: "One part of the story can only be fully understood in the context of the whole."[6] In other words, understanding both Tang and late imperial love stories as having developed in relation to a sustained literary tradition will offer a better basis on which to understand them. Hence, this study has implications for the study of Chinese literature outside of the love story corpus and beyond the period under study.

Neglect of Song dynasty short stories has been largely due to the prejudice of China's May Fourth–period (1919 through the 1920s) intellectuals, particularly the influential fiction writer and scholar Zhou Shuren (1881–1936), better known by his pen name, Lu Xun. In his extensively quoted *Short History of Chinese Fiction* (*Zhongguo xiaoshuo shilüe*) and his *Historical Changes in Chinese Fiction* (*Zhongguo xiaoshuode lishi yanbian*), Zhou belittled Song dynasty (960–1276) classical language short stories while extoling those of the Tang. "Stories of the strange written by authors of the Song period are insipid and lack literary polish. Their short stories tend to focus on old stories while avoiding the contemporary. Their imitation of the earlier tradition falls short and, moreover, lacks innovation."[7] Elsewhere, Zhou writes, "Authors of the Tang largely described contemporary affairs whereas those of the Song mainly spoke of old stories. Where Tang period fiction contains infrequent didactic content, that of the Song was largely didactic."[8] When praising the literature of the "common people" (*pingmin*), which he contrasts to classical language stories written by the elite, Zhou further opines, "In regard to innovation, the scholar-officials of the Song really offered no contribution."[9] Given Zhou's enormous stature as both a leftist writer and scholar, particularly in the People's Republic of China, his opinion on the Song dynasty short story has proven immensely influential. Hardly a scholarly paper published in the People's Republic that addresses traditional literature does not pay him homage. Another important May Fourth–period scholar, Zheng Zhenduo (1898–1958), all but ignored the Song dynasty's classical language short stories in both his pioneering anthology of traditional Chinese fiction and critical work on its history.[10] Yet, Zhou's disparagement and Zheng's disregard undoubtedly have more to do with their own values and the May Fourth cultural agenda than inherent deficiencies in the Song dynasty literature itself. Critical of how traditional Chinese culture had supposedly impeded China's political and economic development, May Fourth intellectuals overwhelmingly rejected tradition as they looked to Western ideas for modernization. Confucian thought became the target of particular vehement criticism for its moral conservatism, considered the antithesis of modern, Western, progressive values. It was in such an intellectual background that Zhou Shuren wrote his literary history. In view of the value he evidently attached to generic and conceptual innovation as enshrined by modern Western aesthetic theories, Zhou clearly used such concepts to measure the significance of traditional literary works. His appraisal of Tang dynasty stories was, furthermore, colored by his view that its authors were consciously creating fiction, as opposed to the Song dynasty tendency to narrate historically reliable events.[11] Given that short stories of the Song period generally remained formalistically unchanged in comparison to their Tang precursors, Zhou accordingly underrated them. His binary of elite versus popular literature and his disparagement of the former further reveals his Leftist intellectual bias.[12]

Nevertheless, given the vastly different social and intellectual environment under which literature of the Song and Yuan dynasties was written, it is hardly surprising that its forms and conventions do not equate to modern notions of good literature. Authors and storytellers of the period were not necessarily concerned with stylistic or formalistic innovation, which became an all-important standard to measure artistic merit only in the modern world. Even a cursory reading of the period's stories reveal that its authors harbored vastly different concerns and intentions than their post–Romantic era counterparts, who often subscribed to the idea of art for art's sake—that is, art devoid of utilitarian value. As Li Shiren argues, placing undue importance on artistic and stylistic features as an evaluative tool vis-à-vis Tang versus Song dynasty narrative literature contributes little to the field.[13] Indeed, as I will discuss below, the very concept of fiction and authorship during the Song and Yuan dynasties vastly differed from that of the May Fourth era.

If Zhou Shuren did not value short stories of the Song period, Ming-dynasty writers and storytellers certainly did. It is highly significant that leading authors of vernacular fiction, such as Feng Menglong (1574–1646) and Ling Mengchu (1580–1644), based their short stories on earlier classical language versions, notably those of the Song and Yuan. Similarly, numerous playwrights of the Yuan and Ming (1368–1644) dynasties adapted both earlier and contemporary classical language stories for their plays and operas, many of which became equally—if not better—known than their sources.[14] Therefore, as Cheng Yizhong perceptively observes, "Without short classical language stories of the Song period, there would be no short classical stories of the Yuan or Ming dynasties, nor could one explain the rise of *Liaozhai's Records of the Strange* (*Liaozhai zhiyi*) during the Qing period."[15] The fact that short classical language stories of the

Song and Yuan were extensively borrowed and rewritten both within and outside the genre attests to their importance for traditional men of letters. I would, therefore, take Cheng's assertion further and say that without the short classical stories of the Song and Yuan period, there could not have been new genres such as vernacular fiction or, indeed, operas, given the enormous debt the latter owed the former.

Despite the general neglect of the Song and Yuan short story, some admirable studies have been undertaken, particularly in the People's Republic of China among which the work of Li Jianguo is especially notable. Li's extensive coverage of not only the Song and Yuan dynasties, but also other periods, is a rare achievement for one scholar. His in-depth analysis of individual stories within their historical backgrounds, together with his painstaking research on textual history, constitute a major contribution to the field. Similarly, Cheng Yizhong's authoritative and wide-ranging analysis of several major narrative genres spanning several periods is no less significant. His work on Chinese opera is also noteworthy. Together with Li Jianguo, he clearly enjoys Song and Yuan dynasty narrative literature and approaches the topic with insight and sensitivity. In Taiwan, the work of Yu Shiu-yun deserves a special mention. Her volume on Song dynasty classical short stories proved especially valuable for my own research, given her attention to the love story. Unlike most scholars from the People's Republic, Yu is justifiably critical of Zhou Shuren's role in the general neglect of Song dynasty short stories. Her detailed overview of the most important individual stories and anthologies has provided an important basis for anyone interested in the narrative literature of the period.[16] Nevertheless, literary studies produced in both Taiwan and the People's Republic tend to present broad overviews of a particular period's literature or else focus exclusively on one text. Others are largely bibliographic in nature. Literary histories organized by dynasty tend to arbitrarily divide the period under study into formative, high, and declining stages while overlooking developmental continuity across dynastic boundaries. In other words, period divisions are based on political, not literary, history.

The current study, while recognizing the importance of dynastic division as an organizational principle, traces the thematic development of the short story over the course of several dynasties. New developments are analyzed in the context of this broad trajectory rather than within an arbitrary timeframe offered by a single dynasty. Given the considerable quantity of extant Song and Yuan narrative literature and its generic diversity, focusing on romantic love enables me to reduce the study's scope to manageable proportions. Moreover, while the importance of love as a literary theme has been widely recognized, in view of its enduring popularity, sustained production over several centuries, intertextual affinities, formulaic plot devices, not to mention its extensive influence, the love story deserves recognition as a corpus of literature—a genre, perhaps—in its own right, similar to the way in which the Gothic has been considered a genre in the Western literary tradition. Therefore, a specialist study of the love story for the underrated Song and Yuan is sorely needed.

Since the mid- and late Tang dynasty acted as a formative period for the short classical story, a concise overview of Tang period works is necessary before analyzing later ones. Such a survey will reveal several reoccurring themes and plot devices that were adopted and transformed by later storytellers. Tang love stories will, therefore, act as a crucial point of comparison with those of the Song and Yuan. Such an approach will enable us to identify and evaluate new themes. Accordingly, chapter 1 will survey mid- to late Tang dynasty love stories, synthesizing the work of others while offering my own insights. Song dynasty stories discussed in chapters 2 and 3 will then be compared with those of the earlier period. Similarly, stories of the Yuan and early Ming periods discussed in chapter 4 will be compared with earlier ones, thereby tracing the thematic development of the love story from the eighth to the fourteenth century—some seven hundred years of the Chinese love story. Stories have been selected based on thematic innovation. In other words, what new ideas they contribute to the development of the corpus rather than literary polish *per se*. Hence, not all of them represent the best-written examples. Such a comparative approach will evaluate the literary works in question within their own literary tradition, rather than impose modern theory developed under differing cultural and economic circumstances. While this approach is not unique to the field, the systematic comparison of the same literary corpus over a period of several dynasties distinguishes this study from similar ones of limited scope.

Although professional female storytellers existed during Song times and women participated in informal storytelling networks, all extant written stories—as far as we know—were recorded by educated, upper-class males. Accordingly, an analysis of the way in which both class and gender influenced the male author-compiler's portrayal of women forms an important aspect of this study. While it is tempting to consider women's portrayal as an authentic reflection of social reality, the male storyteller's[17] mediation cannot be ignored. As Paul Rouzer has observed in the context of Tang dynasty narrative literature, "women were more than objects of desire. They were pawns in marriage alliances, cement for the social bonds of friendship or political faction, and prizes that allowed for competition and male display. The vast quantity of Tang informal narrative provides a rich source for social history (women's history in particular), but also continues to illustrate male concerns and provides not so much a mirror for Tang society as a key to male writers' dreams and obsessions."[18] Rouzer's insightful recognition of the gendered storyteller during the Tang dynasty is, to an extent, relevant to the Song and Yuan. Accordingly, my close reading of selected examples attends to both gendered and class aspects of authorship. Related questions I would like to address are these: How were women portrayed? How accurate might such a portrayal be when measured against what we know about social history? What does the portrayal of women tell us about male storytellers: their identity, anxieties, and fantasies?

Historical Overview: The Early Tradition

Outlines of many famous love stories may be found in historical works since at least the Han dynasty (207 BCE–220 CE). Among the earliest is King Mu of the Kingdom of Qin's legendary meeting with the Queen Mother of the West, a Daoist deity thought to reside in China's distant west.[19] Similarly, there is King Huai of Chu's sexual encounter with the Goddess of Witch's Mountain. On the morning after, when the King inquired as to the Goddess's identity, she professed to be none other than the morning clouds and evening rain. Henceforth the term "clouds and rain" became a ubiquitous euphemism for sexual intercourse.[20] Imperial prince Cao Zhi's (192–232), frequently cited poem about an elusive encounter with the Goddess of the Luo River also influenced later works.[21] Unlike King Huai's experience, no physical union followed this goddess's brief appearance, although the poet's sexual yearning is clear. Indeed given the quest for immortality during the centuries preceding the Tang dynasty, numerous anecdotes circulated about fantastical affairs between elite males and female goddesses, premised on the idea that divine women could confer longevity on their sexual partners. During a time when some men attempted to gain eternal life through alchemical means or sexual hygiene techniques, copulation with a goddess was none other than a shortcut to immortality.[22] The legend of the Oxherd and Weaver Maid is a very old example whose protagonist is not of elite status. The Weaver Maid was originally a handmaiden of the aforementioned Queen Mother of the West. After she came to earth and had an affair with the humble Oxherd, as a punishment the Queen Mother transformed them into stars: the bright star in Altair and the star Vega, respectively. Separated by the Milky Way, they were permitted only one meeting per year, on the seventh day of the seventh lunar month when a bridge of magpies enabled them to cross the "Heavenly River"—that is, the Milky Way. This is the basis of the *tanabata* festival in Japan.

Yet other historical accounts recorded love affairs between human subjects, such as the elopement of the celebrated Han dynasty poet, Sima Xiangru (179–117 BCE), and Zhuo Wenjun (fl. second c. BCE), the young, widowed daughter of Sima's wealthy benefactor. The couple eloped after Wenjun spied on Sima from behind a blind as he performed music for her father. Confronted with the father's anger, the couple were forced to keep a tavern until a reconciliation could be effected. Another famous story recounts the clandestine affair between the handsome Han Shou (d. 300?) and his lover, Jia Wu, that came to light only when Jia Wu's rare and long-lasting incense was detected on Han's sleeves.[23] Perennial favorites such as these were extensively retold throughout the centuries and eventually became pervasive intertextual markers in later poetry and stories.

Not all early narratives celebrated human love or attainment of immortality through sex with a goddess. Short stories about the "supernatural,"[24] known as *zhiguai* (literally "recording the paranormal"), the writing of which flourished from the fifth century onward, tended to portray pre- and extramarital sex as morally and physically dangerous. Accordingly, male protagonists would unwittingly enter into carnal affairs with beautiful young women only to discover that their lover was a ghost or demon in disguise. Without timely intervention by friends or ritual specialists, the protagonist's lust would often result in death. Seductive female fox-spirits with the ability to assume human form also constituted dangerous sexual partners in these stories. Less frequently, women were seduced by shape-changing male foxes and other were-creatures, or else gods, ghosts, and demons, often with similarly fatal consequences. A major apparent function of such didactic tracts was to deter elite readers—especially male—from engaging in illicit sex. In a patriarchal society which criminalized pre- and extramarital sex among the commoner and upper classes and which strove to ensure the unsullied transmission of the male genealogical line, such stories—exceptions notwithstanding—helped uphold orthodox values.

New Developments

In contrast to the ubiquitous *zhiguai* tradition, the mid–Tang dynasty witnessed a paradigmatic shift in literary production that Stephen Owen has termed the "culture of romance."[25] Coinciding with the "development of individual acts of interpretation or valuation and the demarcation of private space," men of letters began to valorize romantic love between human protagonists, often without reference to the paranormal.[26] Henceforth love poems and songs were composed, sung, and disseminated according to this new discursive practice. Short prose stories examined freely chosen romantic attachments, as opposed to customary arranged marriages. Even funerary inscriptions sometimes addressed one's romantic life.[27] For the Harvard-trained scholar Hong Yue, this was a "burgeoning counter-culture" in which "officials were celebrated as devoted lovers," as distinct from filial sons or righteous civil servants. Likewise, "esteemed literati recollected their associations with courtesans in their youth, and gifted poets wrote of themselves as participants in romantic affairs."[28] Paul Rouzer similarly observes how women became more important as literary topics during this period."[29]

Howard Levy links the emergence of love poetry and exploration of amorous themes in narrative literature to the rise of "individualist thought" during the Tang-era. He explains how, in contrast to the post–Han dynasty period (third to sixth centuries) during which aristocratic families tended to marry exclusively among themselves, the Tang-era's influential aristocratic clans were officially censured for this practice. In fact, these illustrious clans were at one time forbidden to intermarry, although sustained enforcement proved problematic. Levy argues that a new attitude toward romantic love emerged in which rigidly demarcated class boundaries were not always observed. Consequently, romantic themes became common topics for the storyteller's writing brush.[30] As Levy does not provide historically grounded evidence, it is nevertheless unclear whether he bases his argument on the love stories themselves.

Although liaisons between humans and paranormal beings were not expunged from short stories of the period and the recording of such phenomena as a separate genre continued, from about the early ninth century onward, love stories were freed from the shadow of the paranormal, particularly in its didactic form. Fresh themes and authorial concerns informed the new stories, such as female fidelity, romantic freedom of choice, marital predestiny, and the like. Although a strong, didactic tenor may still be discerned in many, the focus shifted from moralistic warnings premised on the belief in ghosts and retribution to a more complex exploration of human desire and morality. This new approach even affected the writing of *zhiguai* stories. Dai Fu's (fl. mid- to late eighth century) *zhiguai* collection titled *Extensive Collection of the Strange* (*Guangyi ji*) includes several stories in which young men have affairs with deceased young women who later come back to life and marry their self-chosen lovers.[31] Such stories rarely, if at all, appeared before the late eighth century.[32]

As noted above, after the fall of the Tang dynasty, the oral telling and recording of love stories continued throughout the Song and Yuan period. New stories purportedly based on contemporary gossip were circulated, while old ones were repeatedly anthologized. Many fine collections from the Tang-Song dynastic transition period have survived. Fan Shu's (fl. late ninth century) *Conversations beside Cloud Creek* (*Yunxi youyi*), for example, contains short stories on diverse themes, including romantic love. Similarly, both Chen Han's (fl. ninth century) *Collection of Strange Tales Heard* (*Yiwen ji*) and Pei Xing's (825–880) no longer extant *Transmitting the Remarkable* (*Chuanqi*) included many famous love stories. Zhang Junfang's (fl. early eleventh century) milestone, *Collected Love Stories* (*Liqing ji*), is the first extant (redacted) compilation to specialize in love stories. Following these, many others were produced throughout the three hundred or so years that spanned the Song dynasty, with extant collections from the twelfth century being particularly numerous. Among these, Liu Fu's (1040–after 1113) *High-Minded Conversations beside the Green Lattice Window* (*Qingsuo gaoyi*) is a treasure house of well-written, sophisticated short stories, many of which focus on love. Li Xianmin's (fl. twelfth century) *Comprehensive Record of the Cloud Studio* (*Yunzhai guanglu*) is a topically arranged short story collection that includes two chapters categorized as "love stories"— that is, *liqing*, an identical term that also appears in Zhang Junfang's title. *New Stories from a Green Lattice Window* (*Lüchuang xinhua*), written under the pseudonym Romance Master of the Imperial Capital (Huangdu fengyue zhuren), likely compiled in the late twelfth century or somewhat later, is another exclusive collection of love stories, as is Luo Ye's (dates uncertain) *Drunken Man's Talk* (*Xinbian zuiweng tanlu*). Miscellaneous

Stories from the Green (*Zhiqing zashuo*), attributed to the famous man of letters and statesman, Wang Mingqing (1127–after 1214), also contains several well-written love stories. Besides these notable works, a perusal of Song dynasty bibliographies reveals several other no-longer-extant collections whose titles strongly suggest a focus on romance. For example, *Stories from a Green Lattice Window* (*Lüchuang jishi*), cited by later anthologists, appears to have been a mid-thirteenth-century work. The *Trousseaus Recorded with a Brush* (*Bilian lu*), written around the mid- to late eleventh century, appears to have been another.

Although the circulation of love stories continued throughout the fourteenth century, few survive. The late thirteenth and fourteenth centuries were a formative period for opera, and this may partially explain the dearth of surviving short stories, as men of letters tended to have produced love stories in genres other than the short story. The longest and most detailed love story, *Bella and Scarlett* (*Jiao Hong ji*), was nevertheless produced during this period. Several short story anthologies were compiled in the early years of the Ming dynasty, foremost among which is the famous *New Stories Told while Trimming the Lamp-Wick* (*Jiandeng xinhua*), which spurred several copycat compilations. While the reasons for such copious literary production are complex and not unworthy of a separate study, suffice to note here is the sustained and widespread interest in the love story over the course of several centuries.

The Traditional Status and Bibliographical Classification of Love Stories and the Concept of Authorship

Most love stories were written in a structurally homogenous genre known as *chuanqi*. The term was first coined by Pei Xing as a title for his aforementioned short story collection, although not in a generic sense. The term was first used generically by poet and writer Yu Ji (1272–1348) when referring to the practice of Tang authors who composed narratives to match poetry—that is, both a poem and a narrative may have been produced on a given topic. Many short stories were written in this way.[33] Translated literally as "transmitting the remarkable," Chinese scholars of the May Fourth period adopted the term *chuanqi* to label short prose narratives ranging from 800 to approximately 3,500 characters in length.[34] They were written in classical Chinese, which was to the Chinese literary tradition what Latin was to Europe after the fall of the Roman Empire—that is, the written language of the educated elite as opposed to the spoken vernacular. As its conventions were developed and atrophied centuries before the Common Era, an increasingly wide gap opened between classical and spoken forms over time. Accordingly, the worldview projected in such texts is mediated through the mindset of the educated, male elite. Although *chuanqi*-type short stories acted as a vehicle for many of China's most influential love narratives, their content was broad ranging and included diverse subjects, such as martial artists, historical narratives, and paranormal occurrences. Nevertheless, a marked focus on humanistic themes characterized the genre.[35]

From the eleventh century onward, bibliographers classified texts characterized by modern scholars as *zhiguai* and *chuanqi* under the larger rubric of *xiaoshuo*, or "petty stories," itself a highly amorphous category. In terms of content, *xiaoshuo* was a catch-all category for an enormous body of heterogeneous literary work that included narratives, textual criticism, historiography, anecdotes, humor, and the like. Given its enormous breadth of subject matter, it is difficult—if not impossible—to define the term *xiaoshuo* as a literary genre according to modern formalistic methods. During the Song and Yuan dynasties, works considered *xiaoshuo* had already been subsumed into a quadripartite bibliographical taxonomy. First in this schema were the Confucian classics, a canonical set of texts purportedly related to Confucius that remained unchanged. Next were official histories, reflecting the high status that historical works enjoyed in traditional China. The remaining two categories were "philosophers" and *belles letters*, respectively. *Xiaoshuo* works were generally catalogued under "philosophers," itself an eclectic assortment of heterogeneous writing ranging from what may be understood as philosophical treatises to works on agriculture.

Although proponents of the May Fourth literary revolution employed the term *xiaoshuo* to denote "fiction" in the modern, Western sense,[36] the term's pre-twentieth-century connotation is fundamentally dissimilar. In line with Confucius's famous remark that he was a transmitter rather than a creator, the transmission of purportedly "true" events was common in imperial China. Accordingly, storytellers throughout the Song and Yuan tended to base their written stories on orally circulated gossip, hearsay or, in the words of Howard Levy, "on actual historical episodes."[37] Versions proliferated, particularly in their oral forms, but even supposedly fixed, written texts exhibit considerable variation. As is often the case with gossip, stories were gradually embroidered, improvised, filtered through a variety of dissimilar worldviews, and adapted to suit new contexts until they were recorded. In this chain of oral transmission, much unreliable detail was undoubtedly added while original events became distorted. Occasionally, a story preserved in a lost book was even recorded from memory.[38] Under such circumstances, imperfect memory may well have been occasionally responsible for inaccurate transmission. Contemporary readers, recognizing the possibility of factually spurious content, evaluated the reliability and plausibility of what they heard and read in their prefaces, metatextual and marginal commentaries, as well as anecdotal jottings.

Nevertheless, stories were sometimes consciously fabricated. Indeed, the famous aforementioned man of letters, Zhang Junfang, was reportedly assaulted in the street by the son of a man whom he had portrayed as a reincarnated turtle in one of his *zhiguai* accounts.[39] Similarly, in the renowned Tang dynasty *chuanqi* story "Tale of the White Ape," historical dates were manipulated to slander a famous courtier.[40] The renowned statesman, historian, and collector of anomalous accounts, Hong Mai (1123–1202), told how a storyteller attempted to pass off a wholly fabricated story as factually true.[41] In a preface to the third installment of his *zhiguai* collection, *Record of the Listener* (*Yijian zhi*), where he expresses regret for the factual inaccuracy of some of his stories, he remarks, "[after citing several story titles] are all largely unlike [the facts] and even border on the slander of good people." He shortly after says, "This is probably partly due to the fault of the tellers, and partly due to my listening and not having verified the details—for this I am deeply ashamed."[42] Here, then, is an admission to the factual unreliability of Song dynasty short stories by an author-compiler who boldly claimed that stories that he spent his lifetime collecting and recording recounted real-life events.[43]

Despite the possibility of fabrication and factual unreliability, readers throughout the Song and Yuan tended to interpret narratives literally—that is, based on what they considered more or less a factually reliable source or chain of events.[44] Even prior to this period, readers and compilers of the Tang and Six dynasties tended to understand narrative in a similar way.[45] Ming Dong Gu characterizes this tendency as "the tyranny of history"— that is, prior to the late sixteenth century, official historiography was so esteemed that the reading and writing of narrative was largely justified by claims of historical factuality.[46] In the context of Tang dynasty storytelling, Sarah M. Allen understands such a discursive and interpretive approach as one of "documentary intent"—that is, "events recounted may not have actually happened, but the recorder probably believes that they did and recounts them with the expectation that his audience will take them at face value."⁴⁷ Accordingly, the famous poet and statesman Su Shi (1037–1101) read the ninth-century "Story of Yingying" as biographical and considered Zhang Ji (765–830) its historical male protagonist.⁴⁸ The twelfth-century author Wang Zhi (dates uncertain), rejecting this attribution, argued that the protagonist was none other than its recorder, the famous poet Yuan Zhen (779–831), a viewpoint that remains influential today.⁴⁹

An end commentary to one of Shen Liao's (1023–1085) stories superbly illustrates this phenomenon. In chapter 8 of his *Cloud Nest Compilation* (*Yunchao bian*), Shen records a story titled "Miss Ren She's Story," which tells of how a courtesan serving the Southern Tang court, just prior to its annexation by the Song state, was commanded to seduce Tao Gu (903–970), a diplomat sent by the Song emperor. Historical sources testify to Tao's hypocritically serious nature. So as to discredit him, the Tang ruler, in collaboration with his minister Han Xizai (902–970), sent a courtesan to seduce him. After spending a night with the courtesan, Tao composed a commemorative lyric poem that circulated widely and, indirectly, exposed his indiscretion. At the conclusion of the narrative, Shen remarks: "When I first heard of Tao's lyric, the events leading to it were said to have occurred in the North. I did not quite believe it. To be sure, from what we may infer from the lyric's import, events should have occurred elsewhere. When I heard about the Renwang Temple and one of my guests related the story from beginning to end, I recorded it since it was different from what I had previously heard. I have heard of many such cases whereby courtesans have donated to temples."⁵⁰ Several aspects of Song and Yuan period storytelling may be gleaned from this small snippet. First, the written record is based on oral telling, probably having passed through several hands before Shen heard it. The narrative was circulated together with a poem; as noted above, this was a common aspect of narrative production. Shen's initial disbelief demonstrates his tendency to read the lyric and its associated narrative literally—that is, as having a factual basis. It was only after he "verified" the story's historical foundation that he considered it worthy of recording. The convincing detail for Shen was the existence of the Renwang Temple, for whose construction the courtesan was said to have donated money in her middle age. Shen considers this plausible based on his existing knowledge. Finally, although Tao Gu was a historical personage who would have been known to men of Shen's generation, even though his lyric circulated widely, news of his peccadilloes with the courtesan was evidently not well known given the passage of time. This would explain the discrepancy between the courtesan's historical name, Qin Ruolan, and the narrative's heroine, Miss Ren She. Shen's ultimate motivation to record the story was the new information it offered. This is but one example of how stories of the period were circulated and recorded.

The persistent tendency to read literally may further be seen in the famous bibliophile and literary critic Hu Yinglin's (1551–1602) discussion of *zhiguai* accounts. When assessing the literary merit of tenth-century author-compiler Xu Xuan's (915–991) *Investigation into the Spirit World* (*Jishen lu*), Hu blames Xu's guests for spinning spurious stories in order to curry favor. Hu similarly criticizes Hong Mai's overreliance on informants for his massive twelfth-century collection of paranormal accounts, *Record of the Listener* (*Yijian zhi*). So as to substantiate his assertion, Hu cites several examples of stories found in either Xu or Hong's compilations that were largely identical to earlier ones. He concludes that the tellers simply changed the names and dates, thereby fooling the two author-compilers who unwittingly recounted old stories as new. Hu's reasoning that the existence of an earlier story discredits the historical veracity of a later one reveals an expectation that the latter should be unique and, therefore, have a historical basis. His emphasis on the reliability of a written text is also interesting because it disregards possible mutability introduced by oral sources.[51]

Given that stories generally circulated orally as gossip before being recorded, and that both tellers and recorders alike, influenced by historiographic practice, tended to receive and relate such material with "documentary intent," the modern Western notion of a single, self-autonomous "author" is largely irrelevant. The "author," in most cases, was merely the recorder. This is not to say that men of letters did not fabricate stories, as illustrated above. In this respect, Zhou Shuren's idea that Tang dynasty writers were beginning to "consciously create fiction" (*yi wei xiaoshuo zhe*) is, to an extent, justified.[52] Nonetheless, intentional fabrication appears to be the exception. Much more common was well- or ill-intentioned elaboration of stories as both written and oral versions proliferated. Therefore, as Wilt Idema has observed, it is not accurate to speak of Chinese "fiction" in the modern sense until the large-scale importing of Western ideas into China during the early twentieth century.[53] Cognizant that individual recorders relied on a wide network of informal storytellers and gossips, I replace "author" with terms such as "storyteller," "recorder," and "author-compiler" throughout this study. Well-known historian and statesman Hong Mai is a case in point. Hong spent most of his life collecting and recording paranormal events that he complied into the aforementioned 420-chapter serial, *Record of the Listener*. Hundreds of storytellers from diverse class backgrounds provided him with material over a vast geographic area.[54] As Hong was not a professional storyteller, his discursive practice may be understood as informal storytelling. Nevertheless, we know that Hong's magnum opus was later consulted by professional storytellers; that is, numerous professionals utilized it as a source for oral stories that they related to paying customers (presumably both elite and non-elite) in the marketplaces and specialized urban entertainment centers.[55] My understanding of traditional short stories is, therefore, premised on the idea that (1) they tended to be read literally given their purported factual basis, and (2) they circulated in both oral and written forms akin to common gossip, notwithstanding exceptional cases.[56]

The fact that stories recorded by an amateur story collector based on an informal network of raconteurs and gossips ultimately provided the material for professionals blurs the boundary between "popular" and "elite," "professional" and "informal," and "oral" and "written" in the literature of the period.[57] In the twelfth century, what were initially "popular" (among the general populous) stories became "elite" (Hong Mai and his upper-class peers), and what were "elite" returned to the "popular" (the professional storytellers' general audience). The late Ming dynasty play "Encouragement for Goodness" is another example. Based on the popular Buddhist story of Mulian, the storyline was heard and recorded by a minor literary figure, Zheng Zhizhen (fl. 1582), during a visit to Anhui. After initially circulating in manuscript form, popularity led to its publication. Some decades later, it was again being performed in villages to a general (popular) audience. As Anne McLaren notes, the "play is thus an example of a work which was derived from the villages, rewritten by a literati figure, circulated in manuscript form then published by someone who is aware of popular demand."[58] Given the symbiotic relationship between popular and elite raconteurs, I would therefore argue that, in regard to the classical language short stories of the Song and Yuan, it makes little sense to distinguish between "popular" (*tongsu xiaoshuo*) literature and that of the educated elite.

As noted above, *xiaoshuo* as a discursive practice was accorded comparatively low status by the intellectual elite. It is therefore not surprising that author-compilers of short stories tended to avoid metatextual discussions about it. This, however, vastly differs from their approach to poetry and the classics. For the educated men of imperial China, the study of Confucian classics and the histories was considered far more important than the reading and compiling of short stories given the moral edification thought to be derived therein. Short story writing or anthologizing was generally considered a dubious pursuit. Related to this is the factually unreliable nature of *xiaoshuo*, especially when compared to supposedly more reliable and morally edifying historical works. Accordingly, many anthologies contain a decidedly apologetic preface. Despite this, the practice continued.

Anthologizers of love stories, as opposed to those of other subject matter, therefore faced a twofold dilemma: if compiling prose narratives derided as *xiaoshuo* was bad enough, focusing on romantic love was equally dubious, especially if the love stories in question deviated from orthodox social mores. Many a love story featured illicit premarital and extramarital sex and, in contrast to their male counterparts, adulterous female characters were rarely, if ever, allowed to escape unscathed. Likewise, interclass marriage was generally considered potentially subversive vis-à-vis the structured social hierarchy of the Song and Yuan, as was the portrayal of young unmarried couples who eloped or else arranged their own marriages. All this contradicted orthodox social values and moral standards in addition to threatening social control. Such is the evident embarrassment of several author-compilers that they wrote under pseudonyms.

Given the material and social conditions of the period, it is not surprising that educated men derived pleasure from circulating and recording gossipy stories. A famous love story or sexual encounter, such as pertaining to the aforementioned Tao Gu, or else an inexplicable paranormal phenomenon, would have often inspired informal gossip, much to the entertainment of participants, be they members of the ruling elite or humble farming folk. Worthy stories brought to the attention of educated men were consequently recorded, sometimes with matching poems. Given advances in printing technology, written versions were then re-recorded, anthologized, edited, and, where further information was available, enhanced. New editions and narrative anthologies fed an ever-increasing consumer book market hungry for novelty. At the same time, such written version fed verbal retelling both informally and during formal, professional performances. In this way, storytelling in both written and oral forms supported several cottage industries, such as printing and publishing, professional storytelling, the dramatic arts, et cetera. And, to be sure, the populous as a whole was kept entertained as a consequence.

Finer Bibliographic Distinctions

Although love stories were widely understood as *xiaoshuo* from the Song dynasty onward, a somewhat finer distinction was made by the compilers of *Extensive Records from the Era of Supreme Peace* (*Taiping guangji*). Completed by 978, this was a state-sponsored editorial project charged with collecting, classifying, and preserving the narrative *xiaoshuo* works of previous dynasties. The result was an unprecedentedly voluminous work comprising 500 chapters (i.e., *juan* or scrolls). Individual narratives were topologically arranged under ninety-two main categories and 150 subcategories. Many of the finest prototypical love stories were classified as "miscellaneous biographies" (*zazhuan*, chapters 484–92). The term "miscellaneous" (*za*) connotes the idea of "mixed" or "mongrelized," which, in Chinese culture, is decidedly derogatory. That love stories were so labeled in the late tenth century is perhaps not surprising given the low status of short stories in general. Nevertheless, the *zazhuan* as a bibliographical category was clearly created as a supplement to historical works, thereby revealing the influence of historiography on *xiaoshuo* writing at the time. To be sure, the fact that many love stories' titles are derived from the main protagonist's name indicates their affiliation with historical biography. The same may be said for other types of stories now considered *chuanqi*. Five other categories from the *Extensive Records* (chapters 271–73) labeled "sagacious women," "talented women," "beautiful women," "jealous women," and "courtesans" contain romantic stories whose themes were developed in later anthologies. The following chapter, 274, is labeled *qinggan*. This term may be understood as "transformation brought about through *qing*" (love/emotion). Narratives thus categorized feature instances whereby the power of romantic love engendered a significant change of behavior, caused death, or else brought about resurrection from the dead. Many prototypical love stories featuring such occurrences were classified under the *qinggan* rubric. On the other hand, if a love story's main protagonist was a ghost, it was classified under one of the many chapters labeled "ghosts." Similarly, if the story featured a fox, it was classified under "foxes." Therefore, no distinct, unified category that recognized the love story's romantic focus had been devised by the late tenth century.

The first individual to classify love stories as a discreet literary corpus was Zhang Junfang, above-mentioned author-compiler of *Collected Love Stories* (*Liqing ji*, completed approximately in the mid–eleventh century).[59] Zhang's titular use of the term *liqing* for an anthology exclusively focusing on romantic love indicates recognition of the love story as a quasi-generic group distinct from other story types. All his (extant) stories are of Tang dynasty provenance, except for three from the early Song era. As current editions have been redacted, unfortunately we can no longer access Zhang's original. Whether he wrote an explanatory preface is unclear, and we may only guess his motives and interests from the nature of his collection. Famous twelfth-century book collector Chao Gongwu (d. 1171) referred to *Collected Love Stories* as an anthology of *qinggan* stories.[60] Although Zhang's selected items did not confine themselves to physical transformations engendered by romantic attachment, it is significant how Chao conflated *qinggan* and *liqing* as a bibliographical category. In the history of the love story, Zhang's *Collected Love Stories* constitutes a landmark not only of classification but also in regard to establishing a canon given his inclusion of the most famous, well-written love stories of the eighth and ninth centuries.[61]

Besides Zhang Junfang, Li Xianmin (fl. early twelfth century), also used the term *liqing* as a classification for love stories in his *Comprehensive Record of the Cloud Studio* (*Yunzhai guanglu*, completed 1111). This work is a topically arranged collection of narrative and anecdotal literature that included two entire sections labeled "New Love Stories" (*liqing xinshuo*). Unlike Zhang Junfang, Li selected contemporary accounts. In his bibliography, Chao Gongwu described the *Comprehensive Record* as containing remarkable (*qi*), romantic/beauteous (*li*), and miscellaneous (*za*) stories of the age.[62] Li Xianmin and Zhang Junfang's use of the term *liqing*, in addition to Chao Gongwu's citation of *li*, strongly suggests that it was a widely accepted term used to classify love stories from the mid-eleventh to the early twelfth century.

Curiously, no extant instance of the term *liqing* may be found after this time. Nonetheless, an extended discussion of the love story is found in the first chapter of Luo Ye's (dates uncertain) *Drunken Man's Talk* (*Xinbian zuiweng tanlu*), an extensive collection of love stories compiled anywhere between the late twelfth to late fourteenth centuries. Its first chapter, "Beginnings of Storytelling" (*xiaoshuo kaipi*), in a discussion of professional (oral) storytellers and their art, posits no less than eight subcategories of *xiaoshuo* based on subject matter.[63] Given the symbiotic relationship between written and oral stories, the eight categories may equally apply to the written short story. They are: stories of the paranormal (*zhiguai*), "romance" (*yanfen*), short stories (*chuanqi*), legal cases, swordsmen, stave-wielding, immortals, and sorcery. The author illustrates each category with sample titles. Several famous extant love stories are classified as *chuanqi*. Unfortunately, such a classification fails to distinguish love stories from other story types given that *chuanqi* stories, as previously noted, include a variety of subject matter besides romance.[64] A contracted form of *yanhua daifen*, the intriguing category *yanfen* may be translated literally as "powder and incense." The term *yanhua*, often mistranslated as "mist and flowers," denotes "incense (smoke) and flowers." The term *dai* (kohl) was the premodern equivalent of mascara, while *fen* signifies face powder. In the literature of the imperial period, these metaphors all refer to women. Women's faces were often compared to flowers, while in lyric poetry female personas frequently evoke the image of burning incense. Furthermore, as may be seen from love stories themselves, incense was often burned during sexual encounters. Although a few of the titles cited under this *yanfen* category are extant love stories, why they were considered *yanfen* and not *chuanqi* is unclear. Based on Ming dynasty versions bearing similar titles to Luo Ye's list, Tan Zhengbi argued that *yanfen* signified love stories that included significant paranormal elements. Drawing such a conclusion based on titles when Song or Yuan era stories are no longer extant is, nonetheless, unsound.[65] In any case, Luo Ye's categories are extremely important to the love story's development and I will return to them below.

Thirteenth-century writers corroborate Luo Ye's categories, albeit in less detail. Nai Deweng's *Recording the Splendor of the Capital* (*Ducheng jisheng*, completed c. 1235), possibly contemporaneous with the *Drunken Man's Talk*, posits four subcategories of professional storytelling among which *chuanqi*, *zhiguai*, and *yanfen* appear under the broad rubric of *xiaoshuo*. Wu Zimu, author of *Dream of Liang* (*Mengliang lu*, completed c. 1275), devised a similar schemata that included both *chuanqi* and *yanfen*.[66] Although the above schemas are extremely valuable, lack of an articulated theoretical basis hinders our understanding of how love stories were formalistically conceptualized during this time.

Feng Menglong (1574–1646), generally acknowledged compiler of the voluminous *History of Affection* (*Qingshi*), anthologized over 850 love stories that he classified both thematically and by subject in twenty-four chapters (or *juan*) that were further subdivided. Besides short classical language stories (*chuanqi*), additional items were drawn from other genres, such as paranormal accounts (*zhiguai*), anecdotes, and historical records. Rather than approaching love stories as a literary genre, Feng's interest clearly lay with the concept of *qing* as a cultural phenomenon. The term *qing*, as a semantic category, encompasses diverse concepts such as love, passion, ardor, sentiment, sensibility, emotion, feeling, and empathy, and identifying a one-to-one English equivalent is not impossible. During the imperial period, *qing* also denoted "affection" among the seven emotions: joy, anger, sorrow, fear, affection, hate, and desire. Although *qing* was closely associated with sexual desire and unbridled emotions in traditional Chinese thought, late Ming dynasty thinkers salvaged the concept so that it assumed virtual cult status vis-à-vis literature and culture. Feng's major categories are chaste affection, predestined affection, clandestine affection, knights-errant of affection, heroes of affection, passionate affection, infatuated affection, affection that moves the heart (*qinggan*), illusory affection, efficacious affection, transformations of affection, matchmakers and affection, affection and regret, affection and hate, the sprouting of affection, affection and retribution, affection and degeneracy, harm caused by affection, implausible affection, ghosts and affection, monstrous beings and affection, homosexual affection, anthropopathic affection, and vestiges of affection.[67] Although these categories do not help us identify a suitable generic label for the love story, Feng's emphasis on *qing* as an organizing principle for short stories indicates his tacit acknowledgment of the love story as a sustained discursive practice, while his categorization schema echoes Luo Ye's subcategories. The *History of Affection* is, furthermore, a famous example of the love story's dedicated anthologizing in late imperial China.

Content to classify love stories under the catch-all rubric of *xiaoshuo* in traditional bibliographies, later literary critics did not address the issue of classification. If any bibliophile of the late imperial period were to have formulated a theoretical basis for the love story, the influential bibliophile Hu Yingling was likely to have done so. His almost cursory citing of four famous love stories under the label of *xiaoshuo* is, therefore, disappointing and does not help us understand how he and his contemporaries understood what, by his lifetime, had developed into a significant corpus. Hu *did* posit the *zhiguai* genre, which he contrasted to both the *chuanqi* and *zalu* (miscellaneous records).[68] Nonetheless, once we consider the overlap of both subject matter and narrative technique, Hu's distinction as a structuralist generic category largely disintegrates.[69] His delineation of the two is premised on the dominant subject matter of individual narratives. Although incommensurate with modern Western genre theory, given the overwhelming tendency of traditional Chinese bibliophiles to classify literature by subject matter, particularly in regard to narrative, Hu's solution was, perhaps, the best way to proceed at the time. Interestingly enough, his dominant subject matter idea anticipates the notion of "dominance" as developed by the Russian formalists in the twentieth century.[70]

Luo Ye's Categories as a Basis for Prototypical Analysis

Returning to the categorization schema outlined in the *Drunken Man's Talk*, of even greater interest than the first chapter's eight subcategories are those under which individual stories are organized. Omitting those not pertaining to narrative leaves us with: "clandestine love and legal cases," "romantic union," "humorous tales," "records from the red light district," "rare liaisons with immortal women," "broken promises," "promises kept," "predestined meetings," "faithful hearts," and "reunion." The "romantic union" category is erroneously reduplicated, as is that of "reunion." The "broken promises" category is also repeated (using two variant terms, *fuxin* and *fuyue*).[71] Such repetition indicates that the extant imprint derives not from an original edition but is a reprint based on a poorly preserved original text or fragments thereof. Nevertheless, reliance on categorization by subject matter leads to inevitable overlap. For example, when considering the love story as a substantial corpus beyond Luo Ye's narrow selection, stories of "romantic union," "reunion," or "broken promises" often narrate "clandestine love" and may evince similarities to those categorized as "humorous," or else may have been set in a brothel district. Nevertheless, Luo Ye's schemata implicitly recognizes the formulaic nature of many a story's plot and provides a basis for prototypical analysis.

"Romantic union" is a useful category because it points to the love story's central concern: the joining, albeit temporarily, of a heterosexual couple. Similarly, as many love stories featured reunion, this provides another productive category. Affairs between human protagonists and immortal beings, particularly between mortal men and immortal women, may well be subsumed under either of these, but since orthodox moral standards vis-à-vis sexuality were not generally applied to the protagonists of such narratives, as I will discuss in chapter 1, retaining "rare liaisons with immortal women" as a separate category is helpful. Similarly, stories of "broken promises" may be collapsed into either "romantic union" or "reunion," but retaining a separate category acknowledges the formulaic nature of such narratives while emphasizing the censure accorded to betrayers of women vis-à-vis the culture of romance. So as to further refine these subcategories, we may consider whether the conclusion is happy or tragic. That is, does the plot conclude with a freely chosen "state of permanent bliss"[72] or the protagonists' perpetual separation, perhaps even death? Hence, a happy or tragic conclusion may further delineate the above four subcategories. As such subcategories are based on broad structural differences, regardless of plot variation, they provide useful analytical tools to acknowledge commonality across individual stories while avoiding the pitfalls of essentialism.

Although Zhang Junfang recognized the love story as a discreet story type, if he ever attempted to delineate a boundary with other texts, no such explanation survives. Likewise Li Xianmin, while content to label love stories as *liqing*, refrained from theorizing. Nonetheless, the current study cannot ignore the question: what constitutes a love story? Which narratives should be considered? Articulating a definition along structuralist lines would seem doomed to failure, despite the traditional Chinese bibliographer's predilection for categorizing literary texts—especially *xiaoshuo*-type narratives—according to subject matter. It is little wonder that Glen Dudbridge "rejects the attempt to establish a definitive category of stories which might give formal substance to the '*chuanqi*' label, or erect some other in its place," further arguing that, "such categories as these mislead and hinder our efforts to read Tang narrative sensitively."[73] To help navigate the thorny question of generic boundaries, I will use a functional-systemic approach developed by Dirk de Geest and Hendrik van Gorp based on prototype theory.[74]

Unlike structural literary and linguistic theory that posits fixed, inflexible generic categories, prototype theory acknowledges the existence of discreet categories while recognizing considerable variation among individual works. In color theory, for example, not all whites are an identical hue; some may be tempered with gray, blue, green, and the like, but the concept of "white" remains. Similar to literary texts, some colors simultaneously straddle a line between two or more categories and thereby attract labels such as "blueish-green" or "orangey-red." This has long been recognized and exploited by artists. Accordingly, it no longer matters to which group the instance ultimately "belongs." Zadeh's mathematical topology of "fuzzy sets," whereby numbers are not restricted to binaries (0, 1) but rather cover the entire interval (0 1), also relates to this concept.[75] Accordingly, familial resemblance in a Wittgensteinian sense replaces the rigid Aristotelian concept of generic classification; one might note genetic resemblance between two family members without assuming the two act and think identically.[76]

Such a conceptualization enables us to explain the way authors may consciously subvert generic norms in quest of innovation. The structuralist notion of a *prima facae* example is replaced by the prototype: that is, a typical instance of a given category. Texts that maximize categorical features while minimizing those of adjacent groups may be considered prototypical of that category. In view of this, it is a text's *degree* of membership to a given category that comes to the fore. The notion of center versus periphery is also a helpful way of conceptualizing a text's conformity or deviance from its prototype, such as Campany's solar system metaphor to account for textual variety in relation to the *zhiguai* genre. For Campany, the distance a given text may be plotted from its taxonomic/prototypical center may be likened to a given planet's distance from its solar center.[77] This open-system approach to literary genres acknowledges the love story's disparate elements while allowing a comprehensive investigation of its intertextual complexity. What might be considered a problem of overlapping features under a structuralist conception of genre may now be understood as an inevitable process of borrowing whereby tellers innovatively manipulated established generic patterns, thereby ensuring the corpus' sustainability.

Guided by prototype theory, *chuanqi* narratives that appear in *Collected Love Stories*, those appearing in the *liqing* sections of Li Xianmin's *Cloud Studio* anthology, in addition to those from Luo Ye's collection discussed above may be considered prototypes; some stories, to be sure, are found in more than one anthology. Short stories from other works that closely resemble these may be deemed central to the corpus, while those that exhibit other generic elements may be considered more or less peripheral to the corpus yet not excluded entirely. Therefore, for the purposes of this study, I would characterize a prototypical love story (*liqing xiaoshuo*) as a relatively short prose narrative written in classical Chinese that may include poetry and whose narrative interest focuses on humanistic, heterosexual,[78] romantic love whether or not one of the protagonists is a paranormal entity. This recognizes dialogic interconnectivity with related genres and subsets, particularly that of the *zhiguai*. Indeed, what post-Enlightenment scholars would understand as paranormal elements in both the love story and other traditional genres are so numerous that any attempt to exclude such stories would disregard the longstanding Chinese belief in the paranormal (i.e., *guai*). While stories that foreground paranormal events may not be considered close to the love story's "generic center," prototype theory allows us to include rather than expunge them outright. While *zhiguai* narratives generally vilify sexual congress by treating the heterosexual lover as an ontological Other, or else focus on the paranormal for its own sake, the love story portrays romantic affairs between humans and supernatural beings in a humanistic, celebratory manner; herein lies a crucial difference between the two corpuses. This is particularly true of Song dynasty love stories whose male protagonists knowingly engage in affairs with female ghosts and fox-fairies, much more so than those of earlier periods.

Chapter 1

The Mid- and Late Tang Dynasty

Informed by previous studies, this chapter surveys major reoccurring themes from the Tang dynasty so as to provide a point of comparison with later texts. Although I offer new insights, I am not attempting a groundbreaking analysis. As Daniel Hsieh has observed, "many of the issues and approaches first explored in a systematic manner in the Tang would be revisited throughout the later period."[1] Comparing these "issues and approaches" with those of the later period will illustrate the nature and degree of subsequent thematic change.

The majority of surviving sources from the Tang are found in the aforementioned *Extensive Record*. Although some of the love stories preserved therein are set during the early Tang period (seventh century), the earliest extant anthologies to include them date from the eighth and ninth centuries. Hence "Tang dynasty" throughout this book refers to these latter two centuries. Before embarking on close reading of selected works, a brief overview of Tang dynasty society and its relation to the stories' subject matter will be useful.

Tang society comprised highly stratified and distinct social classes. Broadly speaking, we may differentiate between an educated elite known as scholar-officials (*shi dafu*) who were largely influential at the local level, as opposed to commoners, such as farmers, artisans, and merchants. There were also "debased people" (*jianmin*) that included various types of indentured laborers, such as courtesans, female servants, and their family members. The social apex was dominated by a hereditary aristocracy whose immense wealth and power had endured for generations. This group consisted of clans that traced their lineage to a common ancestor and identified with a particular locality, although specific branches did not necessarily remain in the same area over an extended period.

The most powerful and prestigious were the four great clans of the Northeast ("east of the mountains"—that is, modern Hebei) who considered themselves torch bearers of the purest Chinese cultural tradition. Equally influential, if somewhat less self-important, were those of Guanzhong (within the mountain passes) in the Northwest, including the Tang imperial family and clansmen. As these northwestern clans had risen to prominence under a succession of non-Chinese ruling houses during the period of disunity preceding the Tang, intermarriage with outside ethnicities had been common. As a consequence, their partial adoption of central Asian and steppe culture belittled them in the eyes of the pure-blood, northeastern clans. Somewhat less powerful were the clans of northern Sha'anxi whose mixed blood was still stronger than their Guanzhong counterparts. Last were the wealthy clans of the Yangzi River valley who had risen to importance under successive southern dynasties.[2] These super-elite clans virtually monopolized government positions and influenced policymaking.[3] They married their daughters with considerable selectivity, generally among themselves. Hence extraordinarily large bride prices became the norm. In fact, marrying a woman from a great clan was considered a major life aspiration for an upper-class man.[4] Such was the influence and self-importance of the super-elite that they considered the Tang imperial family inferior and there were instances whereby aristocratic bridegrooms preferred their own kind to an imperial princess.[5]

In view of the enormous political power wielded by eminent clans, successive emperors sought to limit their power and bring them under central government control. Among such measures was the Gaozong emperor's (r. 650–684) edict forbidding intermarriage among the premier northeastern clans, although this eventually proved ineffective.[6] During the seventh and eighth centuries, several official genealogies were produced and presented to the throne in an attempt to record, quantify, evaluate, and control claims to aristocratic lineage. A more far-reaching measure was the expansion of the examination system established by the previous, short-lived Sui dynasty (581–619). As an alternate method of recruitment to the supremely prestigious bureaucracy, the examination system theoretically enabled candidates from relatively humble backgrounds to secure bureaucratic positions based on academic prowess, as opposed to direct appointment or other means that were controlled by the ruling class. Admitting a wider pool of entrants into the bureaucracy could curtail the super-elite's dominance since successful candidates would theoretically owe their allegiance to the throne rather than an aristocratic clan. Controlling entry to the bureaucracy was all the more crucial given that government service was considered part and parcel of a Confucian gentleman's social obligation. Furthermore, in view of the monetary and legal privileges bureaucratic status conferred on successful candidates, such as exemptions from tax and corvee labor duties, as well as immunity or reduction in punishment for certain crimes, public service was generally attractive to the upper classes. The prestige commanded by the "presented scholar" degree (*jinshi*, hereafter "advanced" degree) in particular was such that it became highly sought after, even among distinguished aristocrats. Accordingly, the attainment of an advanced degree ranked among the superlative achievements for an educated man of the era.[7] In view of these advantages, bureaucratic service through the examination system became an important means by which the ruling class established their claim to elite status. Nonetheless, only a minute proportion of bureaucratic positions were filled by examination throughout the dynasty; attaining a position by other means, such as direct appointment or hereditary privilege, remained the norm.[8]

Passing the examination for the advanced degree did not immediately confer a bureaucratic position; this was secured by additional placement examinations. Attainment of the advanced degree did, nevertheless, secure official rank, title, and enhanced social standing, in addition to the aforementioned judicial privileges. Until a posting was received, however, successful candidates joined the ranks of supernumery officials who waited in the wings. As only a minute percentage of candidates were successful, passing the examinations was seen as a mark of intellectual distinction. Successful candidates were thus feted in a manner not unlike today's celebrities. They also became prime potential sons-in-law for established patriarchs wishing to improve their own social standing through the marriage of their daughters. Since the examination system figured so prominently in both the lives of elite storytellers and their narratives, a brief overview of its pertinent features will help contextualize the ensuing literary analysis.

There were two major pathways to examination success. One was through study in one of the several universities or academies located in the dynastic capital, Chang'an. The other was through successful completion of a provincial examination that qualified a candidate to undertake those held in the capital. Metropolitan institutions, such as the Academy for Sons of the State (*guozi jian*) and the National University (*taixue*), prepared candidates for the main two examination categories, the *mingjing* (elucidating the classics) and the above-mentioned advanced degree. Curriculum, particularly for the first category, largely focused on the Confucian classics while the advanced degree emphasized literature. Besides these, less prestigious degrees in specialist fields were offered, such as law, mathematics, and philology. Candidates would typically spend several years studying in the capital during which time they could establish connections with influential men, including future examiners. Unlike the more rigorous system of later centuries, Tang-era procedural protocol differed significantly and it was common for candidates to have contact with their examiners before undertaking the examination.[9] Little wonder, therefore, that considerably more graduates from these metropolitan academies passed than their provincial counterparts.[10]

Provincial candidates, on the other hand, first needed to obtain the recommendation of a local authority. Needless to say, this necessitated and perpetuated a local system of patronage that proliferated into later centuries. If candidates passed the provincial examination, they were permitted to travel to the capital for the metropolitan round. This would typically involve a stay of several months from the fall—when examinations were routinely held—until the following spring when results were announced. Candidates who undertook the examinations in this way were at a disadvantage because they could not hope to make as many social connections in such a short timeframe as those whom had been established in the city for several years studying under the best teachers.

The successful few who attained the top grade were able to undertake a further examination at the palace. This examination was particularly prestigious as the emperor himself frequently set questions and may have interviewed candidates. Passing this round ensured a successful candidate's procurement of a high-ranking bureaucratic post, most likely at court. Besides this palace examination, sometimes an even higher-level, special examination was held so as to distinguish the *crème de la crème* of that year's graduates.

During the ten or so days following the announcement of the first-round results in the second lunar month, it was customary for several sumptuous banquets, both state and private, to be held in honor of successful candidates. Wang Dingbao (870–c. 954), writing from memory in the late ninth century, noted no less than nine types of banquet in his anecdotal collection titled *Gleanings from the Tang Dynasty* (*Tang zhiyan*).[11]

Most were held at or nearby the Serpentine Pool and the nearby Apricot Garden, both popular destinations for leisurely outings. It is easy to imagine candidates and their examiners toasting each other while forming important sociopolitical bonds in the mild springtime weather. At one of the state-orchestrated banquets, top-ranking candidates were allowed to pluck a branch of blossom and were therefore known as "gentlemen who plucked a flower" (*tanhua lang*). This became a popular metaphor signifying advanced degree holders in general.

In imperial China, as in many traditional cultures, feasting and drinking went hand in hand with female servers and entertainers. So as to organize and train public performers, as well as ensure a sufficient number of courtesans to perform music and supply entertainment during state-sponsored festivities, the Xuanzong emperor (r. 712–756) established the Music Bureau (*jiaofang*). This undoubtedly did much to legitimize the courtesan's already entrenched social role. Courtesans who officiated at state-sponsored banquets provided a wide range of functions that included pouring drinks, singing, performing with musical instruments, engaging in witty repartee with guests, or else acting as adjudicators of drinking games and the like. At private functions a senior courtesan might have acted as master of ceremonies, ensuring the enjoyment of all present. For young men in a society that generally segregated upper-class males and females, this would have been a rare occasion for contact with young, attractive, unmarried women who were sexually available. After a banquet's conclusion, young scholars might visit Chang'an's brothel districts where they could be entertained by courtesans in an informal setting, to which many love stories bear testament. Hence romance was intimately related to both examination and courtesan culture. Indeed, Xuanzong's Music Bureau and courtesans' consequent enhanced status may well have contributed to the rise of the culture of romance.

We know something of the lives and organization of Chang'an's courtesans from two extant sources, Cui Lingqin's (fl. 749) *Record of the Entertainment Bureau* (*Jiaofang ji*) and Sun Qi's (fl. 880s) anecdotal collection *Record of the Northern Quarter* (*Beili zhi*). The latter is by far the most informative. Sun was a minor bureaucrat residing in the capital during the late ninth century and, after the city was largely destroyed by the Huang Chao rebellion in 880, he wrote a notebook-style collection (preface dated 884) ostensibly to "provide a topic of conversation in later ages."[12] Through Sun's vignettes, it is easy to conceive the symbiotic relationship among urban entertainment, courtesan culture, and the culture of romance as recorded in stories. The Northern Quarter, otherwise known as the Pingkang ward, was home to Chang'an's high-class courtesans and, in the post–Tang era, became a euphemism for brothel districts in general. It was here that young and talented courtesans entertained wealthy male clients, including well-to-do examination candidates. Courtesans of this period were similar to Japanese geishas—that is, they were highly talented entertainers who not only provided the types of entertainment outlined above but could also extemporize poetry. Feminine beauty was undoubtedly one of their attractions and, like prostitutes, they were sexually available. Nonetheless, their talents rendered them far superior to common prostitutes, of which there would have been many, but Sun Qi glosses over lower-class sex workers in the briefest of terms. He tells us that the Pingkang ward was located southeast of Chang'an's imperial palace complex, adjacent to the East Market. Near the courtesans' residences were several Buddhist temples and the stately homes of formerly powerful courtiers. In his introduction, Sun speaks of courtesans residing in clean and spacious residences replete with gardens that sported exotic rocks and potted trees.

Most courtesans were registered with the Music Bureau. This obliged them to perform or serve at state banquets as required, such as at banquets given in honor of successful examination candidates. State registration also prevented them from quitting their profession without official approval. Besides state functions, they also served at private gatherings, in which case, Sun tells us, they could expect higher remuneration. Courtesans lived under the guidance and control of adoptive "mothers" who, in turn, appeared to operate under the protection of local strongmen. Courtesans were usually recruited from an early age, although some older girls were sold to the establishments. Sometimes trickery or kidnapping may have been used to coerce young girls into service. Those recruited at a young age were taught performing arts and the rules of drinking games while higher-class courtesans were taught poetry and possibly a rudimentary curriculum of classical literature. They were generally not allowed to leave the brothel precinct unless accompanied by a fee-paying client. Sun Qi mentions how they would attract the male Gaze when worshipping at a local temple on days of religious observance.

Sun Qi tells of how newly minted bureaucrats surreptitiously visited the precinct, suggesting that although being entertained by courtesans at officially sanctioned functions was permissible, privately seeking their company may have been considered disreputable. He himself admits to visiting courtesan establishments in the company of other men when tired or depressed.[13] At such times he could be cheered by witty repartee while regaled with tea or wine along with a range of delicacies. Poetic exchange figured prominently in interactions between elite men and courtesans, as we will see from the stories. One of Sun's longer items tells of a fleeting affair he experienced with a courtesan known as Yizhi. One among several courtesans in the same household, Sun describes her as "very bright; she matched the ideal in plumpness and was breezy and elegant in conversation. She was also talented in letters."[14] "Plumpness" is significant here as men of the period tended to prefer voluptuous women. Sun narrates her appreciation of a poem he composed in which he compared her with Western Grace (Xishi), a famous beauty of the Warring States period (475–221 BCE). After that, she invited Sun to write more poems on the wall of her room. After a time, Yizhi expressed her willingness to become Sun's concubine in a poem she presented him. Mindful of the social disgrace and possible legal repercussions that may have arisen had he accepted, Sun refused. " 'I understand full well your implied meaning, but this is not suitable for an examination candidate. What should we do?' Weeping again, she replied, 'Luckily I'm not yet on the registers of the Imperial Music School; so if you so desire, only one or two hundred pieces of silver should be enough [to redeem me].' Before I could reply, she handed me a writing brush and asked me to match her poem."[15] Sun conveyed his refusal in a poem, after which their relationship cooled. Yizhi was eventually bought by a wealthy patron. The anecdote continues as Sun waxes wistfully about his affection for her when their paths later crossed. Sun's testimony is a good example of a love affair written with clear documentary intent. Its sober outcome certainly contrasts with the fully developed stories analyzed below. Nevertheless, his candidness illustrates the value placed on one's romantic life that characterized the culture of romance.

Loyalty and the Love Story's Formative Period

Daniel Hsieh hypothesizes that the An Lushan Rebellion (755–763) acted as a catalyst in regard to the culture of romance. For Hsieh, ideas and literary forms contrary to Confucian orthodoxy, such as the erotic and the emotional, along with short stories, were the result of a newfound questioning of orthodox thought in the rebellion's wake.[16] Similarly, Paul

Rouzer has noted how men of letters wrote about a significantly wider variety of topics thereafter.[17] The catastrophic rebellion saw the occupation of the imperial capital, during which time some members of the imperial family and bureaucracy who had not already fled were executed. It also witnessed the long-reigning Xuanzong emperor's abdication, wrought general mayhem, and so shook the dynasty's foundations that it never completely recovered. China's staggering population decline after the rebellion points to enormous social upheaval; recorded population figures fall from 52.9 million in 755 to 16.9 in 764—a drop of nearly two-thirds in less than ten years.[18] Around eight years were required to suppress the rebellion. Even so, the dynasty was plagued by smaller uprisings for decades thereafter.

While the causes of the rebellion are complex, the Xuanzong emperor's infatuation with his favorite, Precious Consort Yang, became fixed in the popular imagination as a significant factor. This was partly due to the historiographic tradition of blaming dynastic decline on seductive women, as Helen of Troy was blamed for launching a thousand ships in Bronze Age Greece. Although Xuanzong had diligently discharged his responsibilities as emperor throughout the first half of his reign, his subsequent pleasure seeking coincided with his devotion to Lady Yang. Concurrent with Lady Yang's rise in fortune was that of her relations, notably her brother, Yang Guozhong (d. 756), who was vilified by traditional Chinese historians as a corrupt and evil chief minister. Later historical accounts, stories, and poems link Lady Yang and her family to extravagance at court. Gossipy stories perpetuated rumors about an alleged sexual affair between her and the rebel leader, whom she had adopted as a son prior to the rebellion's outbreak. When the rebellion begun, Lady Yang became such a focus of hate that troops loyal to the throne mutinied during the emperor's flight from Chang'an. The only way Xuanzong could pacify them was to allow her execution.[19]

Among the earliest stories and poems about Lady Yang and Xuanzong is Li Yue's (fl. mid- to late eighth century) poem, "Passing Floral Purity Palace" (*Guo Huaqing gong*). The poem explicitly criticizes the emperor's extravagance and neglect of state affairs. Its title refers to the hot spring resort much frequented by the imperial couple.[20] In "Northern Journey," the illustrious poet Du Fu (712–770) compared Lady Yang to notorious *femme fatales* of China's past who were blamed for dynastic decline.[21] Renowned poet Bai Juyi's (772–846) "Ballad of Eternal Sorrow" (*Changhen ge*) and its accompanying narrative, "Account of the Ballad of Eternal

Sorrow" (*Changhen ge zhuan*), written by Chen Hong (fl. 785–830), are also famous.[22]

Unlike Li Yue's earlier poem, Bai and Chen's work largely sought to salvage the Emperor's reputation by refashioning him as a devoted lover rather than a debauched shirker of responsibility—quite in keeping with the then emerging culture of romance.[23] Glossing over the fact that Lady Yang was originally the emperor's daughter-in-law (considered tantamount to incest by contemporary standards), Bai and Chen celebrate the couple's mutual devotion. The poem does, however, note the emperor's consequent neglect of state affairs and catalogues the luxury at court, albeit in a neutral tone. After Lady Yang's execution, the emperor-protagonist briefly reunites with her thanks to the aid of a Daoist priest. In this latter part of both the poem and account, Lady Yang has become an immortal dwelling on the legendary islands in the Eastern Sea. The poem's concluding lines are significant:

> On the seventh day of the seventh month in the Palace of Eternal Life,
> At midnight, when no one was around, they whispered to each other:
> In heaven, we wish to become two birds with paired wings;
> On earth, we wish to be twin trees with branches interlocked.
> There will be a time when the long-lasting heaven and earth cease to exist;
> Yet this sorrow will linger on and on, never ending.[24]

The references to "twin trees with branches interlocking," as with "two birds with paired wings," were to become oft-cited images of romantic devotion in later love stories and poems, as was—to a lesser extent—the idea that a deceased lover could become an immortal. The first alludes to the legend of Han Ping, whose wife was sequestered by his master, Prince Kang of the State of Song. Unable to recover her, the disconsolate Han committed suicide. The wife did likewise after learning of her husband's death. The furious Prince refused her request (in a suicide note) that she be buried with her husband. Instead, he interred them in nearby graves, sarcastically promising to honor her wish were the graves to join themselves. After this, two trees grew from each grave whose branches and roots subsequently intertwined.[25]

Of particular interest is Chen's postscript. This tells how both the poem and short story were written during a winter sojourn to the Monastery of Celestial Roaming in late 807. During this time Bai, Chen and others discussed the events of Xuanzong's reign. Bai was persuaded to compose his poem while Chen undertook to write a prose account. Significantly, Chen's postscript reveals how these literary works were recorded from orally circulated stories and gossip—that is, informal *discussion* of received events. If Bai, Chen, and their friends were still talking about the imperial love affair decades after the deaths of both the emperor and his consort, many others certainly would have done so both before and after. Indeed, the existence of several early Song dynasty love stories about Lady Yang indicate elite men's long-lasting fascination with the imperial love affair for centuries thereafter.[26] In view of the Emperor and Lady Yang's very public affair and the impact it had on later generations, the expression of romantic love consequently gained a degree of legitimacy not previously felt, quite in keeping with the then burgeoning culture of romance.

That both emperor and consort were imagined as loyally devoted to each other in the "Ballad of Eternal Sorrow" and the "Account of the Ballad of Eternal Sorrow" is also significant since loyalty, as a socially constructed moral virtue, lies at the heart of both the culture of romance and the love story. In contrast to real-life arranged marriages in which, from a male's perspective, the wife's role was institutionalized and her loyalty to both husband and his household was socially expected, freedom of choice in love became a testing ground for loyalty; would a woman freely choose a man and remain faithful without the social imperative arranged marriage demanded? In virtually any narrative account of romantic love, loyalty serves as a pivotal theme on which all others turn. This may seem self-evident, but its importance warrants stressing before other aspects are considered.

Loyalty became even more important in a culture that mapped political loyalty onto personal and familial allegiance. Confucian thought conceived of a political system based on that of the family—that is, ruling the empire was equated to controlling one's family. Accordingly, sons, daughters and wives were to their fathers and husbands as were ministers to their sovereign. Such a social hierarchy engendered a mutually dependent network of social obligation. First promulgated by the Confucian thinker Dong Zhongshu (c. 179–c. 104 BCE), the subservient relationship of wives to husbands, sons to fathers, and ministers to their sovereign was known as the three cardinal relationships (*san gang*).[27] Both political and personal loyalty, therefore, were considered two sides of the same coin.

Rebellion vis-à-vis the Chinese imperium, by its very nature, was considered an act of disloyalty. Hence, in the wake of the An Lushan

Rebellion, loyalty almost certainly acquired increased importance as members of the aristocracy and commoners alike came to terms with the rebellion's causes. The love story and its stress on personal loyalty between lovers would have afforded an ideal vehicle with which to explore this important theme. This may at least partly account for the intense literary production that the culture of romance engendered throughout the late eighth and ninth centuries.

"Ren's Story" (Renshi zhuan), recorded by the man of letters Shen Jiji (c. 740–c. 800), is an excellent illustration of romantic loyalty, written with the historical romance between Lady Yang and the Xuanzong emperor in mind. The temporal setting is 750, just prior to the outbreak of the An Lushan Rebellion. According to its end commentary, it was recorded from an oral version circulating during the *dali* reign period (766–779). The heroine is a fox-fairy—that is, a were-creature who could change shape between a vixen and a woman. As previously mentioned, didactic *zhiguai* narratives often portrayed such creatures as dangerous in view of their ability to cause death by draining a man's vital *yang* energy. Untrustworthy, treacherous, and not unlike female ghosts, fox-fairies were an ideal bogey-(wo)man with which to deter young men from engaging in illicit sex.[28] In contrast to this typical depiction, the affair between Miss Ren and her lover, Mr. Zheng, is treated no differently from human love. The beautiful heroine's womanly traits are highlighted as her ontological Otherness is minimized.[29] Indeed, she is portrayed as a paragon of female virtue, despite her humble social status as one connected with the Entertainment Bureau. In other words, she was an entertainer with whom sex was legally permissible according to the Tang legal code. Hence both ontologically and socially, Miss Ren is a figure for the Other from an elite male perspective.

The plot follows the action of a Mr. Zheng who, due to financial constraints, is compelled to live with wealthy, aristocratic in-laws in Chang'an. Whether Zheng himself is an aristocrat is not specified, but we may reasonably assume so given the marriage connection. His surname certainly coincides with that of a well-known aristocratic clan. Early in the story, "He came upon three women walking along the street, of whom the middle one, dressed in white, was a rare beauty. No sooner did he see her than Zheng was infatuated." He follows her home and, while on the road, the pair engage in witty banter: "'And how is it that such a beautiful woman as yourself is going on foot?' The woman in white laughed, 'What can I do but go on foot if someone doesn't lend me his mount?'" They engage in sexual intercourse that night. He does not realize her true identity until the following morning after a tipoff from a local food vendor who informs him of a fox-spirit that often seduces men. Yet such is his passion that he relentlessly pursues her. He eventually finds her in a clothing store where he pledges fidelity, fully aware of her true form. She, in turn, agrees to "serve him in regard his cap and comb," a well-established metaphor signifying wifely duties to a husband. So as to install her as his mistress in a nearby apartment, financial constraint compels Zheng to borrow necessary items from his brother-in-law, Wei Yin, who thereby learns of Miss Ren's existence. Wei waxes sarcastically, "Considering your looks, you must surely have gotten yourself a spectacularly ugly woman." Curious as to her appearance, Wei sends a servant to appraise her under the pretext of delivering necessities. In a series of questions and answers worthy of Vaudeville, Wei Yin asks the servant to compare her beauty with a host of other beautiful women. The latter invariably answers, "Not of that caliber." Intrigued, Wei visits the love nest during Zheng's absence and, when he sees that Miss Ren's attractiveness even surpasses the servant's report, he attempts to rape her. Although she strenuously resists, her strength eventually proves unequal and so she resorts to reason:

> Realizing that she couldn't escape, she let her body relax and didn't resist anymore, yet her expression changed to one of heartfelt sadness. Wei Yin asked why, saying, "How unhappy you look!" Ren gave a long sigh. "It's just that I feel sorry for Zheng." Wei Yin said, "What do you mean?" She replied, "Zheng is six feet tall yet is unable to protect one woman—how can he be a real man! You, sir, have led a life of wild excess since your youth and have had many beautiful women—a multitude of those you have encountered have been comparable in beauty to me. Yet Zheng, who is poor and of humble background, has only myself to suit his fancy. Can a heart who has had something in abundance be so hardened as to plunder the same from someone who does not have enough? I feel sorry for his poverty and want, that he is unable to stand on his own. He wears your clothes and eats your food, and thus he is bound to you. If he could provide even simple food for himself, he should not be brought to this."

Wei then desists and henceforth provides the couple's necessities, thereby enjoying a platonic love affair with the heroine. "Wei Yin would go about with her every day, and be extremely happy to do so; the two grew very familiar and intimate with one another, and there were no barriers between them, except for sexual intimacy."

Mindful of Wei's love yet unable to physically satisfy him, "so as to repay his kindness toward her," Miss Ren procures women on his behalf. As she is bound by loyalty to her chosen lover Zheng, the young women she selects act as surrogates for herself. Although this may appear unconscionable to modern readers when measured against Judeo-Christian morality, the author possibly intended to illustrate Miss Ren's lack of jealousy, which was considered a womanly virtue in traditional China. Miss Ren's acquiring women for Wei furthermore complements her willingness to act as Zheng's concubine without exhibiting jealousy toward his wife, whom the story ignores. Nonetheless, the methods she adopts to attain women for Wei Yin, including deception, anticipate literary seduction found in erotic novels and middle-length stories of late imperial China. Even if her behavior on this point was not meant to be excusable, such a nuanced characterization avoids portraying her oversimplistically. In a touch of literary realism, one of the young women she procures for Wei even falls pregnant. Given that biological realities such as pregnancy are almost always suppressed in love stories, this realistic vignette further distinguishes "Miss Ren's Story" as a masterwork. At this point, the narrative undergoes a lengthy diversion as it tells how the heroine would use her superhuman precognition to assist Zheng in commercial enterprises, which need not concern us.

The ultimate test of Miss Ren's loyalty comes when Zheng insists she accompany him to a recently acquired bureaucratic posting in the provinces. Forewarned by a fortuneteller that catastrophe would strike should she travel west that year, she reluctantly acquiesces. En route, as the pair reach Mawei, she is torn apart by hunting dogs that instinctively detect her true identity. "One of his (the huntsman's) dark gray dogs leaped out from among the grasses, and Zheng saw Ren fall to the ground in a flash, reverting to her original shape and running south. The gray dog chased her. Zheng ran after it shouting, but he couldn't stop it. After a little more than a league the dog caught her." When Zheng returns to Chang'an, he relates the tragedy to an astounded Wei Yin who, until this point, was unaware of Ren's true identity. The narrative concludes with a brief mention of Zheng's subsequent social status and an extensive end commentary.[30]

Mawei—as the location of Miss Ren's death—is highly significant in the context of the post–An Lushan Rebellion period.[31] This was where Lady Yang was strangled. Regardless of what hermeneutic importance we might attach to the political allusion, the link between the love story and the historical romance is clear, as it would have been for contemporary readers. Related to this is the detail about how Miss Ren's clothes were found on her saddle while her stockings and shoes were left hanging from the stirrups, as if shed (*tui*) like a cicada sheds its skin. Such description was occasionally offered as proof of an anomalous occurrence in *zhiguai* accounts whose conclusion may have otherwise remained ambiguous. This is all the more applicable given Miss Ren's identity as a fox-spirit. Yet, in this context, the reference to Miss Ren's stockings and its association with Mawei must almost certainly have resonated with Song dynasty readers familiar with the apocryphal story about how one of Lady Yang's stockings was supposedly recovered and kept as an antique.[32] Here, then, is evidence that "Miss Ren's Story" was recorded with Xuanzong and Lady Yang's love affair in mind. This affords a glimpse of how the imperial love affair may have influenced the telling of love stories during the late eighth century. Indeed, it may have even spurred the circulation and recording of similar stories.

The idea of women dying for their lovers was a common motif in the love story from the Tang onward. It was not, however, without historical precedent. King Xiangyu of Chu's (232–202 BCE) concubine, Lady Yu, for example, committed suicide on the night before his final defeat by the founder of the Han dynasty. Tracing the phenomenon further, it was not unknown in ancient China for a queen and, indeed, an entire court to be buried with a newly deceased king as an ultimate demonstration of loyalty. The ubiquity of this motif in the love story reflects a Confucian-guided, patriarchal system in which those of lower status, such as wives, younger brothers, children, and the like were expected to remain loyal to their social superiors. Social seniors, in turn, were expected to protect and care for inferiors with whom social obligation had been established. And, as already noted, this model of mutual familial obligation was mapped onto sociopolitical organization. Therefore, when Miss Ren as an individual demonstrates loyalty to her lover, she also affirms loyalty to the patriarchal system in general. Her ability to willingly sacrifice her life, in addition to defend her chastity, establishes her as a faithful woman who freely chooses the central male protagonist.

Loyalty is foregrounded in Shen Jiji's metatextual commentary as he contrasts Miss Ren's fidelity with that of other women. "I am struck that such humanity could be found in the feelings of a creature so alien. When someone used violent force on her, she did not abandon her principles, and she met her death by sacrificing herself for someone else. Among women today there are those who are not her equal."[33] Bai Xingjian, author-recorder of the famous "Story of Li Wa," makes a similar contrast between his lower-class courtesan-heroine and women—presumably upper-class ones—of his social milieu: "Alas! A woman of the *demimonde* showed such virtuous conduct! Even exemplary women of ancient times could not surpass her."[34] Shen Jiji's comment that "Among women today there are those who are not her equal" foregrounds the contrast between Miss Ren's exemplary conduct and that of real-life women of his social circle, implying that the latter are morally deficient. Miss Ren's Otherness as both a *demimondaine* and fox-fairy intensifies such censure as it further implies that upper-class women are being no better than vixens or prostitutes. This suggests a dichotomy between freely chosen love affairs and the institution of arranged marriage. On one hand, the love story grants the possibility that a beautiful woman would love and remain staunchly faithful to an impoverished, possible ungainly looking man (think of Wei Yin's sarcastic comment that Zheng's lover could only be remarkably ugly).[35] On the other hand, this may be contrasted with arranged marriages contracted between families for socioeconomic purposes unrelated to romantic love or the inclinations of the parties involved. Any loyalty owed to a husband by a wife, under such circumstances, was evidently considered coerced and, therefore, suspect. Shen Jiji all but ignores Zheng's wife, who is only mentioned once or twice. Perhaps upper-class wives represented by this marginal character were the target of Shen's sarcasm, although how far he meant to carry his criticism is unclear. Nonetheless, while outwardly "Miss Ren's Story" is a poignant romance celebrating freedom of choice in love and extramarital affairs, the author-recorder's end commentary reveals a didactic impulse that promotes androcentric values—that is, female fidelity to a male.

Accordingly, the story's didactic strain and its valorization of the heroine as a virtuous paragon reduces her to a spokesperson for patriarchal values. She is interpellated, in the Althusian sense, insofar that she exemplifies a male-constructed ideal of feminine virtue and is singled out as an exemplar, as opposed to projecting her own subjectivity.[36] Her words and actions affirm male values, just as she maintains her chastity while ensuring that male sexual competition does not violate social obligations. Throughout the narrative, she plays the role of an ideal lover: she engages in witty banter, she grants the main protagonist sexual favors and remains resolutely faithful, and she is not jealous and procures other women for their patron; she also assists her lover's business ventures and helps increase his wealth. In short, although she occupies much narrative space and her character is rendered with a high degree of verisimilitude, she remains a male-constructed ideal of feminine beauty and virtue.

Even so, the valorization of Miss Ren's virtue contradicts dubious aspects of her conduct. Before she met Zheng, the food vendor tells how she, as a fox-spirit, had seduced many men. That a woman should grant sexual favors to more than one man was deemed a gross violation of the Confucian moral code and, indeed, sexual exclusiveness was central to the culture of romance. Yet the storyteller all but ignores this aspect of her past character. It was, of course, legal for debased classes, such as courtesans and prostitutes, to engage in extramarital sex as this class was considered beneath orthodox moral expectations applied to commoners and the upper classes. Nonetheless, the author-compiler's singling out Miss Ren as a virtuous paragon implicitly subjects her to ruling-class moral standards. Furthermore, the fact that a woman of dubious morality (she was, after all, affiliated with the Music Bureau and, therefore, of debased social status in the eyes of contemporary readers) would remain faithful to Zheng appears unlikely according to both the social norms of the time and the financial realities of the *demimonde*. Here, therefore, we may discern a degree of wish fulfillment found in many a love story—that is, the hope of encountering a witty and beautiful young woman who would remain staunchly faithful to the protagonist, despite the probability against it.

Shen Jiji's end commentary is also significant as it reveals the circumstances under which "Miss Ren's Story" was recounted and recorded. "We floated down the Ying River and then the Huai, our double boat carried along by the current. By day we would feast and at night tell stories, with each of us presenting strange tales. When these gentlemen heard of the events surrounding Ren, all were deeply touched and amazed. As a consequence they asked me to transmit it as an account of strange things."[37] To while away the hours during a boat trip, Shen and acquaintances swapped stories, not unlike the fictitious pilgrims in Chaucer's (b. *circa* 1342)

Canterbury Tales or the refugees in Boccaccio's (1313–1375) *Decameron*. Shen was presumably chosen as recorder in view of his literary talent.[38] Hence, "Ren's Story" was—in effect—voted the best among several. Shen furthermore claims to have heard of the story from Wei Yin, with whom he was acquainted. Wei Yin was, indeed, a historical person mentioned in the *New History of the Tang*.[39] Although we may lament the loss of the unrecorded stories, Shen's commentary reveals the manner in which many oral ones, considered inferior by contemporaries, have been lost for want of recording. Also significant is that the story appears to have been related for its paranormal interest. This further demonstrates the shared affiliation between the love story (*liqing*) and the *zhiguai* genre during the culture of romance's formative period. To be sure, Zheng's meeting with Miss Ren and the sexual intercourse that followed in the first part of the narrative could constitute a *zhiguai* story in itself without further plot development. Indeed, the episode in which Zheng reencountered Miss Ren after he became aware of her paranormal nature seems abruptly sutured with the narrative's first phase, which concluded with the revelation of Miss Ren's ontological Otherness. This first phase may well have initially circulated as a stand-alone *zhiguai* piece that was later amended, perhaps by Shen Jiji himself.

Male Bonding and Competition

"Miss Ren's Story" nicely illustrates what Hong Yue terms an "erotic triangle" whereby two men compete for the same woman's affection.[40] This was an extremely common plot device, particularly during the ninth and tenth centuries. It is also a useful analytical tool to better understand the love story's androcentric aspects, such as male sexual and social competition, fear of losing one's woman, and the value men placed on friendship. We are told early in the narrative how Zheng and Wei were often together. Nevertheless, the threat that the wealthier man would steal his lover initially prompts Zheng to conceal her existence. Zheng also concealed his having spent the night with her early in the narrative. His fear is vindicated by Wei's attempted rape. Were Ren not a paragon of virtue, endowed with superior rhetorical prowess, she may well have succumbed. So as to preserve her chastity, she appeals to Wei Yin's sense of righteousness and his social obligation by addressing his and Zheng's socioeconomic disparity. Wei Yin's social position as Zheng's brother-in-law, coupled with his superior financial resources, obligate him to protect the latter's interests. Hence, friendship intersects with familial obligation. In fact, such was the importance of (male) friendship that eminent Sinologist Arthur Waley asserted that elite males of the period valued it over romantic relationships (with women).[41] Nonetheless, Wei's attempted assault suggests that unreported rape by a friend or family member was not uncommon in the storyteller's social milieu. As an example of the extraordinary, the narrative conveys male anxiety over female chastity, male sexual competition, and an inability to protect women while articulating an optimistic resolution. Although Miss Ren is not possessed by the male competitor, the heroines of other stories were not so fortunate.

In numerous love stories featuring the erotic triangle device, plot development was driven when the woman was abducted or judicially separated from her protagonist-lover. A deceptively straightforward yet instructive example is "Miss Liu's Story" (*Liushi zhuan*), classified as a reunion prototype by Luo Ye. As with "Miss Ren's Story," it too is set in the imperial capital—just prior to and during the chaos of the An Lushan Rebellion. Significantly, in the context of male-centered narratives, the storyteller first introduces the main male protagonist, Han Hong, and his protégé, one Mr. Li, before introducing the eponymous heroine. Han, we are told, was reckless and poor albeit poetically talented. As with other educated, non-aristocratic men in Tang China, he relied on the recommendation of others for social advancement. His patron, the wealthy Mr. Li, appreciates and promotes talent. Li's favorite concubine, Miss Liu, was "an outstanding beauty of the age; she enjoyed conversation and joking and was good at chanting poetry."[42] After Han moves into Li's household, Miss Liu is able to catch glimpses of him through a doorway. Here, perhaps, is an allusion to how Zhuo Wenjun spied on the famous poet Sima Xiangru when he was entertained at her father's house. Even before the narrator tells us of Miss Liu's romantic attraction to Han, her thoughts are revealed in a rhetorical question that she asks of her servant: "Is it possible that a man like Han will always be poor and obscure?" Once Li learns of her feelings, he gives her to Han during a banquet; in imperial China, it was permissible for a master to dispose of his concubines as he pleased. Similar acts are found in numerous other love stories in which women— particularly concubines—are given or introduced to men as a reward for either talent or meritorious feats. As Paul Rouzer observes, women acted as "prizes" for male competition and display.[43] Indeed, Li further gave Han a large sum of money; hence the female body and monetary gain go hand in hand. Nonetheless, Miss Liu's preference for Han establishes a private space in which "freely elected" romantic feeling may be explored, which Owen considers a key characteristic of the culture of romance.[44]

The contented couple are parted the following year when Han is recommended for an examination to enter the bureaucracy. While he is away, the twin capitals—Chang'an and Luoyang—are overrun by An Lushan's rebel army. Miss Liu, consequently, takes refuge in a Buddhist nunnery. After the rebels' retreat, Han, who was then serving as a military attaché, sends an intermediary with gold and a poem in search of her. She responds with a poem of her own. Hence, as in numerous other love stories, this one uses poetic exchange to reveal both the lover's psychology and the storyteller's literary talent while engaging the reader's emotions. Shortly after this exchange, Miss Liu's beauty leads to her abduction by a Turkic general, Shazhali. Her rescue is eventually brought about after Han returns to the capital in the service of a newly appointed civil official. He happens to meet Miss Liu as she rides in an ox-cart. During this poignant scene, Miss Liu gives him a jade box filled with scented oil as a parting gift, supposing they will never meet again. Shortly after, Han meets a knight-errant figure, Xu Jun, who is a military inspector. On learning of Han's injustice, he immediately undertakes Miss Liu's rescue. Wearing armor and equipped with arrows and a sword, he forces his way into Shazhali's residence, claiming that the general is ill and requests his wife. In their master's absence, the frightened servants do little to prevent him from seizing Miss Liu and returning her to Han. Such a daring act of military prowess carried political risks. Given Shazhali's influence at court, Han fears retribution. This, however, is forestalled when his superior, Hou Xiyi, submits an explanatory memorial to the throne. The emperor rules that Miss Liu be returned to Han and that Shazhali pay a hefty fine (see figure 1.1).[45]

This story exhibits no fewer than two erotic triangles. The first constitutes Han, Miss Liu, and her original master, Mr. Li. The underlying male competition between the young, socioeconomically dependent male and his wealthy patron is established with Miss Liu's preference for the former. The potential competition, however, is readily resolved when Li voluntarily relinquishes Miss Liu. More disruptive is the triangle between Han, Miss Liu, and Shazhali. Han, as an impoverished member of the upper classes, reliant on the patronage of others, is almost powerless to protect his woman and stand against a powerful general with influence at court. Resolution of this second triangle promotes male solidarity.

48 | The Chinese Love Story from the Tenth to the Fourteenth Century

Figure 1.1. A Tang dynasty style oxcart.

Xu Jun's martial valor, along with Hou Xiyi's literary prowess and political influence, prove instrumental in rescuing Miss Liu and assuring the couple's happy ending. The male bureaucratic establishment, represented by the knight-errant and the influential administrator, who is also Han's superior, unite to assist the hero. Sociopolitical as well as friendship ties are thereby forged and strengthened. Hence Han Hong relies on the assistance of several other characters, lending the story the flavor of a folktale in which helpers often prove invaluable to the hero's quest.

Li's gift of his favorite concubine illustrates the inverse of male competition: male patronage. Furthermore, at the conclusion, the emperor acts as the ultimate patron. To be sure, younger men attaining women through social superiors was an especially productive literary motif in the love story, reflective of the period's social conditions. Throughout the imperial period, both social and career advancement depended on the help of powerful supporters. This was particularly important during the Tang dynasty, when bureaucratic entrance relied on a patronage network controlled by the aristocratic ruling class.[46]

As in "Miss Ren's Story," the erotic triangles reveal male sexual competition and anxiety over female loyalty. The first triangle reflects the socioeconomic reality of the period that beautiful and sexually desirable women were collected by somewhat older (or so it is implied) and socioeconomically powerful men. This hints at the likely frustration felt by readers who identified with Han—that is, social juniors yet to establish themselves. Through the second triangle, the narrator reveals Han's grief over the loss of Miss Liu and, indeed, his apparent unhappiness brings about Xu Jun's involvement. Han does not expect to see his love again at this juncture. Yet, the poetic exchange reveals, even before the abduction, his fear that she may not willingly return:

> Zhangtai willows, Zhangtai willows,
> Green in former days, might they still be here?
> Even though their long branches as of old appear
> By now they have been likely plucked by another fellow.

Mistress Liu responds:

> Branches of the willow, how heartily they grow!
> How I hate that, every year, in parting they're bestowed.
> A single leaf follows the wind, abruptly announcing fall,
> Even were my lord to come, would any remain at all?

Zhangtai was the name of a street in Chang'an famous for its brothels. The appellation later became a euphemism for brothel districts in general. In this context, it may have simply referred to the location of Miss Liu's residence given that events supposedly occurred in Chang'an. Yet, in connection with an abducted woman, the allusion seems significant. Furthermore, in Chinese poetry, willows were frequently used to symbolize beautiful women because their thin, pliable branches were considered comparable with a woman's soft hair or slim figure. The term "willow" (*liu*) furthermore puns with Miss Liu's surname. Therefore, Han's allusion to willows in the opening line clearly alludes to her. Accordingly, the line about their being plucked unambiguously discloses anxiety that his lover may acquiesce to another man's advances. It was furthermore customary during the Tang to farewell someone by presenting them with a willow twig since "willow" (*liu*) also punned with the word for "stay," hence Miss Liu's allusion in her second line. As with modern spaghetti westerns in which the heroine is abducted, contemporary readers would almost certainly have been anxious for Miss Liu's safe rescue. Such desire for justice and rectification of the proper social order would have engaged readers while resolving the plot. Conversely, some male readers may have derived pleasure from the thought of a kidnapped woman at the mercy of her captor.

Although romantic attachment engenders the story's plot, Miss Liu's feminine agency is rendered almost invisible by predominant male-centered concerns. She becomes a pawn in an androcentric sociopolitical exchange, one that prioritizes male friendship and competition, social climbing, and bonding, in addition to the patron–client relationship. Little individualized attention is given to her physical features. The author-recorder simply evokes the cliché that she was a consummate beauty of her age. The storyteller also specifies that her good looks led to her abduction, hinting that she may have been considered a *femme fatale*. Nonetheless, that a great beauty of the age would so readily transfer her affections from her powerful lord and master to a comparatively poor poet suggests a male fantasy of female emotional and sexual availability. Her having remained faithful to Han in the face of abduction and, presumably, coerced sex or rape in Shazhali's household, foregrounds the importance of loyalty to the love story while, at the same time, implies male anxiety.

Similarly, no physical description of Han is offered throughout. The reader must be content with Miss Liu's female Gaze, which acts as a mirror affirming the male articulating subject. By using both Miss Liu's gaze and her rhetorical question in place of conventional description ("Is it possible that a man like Han will always be poor and obscure?"), the narrator implies a range of possibilities: good looks, the protagonist's air, his possibly erect carriage, his gait, not to mention intellectual abilities. As with the storyteller's treatment of Miss Liu, Han's physical features are downplayed in favor of the social connections he makes and his career advancement.

Regardless of the anxiety that "Miss Liu's Story" exposes, it concludes on a happy note, as do many Tang-era stories. Such felicitous conclusions achieved through the patronage of a social superior, I would argue, reveal optimism about the storyteller's social network, even though it may have reflected little more than wish fulfillment. That is, talent and diligence could be and was rewarded. And, if things went wrong, ultimately the sagacious emperor would rectify matters. This spirit of optimism, as we shall see, stands in contrast to later periods whose authors were not so sanguine.

If stories such as Miss Liu's convey male anxiety about loss of one's woman, others reveal the desire to possess that of another. Such stories invariably align the reader with an educated protagonist of elite background, yet one sufficiently young not yet to have shouldered a leadership role in society—what Linda Rui Feng terms "para-literati."[47] The female protagonist tends to be either the young, sexually frustrated concubine of an aging magnate, or else a palace lady whose sexuality belonged to a neglectful emperor. A relatively late story titled "Bu Feiyan" is a good example of this type. Initially recorded by Huangfu Mei (fl. 874–910) in his *xiaoshuo* collection *Minor Documents from Sanshui* (Sanshui xiaodu), its later inclusion in *Collected Love Stories* and the *Drunken Man's Talk* indicate its centrality to the love story. Huangfu was a grandson of the chief minister, Bai Minzhong (792–861), and cousin of the famous Bai Juyi and Bai Xingjian. Events related in the story supposedly occurred during the *xiantong* reign period (860–874). Li Jianguo dates the story's recording to 873 or 874.[48] The eponymous Bu Feiyan is the concubine of Wu Gongye, a powerful courtier. She is described in terse clichés: of "beautiful face and slender figure, so much so that she seemed unable to support her silken dress." The male protagonist is Zhao Xiang, the twenty-year-old (*sui*) son of a neighboring scholar-official household. No sooner does he see Bu Feiyan through a crack in a wall, than "his spirit and breath both take leave of him; he forsakes food and forgets sleep." Hoping to instigate an affair, he bribes Wu Gongye's gatekeeper and, through the latter's wife, is able to exchange poetry and letters with his beloved. When the gatekeeper's wife broaches the subject with her, Feiyan confesses to having seen young Zhao and liking what she saw: "I, too, have caught a glimpse of Master Zhao. I greatly admire his good looks and [literary] talent. Unfortunately, I am unlucky in this life and have no means to serve him [as a wife]." An extended exchange of poetry and letters convey the lovers' mutual feelings while soliciting the reader's sympathy. One of these letters affords insight into Bu Feiyan's dissatisfaction with her lord and master: "Unluckily my father died while I was a child. I was deceived by a matchmaker and so came to be mated with a small-minded man." She avails herself of her master's absence to arrange a tryst with Zhao. Since their residences abut, she piles two beds against a common wall that he manages to scale with the aid of a ladder. During their first meeting, the couple "entered Feiyan's boudoir from the rear door, hands joined. Then, with their backs to the lamp, they lowered the bed curtains and proceeded to give full reign to their passion." In the dialogue that follows, Feiyan expresses guilt over having betrayed her master as she attempts to justify her actions: "Tonight's meeting was ordained in a previous existence. Don't believe that I am without chaste principles to do something as dissolute as this, but having encountered your bearing and demeanor, I can't help myself. I wish to reflect deeply in it." The lovers continue to meet for a further year. Wu Gongye remains ignorant until tipped off by Feiyan's servant, whom her mistress had beaten over a misdemeanor. Feigning all-night business, Wu leaves home, only to retrace his steps. He then witnesses Feiyan reciting poetry by her window just as young Zhao climbs the rear wall to reach her. Having unsuccessfully attempted to accost him, Wu instead interrogates Feiyan. Angry at her lies, he has her tied to a pillar and savagely beats her. She dies soon after, unrepentant: "Having had someone affectionate in life, I have no regret to die." Wu pretends that she died of an illness, but the neighbors know the truth.[49]

The narrative includes a brief metatextual story that tells how two of Wu Gongye's educated acquaintances, Misters Li and Cui, heard what had happened and wrote poems about Feiyan. Cui's sympathetic poem includes the lines: "It is just like the scattering of people who passed flowers in drinking games, the most luxuriant branch is left on an empty couch." Li's poem, however, reflects moral conservatism: "If her beautiful and fragrant soul indeed had an afterlife, she would have felt ashamed to meet the girl who threw herself down from the tower."[50] Li alludes to the story of the loyal concubine Green Pearl who committed suicide when threatened with rape. Such devotion enshrined her as a faithful paragon throughout the imperial period.[51] In a final narrative twist that draws on the *zhiguai* tradition, Feiyan's ghost appears in dreams to thank Cui and berate Li, threatening to confront him in the netherworld. He dies soon after.

In contrast to "Miss Liu's Story," that of Bu Feiyan positions readers on the other side of the erotic triangle. Instead of foregrounding the male protagonist's fear of losing his lover, here we are invited to empathize with the adulterous couple as the husband's role is diminished. The sympathy accorded Bu Feiyan contrasts with authorial attitudes to adulterous first wives in other Tang-period narratives.[52] Nonetheless, although cast in a sympathetic light, the immorality attached to female infidelity remains. Consequently, Bu Feiyan sacrifices her life for romantic freedom and satisfies the demands of both romance and patriarchy.[53]

The apologetic metanarrative about the two poets furthermore offers an insight into contemporary reader reception. Cui's compassionate response, as Manling Luo observes, foregrounds the story's tragic aspect and offers no moral judgment.[54] Li, on the other hand, reflects a moralistic attitude informed by Confucian orthodoxy. While twenty-first-century readers may see this as overly conservative, Li's values were, nonetheless, mainstream for the period. Competing views similar to those of Cui and

Li are found in many love stories and erotic novels of late imperial times. Even when no overtly orthodox judgment is offered, Li's critique allows us to imagine how such a socially conservative stance informed actual readers' horizon of expectation vis-à-vis literary sexual encounters.

In contrast to Mr. Li is Huangfu Mei's authorial end commentary. This exhibits considerable sympathy for Bu Feiyan while acknowledging the threat her action posed to patriarchal values.

> Alas! Every age has known alluring faces, yet seldom do we hear of unsullied virtue. For this reason, the gentleman who boasts of his talent will be of deficient virtue; the woman who flaunts her beauty will develop romantic liaisons. In life, if one could carry a basin full of water (without spilling any) or stand on the edge of a bottomless pit (without falling), then we would all be proper gentlemen and prim ladies. Although Bu Feiyan's crime is not excusable, we may feel pity for her when we consider her (sincere) heart.[55]

Although Huangfu's comment about talented gentlemen invites the reader to apply the story's lesson beyond narrated events, his focus on the culture of romance is clear and the plausibility of historical factuality remains. He explains Bu Feiyan's infidelity as natural human weakness stemming from her beauty and emotional sensibility. Yet despite overt sympathy, his overgeneralization about beautiful women belies male anxiety over female infidelity, echoing the end commentary to "Miss Ren's Story." Therefore, even for empathetic author-compilers such as Huangfu Mei, orthodox morality was too strong to ignore.

In regard to possession of another's woman, what more ambitious hope might the male subject harbor than possession of an emperor's lady? Several stories tell of men who either married or acquired palace ladies—that is, women who had pledged sexual and personal fealty to the emperor in return for the privilege of serving him in the palace. The poetic image of a palace lady was well established by the mid–Tang period as poets and storytellers, fueled by historical precedent, often fetishized their supposed lonely existence. Intense competition among them for the emperor's favor was thought to have caused loneliness and sexual frustration, thus rendering them ripe for male attention. "Vice-Censor Zheng" is a good example. The story's male protagonist, Liang Houben, rescues a palace woman from a coffin that floated downriver next to his country residence. The woman's relative, the title's eponymous Vice-Censor Zheng, had incurred the emperor's displeasure. Having shared his downfall, the woman had been strangled and placed in the coffin, yet miraculously survived. Liang married her, although whether as a first wife or concubine is unclear. As a talented lute player, her musicmaking eventually led to detection by a palace official. When informed, however, the emperor granted her clemency as penance for his violent act.[56]

This story's hero fulfills a male fantasy that, under normal circumstances, would have been nigh impossible—that is, sexually possessing a talented and, presumably, beautiful young palace woman.[57] Hence the improbable device of the floating coffin is necessary to engender the felicitous denouement. Accordingly, the rescue of the woman from the river and the circumstances of her expulsion from the palace absolve the protagonist from *lèse majesté* that possessing an emperor's woman would have otherwise entailed. No less a figure than the emperor himself forms both the third party in an erotic triangle and, at the same time, a benevolent social superior who bestows the heroine on our protagonist. Again we have an optimistic ending predicated on imperial clemency and one that affirms imperial rule. The emperor's violent act is all but glossed over, while his generosity is celebrated. In his *History of Affection*, Ming scholar Feng Menglong included this story under the category of "predestined affection." Feng no doubt recognized the extraordinary, if not implausible, coincidence of the lover's meeting as evidence of predestiny, another well-explored theme that I will discuss below.

Marriage

Marriage was a fertile theme for many a Tang dynasty storyteller. Nonetheless, such stories either illustrated the idea of predestined marriage or else focused on paranormal phenomena, such as a marriage between a man and a female ghost. From this we can see the influence of earlier and contemporaneous *zhiguai* accounts that Daniel Hsieh refers to as "animal-bride" and "animal-groom" stories.[58] On the other hand, "Li Wa's Story" (discussed below) is a rare example of marriage between human protagonists without paranormal occurrences.

Marital predestiny as both a widespread folklore and literary theme endured throughout the imperial period.[59] Besides popular fatalistic belief, it sometimes reflects Buddhist ideas about reincarnation—that is, that unrequited love in a previous lifetime may find fulfillment in later incarnations. Indeed, Bu Feiyan's remark that "tonight's meeting was ordained in a previous existence" refers to this. Coincidental meetings under unlikely circumstances were sometimes thought to evince conjugal predestiny. At other times the storyteller directly addresses such belief in a metatextual commentary. The narrator or protagonists themselves might remark how their meeting was "not random" (*fei ouran*) or was "a match made in Heaven" (*tian zuo zhi he*), while in other stories predestiny is merely implied.

An extremely famous yet simple story, "Hou Xutu," and its variants lucidly illustrates the theme. In this, a gentleman finds a leaf on which a love poem has been written. Years later, when he marries, he is astounded to discover that the poem's author and his new wife are one and the same. In most versions, the leaf is found floating from the moat outside the imperial palace, thereby linking the location with the poem's author who happens to be a lonely yet romantically inaccessible palace lady. In another version, the leaf floats on an autumn breeze.[60] In light of this, the fact that Liang Houben's concubine floats to her lover on a river is significant as the woman's body itself replaces the leaf, strongly suggesting that "Vice-Director Zheng" was conceived after the leaf motif became popular.

In another famous story, when the emperor's palace ladies are ordered to make army jackets for soldiers serving on the western frontier, one woman secretes a love poem inside the jacket she is making. Its later discovery warrants severe punishment as the woman's infidelity constitutes disloyalty—indeed treason—to the emperor. Yet in an unexpected act of clemency, his majesty marries her to the poem's recipient. The predestined nature of their union is made explicit at the conclusion when the woman tells her new husband that she is tying the knot with him in *this lifetime*, not the next.[61] Again we see the desire to possess a palace lady, in addition to an affirmation of imperial justice: "From this time onwards, there was not one among the border people who did not think fondly of the emperor's clemency. They defended with the utmost loyalty and the border, thanks to this, remained peaceful."[62] Again the emperor becomes the ultimate arbitrator of a couple's happiness.

Perhaps no other well-developed story illustrates marital predestiny more explicitly than "Inn of Betrothal," in which Wei Gu meets the legendary Man in the Moon. Wei was the son of a scholar-official, although whether he is an aristocrat is unclear. As his father died while he was young, Wei wished to marry early so as to continue the family line, yet his previous proposals had been unsuccessful. Very early one morning, before the moon had faded, he went to discuss yet another marriage proposal at a nearby temple. There he came across an old man reading a book that he could not understand. When asked, the old man told him that it was a book from the otherworld (*youming zhi shu*). In the ensuing conversation, the old man revealed himself as the arbiter of matrimony, a divinity responsible for marriage. He then explained the function of magical red cords vis-à-vis conjugal predestiny: "Once a couple are joined with this string, they can never remove it, no matter if their families are enemies, should they be rich or poor, should they be separated by countless miles or whether they travel to far-flung localities." When the anxious Wei inquired about his own conjugal destiny, the old man foretold that he would marry in fourteen years' time a bride who was currently the three-year-old (*sui*) daughter of a melon seller. Wei asked to see her, so the old man led him to a local fruit and vegetable market. When Wei saw an aging woman carry an ugly infant through the market place, he was disappointed that his future wife was of such humble status. So he asked the old man if he could kill the child. The old man replied, "She is destined to enjoy a great fortune. It is because of her son that she may enjoy it." When Wei asked if his servant may kill her, the old man disappeared. Reminiscent of the fairytale "Snow White," Wei offered his servant a large reward to murder the child. Although the eager servant attempted to do so, he succeeded only in wounding her. The story then jumps fourteen years into the future when Wei inherits a civil service posting from his father due to the hereditary *yin* privilege.[63] He soon after marries the attractive daughter of a bureaucrat who admires Wei's ability. When Wei notices that, after a year of marriage, she never removes a beauty patch worn on her forehead, she reluctantly explains the reason. "I am the prefect's foster child, not his real daughter. In the past, my father governed Song City and I was still a baby when he passed away. My mother and brother died one after the other. The only house we had was in Song City South. I lived there with my wet nurse, Madam Chen, not far from the inn. Madam Chen would sell vegetables so as to make ends meet. She took pity that I was a baby and couldn't bear to abandon me. When I was three, she carried me to the market where a maniac stabbed me. The scar is still there, so I cover it with a flower." Wei then confesses that he was the culprit. Rather than become resentful, she marveled at the workings of fate and devoted herself even more dutifully to her husband. The narrative concludes with information about her son who became a bureaucrat, in addition to an imperial title she received because of his social position, which fulfilled the old man's prophecy. A metatextual comment remarks on how such matters are predestined.⁶⁴

Concluding with biographical information in this manner is premised on the belief that life's milestones, such as career, social standing, progeny, and time of death, all depend on fate. Given contemporary readers' tendency to read such stories as grounded in historical fact, such a concluding device offers further proof of destiny. This formula was frequently used by short-story tellers throughout later periods.

Stories such as this were clearly intended to demonstrate the workings of conjugal fate and to reconcile couples to arranged marriage. Contemporary readers would have understood Wei Gu's inability to change his destiny as a powerful illustration of fate's inevitability. The Old Man of the Moon reflects the widespread belief that deities could arbitrate one's destiny. His use of red thread to bind conjugal ties was also an enduring, popular belief. In love stories and poetry of the imperial era, red thread became a well-established metaphor of marital predestiny; indeed, the color red remains the traditional Chinese wedding color. Hence, as with their counterparts in Europe, so too did lovers "tie the knot"; in old China, however, it was done with red thread. Nonetheless, both the story's focus on paranormal phenomena and its denial of free choice render it marginal to the culture of romance.

As Manling Luo has observed, the story's heroine received the worst of the bargain as she was compelled to accept a husband seventeen years her senior. Wei, by contrast, received a beautiful, young wife. It seems that fate, therefore, favored the male.⁶⁵ Similarly, in the story series of the floating leaf or that of the poem concealed in a battle jacket, even though the female takes the initiative, the male protagonist and male articulating subject closely align. The female, by contrast, is clearly the object of a male fantasy that centers on beautiful, albeit lonely, sexually unfulfilled women who are dependent on men for ontological meaning. The conjugal destiny motif, although romantic, camouflages such fantasies.

Many stories found in *zhiguai* collections of the mid- and late Tang period combine both paranormal (*zhiguai*) and romantic (*liqing*) elements. Although narratological interest foregrounds in the anomalous event, their plots commence or develop as would a love story given their inclusion of romantic freedom of choice. Dai Fu (fl. 757) recorded several such stories in his collection of mainly paranormal events titled *Extensive Collection of Marvels* (*Guangyi ji*). In "Clerk Liu's Daughter," for example, the eponymous protagonist's daughter dies during her father's tenure as a provincial bureaucrat. On completion of his term, Liu leaves by boat, taking his deceased daughter's remains with him for later burial. His friend, Gao Guang, follows him aboard a boat of his own. Late one night, while the two boats are moored by a riverbank, a young serving-maid of comely appearance boards Gao's boat to borrow candles. When Gao's son flirts with her, she offers to arrange a meeting with her mistress, who she claims is of "peerless beauty." Thinking that the maid refers to Liu's living daughter, he agrees and so, on the following moonlit night, he saw "a woman emerge from the rear of the vessel, accompanied by the maid, heading in his direction. When she was ten (double) paces away, her radiance shone forth while her fragrance assailed his very being. Gao could barely maintain concentration. He stepped forward and embraced her. The girl melted into his arms, her loveliness overflowing. They proceeded into the interior of the boat where they redoubled their intimacy. After this, she came every night." A month or so elapses, after which she reveals her true form: "I am my father's deceased daughter. It is my fate to come back to life and my karma to be your wife. If you would have me, you should inform your father." She predicts the time of her rebirth and gives instructions on how to nurse her back to health. Young Gao tells his father, who in turn relates the story to Liu and his wife. The latter is particularly angry. Believing that her daughter's corpse is in a state of decay, she refuses Gao's proposal. The parents change their mind, however, after they both dream of their deceased daughter who explains her impending rebirth in terms of karma. Three days later, when both families open the coffin, they find her perfectly preserved. Removing her from the coffin, they follow her instructions for resurrection and marriage. As final proof of the girl's providential revival, the narrator tells how she later gave birth to several children.[66]

As may be seen, the storyteller's interest clearly lies with the anomalous event, which nicely fits the *zhiguai* genre. Nevertheless, if we ignore the fact of the daughter's decease, the couple's romance is no different from that of a prototypical love story. Furthermore, the formulaic descriptions of the heroine and the device of a maid-as-intermediary were hallmarks of later love stories. The subversive nature of the couple's sexual union is neutralized as their eventual marriage returns them to the patriarchal fold. Moreover, freely chosen love is the catalyst for the heroine's rebirth. To contemporary readers, this would have evinced love's ability to enact physical transformation (*qing gan*)—in this case, resurrection from the dead.

Popular Buddhist ideas of karma and fatalism are further evoked to explain and justify what would otherwise be inexplicable. What distinguishes this story from mainstream, didactic *zhiguai* accounts is its endorsement of romantic freedom of choice. Unlike most other anomalous accounts, the male protagonist neither dies nor suffers ill effects after intimacy with the ghost. There is no hint of moralizing. The homage paid to the power of love/*qing* ensured its inclusion in the seventeenth-century compendium *History of Affection*.

"Wushuang's Story," first recorded by Xue Diao (830–872), remained extremely popular throughout the imperial period.[67] While almost all marriage-related stories of the period resembled those discussed above, this is a rare example of romance that leads to marriage between human protagonists. It also affords further insights into both the love story's portrayal of women and its androcentric aspects. Its inclusion in both *Collected Love Stories* and Luo Ye's *Drunken Man's Talk* indicate its centrality to the love story. Luo Ye classifies it as an old story of reunion. It is also a story of union between two cousins, Wang Xianke and the eponymous Wushuang. Her name, meaning "without peer," stereotypes her as a lass unparalleled. After the death of Wang's father, he and his mother move into his uncle's residence in Chang'an. His uncle, Liu Zhen, is a powerful courtier. Since Wang Xianke and Wushuang play together as children, Wushuang's mother playfully refers to Wang as "the Young Master," as she would a son-in-law. Wang's mother admires Wushuang, whom she describes as "beautiful and quick-witted." On her deathbed, she asks her brother to marry Wushuang to her son. The uncle, however, demurs. When his mother dies, Wang returns to his native Xianyang, where he says to himself, "I am orphaned and am alone in the world. I should marry and continue the family line." After the morning period, he packs his bags and returns to his uncle's house. There, through a crack in the wall, he glimpses the, by now, grown Wushuang, who is described as of "graceful bearing and radiant beauty, equal to that of deities and immortals." Having thus beheld his beloved, he "goes crazy." So as to ply his uncle's household with gifts in the hope that they will support his suit, he proceeds to sell his possessions. He even buys exquisite hair ornaments for his aunt's birthday. The delighted aunt promptly presses his suit with her husband who, nonetheless, rebuffs her. Given his elevated social position, it is implied that Liu would have had the choice of many excellent young men as potential sons-in-law.

The situation abruptly changes in 783 when the military governor of Huaixi, Li Xilie, rebels and troops led by Yao Lingyan, summoned to quell the rebellion, instead join it. The uncle unexpectedly returns from the palace one morning to report how rebels have forced the emperor and his court to flee. He then calls for his nephew and promises him Wushuang's hand in marriage. "Liu Zhen had some twenty carts packed with gold, silver, silk, and brocade, and instructed Wang. 'Change your clothing and conduct these goods through the Longview Gate. Find a secluded inn and take lodging there. I'll escort your aunt and Wushuang out of the city through the Cathay Gate and take a roundabout route to join you.'" Unfortunately, the uncle and his family are arrested while attempting to escape. When Wang learns of this, in view of the turmoil, he returns to Xianyang.

Three years later, after the rebellion has been crushed, Wang returns to Chang'an in search of his relations. There he meets a former servant, Saihong, who informs him that his aunt and uncle were executed as traitors and that Wushuang was pressed into the imperial harem. On hearing that a former maid, Caiping, is still alive and serving in the household of a general, the distraught Wang redeems her. The sympathetic general pulls strings to have Wang appointed as a minor government official in charge of a state-run guesthouse. After Wang has served there for several months, a group of palace ladies come to stay overnight, among whom is Wushuang. Given the customary segregation of palace ladies from outsiders, Wang is unable to communicate with her directly. Saihong, however, manages to do so surreptitiously. Wushuang, for her part, leaves a letter under a cushion for Wang to find. Although he is unable to speak with her, he manages to catch a glimpse of her departing carriage: "As the third carriage passed by, the curtain parted and it was indeed Wushuang. It was a sight which filled Wang with as much grief as it did longing." The letter included a postscript that read, "I have heard several times that there is a man of chivalrous spirit in Fuping County, an officer named Gu. Can you seek his help?"

Officer Gu proves to be a knight-errant. Through an elaborate scheme lasting several months, he eventually engenders Wushuang's rescue by feigning her death. Having first acquired a magic pill that induces a cataleptic-type trance, he dispatches Caiping to deliver it to Wushuang. In order to prevent news of the rescue—kidnapping an emperor's palace lady was no light crime—he not only kills Saihong and sundry others but also himself. Wang Xianke and Wushuang relocate to Wang's country residence in Xianyang where they have several children and enjoy fifty years of married life.[68]

Focusing on romantic aspects, I have summarized the story's last phase in the briefest manner; the scheme to liberate Wushuang actually occupies about a third of the narrative. Hence, the story is a blend of prototypes: that of romantic love as well as the knight-errant tale, not to mention strong *zhiguai* elements. My analysis will concentrate on the romantic theme. Unusual for a Tang dynasty love story, which tends to tell of transitory affairs between elite males and lower-class females, the heroine of this story is the male protagonist's social equal. Since a *femme fatale* theme (discussed below) is not intended, the pathway to matrimony drives plot development. Therefore, romantic freedom of choice and marriage are not mutually exclusive as they are in almost every other Tang dynasty love story.

Wang Xianke and Wushuang certainly have a strong claim to be married. It is the wish of both their mothers. Furthermore, Wushuang's mother addressing Wang as she would a son-in-law establishes an expectation that they will eventually marry. Given the death of Wang's parents, his wish to produce heirs for his family's ancestral cult was no less than socially expected. Indeed, no more urgent a reason for marriage could be found throughout the imperial period. Hence, the protagonists' pursuit of happiness through marriage also demonstrates filial piety. As he and Wushuang are social peers, little objection may be made against their union on grounds of class disparity, discounting the uncle's wish to improve his social position. Indeed, given the established custom to marry cousins throughout the imperial period, providing the surname did not coincide, Wang Xianke and Wushuang's familial relationship strengthens the case.

Wang's relationship with his uncle institutes a love triangle of a different kind than previously discussed; while the uncle is not a sexual rival, he is certainly a social superior with whom the junior must contend. Prior to the rebellion, the greatest obstacle to lover's happiness is the uncle's implied desire to social climb. Yet, when the rebellion destroys sociopolitical normality, so too are such socioeconomic considerations. The story, therefore, tacitly critiques the deep-seated custom of marriage for socioeconomic advancement. As we will see, the story's endorsement of informal betrothals, the parental roles in facilitating romantic happiness, and the expectation that cousins would marry after having growing up together would frequently reoccur in stories of the Song dynasty. Hence, "Wushuang" is no less than a landmark of narrative literary history.

Although the story takes its title from the heroine's name, Wushuang remains a shadowy figure throughout. Direct description of her occupies only a small portion of the overall narrative and, even then, we rarely "see" her. Early in the story, she becomes the object of Wang's gaze as he peers through a crack in the wall. Prior to this, the narrator briefly introduces her and explains her relation to Wang. We are told about her character and appearance through Wang's mother's monologue, yet we neither hear about nor see her during the political crisis. Toward the end of the narrative, the storyteller describes her lifeless form and how Wang nursed her to a speedy recovery. The only occasion on which we hear her speak is when she communicates to Saihong through the guesthouse's bamboo blind; we do, however, see her departing face through Wang's gaze. Unlike other heroines, the reader is offered little dialogue with which to understand her thoughts, and there is little or no characterization. Like Miss Liu, she remains an object of male desire and fuels male competition, first between Wang Xianke and his uncle, and second between Wang and the briefly mentioned men of quality which, presumably, the uncle has in mind as potential sons-in-law. A third erotic triangle emerges between Wang and the emperor. Indeed, the latter's narrative function is comparable to Zhashali in "Miss Liu's Story" after Wushuang is taken into the imperial harem.

Besides the multiple love triangles engendered by Wang's desire for Wushuang, the friendship he patiently builds with Officer Gu, the knight-errant helper, foregrounds traditional male friendship. Gu, in turn, sacrifices his life for his friend, as does the servant, Saihong. As in "Miss Liu's Story," loss of the female provides a catalyst for male bonding and assistance. Furthermore, male anxiety over loss of a female is dramatized by Wang Xianke and Wushuang's traumatic separation. Even prior to this, Wang worries that his suit will be unsuccessful and so empties his purse to bribe members of his uncle's household. This action foreshadows the gifts he later gives Officer Gu. Not unlike "Miss Liu's Story" therefore, this story's androcentric aspects are so strong that, to a large extent, they eclipse romantic themes. The multifarious themes and generic elements suggest a pastiche comprised of several—possibly once separate—stories.

A rare story focusing on freedom of choice that leads to marriage, devoid of paranormal elements, is "Li Wa's Story." As with "Wushuang," its inclusion in both *Collected Love Stories* and the *Drunken Man's Talk* render it central to the love story corpus. Likely to have been recorded in the early ninth century, it recounts events that purportedly occurred during the *tianbao* reign period (742–756). Its male protagonist is a twenty-year-old aristocrat. In view of the youthful misdemeanors that the story exposes, his name has been suppressed—assuming the story is based on actual events, although it was traditionally read this way. He is referred to as "Master Zheng" throughout. His father characterizes him as the family's "thousand-mile colt" given his precocious intelligence and literary talent. He therefore endows his son with no less that two years' worth of living expenses and sends him to Chang'an to prepare for the imperial examinations. One day, the young Zheng sees the beautiful courtesan, Li Wa, standing in her doorway. A terse formula encapsulates her beauty: "a woman whose bewitching looks were beyond compare." Li Wa returns the male Gaze to show her "feelings of deep admiration." Smitten by her charms, the young man soon visits her in the company of friends. The narrator describes her "bright eyes, white wrists and movements that were voluptuous and captivating" as she emerges to greet him. The young man stays for the night and, the following morning, arranges with Li Wa's adoptive mother to move in. Henceforth he isolates himself from polite society and associates solely with members of the lower classes. He soon starts selling his possessions and, in little over a year, is destitute. Wishing to rid herself of an insolvent client, the mother hatches an elaborate plot with Li Wa unbeknownst to the young man. One day she suggests, "My daughter has known you for a whole year, but she is still not with child. I often hear tell that the Spirit of the Bamboo Grove responds to prayers as surely as an echo. Would you agree to offer a libation and pray for a son?" The unsuspecting protagonist readily agrees. On their return journey, they stop by Li Wa's "auntie's" house, a magnificent residence replete with gardens and courtyards. During the visit, a rider suddenly bursts in announcing that Li Wa's mother has been taken dangerously ill. As Li Wa has been, up to this point, traveling by carriage, it is decided that she should take the young man's horse and send it back later. When considerable time passes and she does not return, the "auntie" urges him to investigate. When he reaches Li Wa's residence, he is told that the mother moved out two days ago. Distraught, he retraces his steps. When he finally reaches the "auntie's" mansion, he is told that it belongs to Minister Cui and had been rented for a family gathering the previous day.

When he returns to his former residence, not knowing what to do, the empathetic landlord offers him temporary accommodation. Too distraught to eat, however, he soon falls ill. Fearing the worst, the landlord abandons him in a funeral home. There, thanks to the owner's generosity, he eventually recovers and earns his keep by holding the funerary curtains during services. He also utilizes a newfound talent for singing funeral dirges. At this point, the plot diverges with a lengthy narration of the funeral home's rivalry with another establishment. This culminates in an elaborate competition between the two in which the young man brings a gathered crowd to tears with his rendition of the funeral dirge "Dew on the Shallots." The commotion wrought by the competition attracts even upper-class spectators including, coincidentally, the young man's father who happens to be in town. At its conclusion, the father's servant recognizes and accosts the young Zheng. His father deals with him severely: "With ambition and conduct no better than this you have soiled and dishonored my house. How can you have the face to meet me again?" He then takes his son to, ironically, the Apricot Garden where it was customary to fete newly passed examination candidates. There he beats him severely and leaves him to die. The young man is again saved by the funeral home owner. The beating, however, leaves him in a desperately sorry state. Unable to move his limbs for several days, his wounds soon become ulcerated. Repelled by the smell, the funeral home's employees cast him into the street. Passers-by give him food scraps and, once he is able to move again, he resorts to begging. In this manner, the once proud "thousand-mile colt" must sleep in hollowed-out dung piles.

One snowy, winter's day, Li Wa hears the young man's piteous calls for food. Recognizing his voice, she hurries out to help him.

> She went out with rapid steps and saw him, emaciated and full of sores, scarcely looking human. Li Wa was moved by the sight. She said to him: "You must surely be Master—!" He collapsed, overcome with indignation. Unable to speak, he merely nodded. Li Wa went forward and put her arms around his neck. She wrapped him in an embroidered jacket, took him back to the west chamber and burst into a long lament, saying: "I am to blame for bringing you so suddenly to this pass." She swooned and revived again.

When her mother enters, an altercation ensues as the mother wishes to throw him out. In a lengthy monologue, Li Wa admits duplicity in the young man's demise. Taking the moral high ground, she professes her intention to rectify their former wrongdoing. She proposes to redeem herself with the proceeds of twenty years' "wages" so as to nurse the young Zheng back to health; in effect, she becomes his surrogate mother. When he recovers, she persuades him to resume his studies, buys him books, and supervises his progress as would a schoolmarm. She even pontificates about his readiness for the examination. After he passes the first round, she urges him to take the second, more prestigious one so as to attain first rank among his peers. Once he passes this and is granted a bureaucratic posting, so as to facilitate his marriage to an aristocratic woman, she generously resolves to leave him. "You must marry a girl from a great family, for her to serve at the ancestral sacrifices in the winter and autumn. By a marriage with one of your own cousins you will avoid bringing shame upon yourself. Do your best to take care of yourself! Now I shall be gone." The young man reluctantly agrees on the condition that she accompany him for the first leg of his journey to his provincial posting. During this, he meets his father who is en route to a posting of his own. In a poignant reunion, the father declares: "I and you are father and son as before." When he hears about Li Wa's role in his son's rehabilitation, he installs her in a purposely built house as a prelude to accepting her as his daughter-in-law. The narrative concludes with information about the four sons that she bore and how they all became bureaucrats. Li Wa herself was awarded the title of Lady Qianguo, an extremely prestigious one reserved for the highest echelons of the Tang aristocracy. These last details would have been purportedly intended as proof that their marriage was predestined.[69]

In a metatextual commentary, Bai Xingjian claims to have recorded the story at the request of the famous man of letters, Li Gongzuo (c. 770–c. 848), after having related it to him in 795. This date, however, is almost certainly incorrect and no modern scholar has accepted it; probable years of composition range between 806 and 819.[70] Bai's professed authorial motivation is to extol Li Wa's "remarkably true and loyal conduct." In his end commentary, he further states: "O—that a wanton singing girl (i.e., courtesan/prostitute) could prove so true! Even the paragons of womanly virtue in ancient times could not do more. How can we help sighing in admiration for her?"[71] Li Wa's "true and loyal conduct" was predicated on her having saved the young man from destitution, nursing him back to health and supervising a resumption of his studies that led to examination success—in short, his social rehabilitation. Li Wa was, therefore, hailed as an exemplar.

Nonetheless, her conduct is far from blameless when we consider her role in the young man's demise. In the words of the famous sixteenth-century bibliophile, Hu Yinglin, "That Li Wa later took in Li [the young man] was just enough to atone for her guilt in abandoning him. It is utterly ridiculous for the author to praise her virtue."[72] Similarly, Feng

Menglong observes, "It was unfortunate that the young man met Li Wa, but how fortunate it was for her to meet him again!"[73] Such comments illustrate the way in which Li Wa's constructed virtue would have been viewed by many contemporary and post-Tang readers alike.

Furthermore, as Liu Kairong observes, it is highly unlikely that a premier aristocratic clan such as the Zheng's would have accepted a former courtesan as a daughter-in-law.[74] As already noted, the preeminent aristocratic families preferred intermarriage with their peers and at times disdained even imperial princesses. Given, moreover, a courtesan's debased social status and dubious morality, it was illegal for upper-class males to marry them and, as Dudbridge points out, even taking them as concubines met with disapproval.[75] It is no more likely that aristocrats such as the Zheng's would have welcomed gossip about a former courtesan marrying into their clan than their Victorian counterparts. While modern readers, conditioned to viewing films such as *Pretty Woman*, may overlook this aspect of the story and read it as one that celebrates interclass marriage, many traditional readers may not have seen it that way. At best, Li Wa's "true and loyal conduct" mitigates her former duplicity. Her disloyalty, by dint of contrast, enhances the merit of her later good deeds.

Given the storyteller's professed intention to conceal the protagonist's identity, it is curious he does so in such an obvious manner. As he provided not only the protagonist's surname but also the location of the Zheng clan's ancestral seat, contemporary readers would have easily identified the family. Moreover, if Bai Xingjian's authorial intention truly was to praise Li Wa's virtue, why should he conceal the young man's name? The story's first line, which gives Li Wa's title, accentuates this contradiction as it unambiguously identifies both her and the protagonist. This opening line, therefore, may well have been a later addition, as both Dudbridge and Cheng Yizhong point out.[76]

Given the salacious aspects of both Li Wa's social status, her initial treachery, and the unlikelihood that an aristocratic family would accept her, in addition to the half-hearted concealment of the protagonist's name, readers from at least the Song dynasty onward have understood the story as malicious gossip directed at members of the Zheng clan. Besides Liu Kairong, however, few modern scholars maintain this reading, and Glen Dudbridge has argued against it. Nonetheless, as Dudbridge observes, such a reading's central assumption remains good: "contemporary readers must have recognized that behind the deliberately flawed device of anonymity, the *Li Wa chuan* concerned one of the great clans of the old northern aristocracy."[77] As this has no bearing on the current study, I will not pursue the matter further—suffice to note this Song dynasty reading of the story.

If the story is not read as malicious gossip and we take the storyteller's praise for Li Wa at face value, guided by its end commentary it may be alternatively read as a didactic work—that is, to uphold the heroine as a paragon of female virtue in view of her "true and loyal conduct." Accordingly, her elevation into society's upper echelons through marriage is her just reward. The story's denouement neutralizes the subversive nature of unsanctioned sexual relations and the threat of the courtesan–*femme fatale* by incorporating the latter into the patriarchy, thereby preserving orthodox social standards. Nonetheless, Li Wa's characterization as both *femme fatale* and supporter of patriarchal values create competing voices within the text that elude straight-forward interpretation. No doubt this has enhanced the story's enduring attraction. Its dualistic nature furthermore echoes that of Miss Ren, who was both a paragon and morally dubious fox-fairy.

Rather than foreground romantic love, much of the narrative follows momentous events from the protagonist's perspective as he disgraces himself and almost dies (twice) until his eventual rehabilitation. Although this fits the reunion prototype, it is hardly a straight-forward celebration of romance, and whether the storyteller wished to endorse interclass marriage is unclear. Narrative details even resist Owen's criteria for the culture of romance—that is, one in which financial realities of the *demimonde* are suppressed.[78] To be sure, pecuniary self-interest on which the lover's seemingly freely chosen affair was based is later exposed. The couple's permanent reunion is arranged and sanctioned by the young man's father, at which point the couple had both agreed to separate. Hence it may also be read as a story of arranged marriage in which romantic aspects are outweighed by moralizing ones. In fact, the story's exposé of the profit-driven basis of a courtesan's relationship with her clients is highly unusual for a love story. From this perspective, the story is something of an aberration among prototypical love stories.

The story's focus on marriage between human protagonists is of great importance vis-à-vis the love story's history. The closest comparable example is "Wushuang's Story." Nonetheless, as already noted, paranormal means were necessary to affect Wushuang's rescue, which somewhat marginalizes it vis-à-vis the reunion prototype. In Li Wa, on the contrary, no paranormal element exists. Nonetheless, marriage between an upper-class young man and a virtuous courtesan—at least the literary construction

68 | The Chinese Love Story from the Tenth to the Fourteenth Century

of a virtuous courtesan—was to become common from the Song dynasty onward. As we will see, borrowed elements from "Li Wa's Story" by later raconteurs attest to its enduring influence.

FEMME FATALES

Many stories discussed thus far take romantic loyalty as their central theme and reward the heroine for her constancy. Some stories, however, evoke the *femme fatale* stereotype to address disloyalty. The idea that a seductive woman could cause dynastic ruination was a long-established cultural construct supported by numerous historical and/or apocryphal examples. Among the earliest is Lady Bao of Si, queen of King You (r. 781–771 BCE), last ruler of the Western Zhou dynasty. In a culmination of undue favor lavished on Lady Bao merely to make her smile, the King repeatedly lit a series of beacon fires used to summon his feudal lords in case of attack. Eventually, when an enemy *did* attack, the exasperated lords failed to come. The King was consequently killed, Lady Bao captured, and the capital pillaged, thus marking the end of the Western Zhou.[79] As discussed above, Precious Consort Yang was similarly blamed for the Xuanzong emperor's extravagance and near dynastic collapse. Moreover, as empire-wide governance was based on the Confucian model of family management, a consort or empress thus blamed for dynastic downfall was considered akin to an unfaithful wife. Such women were referred to as *youwu*—literally, "supremely beautiful creatures," whose beauty was considered sufficient to bewitch males and destroy their resolve.[80] While modern readers may rightly deem this idea misogynistic, it was nevertheless a well-established notion enshrined in (male-authored) historiography.

The idea that virtue untested is not true virtue occurs in the multithematic, hermeneutically subtle "Yingying's Story," whose heroine was portrayed as a femme fatale. Recorded by the poet Yuan Zhen (779–831), many scholars have read "Yingying's Story" as autobiographic.[81] Its inclusion in both *Collected Love Stories* and the *Drunken Man's Talk* established its centrality to the love story. Such was the story's popularity that it inspired an exceptionally famous opera, "Story of the Western Chamber" (Xixiang ji). It was also anthologized in numerous narrative collections throughout the imperial period. Set in the year 800, the story opens with a description of its male protagonist, Master Zhang, who is "of a gentle nature and handsome appearance. He held steadfastly to his personal principles and refused to become involved in anything improper." He had, furthermore, "never been intimate with a woman." When charged by anonymous interlocutors of indifference to feminine beauty, he counters by owning never to have met with "creatures of supremely bewitching beauty" (youwu) to whom he is especially vulnerable. The plot unfolds when Zhang visits Pu Prefecture, about 100 kilometers west of the Tang capital, Chang'an, on the Yellow River. While lodging at a Buddhist temple, he meets his widowed maternal aunt, Madam Cui, who is en route to Chang'an. When a local military insurrection breaks out, Zhang uses his connection with the rebel commander to spare his aunt and children. The grateful aunt consequently introduces him to her son and daughter. So as to avoid the impropriety of an outside male's meeting an unmarried daughter, she has her children recognize Zhang as an elder brother. Hence, the senior matriarch unwittingly has a hand in the female protagonist's "fall from virtue." Zhang is smitten at the first sight of Yingying and promptly instigates a scheme to deflower her by acting through her maid, Hongniang.[82] When Hongniang asks why he cannot simply propose marriage, he replies:

> Ever since I was a child I have by nature avoided unseemly associations. When I have been around women, I would never even give them suggestive glances. I never would have thought a time would come when I found myself so overwhelmed with desire. The other day at the party I could scarcely control myself. For the past few days I have walked without knowing where I am going and eaten without thinking of whether I am full or not. I'm afraid I won't last another day. If I had to employ a matchmaker to ask for her hand in marriage, with the sending of betrothal tokens and the making of formal inquiries and names, it would be another three months, and I would be a fish so long out of water that you would have to look for me in a dried fish store.

At Hongniang's suggestion, he initiates an exchange of poetry, which eventually leads to a nocturnal rendezvous in the western chamber; henceforth the western chamber was to become a ubiquitous intertextual marker in the literary culture of romance. Yingying uses this opportunity to repel his advances with impeccable moralistic arguments. Accusing him of exploiting the family's moral debt to extract sexual favors, she explains how she has come in person lest written communication cause misunderstanding. Inexplicably, however, she willingly spends the night with him a few days later. "From that point on she allowed him to come to her. He would go out secretly at dawn and enter secretly in the evening. In almost a month they shared happiness in what had earlier been referred to as the 'western porch.'" Again, at this point, the narrator addresses Zhang's failure to propose marriage. "Zhang constantly asked about how Madame Cui felt, and she would say, 'I can't do anything about it.' And she wanted him to proceed to regularize the relationship."[83] This detail raises more questions than it answers. If Zhang was unwilling to marry Yingying, why did he concern himself with Madame Cui's opinion?

The lovers temporarily separate as Zhang completes his journey to the capital. Yet, when they soon reunite and continue as before, the narrator mentions an earlier vow Zhang made to Yingying while omitting any detail of it. After further dalliance, Zhang returns to the capital to sit for an examination, albeit unsuccessful. He nevertheless remains there preparing for the next one. Despite a moving letter Yingying sends to him in which she expresses her wish to become his wife, Zhang declared her a *femme fatale* and thus "hardened his heart against her." Eventually the pair permanently separate and marry other partners.[84]

In contrast to her later behavior, Yingying is initially decorous and reserved. During a conversation with Zhang early in the story, her maid discusses her character: "Miss Cui is virtuous and guards herself scrupulously. Even someone she held in the highest regard could not lead her into misconduct by improper words." Yingying furthermore exhibits exacting propriety when she initially refuses her mother's request to meet Zhang: "'Come out and pay your respects to your elder brother. You are alive because of him.' A long time passed, and then she declined on the excuse that she wasn't feeling well. Madame Cui said angrily, 'Mr. Zhang protected your life. Otherwise you would have been taken captive. How can you still keep such a wary distance from him!' After another long wait, the daughter came in."[85] Similarly, when Zhang initially propositions Yingying, her refusal is based on sound Confucian principles. Nevertheless, presumably once tempted by sensual gratification, she readily succumbs. This pattern of initial punctilious virtue more or less easily seduced found in other Tang period stories implies male anxiety over women's chastity. In this story, Yingying cannot be considered a truly virtuous woman until her virtue is put on trial.

Yet the story is not primarily a trial of feminine chastity: more importantly, it is the male protagonist's character that is at stake. This is made clear from Zhang's contradictory monologue at the narrative's opening. When questioned by friends about his inexperience with women, he replies, "The famous lecher of antiquity, Deng Tuzi, was not a man of passionate desire; his were the actions of a brute. I am someone who is truly capable of passionate desire, but simply have not encountered it. How can I say this? Creatures of most bewitching beauty never fail to leave a lasting impression on my heart, and this tells me I am not one of those free of passion." This monologue establishes an expectation that Zhang's passion will be tested. Furthermore, the initial narrative focused on the male aligns readers with the young protagonist. Zhang's claim that he has not encountered passionate desire refutes the claim that creatures of bewitching beauty have "never failed to leave a lasting impression" on him. This contradiction notwithstanding, the testing of male virtue and resolve remains a central theme.

Yingying's *femme fatale* stature is largely premised on the protagonist's above claim—that is, a woman of bewitching beauty is able to seduce a hitherto demure young man. Toward the story's denouement, Zhang further develops this idea in response to the constructed storyteller's question.

> Zhang then said, "All such creatures ordained by Heaven to possess bewitching beauty will inevitably cast a curse on others if they don't do the same to themselves. Had Cui Yingying made a match with someone of wealth and power, she would have taken advantage of those charms that win favor from a man; and if she were not the clouds and rain of sexual pleasure, then she would have been a serpent or a fierce dragon—I do not know what she would have transformed into. Long ago, King Shouxin of Yin and King You of Zhou controlled domains that mustered a million chariots and, their power was very great. Nevertheless, in both cases a woman destroyed them. Their hosts were scattered, they themselves were slain, and even today their ignominy has made them laughingstocks for all the world. My own virtue is inadequate to triumph over such cursed wickedness, and for this reason I hardened my heart against her." At the time all those present were deeply moved.[86]

Zhang's construction of Yingying as a *femme fatale* comparable to the most notorious examples of Chinese history complements his discussion of *youwu* at the narrative's outset.[87] For Zhang, Yingying's beauty and sullied virtue would have brought about his demise. His fear that she may become the "clouds and rain" of sexual gratification points to anxiety over possible future infidelity. This is echoed in her own final letter to Zhang toward the story's conclusion. "Since I suffer the shame of having offered myself to you, I may no longer serve you openly as a wife."[88] Therefore, Yingying's guilt over having succumbed to Zhang's improper sexual advances implies that she may do so again as a wife. It also indicates her own perceived unworthiness given her promiscuity. When read from a conservative, patriarchal perspective that many contemporary readers would have brought to the story, Yingying's marrying another man after the affair with her cousin—hence her serving two masters—justifies the narrator's depiction of her as a *femme fatale*. In this light, her initial resistance may be seen as little more than a façade masking latent sexual "depravity" that threatens the patriarchal family order.

Yet despite the intellectually orthodox male storyteller's control of the story, Yingying is accorded considerable sympathy. I have already noted her decorous behavior at the outset. Equally important, she occupies a significant proportion of the narrative; to be sure, she constitutes the pivot around which all events turn. Both her character and physical features are described in a naturalistic style rather than formulaic phrases applied to the two-dimensional paragons of other stories. Moreover, her dialogue, poems, and letter afford the reader access to her thoughts and emotions, including her repeated wish to marry Zhang. In her letter, she asks, "If by chance in the goodness of your heart you would condescend to fulfill my secret hope (to marry me), then even if it were on the day of my death, it would be for me like being reborn." When professing her love, she says, "When it comes to my vow to love you forever, that is steadfast and unwavering."[89] Such sentiments are in keeping with the culture of romance and undermine the *femme fatale* stereotype.

Guided by the narrator, readers may readily empathize with Yingying. Consequently, many contemporary readers may well have viewed Zhang as a betrayer of women. This is implied toward the conclusion. When the narrator tells us how, "Every one of Zhang's friends who heard of the affair was stirred to amazement. Nevertheless, Zhang had already made up his mind." His decision to jilt Yingying is contrasted with his friends "amazement"; their reaction points to a sympathetic view of the heroine. This compromised portrayal of Zhang therefore allows readers to understand Yingying as a romantic heroine, as numerous allusions to her in later love stories confirm.

Zhang's decision to betray her creates a further irony. The sexual favors Yingying freely grants him, despite her professed awareness of impropriety, fits with Owen's characterization of the culture of romance—that is, a freely elected private space in which private concerns may be pursued regardless of social obligation.⁹⁰ She has, in effect, proven devotion to her chosen lover unencumbered by the institution of marriage. Yet by doing so she becomes a *femme fatale* in both his eyes and those of morally conservative readers. By her own admission—or at least according to the male storyteller who speaks through her—her lapse of propriety renders her unworthy to be Zhang's future wife. This paradox, therefore, destroys the possibility of lasting romance, the happy ever-after. Hence for Tang dynasty storytellers, it seems that the culture of romance and marriage must inevitably remain separate unless, as already noted, some anomalous occurrence rendered the story worthy of recording in a *zhiguai* collection. In Owen's words, "the boundaries of enclosure are usually broken; the outside world intrudes and lays claim to the protagonists." Nonetheless, as we will see in the next chapter, Song dynasty raconteurs developed different solutions to this conundrum.

As Owen observes, moral ambiguity created by conflicting voices within this story invites multiple readings while preventing a single, clear-cut interpretation. Partly for this reason, he recognizes it as unique among Tang short stories.⁹¹ No doubt this, as well as the nuanced portrayal of its protagonists, is largely responsible for the story's enduring attraction throughout the centuries.

"Ouyang Zhan" is another instructive illustration of the *femme fatale* theme. Its purportedly true events were said to have occurred around 800, the year of Ouyang's death. Written in terse, unadorned prose, it tells of a promising young scholar from a somewhat humble family background. Having recently passed the imperial examinations, he falls in love with a courtesan during a visit to the northern city of Taiyuan. After a brief affair, he leaves to take up an appointment in the capital, promising to send for her once established. For reasons unexplained, however, he misses the agreed time. A year later, his courtesan-lover dies of an unspecified illness. Before dying, she cuts a lock of her hair and encloses it with a poem. Soon after receiving it, Ouyang also dies.⁹²

Ouyang Zhan (755–800) passed the examinations of 792 along with luminaries such as the intellectual and statesman Han Yu (768–824). Their graduating class became known as the "class of dragons and tigers" (*longhu bang*) given the sterling achievements of an unusually large number of its graduates. Ouyang was already renowned for his poetry at the time. Indeed, Han Yu mentions his poetic prowess in an elegy he wrote for him.[93] Ouyang's peer, the famous poet Meng Jian (d. 823), also wrote a poem and a preface lamenting his death, both of which are appended to the *Extensive Record*'s version of the main text. Here Meng tells how he and an acquaintance often discussed and regretted Ouyang's demise. Hence Ouyang's story was well known and orally circulated among this milieu of educated men during the early ninth century.

While Ouyang's lover would not seem to fit the *femme fatale* stereotype, especially for modern readers, this is how Meng Jian understood the story. His preface emphasizes Ouyang's literary and scholastic accomplishments, his ties to the Imperial University, and a bureaucratic post for which he had been recommended. He also draws attention to Ouyang's relatively obscure family background; that is, rather than of noble birth, he hailed from commoner (albeit privileged) stock. Despite this, he "was single-minded and diligent, and did not pay attention to music or female beauty. Before his demise, he was unaware of the poisonous enchantment that could issue from a woman's slender waist." Such encomiums are reminiscent of Mr. Zhang's monologue at the outset of "Yingying's Story." Meng then proceeds to tell of Ouyang's visit to Taiyuan and how, at a banquet given by a local general, a "*femme fatale* from the north" (*beifang zhi youzhe*) inveigled him with her gaze. The female Gaze in this context is clearly tantamount to an ensnaring, evil eye. When Ouyang's career necessitated his return to the capital, Meng Jian explains that Ouyang's decision not to take his lover with him was due to fear of "prying eyes"—that is, gossip mongers. As noted above, government officials were forbidden to marry courtesans, and taking them as concubines was frowned on. No doubt Ouyang worried about being reported. He therefore sent an underling to bring her in secret. After her death, Meng confirms Ouyang's receipt of the courtesan's *memento mori* and, in his poem, tells how Ouyang neither ate nor drank for ten days after receiving the news. Having related the circumstances of Ouyang's death, Meng further opines that he would not have died had he not have succumbed to the charms of feminine beauty. "Generally, if one severs [the romantic tie] in time, one will not be befuddled by female beauty. How could one then come to this?"[94]

For Meng Jian, therefore, transitory dalliances should remain separate from social demands, such as career. This echoes Yingying's words in her letter to Zhang when she tells him that concentration on study befits the male disposition. As Manling Luo observes, the dichotomy between men's social obligations and romance was part of an elite tradition that saw romance as a passing diversion.[95] Ouyang's failure to observe this rule was thought to have caused self-destruction, but Meng Jian largely blames the woman. His portrayal of Ouyang as a focused and conscientious scholar, uninterested in feminine charm, further echoes that given to Master Zhang in "Yingying's Story." Hence, a necessary corollary to the *femme fatale* construct appears to be that of the decorous, conscientious male.

Meng Jian's derogatory reference to a "beauty *from the north*" is also significant. Given that Ouyang's birthplace was Quanzhou in the south, one suspects regional bias. Meng Jian himself, however, came from Shandong in northern China. It is conceivable that he viewed people from Taiyuan as foreign to those of his own region. Nonetheless it is clear that, in the context of the preface, regional, class, and gender biases are conflated.

The poem, furthermore, affords an insight into what Meng Jian considered feminine beauty. He describes her sleek hands and waist, thus undermining the stereotypical Tang-era ideal of voluptuous beauty. Her hairstyle he describes as piled high like an oriole (symbolic of conjugal felicity) and looped at the sides of her face like a jade cicada ("cicada curls" were fashionable at the time). Furthermore, when the woman cast her eyes on Ouyang, Meng Jian likened them to autumnal waves. While modern readers may not find some of these images particularly attractive, we may understand how a woman's hair and slim stature would have attracted the attention of the Tang-era male Gaze. Such features, as we have seen, also formed the locus of the Gaze in other stories.

The ninth-century reception of the Ouyang Zhan story affords a valuable insight into how some men of letters read love stories, particularly those in which the male protagonist suffered misfortune. While modern readers may more readily sympathize with heroines such as Yingying, many ninth-century readers did not. Similarly, Ming dynasty readers such as Hu Yinglin understood Li Wa in a negative light, even though he did not label her a *femme fatale*. Furthermore, Meng Jian's information that Ouyang died ten days after receiving his lover's poem and accompanying *memento mori* is considerably more plausible than the main text, whose crude juxtaposition of the two events suggests an immediate causal relationship (*jian qi shi, yi dong er zu*). Indeed, comparison of the two reminds us that recorded narratives were likely exaggerated. Written narratives of the period were, after all, largely recorded from oral accounts, including biased gossip, and often with documentary intent.

Vengeance

> Heaven Has No Rage, Like Love to Hatred Turned.
>
> —Congreave, *The Mourning Bride*

The *Drunken Man's Talk* includes a "broken promises" (*fuxin/fuyue*) category under which two accounts of romantic betrayal are classified. The "Story of Wangkui" (discussed in chapter 2) recounts vengeance wrought by a jilted courtesan. Similarly, the "Tryst of Crimson Silk" tells of a jilted woman, yet concludes harmoniously thanks to intervention of a social superior. Many union and reunion stories also contain elements of betrayal, or the possibility of such. Indeed, this may be found in "Yingying's Story." Such prototypes, to the extent they impugn heartless male lovers while encouraging reader sympathy with the abandoned female, are closely aligned with the culture of romance. These later stories owe a considerable debt to "Huo Xiaoyu's Story." Highly realistic and well written, this affords many small details of everyday life and, more significantly, establishes narrative conventions that would be utilized throughout the Song dynasty.

"Huo Xiaoyu's Story" is based on events said to have occurred during the *dali* reign period (766–779), although Li Jianguo surmises that it was recorded in 829 or a little after.[96] Its protagonist, Li Yi (746–829), was a notable statesman of the Longxi Li clan—one of the most illustrious aristocratic families of the age. The narrator tells of how older men would bow before his literary prowess. At the narrative's commencement, the twenty-year-old Li is seeking a concubine having recently passed two metropolitan examinations. Rather than serenade some random beauty he happens to see, as in many other stories, he deputizes a high-class matchmaker, Madame Bao, to arrange a meeting with Huo Xiaoyu, the illegitimate daughter of a deceased imperial prince. Early in the story, the Madame summarizes the young woman's talent and beauty: "All my life I've never seen such a voluptuous figure. Yet she has noble sentiments and an independent manner. She surpasses others in every way. She understands everything from music to poetry to calligraphy." Detailed description vividly portrays the couple's first meeting. When Li firsts sets eyes on Xiaoyu, "all he was aware of was something like an alabaster forest and jade trees throughout the whole room, casting their dazzling radiance back and forth, and as he turned his gaze, the crystalline rays struck him." Something of Xiaoyu's character is conveyed through minute gestures, such as when she "lowered her head, giggling, and whispered softly." Predictably, the couple spend the night together. When, however, Xiaoyu articulates her fear that Li will eventually abandon her, he makes a written oath to the contrary; this narrative device was evoked in "Li Wa's Story" and became conventional in later ones. The narrative jumps to the following spring when a banquet is given in Li's honor for having passed a special examination that resulted in a provincial posting. Xiaoyu, knowing that their happy days together are numbered, proposes a compromise:

> I am eighteen now and you are twenty-two. There are still eight more years until you reach that season of your prime when a man should establish a household. During this period, I want to experience a lifetime of love and pleasure. After that it will still not be too late for you to make a fine choice from a noble family and conclude a marriage alliance. I will then cast the affairs of mortal men behind me, shave off my hair and put on the black habit of a nun, and in doing so a long-standing wish will be fulfilled.

In tears, Li Yi reiterates his oath and promises to send for Xiaoyu once reaching his post. Shortly after doing so, he takes leave to visit his parents. There his mother apprises him of a match she has made with a daughter of the Lu family, one of the most prestigious families of the era. "His mother had always been strict and unbending, so that Li Yi wavered in indecision and did not dare refuse." Li Yi's family wealth, however, is unequal to the Lus' bride price, so Li must borrow from distant relatives. During this mission he misses the agreed time to send for Xiaoyu. Having lost hope of being with her given his impending marriage, he decides to abandon her. Xiaoyu, on the contrary, faithfully expecting his summons, exhausts all available means to gain news of him. She spends large sums on gifts to friends and acquaintances who might bring her news, in addition to consulting fortunetellers. After a year of waiting in vain, she falls seriously ill. A particularly moving scene occurs when, too ill to leave her dwelling, she dispatches a maid to sell a valuable jade hairpin given by her father; the sentimental value attached to this object hints that it is her last valuable possession. On the way, the servant coincidentally meets the very carver who produced it. Recognizing his own work, he asks how she came by it.

My young mistress is the very daughter of the Prince of Huo. The household was dispersed and she has fallen on hard times, having given herself to a man. A while ago her husband[97] went off to Luo-yang, and she has heard no news of him. It has been almost two years now, and she has become ill through her misery. She ordered me to sell this so that she could offer gifts to people and try to get some word of him." The jade-carver was moved to tears: "To think that the sons and daughters of the nobility could fall into such misfortunes and end up like this! The years left to me will soon be done, and to see such reversals from splendor to decline is a pain not to be borne.

He then took the servant to Princess Guangxian (daughter of the Suzong emperor [r. 756–762]), who paid a large sum for the pin. Soon after this, news of Li Yi's return to Chang'an is brought to Xiaoyu by a mutual friend. Acting through the friend, she requests that Li visit her, at which point the narrator lays bare his thoughts: "Li Yi was aware that he had not kept the date he set with Xiao-yu and had betrayed his vow. He further knew of Xiao-yu's condition, that her sickness had made her an invalid. In his shame, he hardened his heart against her and absolutely refused to go." Xiaoyu, meanwhile, "lay sprawled helplessly on her bed" and "forgot about eating and sleeping" as "her rage deepened." Li Yi's callous behavior is then contrasted with unnamed "men of delicate feeling" who were all "enraged at Li Yi's casual heartlessness."

The narrative jumps to May, when Li Yi attends a spring outing at a local temple with friends. The description of his admiring the peonies and reciting poetry as he walked along the western gallery (a probable allusion to "Yingying's Story") vividly illustrates his callousness. One of his close friends, disgusted by his cold-heartedness, berates him. The commotion is overheard by a well-dressed aristocrat, who invites the whole party to his mansion. This, however, proves a ruse, for when the group passes Xiaoyu's lane, the aristocrat forces the unwilling Li Yi to see her. This is to be the last time the couple meet. In a melodramatic scene, Xiaoyu curses Li before dying.

> When she saw Li Yi, she held back her anger and gazed at him fixedly, saying nothing. Her wasted flesh and lovely features gave the impression that she could endure it no longer . . . Xiao-yu leaned to the side and turned her face, gazing side-long at Li

Yi for a very long time. She then raised a cup of wine and poured it out on the ground, saying, "I am a woman; my unhappy fate is like this. You are a man; your faithless heart may be compared to this. Fair of face and in the flower of my youth, I perish swallowing my resentment. I have a loving mother at home, yet I will not be able to care for her. My fine silken clothes and the music of pipes and strings will from this point be forever ended. I must carry my suffering to the underworld, and all of it was brought on by you. Li Yi! Li Yi! We must say farewell for good. But after I die, I will become a vengeful ghost and allow you no peace with your wives and concubines for the rest of your days." With that, she grasped Li Yi's arm with her left hand and threw the cup to the ground. With several long and mournful cries, she died. Her mother lifted the corpse and rested it in Li Yi's arms, telling him to call back her soul. But she did not revive.

While mourning her death, Li Yi suddenly sees her ghost beside the coffin. The final phase of the story tells of his subsequent marriages. On one occasion, when lying with his new bride, he sees a man who calls to Madame Lu. Li Yi chases him, but the man disappears. At another time, an unseen person throws a box containing aphrodisiacs and love tokens on Madame Lu's lap. Suspecting infidelity, Li Yi flies into a rage and beats her, later divorcing her. After that, he becomes excessively suspicious and jealous of his subsequent wives, maids, and concubines. Before going out, he would restrain a favorite concubine beneath a bathtub, sealing the edge so as to ensure confinement until his return. He would even threaten his women with a sword, bragging about murdering others who proved unfaithful. The story ends with the information that "He married three times, and each of the others went as it did the first time."[98]

The historical Li Yi was the son of Li Bo, chief minister during the Suzong emperor's reign. His biography in the dynastic history tells how his poetry was considered comparable to that of the celebrated poet Li He (791–817), and his lyric poems were much sought after by Chang'an's courtesans. Significantly, the biography mentions his jealousy of wives and concubines; he was even known to lock them inside while spreading ashes outside so as to detect intruders. Such was his infamy in this regard that a medical syndrome characterized by excessive jealousy was named after him.[99] This information is corroborated by several other historical sources and corresponds nicely with the plot of "Huo Xiaoyu's Story."[100] That his poetry was celebrated in Chang'an's brothel district also indicates his youthful association with courtesans. Other men whose names appear in the story were also historical personages. Nevertheless, there are historical inaccuracies. Prince Huo was executed by Empress Wu (r. 684–704), having been implicated in a plot to overthrow her. Accordingly, any illegitimate daughter he may have sired could not have been seventeen during the 760s and 770s—some ninety years later. Perhaps, given the common surname (assuming that Huo Xiaoyu's name is historical), the heroine's link to the prince was a *post facto* elaboration. According to his grave inscription, Li married twice (not counting concubines), not three times as the narrative alleges. Interestingly, both wives were surnamed Lu. Furthermore, he did not divorce the first one; she died. Notwithstanding such inaccuracies, the story's approximate grounding in historical factuality is intriguing and further illustrates the correspondence between recorded narratives and orally circulated gossip.

The narrative affords much sympathy for Xiaoyu. Indeed, a considerable proportion recounts the impact of Li Yi's betrayal. After Li misses the agreed date to send for her, Xiaoyu remains naively hopeful that he will honor his agreement. Her selling valuable possessions so as to gain news of him drives her to the brink of destitution. Her plight is poignantly illustrated when her maid sells the jade hairpin, the remaining physical link with her father. As shown above, the manner of the scene's narration engenders considerable pathos. The jade-carver's sympathy, furthermore, echoes that of other male characters as it guides the reader's emotional response. To be sure, the argument between Li Yi and his close friend emphasize the seriousness of his betrayal and indicates that love, rather than friendship, is valorized here. The detailed description of Xiaoyu's bedridden state therefore accentuates the reader's sympathy, as does the paternal link between her and the Prince of Huo. Her royal—if illegitimate—birth mitigates her dubious social status and renders her worthier than a debased courtesan, particularly from the perspective of upper-class male readers.

Moreover, Xiaoyu demonstrates important Confucian virtues that undermine any moral dubiousness attached to either her courtesan status or her actions. Her refusal to entertain other clients, even though it impoverished her, demonstrates her loyalty to Li. This, together with her wish to become a nun once the affair terminates, valorizes the Confucian moral code that a woman should not know two masters; indeed, it renders her akin to a faithful first wife, as opposed to a concubine. In other words, Xiaoyu's fidelity helps reclaim the subversive nature of her liaison. Furthermore, urging Li to marry after a period of eight years demonstrates both her lack of jealousy—a cardinal feminine virtue—and her willing conformity to patriarchal expectations. The narrator's sympathy for Xiaoyu, contrasted with Li Yi's duplicity, allows her "voice" to control the narrative while glossing over Li's reasons for leaving her. This strongly suggests that the story may have evolved from malicious gossip directed against the latter.

Given the emphasis and sympathetic treatment of Xiaoyu, androcentric aspects discernable in other stories are diminished here. There is neither a love triangle nor male competition over possession of a woman. Conversely, the aristocratic and upper-class males in the story unite against Li Yi's treachery. The effects of Xiaoyu's curse are nothing less than his just deserts. Male characters closing ranks against a betrayer of women would become a staple of other broken-promise prototypes. This story, therefore, more so than others discussed thus far, celebrates freedom of choice in love, the importance of honoring one's vows, and endorses upper-class men's liaisons with courtesans—so long as they are contained as transitory affairs.

Felicitous Encounters with the Goddess

In the introduction I touched on the legends of Kings Mu and Huai, as well as the renowned poet Cao Zhi's piece about the Goddess of the Luo River. Narratives about such divine rendezvous are copious and, as previously noted, Luo Ye devised a discreet category under which to classify them (see figure 1.2).

For contemporary readers, this motif was linked to the quest for immortality through ancient sexual hygiene techniques. It was thought possible for men to extend their lifespan through sexual intercourse with—ideally—several different partners without ejaculating. Since *yin* energy was considered the reason for women's comparably longer lifespans, it was thought possible for a man to nourish himself from this source providing he not release his own *yang* lifeforce. Hence, prolonged exposure to *yin* energy from various sources was thought to extend longevity in men. Sexual union with an immortal woman, on the other hand, enabled mortal men to attain everlasting life in a single bound. Such ideas were fostered by the

82 | The Chinese Love Story from the Tenth to the Fourteenth Century

Figure 1.2. Goddess of the Luo River.

widespread worship of Daoist deities, particularly the Queen Mother of the West, whose bevy of immortal handmaidens supplied a ready reservoir of literary heroines (see figure 1.3).[101]

Among early prototypes is that of how Liu and Ruan met the immortal maidens of Mount Tiantai—itself important to the cult of immortality—after becoming lost in the depths of its forests. During their sojourn, the men were entertained with not only food and wine but also sexual favors. Once they left the women, however, they were unable to retrace their steps. Uncannily, even though they had enjoyed the women's company for a short time, several months had elapsed in the outside world. One of the earliest extant stories of this kind is *Dalliance in the Immortal's Den* (*You xianku*), generally considered of late seventh-century composition.[102] Its plot is extremely simple: a government official travels to a remote region where he meets and is entertained by two goddesses. Despite his desire to have intercourse with both, they agree only to a one-on-one liaison. He

Figure 1.3. Liu and Ruan meet the immortal women of Mount Tiantai.

leaves the following morning. This simple plot provides a framework on which its author crafts witty rhetoric and poetry. Its first-person point of view is particularly remarkable, as an omniscient, third-person narrator was the norm for narrative of the imperial period. While one-to-one encounters remained standard for almost all love stories of the Song and Yuan periods, the single male protagonists of later erotic novels sometimes had affairs with multiple women.

Given the parallels between the protagonist's experience in the women's company and that of a visit to a high-class courtesan's residence, real-life encounters with courtesans may well have provided the basis for stories of this type. Cao Zhi's "Goddess of the Luo River" was traditionally understood as an allegory of the poet's supposed love for his brother's wife, Empress Zhen, thereby further blurring the boundary between humanistic and other-worldly romance.[103] Similarly, the Xuanzong emperor was considered the son of heaven given his status as emperor, while his lover,

Lady Yang, was later imagined as an immortal dwelling on the Isles in the Eastern Sea. And, to be sure, beautiful heroines of human-centered stories were often compared with goddesses.

"Guo Han" illustrates many typical features of encounters-with-the-goddess prototype. The narrative opens with a description of the eponymous protagonist's good looks and literary accomplishments. Conveniently, both his parents are deceased. One summer night, while sleeping outside to escape the heat, he "looked up into the sky and beheld a figure floating steadily down, eventually alighting before him." No ordinary goddess, this was none other than the Weaver Maid. Dressed in "dark, diaphanous gossamer" and accompanied by two serving maids, she was a sight to "bewitch both heart and soul." She explains that the celestial emperor has allowed her to visit the earth in search of romantic fulfillment and has chosen Guo for his "air of purity." She then orders her maids to cleanse Guo's house and fit his bedroom with choice curtains and mats, after which the pair enjoy a night of sexual bliss. She leaves at dawn, ascending back into the sky. She returns every night for a protracted period, during which she tutors Guo about the celestial realm. Consequently, "of that which mortal men were ignorant, from then on Guo possessed intimate knowledge." The narrative playfully alludes to the legend of the Weaver Maid's annual reunion with the Oxherd, still celebrated in Japan as the Tanabata festival. In the context of the story, this prevents her nightly visitations. As with Liu and Ruan's story, Weaver Maid is absent for several days because, as she explains, "five days in the mortal world are but one night up there [i.e., the celestial realm]." Prior to this, he raises the question of her infidelity to the Oxherd:

> "So where's your lord and master?" teased Han. "How is it you dare sally forth alone?"
>
> "The *yin* and *yang* transform themselves; what business is it of his?" she replied.
>
> "Separated as we are by the Milky Way, there is no means by which he could know and, even if he did, it would not be worth worrying about."

As with numerous stories of transitory affairs, this too must eventually conclude. One night the Weaver Maid comes to Guo in tears, telling him that only one night remains of their heavenly sanctioned liaison. At dawn the following day, the pair exchange love tokens. Poetry is exchanged at a later date, sent by the goddess's handmaidens. The narrative concludes with an air of historical factuality that cites the official rank that Guo later attained.[104]

Several facets of the prototype may be gleaned from this one example. First is the domestic spatial context. Romantic encounters with immortal women often occurred in the domestic space of unspecified locations, as opposed to large urban centers and their related brothel districts. As we will see, this would become a staple feature of later love stories. In this story, as in many others, a goddess of unsurpassed beauty descends from the sky. In other accounts, the protagonist encounters an immortal in disguise on a journey, in which case the road becomes a significant structural device.

Female agency in this story is more or less the mirror opposite to stories of humanistic love. The Weaver Maid's initiating the affair contrasts to stories of human love in which it is almost always the male who pursues the woman, as we have seen. Furthermore, it is she who terminates the affair, unlike in the stories reviewed above in which it is the male who, being called away on public or family business, leaves the female. In stories of the encounter-with-the-goddess prototype, logic dictated that the female take the initiative. The same held true for mortal male's encounters with deceased women who subsequently revived and married the protagonist. During a time in which social customs relegated upper-class women to the confines of their own homes, only emerging to attend religious services or for the carnivalistic frolics accompanying the Lantern festival, it would have been unusual for women to have traveled about alone; of course, this does not include working-class women. In a literary context, the fact of a beautiful, upper-class young woman's being out and about alone would have been understood as a token of the unusual, thus nicely complementing the paranormal aspects of the story in question. Significantly for the love story's development, female agency in love would become more prominent in love stories of the Song and Yuan when heroines would frequently throw themselves at men.

As with human-to-human romantic affairs, this one also remains transitory. A divinely sanctioned period of time is all the lovers have to pursue their freely chosen love, unencumbered by familial or social duty. Interestingly enough, no negative connotation is attached to the sexual nature of the lovers' relationship. In contrast to androcentric love stories, sexual encounters with immortals were always portrayed positively. Indeed, this was no less than the means of attaining eternal life. Furthermore, immortals were not bound to conventional social mores or laws regarding illicit sex. Again a parallel may be drawn with legendary encounters with goddesses and liaisons with courtesans who, as a "debased" class in the eyes of the Tang penal code, were not held accountable to the same laws that governed the sexual behavior of the commoner and upper classes. Indeed, the image of love-making immortals was often evoked to describe copulation in stories of humanistic love. Similarly, as previously noted, the metaphor of clouds and rain from the legend of Witch's Mountain frequently denoted sexual climax. Therefore, sexual encounters with immortals provided an ideal vehicle through which romantic freedom of choice and sexual expression could be explored unfettered by didactic apology, as was often the case with stories of androcentric love.

As we have seen, socially superior males in many Tang-era love stories engaged in transitory affairs with socially inferior females who were sometimes financially or emotionally reliant on the male. In the above example, as with other encounters-with-the-goddess prototype, a more equitable relationship is found. Unencumbered by class barriers and social dictates, Guo and the Weaver Maid are more or less equal partners. If anything, the Weaver Maid holds the upper hand by dint of her immortal status and her narrative agency. Hence, the "development of individual acts of interpretation or valuation and the demarcation of private space"[105] that Owen sees in the culture of romance are, in the goddess prototype, intensified. Here, freely chosen love may be had without the intrusion of social disparity that even liaisons with courtesans would invariably entail. In stories whereby males marry the immortal woman, they attain immortality with one stroke. Whether Guo Han does so is unclear. Nonetheless, his divine lover's status eludes moralistic censure that may otherwise attend a celebration of pre- or extramarital sex.

Concluding Remarks

As may be seen from the foregoing survey, Tang dynasty love stories encompass a wide range of androcentric authorial intentions. Some, such as "Ren's Story," construct a paragon of feminine virtue with which to critique unspecified women of the author-recorder's social milieu. Others, such as "Miss Liu's Story," foreground male social and sexual competition, so much so that female subjectivity dissolves into a network of male-centered social obligation. Numerous stories include paranormal or *zhiguai* elements that sometimes overshadow those of the romantic. Many may have circulated as malicious gossip, while some perpetuate the long-established notion of a *femme fatale* on which male folly and misfortune is blamed. Stories about liaisons with immortal women, while part of Daoist folklore about the quest for immortality, articulate much wish fulfillment vis-à-vis the male articulating subject. And although Zhou Shuren's critique of Song dynasty stories' didactic nature implied that Tang-period works were largely free of such, stories of this period were by no means devoid of moralistic concerns. Such a diverse spectrum of authorial intention qualifies the extent to which love stories, as a literary corpus, constituted a "celebration" of romantic love. Indeed, only a select number focus on freely chosen love affairs unencumbered by alternate agendas.

Typical plots unfold from the perspective of a single male protagonist. He is almost always young. Although merchant-protagonists occasionally appeared, the emblematic hero is a member of the professional elite, if not the aristocracy. The frequency with which aristocratic characters appear may be considered a narrative hallmark of the period. The protagonist's youth, however, places him in a liminal position within his social class—that is, a social junior yet to undertake a leadership role within the establishment. For Manling Luo, the male protagonist is a youthful sexual adventurer who deviates from his proper course in life. This, she argues, was a late-medieval literati invention.[106]

Such narrowness of character type suggests a constructed readership, as well as the gender and social class of actual storytellers. Certainly many were well-known poets or men of letters. As upper-class members of society with ties to the ruling aristocracy, their stories inevitably project elite male values. To be sure, the intimate social connections between nonprofessional, elite storytellers and their aristocratic patrons easily explains the frequent appearance of aristocratic protagonists. This is not to say that women did not constitute actual readers but, as with modern cinema, their reading of recorded narratives would have been largely mediated by an androcentric point of view.

The typical plot of both union and reunion prototypes is set in motion when the young male sojourns to the imperial capital or another large urban center, often to undertake the examination necessary for a bureaucratic career. Independent and without immediate parental control, the protagonist meets a young woman of "unparalleled beauty," typically a courtesan. Indeed, the ubiquity of the urban setting has prompted several scholars to draw a connection between large urban centers and the rise of the culture of romance as a literary practice.[107] As elite males are known to have been entertained by courtesans in the brothel districts of Chang'an and other cities, it was natural that stories and gossip about their romantic peccadilloes would have circulated. After all, such a physical environment constituted one of the few places young men could have met young, unmarried women, with whom they were not related, more or less outside the control of their social superiors. Urban centers, therefore, created unique opportunities for protagonists and their lovers to demarcate personal space in which public business may have been postponed for the pursuit of romance.[108]

Social obligation frequently intervenes to separate lovers from their privately constructed idyll, such as when Li Yi's mother arranged a marriage in "Huo Xiaoyu's Story." Often the need to undertake an examination provides the catalyst. Such a device foregrounds the contending binary between the public and private. And while the former would have generally taken priority over the latter in reality, the possibility that private desires might triumph against all odds may be understood as wish fulfillment. This binary often drives narrative structure and engenders thematic tension.

Owen and others have argued that, "There is, however, one significant form of external compulsion that must be repressed in order for romance to exist. . . This is financial compulsion, the social fact that permitted the demimonde, the site of romance, to exist." Also, "This particular plot element should remind us of the difference between a *fiction* of romance and the social realities of the demimonde, the context to which *fictions* of romance referred" (emphasis mine.)[109] In other words, the "fictitious" romance must transcend the woman's financial dependency on the male for a freely elected relationship to occur. In recognition of the gulf between social reality and storytelling that was mediated via the elite male's consciousness, he goes on to say, "These Tang stories do not represent the social facts of the demimonde; they represent the culture of the demimonde embodied in fictions that are motivated by its deepest concerns. That is, we have here a simple and forceful example of how fictions represent not a society as it is but a society's interests."[110] In a final reference to the question, he observes, "Economic compulsion and financial dependency run everywhere beneath the surface of these stories, but the surface narrative becomes a theater of choice and different kinds of compulsion."[111] Owen's observations are correct. Nonetheless, financial considerations do, at times, rise above "the surface" level. In "Li Wa's Story," financial realities of the brothel district are starkly exposed, as Owen himself acknowledges. Likewise, Huo Xiaoyu's selling of her treasures foregrounds the price of fidelity to one lover. In an end commentary, the eleventh-century courtesan Wang Youyu's exemplary virtue was contrasted with that of average courtesans, whom the writer claimed cared only for monetary gain.[112] Likewise, the end commentary to "Story of Courtesan Yang" praises the heroine whilst acknowledging a *demimondaine*'s pecuniary interests: "Courtesans utilize their beauty to entertain, yet without profit the relationship will fall apart. That [Miss] Yang could repay the general with her life is no less than righteousness; that she returned the general's gifts is no less than honesty."[113] Toward the conclusion of "Li Zhangwu's Story," Li's lover similarly expresses free choice while acknowledging the social realities of commodified sex.[114] Metatextual commentaries and monologues such as these reveal the author-recorder's awareness of these realities and disclose what often runs "beneath the surface." Even when not openly addressed, the tacit acknowledgment of socioeconomic disparity and political influence is a necessary premise on which freely chosen romantic love may occur. Expressed nondualistically, rather than repression of financial reality acting as a necessary condition for romance, *both* pecuniary interest *and* romantic fulfillment are two sides of the same coin. We may, therefore, understand many love stories as a male wish that profit-dependent courtesans/prostitutes would forego pecuniary interests and freely choose a man for his intrinsic worth *despite* such financial necessity.[115] The unlikelihood of this occurring in real life accentuates the stories' poignancy and emotional impact. Moreover, what better place to test loyalty than brothel districts where profit was paramount?

Intrinsic to Owen's argument about the repression of financial reality is his understanding that these stories constitute "fiction." As discussed in the introduction, however, readers of love stories tended to understand them literally—that is, as narrated events largely based on actual occurrences. And, as we have seen, several recorded stories originated as orally circulated gossip, even though later embellishment may have transformed the received versions in the course of retelling. If readers interpreted stories literally, it follows that the storytellers, gossips, and recorders-of-stories would have done likewise. Therefore, a high degree of plausibility would have been assumed. It is unlikely that contemporaries would have circulated stories that grossly ignored social reality. Hence these stories are not "fiction" in the modern, Western sense. Nonetheless, Owen's observation about the suppression of pecuniary interests in love stories largely holds true and, as we will see, is relevant to those of the Song and Yuan periods.

Androcentric values are also discernable in the portrayal of women. Indeed, readers frequently "see" the female through the Gaze of the male protagonist. Reminiscent of the cinematic technique whereby an establishing shot follows or precedes a point-of-view shot, the narrator frequently focuses on the protagonist's action prior to describing the female he purveys. Such narration tends to focus on women's physical attributes in a formulaic manner while avoiding detailed description of individualized beauty. Evocation of hyperbolic phrases is common, such as "of unparalleled beauty," "peerless," "unmatched," or "a consummate beauty of the age." Some stories do not offer description beyond such clichés. The typical heroine is very young, often no more than the minimum marriageable age—that is, around fifteen (*sui*). This suggests a preference for virgins who may be wholly controlled by the male articulating subject. Under the male Gaze, her fair skin is frequently compared to white jade. Fair skin was—and still is—generally considered a marker of both beauty and social prestige in China. The heroine's hair is usually thick and is often compared to billowing clouds. Upper-class women in imperial China, like their European counterparts, would not have appeared in public with their hair down and, to be sure, long hair was considered a status symbol. The narrator often refers to white teeth and red lips, suggesting both beauty and good health. The heroine's eyes often become the locus of the Gaze. Many heroines are described as "slender," sometimes accompanied by the formulaic observation that she is unable to support the weight of her clothing. The idea of slender women undermines the stereotype of a voluptuous Tang-period beauty. Nonetheless, in the absence of individually inscribed beauty beyond such formulaic expressions, male readers could project their own ideal onto the heroine's more or less indistinct features.

In numerous love stories, direct description of women occupies only a small portion of the overall narrative. As noted in regard to "Wushuang," although the heroine's presence looms large and the protagonist's desire for her motivates much of the action, the narrator rarely addresses her directly. Instead, the plot largely follows the protagonist's efforts to ingratiate himself with her household or else his efforts to rescue her. Hence, male social connections and rivalry are foregrounded. Similarly, in "Miss Liu's Story," the heroine is reduced to a token of exchange in a game of male sexual and social competition. When she is given to the protagonist by her master, a client–patron relationship is established between giver and recipient. Her abduction by the Turkic general betrays universal male anxiety over loss of a beautiful woman, while the protagonist's efforts to rescue her rely on a nexus of social connections and foster ties of obligation between male protagonists. Such a pattern is especially notable in stories featuring erotic triangles.

Contrary to this general tendency, some stories do allot their heroines greater narrative focus. In "Yingying's Story," the reader's gaze follows that of the protagonist when he first lays eyes on her, and much attention is paid to her individualized expressions and gestures. Her initial refusal of the male's advances and abrupt turnaround is accorded considerable detail. The reader is later afforded access to her intimate thoughts through poems and a letter. Similar devices may be seen in "Huo Xiaoyu's Story" as well as that of the adulterous concubine, Bu Feiyan. Nonetheless, female monologue and dialogue almost always affirm the male ego, as beautiful heroines praise the male's literary talent, admire his good looks and, occasionally, openly express sexual desire. In short, heroines often become readily available sexual and emotional companions for the male protagonist despite prior social, emotional, or financial obligations.

As previously noted, fleeting love affairs between human protagonists rarely resulted in matrimony. Nonetheless, Tang dynasty storytellers often addressed marriage in which case paranormal, or *zhiguai*, elements were almost always foregrounded. Many prototypical love stories were included in *zhiguai* collections, suggesting that the story's romantic aspects may have been of secondary interest to their storytellers. Even in a lengthy narrative of humanistic love, such as "Wushuang," the heroine's rescue depends on paranormal means and, to be sure, the assistance of a knight-errant figure. In liaisons with goddesses, marriage to an immortal woman was widely viewed as the gateway to immortality, while a substantial corpus of stories emphasized conjugal destiny. To my knowledge, the only Tang dynasty story devoid of *zhiguai* elements that addresses marriage between living human beings is "Li Wa's Story." As we will see, Song-period narratives about marriage differed considerably.

Freedom of choice in love, central to the culture of romance, no doubt posed a threat to the patriarchal institutions that regulated Tang society. Romance, therefore, as a literary discourse, embodied considerable moral subversion. This operated on two major levels. First, sexual promiscuity associated with romance posed a threat to patriarchy in and of itself. As in many societies the world over, Tang society generally disapproved of sexual desire for its own sake and, in much Confucian writing, it was construed as a base, animal instinct. Separation of the sexes and the institutionalization of arranged marriage were considered essential to counter its subversive nature. Accordingly, upper-class women were cloistered within the confines of their inner quarters, generally emerging only for calendrical festivals or religious observance. Hand in hand with this was the criminalization of extramarital sexual intercourse in regard to commoners and the upper classes. Such social control supported ancestor worship and the need to safeguard the legitimate transmission of the male bloodline. Buddhism also included sex as one of its cardinal prohibitions since it, along with other forms of worldly attachment, prevented the attainment of nirvana. Second, sexual intercourse challenged the ruling classes' political control. The "individual's" establishment of private space potentially diminished one's obligation to social institutions, such as arranged marriage and bureaucratic service. Since arranged marriage was a significant form of social control, as well as a means to neutralize illicit sexual desire, social juniors' attempts to subvert the authority of their superiors could have led to disarray. This is especially true when we remember that the imperial Chinese political system was modeled on that of the family. Furthermore, supremely beautiful women, when construed as *femme fatales*, also posed a serious threat to male morality and authority. And if well-educated, elite men were vulnerable to the charms of *femme fatales*, virtuous, upper-class women were also susceptible to well-endowed, handsome men. Nevertheless, key to Tang society was loyalty. This socially enshrined virtue facilitated normative social interactions. When loyalty was lost, disastrous consequences could follow. As already noted, loyalty was furthermore a central theme of the love story—one might say its *raison d'être*. Therefore, tellers of love stories were, paradoxically, utilizing a socially subversive, morally dubious discourse to explore and valorize an ideal that was also of paramount importance to the establishment.

Tang storytellers adopted several strategies with which to resolve the love story's subversive nature and its key themes. One necessitated the heroine's death as a token of loyalty to her lover, as we saw with Miss Ren and Bu Feiyan. In such stories, love becomes a transitory episode in a young, elite male's life during which time he may seek temporary release from patriarchal authority before returning to the fold. In other stories a couple could freely express their private desires for a limited time, until social duty intervened and one or both married other people, as we saw in "Yingying's Story." Sometimes these strategies were combined, such as in "Huo Xiaoyu's Story." Otherwise, a senior patriarch might withhold or steal a beautiful concubine, thereby destroying the lover's constructed private space. More often, however, a benevolent senior would bestow a woman, usually in the form of a concubine, to a young protégé, as was the case with Miss Liu. All these strategies are premised on the separation of romance and marriage. "The Story of Li Wa" and "Wushuang" are notable exceptions which reconcile both romance and patriarchy as their heroines marry elite lovers. Nevertheless, as aberrant as this appears, the couple in Li Wa did not initially seek marriage. Even after Li Wa had nursed her lover back to health and supported his social rehabilitation, the couple did not consider marriage; it was only the father's intervention that led to this. Nonetheless, by far the most common denouement in love stories featuring human protagonists involved permanent separation.

Tragic conclusions in which the heroine died frequently reoccur in Tang-era stories and may have contributed to their enduring appeal vis-à-vis generations of readers. Huo Xiaoyu's demise is especially futile and may remind us of Marguerite's death in Dumas's *La Dame aux Camélias*. The ninth-century heroine, languishing on her deathbed, betrayed by her sworn lover, must have engendered considerable sympathy and sadness in contemporary readers. Similarly, readers sympathetic to the culture of romance must have regretted the adulterous concubine, Bu Feiyan's, death, having been aligned with the lovers throughout the narrative. The fox-fairy, Miss Ren's, death is likewise as senseless as it is poignant. Besides acting as a strategy to neutralize the subversive nature of pre- and extramarital sex, the frequency of such denouements point to predilection for the tragic. A similar sentiment may be discerned in both Chinese and Japanese poetry in which flower petals are scattered by spring rain. In both cases, death, time's passing, and the ephemerality of life are aestheticized, even valorized to an extent. The less frequent development of this motif in Song-period stories suggest that tragic conclusions were a distinctive narrative feature of the mid- and late Tang.

Conversely, many Tang-period love stories concluded happily, especially those in which women were gained through the auspices of a senior male, often as a reward for literary talent or a meritorious deed. Such stories denote a spirit of optimism regarding the benevolence of social superiors, their willingness to rectify injustice and reward worthy men. This appears to reflect a fundamental affirmation of the imperial system, patriarchal order, the rights of the aristocracy and their ability to successfully govern. If, however, we understand these stories as representing out-of-the-ordinary events, such happy endings imply the opposite in regard to real-life situations that passed unrecorded by the storyteller's brush. Nevertheless, from the articulating subject's viewpoint, the constructed spirit of optimism remains. Although a similar spirit is discernable in love stories of the Song dynasty, a substantially greater pessimistic feeling may be found in those from the fourteenth century onward.

Chapter 2

The Northern Song Dynasty (960–1127)

The collapse of the Tang dynasty's central administration in the early tenth century led to fifty years or so of political disunity during which time several regimes vied for dominance. China was not reunified until 960 when Zhao Guangyin (927–976, r. 960–976) led his palace guards in a *coup d'état* against his former master. He became the founding emperor of the Song dynasty, which was known more for its cultural and technological achievements than its military strength. Despite spending enormous sums to support standing armies, Song military forces proved ineffective in a protracted series of campaigns with steppe neighbors during the eleventh century and, in the late 1120s, the dynasty was almost extinguished by a new and powerful enemy, the Jurchen. Although it was reestablished in the south by Zhao Gou (1107–1187, r. as Gaozong 1127–1162), a prince of the blood, the northern half of the Empire remained under Jurchen control until both empires fell to conquering Mongols in 1234 and 1276, respectively. As the northern Song capital, Kaifeng, fell to Jurchen troops in 1127, this year marks the divide between the Northern and Southern Song (see figure 2.1).

In terms of sociopolitical change, the hereditary aristocracy that dominated the Tang central administration largely lost its political sway following Tang dynastic collapse. It was eventually replaced by what Hartwell terms a "professional elite" whose male members specialized in bureaucratic service.[1] By promoting the professional elite, Song rulers hoped to avoid the social and political chaos of the late Tang and Five dynasties period during which time imperial relatives, eunuchs, palace women, and other favorites adversely affected state policy.[2] The professional elite may

Figure 2.1. Busy city street scene in the Northern Song capital, Bianliang (Kaifeng).

be characterized by its members' tendency to reside in either the Song dynastic capital, Bianliang (modern Kaifeng), or one of the subordinate capitals, in addition to their penchant for intermarriage within their own class regardless of place of origin.[3] Although they claimed ancestry from the Tang aristocratic clans, such assertions were not always factual. This privileged group filled a disproportionately high number of select, policymaking positions within the bureaucracy for well over 100 years until a broader cross-section of the scholar-elite came to the fore.

Despite the emergence of a professional elite, many high-ranking bureaucratic positions in the dynasty's earliest phase were also filled by members of what Hartwell terms the "founding elite"—that is, family members and descendants of military men who assisted Zhao Kuangyin's ascension to the throne, Zhao's personal staff, as well as top-ranking ministers from conquered dynasties who were offered places in the new central administration. Many of them descended from the regional military governors of the post–An Lushan Rebellion period. In contrast to the professional elite, few members of this founding elite filled bureaucratic positions of any importance 100 years or so after dynastic inauguration.

By the turn of the twelfth century, as the Northern Song approached its close, the professional elite's political control was being supplanted by an increasingly powerful group that Hartwell calls "local elite gentry families"—that is, lineages whose influence was felt largely at the local level and whose offspring engaged in a number of pursuits among which government service was but one option. Such a social group had existed since at least Tang times, but their power increased concomitant with the economic development of southern China. As their wealth increased, so did their opportunity to forge sociopolitical alliances through marriage with professional elite families. As Lau Yap-yin observes, few professional elite families possessed the enormous wealth and hereditary pedigree commanded by their Tang dynasty predecessors.[4] Willing to trade social and political prestige for economic advantage, many formed marriage alliances with the generally wealthier local elites of the south. By the reestablishment of the dynasty after its near destruction in 1127, members of these local gentry families all but dominated key positions within the bureaucracy.[5]

The professional and local elite's political rise was facilitated by expansion of the examination system that had been in place during the Tang dynasty. As Hartwell puts it, "the expanded examination system provided the local gentry with a means to define their status group, limit access to it, and establish a political base that was independent from the professional elite."[6] Given the close relationship among social status, scholarship, and state service, the upper class of the period are commonly known as "scholar-officials" (*shi dafu*)—that is, government officials who had entered the bureaucracy mainly due to scholastic success. Notwithstanding a changing curriculum and more stringent supervision, the Song dynasty examination system was largely similar to that of the Tang. Candidates required the recommendation of local magnates to sit for an initial examination at the county level. Successful candidates would progress to a prefectural examination. Success in this round qualified candidates to undertake the metropolitan examination that was conducted every three years. As was the case during the Tang dynasty, success in the capital could lead to a supremely prestigious palace examination that frequently garnered the emperor's attention. The "presented scholar," or *jinshi*, degree remained the most prestigious among other categories. Since the Song emperors relied chiefly on the examination system to fill their expanded bureaucracy, scholastic success rather than direct political appointment—as was the case during the Tang—became the main route to political advancement. Existing office holders—usually a father—could occasionally confer bureaucratic status on a chosen family member through the *yin* privilege. Nonetheless, such appointments were comparatively restricted, and entrance by examination attracted greater prestige. The fact that local gentry controlled access to the first round of the examinations, not to mention their monetary clout and social connections, gave their own class an overwhelming advantage in the system despite its equitable appearance.

Many scholars have optimistically regarded the examination system of the period as a meritocratic vehicle for social mobility given that successful candidates from nonprivileged backgrounds could compete with their more entitled counterparts. Indeed, short stories of the period are replete with young men from non-elite or impoverished families who attain places in the National University or else gain an examination slot. Nevertheless, as Hartwell observes, "There is not a single, documented example . . . of a family demonstrating upward mobility solely because of success in the examinations." On the contrary, it became increasingly common for the sons of wealthy, newly rich families to enter government service through the examination system *after* having married into a local gentry family. This enabled them to make social connections and access resources necessary for scholastic success. Similarly, local gentry families maintained their mutual ties through marriage between cousins, widow remarriage, sororate and uxorilocal marriages.[7] Given the importance of marriage alliances to establish and maintain social standing, marriage as a literary theme attracted unprecedented attention throughout the period.

Concurrent with these changes, the Song dynasty saw the rise of an extremely influential system of thought often translated into English as Neo-Confucianism or, more literally, Learning of the Way (*Daoxue*). Although many specialists prefer the Chinese term *Daoxue* given the ambiguity attached to "Neo-Confucianism," I will use the term throughout this book given its widespread use and convenience. Neo-Confucianism refers to the reinterpretation of Confucian thought brought to fruition by Zhu Xi (1130–1200) in the twelfth century. Premised on the idea that Confucianism had lost its way since the times of Confucius, Zhu Xu posited an orthodox line of transmission from Mencius (fourth century BCE) to the eleventh-century thinkers Zhou Dunyi (1017–1073), Zhang Zai (1020–1077), the brothers Cheng Hao (1032–1083) and Cheng Yi (1033–1108), and thence to himself. Synthesizing Buddhist and Daoist ideas, he formulated a rigorous program of self-cultivation as the sole way in which the human mind might attain sage-like wisdom. Fundamental to this program was a rigorous study of selected Confucian classics: the

Book of Mencius (*Mengzi*), *Doctrine of the Mean* (*Zhongyong*), the *Great Learning* (*Daxue*), and the *Analects of Confucius* (*Lunyu*). Although Neo-Confucian thought attracted adherents throughout the eleventh and twelfth centuries, it was not endorsed by the state until the early thirteenth century when the emperor decreed that the examination curriculum be based solely on its canonical works. Around a century later, the Mongol government followed suit, notwithstanding a relatively brief period from 1279 to 1313 during which they abandoned the examination system. The Ming emperors continued to enshrine Neo-Confucianism as the orthodox state ideology. Accordingly, Neo-Confucianism's intellectual tenets and Zhu Xi's program of investigating metaphysical principles through study gained virtual universal acceptance for the remainder of the imperial era, notwithstanding a period of reevaluation during the late Ming dynasty.

Up until the early thirteenth century when Neo-Confucianism was first institutionalized as state orthodoxy, its influence remained comparatively limited. Nonetheless, as we will see, storytellers as early as the eleventh century began to emphasize certain ideals pertaining to women that were enshrined by Neo-Confucian proponents, notably female fidelity and widow chastity. These concepts are best addressed below where selected stories may illustrate particular cases. Suffice to note here that a distinct moralistic tone is apparent in many stories of the period, much more than their eighth- and ninth-century precursors. At least in this respect, Zhou Shuren's complaint about the didactic nature of Song dynasty stories holds true.

Courtesan culture continued to flourish throughout the Song dynasty as, indeed, it did for the remainder of the imperial period. As Ellen Zhang has observed, female entertainers were a constant presence in the lives of elite men.[8] Bossler argues that courtesan establishments spread exponentially as the dynasty progressed. Concomitant with provincial urban growth and unprecedented commercial development during the Southern Song, courtesan culture expanded into areas beyond the major capital cities.[9] Besides privately owned courtesans, many were registered with the state to serve at official banquets and calendrical festivities. Hence we often read about courtesans who sought deregistration so as to marry commoners or else undertake religious vows in either the Buddhist or Daoist church. Given the heightened importance of the examination system, candidates and courtesans continued to socialize when the former traveled to urban centers for an examination. Indeed, many anecdotal narratives were based on the testimony of bureaucrats who undertook provincial tours of duty before returning to the capital for reassignment. As James Hargett has noted, the travel literature of the period may be characterized by constant empire-wide movement.[10] Although career-related travel undoubtedly occurred during the preceding era, mid- and late Tang author-compilers of love stories tended to focus on the capital, Chang'an.

The flourishing of lyric poetry (*ci*) provided another point of intersection between examination candidates, the educated elite, and courtesans. Although this form of poetry had been developed as early as the mid-Tang dynasty, it reached maturation during the Song, so much so that the terms "Song dynasty" and "lyric poetry" are often lumped together in modern Chinese. As such poetry was generally sung in public by female entertainers, male composers invariably appropriated female personas. Indeed, public performances are frequently depicted in stories and anecdotes of the period. Accordingly, courtesans often requested famous men of letters to compose lyric poems because singing the work of a famous scholar could greatly enhance their own reputation. On other occasions, poetic composition between educated men and courtesans facilitated lighthearted banter and even informal fortunetelling.[11] Given the lyric poem's female voice, frequently evoked romantic themes, their performance by women, and the interaction they engendered between men and women, such poetry acquired a close association with the culture of romance. As we will see, the lyric poem was a favored vehicle with which many protagonists expressed their feelings.

In this chapter, I will survey new literary themes and motifs through a close analysis of selected stories. As previously noted, several such themes were first explored during the mid-Tang. Significant qualitative differences are, however, discernable, as Northern Song storytellers adapted old prototypes to meet the needs of a new era. Although this chapter focuses on stories of the Northern Song period, innovative and thematically related Southern Song examples are addressed here for the sake of convenience.

Social Mobility

One of the most pervasive themes found in the Song dynasty short story is that of social mobility, especially downward mobility. This, no doubt, reflects upper-class anxiety over their social status, power, and wealth during a period of unprecedentedly expanding commerce and when both marriage and the quasi-meritocratic examination system provided major vehicles for social advancement. Hence, social mobility became a new and vastly different literary theme compared to the previous era.

One early example foregrounding downward mobility is "Wang Qiongnu," recorded by Liu Fu in his *High-Minded Conversations*. The story's narrated events purportedly occurred during the *jiayou* reign period (1056–1063) of the Renzong emperor (r. 1022–1063). Somewhat marginal to the love story prototype, "Wang Qiongnu" closely resembles a miscellaneous biography. Nonetheless, this story vividly elucidates aspects of downward mobility illustrated less explicitly in prototypical love stories, particularly in relation to upper-class women. Its eponymous protagonist was the talented and educated daughter of a scholar-official. An interlinear commentary notes how the storyteller suppresses his name and native place, indicating the story's gossipy nature. At the outset, the father was a censorial official in Huainan responsible for overseeing the district administration while guarding against malfeasance. Having relinquished his provincial posting, he returned to his home in the dynastic capital, Bianliang, where he and his wife died shortly after. When the family wealth was divided, as was customary, Qiongnu did not receive her rightful portion, although the reason is not specified. She was subsequently abandoned by her older brother and sister-in-law. Hence from upper-class status, Qiongnu suddenly found herself a destitute orphan. Both poverty and lack of male protection led her fiancé's family to break their son's engagement with her, after which she was unable to find another match. In her own words, or at least those accorded her by the male storyteller, she reveals socioeconomic as well as gender inequality: "Although there was the promise of a matchmaker, I am fated to be alone and without help. How easy it is for them to cut me off now that I can't support myself, yet it would be impossible for me to break off with them." Her poverty and lack of connections starkly contrast with her affluent recent past when she learned poetry and needlework. Straightened circumstances eventually forced her to become the concubine of a wealthy and high-ranking official. Although initially unwilling, a neighboring woman who acts as a matchmaker finally persuades her: "Although your features are all regular and attractive, there is not an ounce of gold in your purse. Who would look at you? There is a Mr. Zhao who is a minister in the Court of Imperial Sacrifice. His family has been privileged for generations and he is immensely wealthy. You could be his concubine. Although you wouldn't be his official wife, it would amount to the same thing. If you don't like this idea, then you'll end up dying in some ditch." Qiongnu tearfully acquiesced.

The husband's first sight of her is worth noting for its idealized depiction of eleventh-century female beauty. "At the time Qiong[nu] was just eighteen. When faced with her fine eyes framed by dark eyebrows, her cherry-like mouth with teeth as white as jade, her lustrous raven locks with rosy cheeks that looked just like red lotus flowers, Zhao was smitten at first sight." In a self-contradictory manner, the narrator tells how she won the goodwill of those around her, yet, by doing so, aroused the jealousy of her *tonglie* (I understand this ambiguous term to signify fellow concubines, as it would not have been unusual for wealthy men to have kept several). These jealous women subsequently slandered her before the official's wife, who then began to physically and emotionally abuse her. In Qinognu's own words, "I was beaten daily and although I wished to die there was no escape. Whenever I wanted to end my life, if I happened to catch sight of a knife or rope, I would gasp in fright and couldn't bear to face them." When she appealed to her husband for protection, he responded how he himself lived in fear of his wife.[12] In this situation, "Knowing there was none to whom she might appeal, Qiong[nu] could do naught but endure the bitterness of the beatings with an ashen heart. And so, when she encountered [fine] spring days or a [refreshing] autumn breeze, or else [the beauty of] morning flowers and moonlit nights, she would remember the past and was unable to prevent from breaking down."

When she later accompanied the official to a provincial posting, she arrived at the very inn in which she had previously stayed during her father's lifetime. Emotionally moved by the contrast between her present misery and former happiness, she wrote her story on the inn wall so as to release pent-up emotion. The narrator then tells how male travelers, moved by her tribulations, memorized what she had written. No less a figure than Wang Anguo (1028–1074), statesman and brother of the Shenzong emperor's (1067–1085) renowned chief minister Wang Anshi (1021–1086), composed a poem about her, the text of which is given at the story's conclusion.[13] Here, therefore, is yet another instance of a narrative composed with a matching poem.

This account exposes the economic woes faced by unmarried, orphaned, or otherwise impoverished daughters of elite families. We are not told why Qiongnu's brother abandoned her. As an unmarried daughter, she was entitled to an additional portion of her father's estate for her dowry according to Tang and, therefore, early Song dynasty law, although in the tenth century it was increasingly common to give unmarried daughters half of each brother's share of the family estate.[14] The elder brother evidently did not follow this new custom, nor did he leave her with a sufficient, if any, dowry. Given her privileged birth, Qiongnu suffered from downward mobility by accepting a concubine's status when she deserved that of a (first) wife, although this was better than starving. Nonetheless, social status was exceedingly important to people throughout the imperial era—much more so than today. Unlike concubines, only a (first) wife could partake a family's ancestral supplications. Furthermore, a wife's place in the family was much more secure than that of a concubine, who could be easily expelled.

That Qiongnu's affianced family broke off the engagement due to her sudden socioeconomic decline lays bare the importance of wealth and property in regard to the tenth-century marriage market—something not found in prototypical love stories. From the early Northern Song, more so than earlier periods, the value of a bride's dowry came to outweigh that of the bride price customarily paid by the groom's family. For Patricia Ebrey, this was a type of "bribe" the bride's parents paid in order to secure a high-status husband for their daughter while forging social connections that would enhance their own social standing. In contrast to the Tang period when exorbitant bride prices prevailed given the aristocracy's general reluctance to marry their daughters beneath their own social circle, the up-and-coming educated elite of the new dynasty needed to make marriage alliances with politically influential families.[15] While their sons could attract upper-class mates given the successful bureaucratic career that would normally follow examination success, daughters required a large dowry to secure a good marriage. Large dowries also ensured high status and, consequently, respect of the bride's in-laws, thereby reducing the likelihood that she would be mistreated.[16] Furthermore, wealthy women's dowries often included substantial tracts of land or real estate. As the bride could legally control her dowry throughout her marriage, the consequent financial independence allowed her to remarry and retain her wealth should her husband die or in the unlikely event of divorce. Given this historical context, Qiongnu's story is a poignant illustration of the financial realities behind upper-class marriages of the period.

Exacerbating Qiongnu's downward mobility were the humiliating physical beatings she endured from her husband's wife. Hence dramatic socioeconomic decline is manifested on her physical body. Reference to these beatings evidently elicited contemporary readers' compassion, as illustrated by Wang Anguo's sympathetic poem. The abused Qiongnu, therefore, presents an image of a suffering young woman who is both beautiful and poetically talented. As Martin Huang has noted in the context of late-imperial love stories, "[f]or male literati writers and readers, nothing was more moving than witnessing a beautiful and talented woman suffering and languishing." He also observes that, "[t]here is a lot of male anxiety invested in this novelistic image of a suffering beautiful *cainü*"—that is, a talented young woman.[17] Although Huang speaks of the late-imperial period, his comments equally apply to the Song dynasty.

Toward the end of the story, a reference to "those of feeling" (*you qing zhe*) is noteworthy: "When those with feeling saw it [Qiongnu's inscription], sadness overcame them and they expressed their approbation." This phrase was an often-cited intertextual marker evoked in many love stories throughout the Song dynasty. In the culture of romance, it implies a constructed, if not actual, readership for love stories centuries before the emergence of the "cult of *qing*" during the late-imperial era when the phrase was frequently applied. Related to the idea of a languishing beauty, references to "one/those of feeling" hint at an intensified concern for women and their emotional hardships from the eleventh century onward. Indeed, empathy for the heroine seems the main *reason d'etre* for recording this story. Unlike many Tang dynasty stories, this one does not posit an erotic triangle, and the androcentrism apparent in many earlier narratives is diminished, thereby underscoring the female's importance. Regardless of whether contemporary readers derived sadomasochistic pleasure from Qiongnu's plight, empathized with her, or both, further analysis of Song-period love stories will show that a subtle yet significant new trend to emphasize the female had emerged.

The physical and mental abuse Qinongnu received from the shrewish wife, conveyed through direct speech, led her to radically air dirty linen in public. Even today in Chinese societies people are reluctant to reveal private affairs, particularly those relating to family scandal. By publicizing her situation, Qiongnu brought both her scholar-official husband and his household into disrepute, which explains why the storyteller suppressed his name and birthplace. While this may seem trivial to us in the twenty-first century, it would have been akin to "libel" for people during the tenth century. And, to be sure, the husband and wife were members of the ruling elite. This, nonetheless, reveals the breaking point when tenth-century personages, accustomed to concealing their feelings for the sake of family reputation, could no longer contain personal anguish. For a powerless woman like Qiongnu, her action was perhaps the best form of revenge she could enact.

Qiongnu's story is also one of female jealousy. While jealousy was rarely addressed in Tang dynasty love stories, it is more common in the Song period, although this may simply be due to an accident of extant sources. In one Southern Song story, a jealous wife abuses her husband's concubine and eventually has her thrown into a ravine.[18] In another, after an initially jealous wife accepts her husband's new concubine, a salacious ditty alleged how the threesome simultaneously slept together under one large quilt.[19] Female jealousy as a literary theme was not, however, as important during this period as it would become in late-imperial China.

One also encounters upward mobility in *"faji"* story types—that is, ones that narrate a rise in fortune vis-à-vis the down-and-out. Although Luo Ye's eight-fold schema did not posit a discreet literary category for this type, his observation[20] of how professional recounting of *faji* stories inspired the down-and-out is evoked in a quasi-generic sense.[21] A gossipy, eleventh-century account narrating the vicissitudes of high-ranking general Zhang Cong'en's (898–966) wife nicely illustrates this theme. Before eventually receiving a noble title through her marriage to the general, Lady Zhang was married to a low-ranking military officer who abandoned her on the road after she contracted a putrefying dermatological disease.[22] An older woman nursed her back to health and arranged for her to marry a scholar. Unfortunately, the scholar was later murdered by a rebel leader, Wang Congjin. After Wang's defeat, the heroine was captured by soldiers who "passed" (sold?) her to Zhang Cong'en. The story concludes by citing the honors and high status that she eventually received, thus implying predestined good fortune.[23] If the story's tenth-century setting is reliable, it is a rare early example of the theme.

In a similar vein, the famous twelfth-century historian and recorder of anomalous accounts Hong Mai (1123–1202), recorded a story titled "Second Sister Zhang," which tells of a female servant who married a family tutor after the couple left their employer's service. The servant, we are told, was quite ungainly. Although she not suffer from a disease, she appeared dried up and wasted; her skin was wrinkled and coarse. Her master, therefore, assigned her rough work such as grinding grain and drawing well water, as well as kitchen duties (which involved exposure to smoke). The tutor was a "traveling gentleman." The wealthy protagonist was sufficiently pleased with his conversation and learning that he employed him to teach his young sons. The wealthy man ordered the servant to serve the new tutor, thinking that her ugliness would prevent hanky-panky. The tutor left once his contract expired while the servant followed suit soon after. When all three accidentally met ten years after, the tutor had become an official, having passed the imperial examination, and the servant had become his wife. The former tutor then explains the circumstances of their marriage. Having serendipitously met the former servant on the road, he has her fetch and carry as they traveled together. Impressed by her diligence, he kept her on. He later married her as a first wife (although there is no suggestion that he had a concubine) due to both her goodness and kindness, as well as her intellect.[24]

Although marginal to a prototypical love story, this may well have inspired the "down and out," as Luo Ye claimed in regard to the *faji* story type, although Hong Mai focuses on the former servant and tutor's gratitude toward their former employer. While both male and female protagonist improved their lot, the woman's rise in social status, from indentured servant to a titled lady by dint of her husband's bureaucratic status, was no less than remarkable. Given her obvious indentured status, she must have originally been a free commoner. Unspoken economic necessity prompts her to debase herself so as to enter service during which time she endured considerable hardship. Her term of indenture expired, she returned to commoner status. Then, in view of her marriage to a scholar who later passed the imperial examinations, she entered the upper class. This nicely illustrates what Bossler has observed about the "breakdown of boundaries between 'respectable' (*liang*) and 'dishonorable* (*jian*) groups in late Tang and Song society"[25]—that is, the blurring of class distinctions between those of free commoner and debased status, such as courtesans, servants, slaves, and the like. Certainly this trend had intensified by the time Hong Mai wrote in the twelfth century. Lower-class women were particularly notable beneficiaries as more opportunities for upward social mobility came their way. The story also gives hope to men who, through education, diligence, and "plain living" (suggested by marrying a plain-looking but capable wife as opposed to a beauty), may join the ranks of the ruling classes. Nonetheless, this example contradicts Hartwell's findings that it was only after a young scholar married into an influential family could he hope to pass the examinations. Therefore, while contemporaries did not consider this story beyond the bounds of reality, if its factual reliability may be trusted, it must have been a rare exception to the general trend and not without a considerable degree of wish fulfillment.

The late eleventh-century story of Tan Yige illustrates both upward and downward mobility while celebrating female virtue. Found in in Liu Fu's *High Minded Conversations*, its valorization of a virtuous courtesan nicely complements similar moralistic tracts in Liu's collection. Its authorship is attributed to Qin Chun (fl. eleventh century), although little is known about his biography. Li Jianguo dates the story to the mid-1080s.[26] Events purportedly occurred in the regional city of Changsha (modern Hunan) where Tan Yige's parents had both died by the time she was eight (*sui*). Although the family's precise social status is uncertain (was the father a merchant, scholar-official, or something else when he died in Yingzhou?), it is clear that they were of a "respectable" class—that is, free-born commoners, if not higher (*liangmin*). At the age of ten (*sui*), soon after her mother's death, Tan was sold to a brothel-madam by an artisan into whose care she had been placed. After a lengthy training period, her poetic prowess and understanding of Confucian thought garnered popularity among local bureaucrats who registered her as a state courtesan. Her understanding of Confucian thought suggests she was a daughter of the educated elite as she would have been unlikely to have access to such learning elsewhere. Her charms were not limited to literary talent and classical learning; she was also beautiful. "Pure of skin and with a delicate physique, [she had] raven locks and long eyes. Her fingers were as slender as young bamboo shoots and her waist was so thin that it could be encircled in one's hands. She was a singular beauty of her time."

Distaining the immorality associated with courtesan status, her request to quit the ranks of government courtesans so as to marry a commoner (*congliang*) was eventually granted. Despite searching, no husband could be found for her until one Zhang Zhengyu arrived as an overseer of tea revenue. She fell instantly in love with him, remarking: " 'I have found my husband.' People questioned her about it, and she replied, 'His bearing, talent and learning all please me.' " Zhang returned her feelings. It was not long before the couple engaged in sexual intercourse on a genial, moonlit night in a riverside pavilion. The following day, an anonymous "person of feeling" (*you qing zhe*), apparently anticipating the lover's wedding, composed a poem in celebration of the occasion:

Talent and beauty both find satisfaction,
A romantic tryst is most sublime.
Once the peony is transplanted into the immortal capital,
Eastern Hunan will henceforth lack beautiful blossom.

Tan packed her belongings (which must have been considerable for she later buys land with which to support herself) and moved in with Zhang as a sort of concubine, reminiscent of Huo Xiaoyu's relationship with Li Yi.

The couple lived together for two years until, following narrative conventions established during the mid-Tang, Zhang found it necessary to leave her when his term of office expired. His parents, furthermore, had arranged a marriage for him. Hence, the compulsion to satisfy social expectations and filial duty prevented him from honoring his pledge to marry Tan. She, in his absence, gave birth to his son. After this she curtailed all but essential contact with the outside world so as to maintain her chastity while awaiting his return. She also taught her son Confucian learning. During this time, she wrote several letters to Zhang, reproduced by the storyteller, that reveal her thoughts and feelings. When Zhang's wife died three years later, he met a bureaucrat recently returned from Changsha who, reminiscent of the sympathy accorded Huo Xiaoyu by Li Yi's circle of acquaintances, extoled Tan's virtue while vilifying her betrayer. Significantly in the context of the culture of romance, he is referred to as "a person of feeling." Stung by his censure, Zhang returns to Changsha, although he did not immediately seek Tan. Wishing to verify reports of her virtue, he first made surreptitious inquires and observed her living quarters from a distance. When they finally met, Tan shut her door on him, refusing to emerge. In this poignant scene, the lovers' thoughts and mutual suspicions are conveyed in a lengthy dialog.

> Zhang said, "Have I crossed countless rivers and mountains, travelled thousands of miles for nothing? My heart is still yours. Why do you refuse me so adamantly? Did I treat you badly before?" Yige replied, "You already have a wife. I wish to live chastely so as to preserve the sincerity of my decision [to give myself to you]. You should go! Don't bother me!" Zhang replied, "My wife is dead. Please don't pay any mind to the past. That may be dealt with. If I can't have you, I swear I'll die on this very spot." Yige responded, "I admired you before. Yet were I to cross your threshold now [as a concubine], it would be easy for you to get rid of me. If you won't forsake me, then find a matchmaker and have them act according to auspicious ritual. Only after that will I do as you say. Otherwise, we'll never meet again."

And so Zhang formally married her—that is, by sending a matchmaker, asking the name, and exchanging gifts.[27] Having had his first marriage parentally arranged, he was free to choose his second wife. The story happily concludes as the couple return to the capital (presumably Zhang's natal home), as had been anticipated in the poem. Tan won the approval of her in-laws through diligent household management and gave birth to another son, who passed the imperial examinations. Finally, in echoes of Li Wa, her marriage to a high-ranking scholar-official made her a titled lady (*mingfu*).[28]

The story's mention of Tan's pregnancy is highly unusual as male storytellers almost always suppressed this aspect of female biological reality. Addressing it here may indicate the Song storyteller's penchant for historical fidelity, assuming its basis in gossip. Nonetheless, Tan's raising a child helps demonstrate her unswerving chastity in the face of hardship after her separation from Zhang. Furthermore, the scholastic honors attained by her second child, along with her status as a titled lady, for contemporary readers would have demonstrated the predestined nature of the lovers' union and thereby partly justified—or apologized for—the illicit sex involved in their unorthodox liaison.

Tan's transformation from daughter of a respectable family to orphan, to a courtesan of debased status, back to a commoner's status, then to the lover of a scholar-official, to a self-appointed virtuous "widow" (i.e., an abandoned woman), and then finally to the wife of a scholar-official with a home in the capital is remarkable even by Northern Song standards. Her story illustrates the comparatively fluid boundary between elite, commoner, and debased (i.e., prostitutes and indentured servants) women's status throughout the Song and Yuan period, as noted by Bossler.[29] The felicitous denouement evokes the *faji* prototype and confirms widespread contemporary belief about destiny, yet the downward social mobility theme remains strong.

Song dynasty storytellers' fear of young upper-class or, at least, free-born women falling into prostitution, or otherwise possessed by unworthy men, recalls the theme of male competition in Tang dynasty stories. Yet no indication of anxiety over downward mobility is discernable in earlier stories. In those of the Song dynasty, fear over the loss of a woman is—significantly—conflated with loss of social status. Moreover, as a woman's social status was contingent on that of her male relatives, as I have observed in relation to Qiongnu, male fear about women's status is interwoven with fear of their own mutable social standing. As Beverley Bossler has observed in regard to similar examples, "these stories also reflect upper-class male anxieties about the tenuousness of (their own) status in their day. Here as elsewhere, male fears and apprehensions are displaced onto the bodies of women."[30] Hence, even though Tan Yige's story outwardly celebrates an individual woman's freely chosen marriage, her rise in fortune, and her observance of traditional social values, intricately related to this are male-centered issues and anxiety.

Related to downward mobility is the image of a languishing beauty, so movingly portrayed in Qiongnu's story. Indeed, our narrator tells how a provincial prefect and other officials "were sad and sympathetic" after hearing how Tan had fallen from a commoner's status to that of a debased courtesan.[31] Such explicit treatment of male emotion no doubt both guided and reflected contemporary readers' sympathy about "damsels in distress." Moreover, the beautiful and talented heroine suffers from sexual servitude. Hence, downward social mobility is further conflated with unspoken moralistic concerns about female sexuality.

The portrayal of male sympathy in the story is undoubtedly related to Tan's poetic prowess through which she upholds traditional Confucian values thought to be embodied in literature itself (*siwen*).[32] Indeed, a considerable portion of the early narrative describes instances of her poetic interactions with local officials. In one such an interaction, when an official disparagingly compares her to a wax gourd (*donggua*), she retaliates by comparing him to a red jujube (*hongzao*): "Seeing what she said, Jiang Tian laughed at her. He therefore called on her to match his line. Pointing at her face, he said: 'A wax gourd, after frost, puts on more make-up.' Yige, seizing the red sleeve of his official's gown, responded: 'Tree-jujubes in autumn also wear red.' His lordship was both embarrassed and pleased, while everyone else praised her in unison."[33] The official's pointing to her face indicates that his line was meant as a personal remark. Wax gourds sometimes referred to girls of marriageable age given the orthographic resemblance to the character for "eight" which, when doubled, made sixteen (*sui*)—the earliest marriageable age for a girl.[34] The final reference to make-up clarifies the allusion. Tan's tugging on the man's sleeve, undoubtedly red, likewise implies that her response refers to him. In this context, the reference to jujubes turning red in autumn likely refers to the man's finally having been elevated to the ranks of officialdom (hence wearing red sleeves) after reaching the autumn of his life. Significant is Tan's knowledge and ready command of the literary tradition. To be sure, her response modifies a poem by the famous man of letters, historian and statesman Ouyang Xiu.[35] Acquisition of such erudition was highly prized by men of the period. Poetic prowess enabled a man to showcase his intellectual superiority and knowledge of a commonly revered cultural heritage. Some daughters of the ruling elite were also taught poetry, but mastery was not expected. Even women who wrote poetry during the eleventh century would rarely have read them in public, let alone circulate them. Therefore, that a lowly courtesan could extemporize matching lines and modify those of enshrined poets garners the male characters' admiration and thereby establishes her place as a literary paragon. Moreover, her upholding of a male-dominated cultural tradition endorses the storyteller's androcentric values and those of his constructed male readership. Guided by the reactions of the scholar-official characters, this—as with her languishing social condition—would have engaged the sympathy of many contemporary male readers.

As with numerous Song dynasty narratives, this reveals a strong moralistic flavor. Tan's consistent display of orthodox morality both mitigates the ill repute associated with her courtesan status while establishing her as a model of feminine virtue which, in turn, confirms patriarchal values. When she first learned of her foster father's intention to sell her into prostitution, she strenuously resisted: "I am not your child, sir. How, then, can you bear to abandon me in the house of a prostitute? If you would marry me off, I would willingly do so even though it be to a poor family." Such a morally correct argument vis-à-vis Confucian thought uttered from the mouth of a ten-year-old (*sui*) girl is almost certainly the voice of the male storyteller. Tan furthermore makes a scene when first taken to the bordello, saying, "I am alone in the world and have wandered myriad [Chinese] miles. I am physically weak and of a tender age. There is no one to care for me. I cannot marry a man of respectable status." Again speaking through a ten-year-old, here the storyteller establishes Tan's preference for marriage, as opposed to the materially comfortable yet immoral lifestyle of a courtesan, while inviting the elite reader's sympathy for a languishing little girl. Her desire to become a respectable woman through marriage is reiterated when she petitions the local prefect to remove her name from the register of government courtesans. Her monologue at this juncture draws attention to the dubious nature associated with a courtesan's profession: "I have been obliged to entertain guests and be at their beck and call as a registered courtesan for a mere year now, so I dare not voice any complaint about fatigue. Now I have been fortunate enough to meet you, your honor. I would thank you with my life would you permit me be released from the register [of courtesans] and become a common man's wife." After her affair with Zhang, her parting words to him are also significant: "You are from a renowned family while I am of courtesan stock. It would not be a fitting match were one of lowly status to marry a man of stature. Moreover, you have no [official] wife and your parents are both elderly. This farewell will be our final one." Besides showing consideration for Zhang's parents—figures of patriarchal authority, Tan's brief speech illustrates her lack of jealousy, which, as a womanly virtue, was enshrined in no less an authority than the *Classic of Poetry*, purportedly edited by Confucius himself.[36] Tan's lack of jealousy is furthermore reminiscent of Li Wa's willingness to relinquish her lover in favor of an upper-class bride. Her semi-reclusive lifestyle subsequent to Zhang's departure, even after news of his marriage, clearly demonstrates her unswerving chastity and loyalty to one man. This, in effect, salvages her integrity after having become Zhang's one-time concubine. Tan furthermore raised Zhang's son and taught him Confucian principles. No celebrated chaste widow of the late-imperial period could have exhibited greater moral rectitude. Such impeccable integrity built her a reputation as a virtuous woman and rewarded her with marriage to an elite man.

Like Tang-era heroines who were valorized as paragons, so too is Tan Yige, yet the reason differs significantly. While Miss Ren, for example, displayed impeccable feminine loyalty in general and Li Wa upheld and repaired patriarchal values, Tan Yige is largely valued for her chastity, notwithstanding her extramarital affair with Zhang and her activities as a courtesan. That is, her refusal to marry another if she could not marry Zhang. Female chastity and fidelity to one man was not an invention of Song dynasty thinkers; such had always been enshrined in the Confucian tradition. Nonetheless, as discussed above, Confucian moralists began to increasingly emphasize this idea over the course of the eleventh and twelfth centuries—particularly widow chastity, eventually making it a cornerstone of Neo-Confucian self-cultivation. While the type of thought discernable in this story may not be considered Neo-Confucian *per se*, it represents conservative male attitudes toward women's morality during a period in which the leading thinkers of the day were reevaluating the Confucian tradition. We will see how similar moralistic ideas pervaded other love stories.

Such morally conservative thought, nonetheless, conflicts with the romantic elements of the story. Early in the narrative when the bordello madam—a supposed example of a conniving prostitute—lavishes Tan with fine food and clothing so as to overcome her resistance, she is likened to a "loving mother." That Tan and her lover suffer no punishment for their illicit lovemaking (punishable by penal servitude) portrays the sexual act as a "legitimate" display of affection, contrary to orthodox morality. To be sure, the sexual intercourse itself is sympathetically described, albeit metaphorically, in a relatively extended manner when compared to its terse treatment under the hands of many Tang dynasty storytellers.

> Zhang arranged a tryst with Tan in a riverside pavilion. At that time, the pavilion was tall and the breeze unusual[37] while the luminous moon cast her rays over the deserted river. High silken curtains cascaded down as a pure breeze caressed the windows. The moon shone through a thin, bamboo blind. Incense smoldered in a silver, duck-shaped burner. Jade pillows were laid side-by-side. An embroidered quilt covered the bed. Like melodious musical instruments, the lovers spoke in low whispers while their amorous hearts took flight like willow catkins in spring. [Their bodies] resembled immortal blossoms on a single branch or else twin fish in the same spring. The pleasure they gave one another could never be erased, even by death.

Gone, here, is the didactic tone of the Confucian moralist, banished by such erotic symbolism as "fish in a spring" and "blossoms on a single branch." The poem composed by "one of feeling," quoted above, is also highly effusive.

Yet, in one of her letters to Zhang, Tan openly contradicts the pleasure she formerly derived. After announcing an intention to pursue a farmer's life while raising her child, she professes: "Other things, such as the pure breeze and large dwellings, bright moonlight and pavilions, gratifying one's heart and mind as well as pleasurable affairs, have not weighed on my mind for a long time." Hence, the overlay of celebratory sentiment and orthodox moralizing constitute two competing voices within the text. The reason for such internal dissonance is unclear. It is, furthermore, uncertain whether the attributed author, Qin Chun, or the anthology's compiler, Liu Fu, or both, or someone else is responsible. Given the story's likely initial circulation as gossip, it is not surprising that minor disparate elements enter the text with each retelling over time. Accordingly, the moralistic elements may well constitute a later retelling of an originally more sympathetic narration, or vice versa. More likely, however, they indicate a sympathetic storyteller's compulsion to mollify orthodox moralistic readers, although one explanation does not preclude the other. I will return to this idea below.

Also celebratory of romance is the phrase "one/those with feeling" (*you qing zhe*), peppered throughout the text. As already noted, the first instance occurs after the assignation by the river when an unnamed "one with feeling" gives the couple a celebratory poem. After their separation, when Zhang showed Tan's moving letter to his relatives, there was not one among "those with feeling" who did not sigh with regret. Finally, the returned official remarks that were "one with feeling" to see Zhang's cruel treatment of Tan, they would call for his execution. This last elicitation of the term indicates that males other than the protagonist-lover could harbor "feeling"/*qing* toward the heroine. This in turn demonstrates that, in regard to the culture of romance, male storytellers and their readers viewed romance as more than simply carnal pleasure. While this was almost always an essential element, "feeling" toward or empathy with the female is conspicuously important. The expectation of fair dealing and loyalty is clearly mutual. We saw how the term *qing* (feeling) also occurs in the story of Qiongnu in a similar sense. Indeed, Liu Fu evokes it frequently throughout his *High Minded Conversations*. Besides its function as an intertextual marker, its reoccurrence is further evidence of a constructed readership vis-à-vis the culture of romance long before *qing* was elevated to cult status in the late Ming dynasty.

Significantly, Tan Yige's story is also one of marriage. As I will discuss below, marriage became a crucially important new theme for Song-period storytellers. In Tan Yige's story, it helps to mitigate the couple's illicit sexual act while reclaiming Tan's reputation. On a more abstract level, it neutralizes the subversive aspects of romance by subsuming them into the establishment. It also rewards the courtesan-lover for her staunch support of Confucian values. Finally, interclass marriage triumphs. Although this theme was first developed in the mid-Tang with stories such as Li Wa's, its frequent reoccurrence from the eleventh century onward reflects women's increasingly indistinct class boundaries throughout the Song-Yuan period.

The Domestication of Romantic Love: Marriage

As noted in the previous chapter, romantic affairs between human lovers in eighth- and ninth-century love stories rarely concluded with marriage.

When they did, often a strong *zhiguai* element was involved. More commonly, many shorter anecdotes and narratives upheld the popular belief that marriage was predestined. To my knowledge, the only Tang-era love story featuring marriage between a human couple without paranormal phenomena is "Li Wa's Story." In contrast to this are numerous Song-period stories that develop marriage as a central theme.[38] While some address interclass marriage, others feature marriage between men and women of equal status. Yet others focus on postmarital events. In this way, Song storytellers consistently reconciled romantic love and marriage; even arranged marriage became grist for the storyteller's mill. If the culture of romance during the Tang era celebrated transitory, freely chosen love affairs as opposed to arranged and possibly loveless marriages, Song dynasty stories envisaged the ideal of freely chosen marriage based on romantic attachment rather than sociomonetary gain. So as to reconcile individual desire and social expectation, the protagonists' parents often became arbiters of a couple's romantic happiness, offering an alternative to the Tang convention of a senior male who could reward the hero with a beautiful woman.[39] The domestic setting, therefore, becomes increasingly important as lovers' meetings between equal-status partners occurred in the home where plots could include parental involvement. Furthermore, in contrast to many earlier stories that diminished the female's importance as it disproportionately focused on the young male, female protagonists often gain equal attention in Song-period stories. Heroines sometimes constitute the narrative subject, as in Tan Yige's and Wang Qiongnu's stories discussed above. Accordingly, marriage became the endgame for many a love story. With this paradigmatic shift, Song-period storytellers explored new themes, such as marital happiness, premarital sex (more openly than in previous works), and the importance of observing marriage contracts, as well as new perspectives on conjugal predestiny and the like.

"Young Mr. Ding's Pleasant Dream" is an unusual union story focusing on events that occurred after the marriage ceremony. Set during the *yuanfu* reign period (1098–1100), it tells of a conscientious Imperial University student who, at his parents' request, returns home to undergo an arranged marriage. His bride, Miss Cui, is from a local gentry family. As was invariably the case with arranged marriages, Ding did not see his bride until their wedding night.[40] The reader glimpses her through the narrator's viewpoint:

> The young man saw his bride. With shoulders draped in a thin scarf that trailed like evening clouds and with phoenixes

embroidered on her silken skirt, she appeared to float—not unlike a goddess. The maidservants left and Madame Cui wished to retire. The young man was as if drunk when he saw mandarin duck-patterned bed-curtains drawn aside to reveal a bright red hue while his wife removed a phoenix comb, releasing her dark, glossy hair. They lowered the curtains and, resting on the pillows, fully enjoyed love's pleasures. Even Sima Xiangru and Zhuo Wenjun, or else Nongyu and Xiao Shi could not compare with them.[41]

After the wedding night, the pair revel in each other's company. Miss Cui proves an accomplished poetess, so they frequently recite poetry together. Hence, besides physical attraction, the couple shares intellectual and aesthetic companionship. Such was their firm friendship that they remained inseparable throughout the day. Evoking the story of Lady Yang and the Tang emperor Xuanzong, the narrator tells how the couple wish to spend their days like a pair of birds joined at the wings.

When the young man, again at his father's request, returns to the University, he cannot stop thinking about his wife. On the evening following the third day of the third (lunar) month (the *Shangsi* festival, otherwise known as *Qingming*, the Clear and Bright festival), when it was customary for both men and women of all classes to go out, the lovesick young husband remains in his dormitory rather than carousing with peers. There he dreams of returning home to find his wife crying as she writes him a letter. Although he cannot remember the letter's entire contents on waking, he records a poem that she wrote. Shortly after this, he receives a letter from home that includes a poem from his wife. And, in keeping with a generic convention common to the *zhiguai* genre, the poem proves identical when compared with the record of the dream-poem. The letter's date—the third day of the third month—is final proof that the young student's soul returned home in a form of astral travel.[42]

The story's anomalous denouement aligns it closely with the *zhiguai* genre. Nonetheless, had it been recorded primarily for the anomaly of the wandering soul, there would have been no need to narrate in detail events leading up to and following the wedding, let alone the wedding night itself and the couple's shared affection. Little wonder, therefore, that its author-compiler, Li Xianming, included it in one of the *liqing* chapters of his *Comprehensive Record*. In fact, as the poem has been transcribed in full, the story's form also resembles the literary genre that framed and explained a poem's context within a brief narrative, known as *benshi shi*—poems based on stories. Hence, this is a good example of a narrative that straddles several generic types. I follow Li Xianming's lead and read it as a love story. In view of the anomalous occurrence, it superficially resembles a Tang-period marriage story such that Dai Fu recorded in his *Extensive Collection of Marvels*. Differing significantly, however, is not only the postmarital bliss but also the focus on *arranged* marriage, something Tang storytellers ignored.

In this story, instead of a male storyteller's jealousy and suspicion over wives discernable in many earlier narratives such as Bai Xingjian's "Record of Three Dreams," one finds a male pining for his absent wife.[43] Nowhere is there a hint of male sexual competition. The narration of events during and after the wedding night unproblematically celebrates the couple's mutual love. The arranged marriage does not preclude the construction of a private space in which a young couple may find reciprocal love, unlike Tang dynasty stories in which the twain largely remained separate. Therefore, in this and similar Song dynasty stories, romantic love is "domesticated" by marriage.

Given the arranged marriage, Mr. Ding's parents replace the Tang senior male who arbitrates over a young protagonist's romantic felicity. The geographic setting is, therefore, largely domestic as this is where parents may plausibly enter the plot. The *post hoc* relationship between the student's industrious habits and his subsequent acquisition of a beautiful wife may also be seen as a variation on the Tang theme whereby protagonists were rewarded with a woman for meritorious deeds. Hence, Song stories such as this reveal a spirit of optimism in regard to parents as a social institution, along with scholastic enterprise and the examination system as a meritocratic means of social advancement. Familial ties are emphasized and, at the same time, harmonized with romantic desire.

Related to arranged marriage is the wife's social status—that is, of comparable social rank with the groom. Here, then, the wife supplants the concubine or courtesan-lover of the Tang love story. Indeed Mr. Ding's wife, given both her poetic talent and ethereal beauty, constitutes any male protagonist's ideal woman. The narrator, accordingly, describes the couple as a beauty and a man of talent (*jiaren caizi*), an idiom that later became so ubiquitous that it was used to coin the scholar-beauty genre of late-imperial literature.

When Mr. Ding expresses his reluctance to return to the University, his wife urges him to do so in a somewhat lengthy speech:

As a young man you wish to attain first grade honors and garb yourself with the green robes [of a graduate]. This is your goal. How could amorous desire lead you to disobey your father's will and miss your goal? Does not the *Commentary on the Spring and Autumn Annals* say: "By gratifying one's ease, one's good name will be lost"? You should go! [On the other hand,] I have heard that the imperial capital has red light districts and wine markets, and that young men frequently stop there to spend a fortune, drinking to excess in houses of ill repute. Such as this has dampened the relationship between many a married couple. If you could concentrate on your studies and put such things out of your mind, think of me often, then although we are apart I will have no regrets.

The wife's encouragement of her husband's studies is also reminiscent of Li Wa. Yet, while "Li Wa's Story" was an exception among Tang-era narratives that reconciled romantic love and public duty, many stories of the Song dynasty did so. As we will see below, public duty—particularly that relating to scholastic cultivation and civil service—no longer necessarily formed a binary opposition with romantic love. Given the heightened importance of examination success so as to establish and perpetuate elite status throughout the Song dynasty, many a love story of the period made scholastic achievement a veritable prerequisite for romantic happiness. To be sure, Miss Cui's monologue carries a heavy burden of orthodox morality. Rather than the authentic voice of a new bride, it appears to be that of a male storyteller. As will be illustrated more clearly in other narratives, didactic content may be considered another distinctive characteristic of the period's love stories. A particularly significant aspect of the wife's speech is her exhortation to obey one's father. Hence, filial piety is valorized as it was in Tan Yige's and other Song-period stories. Therefore, while this story celebrates romance within marriage, orthodox morality affirming the patriarchal family system and public duty are simultaneously upheld.

The male storyteller's mediation is especially discernable from his wedding night description. Not only does the reader "see" the bride through the young protagonist's eyes, but all attention focuses on her physical beauty, her alluring dress, the seductively arranged bed, and the couple's lovemaking. Indeed, the bride's "thin scarf which trailed like evening clouds," the manner in which she let down her hair, and her having initiated the lovemaking are reminiscent of an encounter with a goddess or a visit to a high-class courtesan. Nowhere is attention given to any trepidation that the young bride may have felt at the prospect of sexual intercourse for the first time. Therefore, as the narrative suppresses such emotional reality, particularly from a female's perspective, it conjures a fantasy of male sexual and emotional fulfillment. Furthermore, the visual and emotional pleasure invested in this description seems to stem from an experienced male's perspective, not that of a sheltered young virgin, as Mr. Ding appears to be. From this we may further discern a gulf between reality and wish fulfillment of the textual *weltanshauung*.

Nonetheless, despite the initial emphasis on female beauty, intellectual and cultural attainments are accorded equal standing. The couple's mutual affection after the wedding night bliss, founded on a shared love of poetry, suggests that the male articulating subject was seeking more than mere physical union vis-à-vis romantic love. A meeting of minds, intellectual companionship, if not friendship, is also valued. In an age when women were not encouraged to compose poetry and those who did would not generally have recited them in public, a poetically gifted wife must have been a rarity and, therefore, a worthy topic of the short-story genre.

In "Madam Sun's Story," a would-be illicit relationship leads to marriage. Set in the imperial capital, its educated male protagonist, Zhou Mo,[44] is well versed in medical texts, and his skill as a physician eventually wins the recognition of his acquaintances. One of his neighbors, Zhang Fu, is an impoverished gentleman who privately runs a local school. When Zhang's wife, Madam Sun, falls ill, he asks Zhou to diagnose her malady. When Zhou measures Madam Sun's pulse, the narrator describes her appearance through Zhou's eyes using a narrative technique not unlike a cinematic point-of-view shot. "Zhou saw his [Zhang's] wife, Madam Sun, lying on a small couch. Although she had not made-up her face, the elegance and subtlety of her understated beauty, the delicate and pleasing line of her brow, and her overall glamour as she turned to face him was captivating. Mo beheld her, astounded. He then proceeded to take her pulse." From first sight, Zhou was smitten. After Madam Sun recovered, he persuades his unsuspecting mother to invite her home. "I treated Madam Sun so that she made a recovery. You could invite her to drink with you so as to show neighborly goodwill." Although Madam Sun initially refuses, she accepts a second invitation. "On this occasion Sun had applied a thin layer of make-up. Although she wore jewelry, her clothing was not embroidered with gold thread or verdure. Despite this, her seductive beauty was unparalleled. Her conversation was ethereal, exactly like that of an immortal."

One wonders what an immortal's conversation must have sounded like! The attention paid to the woman's voice, though, is an unusual narrative touch. Little wonder that our protagonist's spirit "disintegrates" (*dangsan*) at the sight of her. Nonetheless, she politely refuses wine offered by Zhou's mother.[45] This visit makes him even more anxious to possess her sexually.

Narrative focus subsequently shifts to an exchange of letters and poetry in which Zhou attempts to seduce the wife by contrasting her aging husband with his own youthful vigor. Sun, for her part, remains so steadfastly loyal to her husband that Zhou eventually desists. The narrator emphasizes Madam Sun's narrative agency as he includes no less than four of her letters and only one of Zhou's. Her initial rebuff reveals her psychology while touching on social mobility:

> You have demeaned yourself to ask after me and I am keenly appreciative of your kindness. Since I have a husband, how might I dare respond in private? Allow me to outline my background. I was originally from a wealthy household and, as a child, often used brush and ink. I met with successive misfortunes growing up. My older brother also died in the provinces while my younger brothers and sisters split up. The family was so poor that we could not support ourselves. I trusted the words of a matchmaker and married this aging man. I won't say anything about my present situation, only that I have no regrets. Women have no other abilities but to conduct themselves with rectitude and chastity. I had not wished to tell you this, sir, but you still have not relinquished your regard for me. For goodness sake, take care of yourself! Do not continue to think of me as this may lead to later regret. My heart is not a stone and I will express it in the enclosed poem.
>
> Rain accumulates in an old pool, eventually filling it up
> The old wood of a wicker cage all at once regenerates.
> You now take pleasure in the scene before your eyes,
> I make-up on the terrace and await my romantic fate.

Sun's following letter addresses conjugal destiny and how she must live on her own. Zhou soon after leaves the capital to take up a provincial posting. Before he departs, he writes her a letter, promising to remain unmarried so as to wait for her. Returning three years later, he learns that Zhang has died and that Madam Sun is living alone. He then sends a matchmaker to propose marriage and is accepted, notwithstanding a decorous delay.

Surprisingly, the story does not conclude there. The narrator follows Zhou and Sun to another provincial posting during which Zhou repeatedly accepts bribes. When Sun discovers this, she remonstrates and threatens to commit suicide. Zhou then agrees to return the ill-gotten gains. The narrative concludes with information about their two sons who both passed the imperial examinations, having been personally educated by Madam Sun. The storyteller's end commentary is highly significant: "One may certainly record [stories of] those women and girls who exhibit chastity and righteousness. There are few [women] in the world today the likes of Madam Sun. As a wife she stood firm against the temptation of impropriety and she persuaded her husband to rectify his errors, thereby laying a foundation for the next generation. It is fitting that she should have become a titled lady!"[46]

Again we see how a woman is extolled as a virtuous exemplar. The contrast drawn between Madam Sun and other women implies a suspicion that many wives may have succumbed to adultery. As with other Tang- and Song-era stories discussed so far, the heroine is interpellated in an Althusian sense as an upholder of patriarchal morality. In contrast to many Tang-period paragons, however, Madam Sun is primarily valorized for her chastity—that is, sexual fidelity to her husband regardless of her own feelings. This she maintains despite the fact that she is clearly fond of the protagonist, as may be seen from her poem and other correspondence. Her ability to suppress her romantic inclinations accentuates her virtue as it anticipates Zhu Xi's exhortation to repress individual desire. In refusing Zhou's advances, she also preserves his integrity as an upper-class scholar-official while supporting patriarchy as symbolized by her husband. In fact, her husband's name puns with the binome "husband" (*zhangfu*), although the storyteller may not have intended a double entendre. Her insistence that Zhou return the bribes resonates with her earlier refusal of his sexual advances. Furthermore, her personally educating her sons paints an ideal vignette of a family organized along Confucian principles, echoing Tan Yige's identical behavior. Unlike Tan, Madam Sun did not engage in illicit sex. Therefore, similar to Mr. Ding's story, this reconciles freely chosen romantic love and orthodox morality, which further distinguishes it from Tang-era love stories. The lack of illicit sex renders it a "chaste" love story, anticipating many erotic novellas of the Ming dynasty that similarly refrained from the inclusion of sexual intercourse. Moral conservative ideas are valorized, particularly that of female chastity, thereby reflecting the growing influence of orthodox Confucian thought as exemplified by the eleventh-century Cheng brothers and others.

The erotic triangle device, so prevalent in Tang-era love stories, reoccurs here. The competition for the female between the young "para-literati" protagonist and the aging patriarch (who was also the local schoolmaster) is explicated in Zhou's addresses to Sun. "Zhou thought to himself, 'I have performed a service for Sun. Moreover, I am young while Sun's husband is extremely old. I far surpass him. I must surely prevail!'" This monologue not only valorizes youth over age (merely implied in other stories), if not superficially, but also directly evokes the idea of woman-as-reward for a meritorious act—that is, Zhou's treating Sun's illness. Nevertheless, unlike Tang-era stories such as "Bu Feiyan," Madam Sun's storyteller defends the husband's rights to his wife's loyalty and sexual labor. The protagonist's improper advances are thwarted and it is only after the husband's death, when Zhou marries his beloved with due ceremony, working through a matchmaker, that his suit is successful. Madam Sun's moralistic, Song-period storyteller allows neither illicit sex nor sexual possession of another man's wife.

Finally, Madam Sun's letter outlining her socioeconomic vicissitudes again highlights social mobility. Here is another example of a woman born into a privileged household who fell on hard times. Like Wang Qiongnu, Madam Sun was impoverished through the male head of household's death and was consequently forced to marry. In fact, toward the narrative's conclusion we learn that she was married no fewer than three times. As will be later discussed, the ease with which many widows remarried during the Song period contrasts significantly with their late-imperial counterparts. Madam Sun's happy ending goes hand in hand with her support of patriarchal values, both of which conform to the moralizing tenor of the story overall. As with the young tutor in "Zhang Cong'en's Wife," this one bears witness to the male protagonist's rise in social status. At the outset, his rank appears marginal and there is no suggestion that his family is particularly wealthy of influential. Nonetheless, through examination success, he is able to better himself, and his virtuous wife contributes to his moral cultivation. The social mobility theme here thus applies to the protagonists of both genders.

Dangerous Liaisons: Illicit Sexual Intercourse

Many Song-period love stories, like their Tang antecedents, narrate incidents of pre- and extramarital sex, as we saw in "Tan Yige." Legal codes of the imperial period, however, rather than distinguish between these two forms of sexual behavior, conflated them under the rubric of "illicit sex" (*jian*) and its variant, "consensual illicit sex" (*hejian*). This was construed as a criminal act between commoners—that is, people of "respectable" status (*liangmin*), which included the upper classes. According to the Tang legal code on which Song dynasty law was based, violators were subject to one and a half years of penal servitude. People of debased status (*jianmin*, such as members of courtesan households, professional entertainers, indentured servants, and slaves) were, nevertheless, considered beneath this law and not held accountable until 1723.[47] Conceptually, illicit sex was similar to the Roman Catholic concept of fornication insofar that it acted as an umbrella term for all forms of pre- and extramarital sex. In premodern China, however, illicit sex was not considered a sin as it was in the West, although it was included among Buddhist prohibitions. Sex in a Buddhist context, like all forms of hedonistic behavior, was believed to inhibit spiritual enlightenment because it maintained undue attachment to the phenomenal world. Failure to abstain was widely believed to result in otherworldly or karmic punishment. According to traditional medical and Daoist ideas, a male's excessive sexual indulgence was thought to deplete his store of *yang* energy; extreme cases could result in death, as illustrated in many a *zhiguai* account.

Illicit sex posed a further threat to China's ancestor-worshipping society that venerated patrilineage. One did not wish one's ancestral line sullied by outsiders, nor was it considered desirable to raise another man's child, unless voluntarily adopting a male heir so as to perpetuate ancestral ritual. Even in Chinese societies today, people's reluctance to raise children not of their own issue remains strong. Therefore, very early in the Confucian tradition, emphasis was placed on appropriate segregation of the sexes. Upper-class women were cloistered within the so-called inner quarters of their family compounds, largely separated from adult males, emerging only for religious observance or calendrical festivals, such as the *Shangsi* festival featured in Mr. Ding's story. Arranged marriage was therefore necessary to avoid unpropitious mixing of the sexes and the immorality that might have ensued.

As observed in the introduction, unlike *zhiguai* accounts that tended to warn of the dangers associated with illicit sex, love stories of all periods generally portrayed it in a sympathetic manner. Although sexual intercourse is integral to numerous ninth-century stories, the act itself tended to be treated elliptically and, when details are given, they are comparatively sparing. [48] In Song-period stories, conversely, illicit sexual encounters are generally described more frequently and in greater detail, albeit metaphorically. Moreover, the manner in which this subversive behavior is neutralized differs significantly between the two periods. As I have already observed, in mid- and late Tang stories, carnal relations that led to marriage almost always included a strong *zhiguai* element. In love stories between two human protagonists who were neither ghosts nor paranormal beings, storytellers tended to separate romance and marriage. When contained as a discreet, transitory dalliance, sexual intercourse and romance were generally condoned so long as the young elite male eventually returned to his rightful social role. Conversely, during the Song and Yuan periods, many storytellers neutralized the subversive nature of sexual relations through marriage. Sex could be aestheticized, celebrated, or condoned so long as it led to matrimony. Nevertheless, such a "permissive" approach ran counter to orthodox Confucian morality. Not surprisingly, many extant salacious stories are presented within a moralistic framework.

"Zhang Hao" (late eleventh century?), found in *High Minded Conversations*,[49] aptly illustrates this new treatment of illicit sex. Moreover, several innovative motifs frequently found in later short stories and novels first appear here. Unlike "Tan Yige," "Zhang Hao" features marriage between partners of equal status. Zhang is the scion of a wealthy scholar-officials family, who attained his bureaucratic status through the hereditary *yin* privilege. In view of his reputation for scholarship, many illustrious families had unsuccessfully sought him as a son-in-law. He explains: "My reputation is as yet unsubstantial and [so] I am not ready to marry." The narrator's broaching the subject of marriage in this way establishes the reader's expectation of plot development.

Zhang's family had laid out an enormous private garden adjoining their sumptuous mansion, replete with waterside viewing platforms, pavilions, and all manner of exotic flora, not unlike the Prospect Garden in the renowned eighteenth-century novel *Dream of Red Mansions*.[50] It is here that he sees a beautiful girl while strolling with a friend in springtime. The girl's choice to remain in his view, rather than to run and hide according to social expectation, tacitly indicates her attraction to him. Later in the story, we learn that she is the daughter of Zhang's neighbor, a Mr. Li, who is also a scholar-official. The narrator carefully describes her "outstanding" (*chuse*) beauty: "With eyebrows thin as a new moon, her face resembled a delicate autumn lotus. Her curls—in the shape of conch shells—cascaded down her temples. Her white teeth were like arrayed jade while her soft, jade-like skin was radiant; she was [no less than] a yet-to-bloom flower." Zhang immediately makes his feelings clear: "I'm not a lustful man, but now I can't comport myself and my soul has all but ceased to exist. What can be done?" When Zhang's friend suggests that he marry the girl, he replies, "It would take too long for a matchmaker to arrange a marriage. By that time, I would be as dead as a dried fish in a shop." At his friend's suggestion, Zhang proceeds to flirt with the girl, who responds: "The purpose of my coming here is really to see you. Now that I've been fortunate to meet you, I hope that you won't be lewd. I wish to serve you as a wife and sacrifice to your ancestral altar." Few heroines of earlier narratives can match Miss Li's forwardness as the object of the male Gaze asserts her own agency. Moreover, her blunt wish to marry Zhang was rarely articulated before the Song period. When Zhang promises to do so, she requests a token of his affection that she might use to persuade her parents. When he proceeds to give her his sash, she insists on a poem as this is more personal. He then composes a verse in which he compares her to a peony, thereby nicely complementing the narrator's prior description. After this, in the typical fashion of lovesick heroes, Zhang behaves "as though he had lost something and could neither eat nor sleep." Unfortunately for him, Miss Li's parents are unimpressed and refuse their consent.

The narrative jumps to the following spring when peony-viewing reminds Zhang of Miss Li. He therefore sends her a bunch of peonies through the intermediary figure of a Buddhist nun who has access to the Li household. With the nun's connivance, Miss Li arranges a tryst one night when her parents attend, coincidentally, a family wedding. Zhang justifies their impending sexual encounter with the notion that the two are already—albeit informally—married. "I met you last year by the railing before the flowers had blossomed. This year the flowers have bloomed and yet we still have not come together. Since we are husband and wife, were we to secretly meet, it would not be indecent. What do you think?" The narrator tells how Miss Li scales a wall (such an act was a well-established metaphor for an illicit rendezvous) to reach Zhang, waiting on the other side with wine and snacks.

The young man took her back to his quarters. By that time, the watch-drum was silent and all was at rest. Light curtains fluttered in a gentle breeze while a thin blind allowed moonlight to shine through (the phrase moon and breeze denoted romantic affairs in classical texts and became a ubiquitous intertextual marker in love stories). Her eyes were like brimming water in fall and her slim waist swayed seductively. She removed her clothes and climbed into bed [with Zhang] where their coy tears coalesced. Zhang felt as though the encounter with the goddess of Witch's Mountain or Hua Xu's dream could not have surpassed their coupling.

In conformity to the love story's conventions, they are soon parted. Unusually, it is Miss Li who leaves the male as she follows her father to a provincial posting. During her absence, Zhang's uncle arranges a marriage for him. In deference to his social superior, Zhang "dares not refuse." When the Li family returns, confronted with two formidable obstacles (the arranged marriage and her parents' refusal), Miss Li attempts suicide, explaining to her parents, "I have already promised to marry [Zhang] Hao. If, Mama and Papa, you do not consent, then there will be only death for me." She soon after throws herself into a well but survives. This extremity leads her father to relent, yet Zhang's engagement remains an impediment.[51] In order to overcome this, Miss Li boldly lodges a legal suit claiming that her engagement to Zhang predates the arranged one and hence demands priority, displaying Zhang's poem as evidence. After summoning Zhang so as to verify the facts, the presiding magistrate annuls his engagement and orders the couple to marry.[52]

In "Zhang Hao," marriage and romance do not preclude each other, as Zhang and Miss Li, social equals, arrange their own match. Miss Li's parents and Zhang's uncle, however, complicate the plot with the former's initial refusal and the latter's arranging an alternate betrothal. Again, parents replace the role of the Tang dynasty story's senior male. Furthermore, sexual intercourse, emanating from strong mutual desire, is condoned. The metaphoric description of the couple's lovemaking even celebrates it. Moreover, illicit sex establishes legitimacy for the intended marriage. To be sure, the magistrate cites their union "beneath the flowers" as constituting a binding engagement that, outside the pages of a love story, would have been punishable by one and a half years' penal servitude: "Your meeting beneath the flowers already contained the promise of a lifetime's devotion;

ceasing halfway would spoil your inclination to grow old together." Under the storyteller's writing brush, illicit sexual intercourse is rehabilitated from a morally reprehensible crime to a legitimate human desire. Along with the giving of the poem and the sash, the sexual act becomes tantamount to an informal marriage ceremony that could be later ratified by a socially sanctioned ritual. In the pages of a love story, sexual union became a beautiful, even sacred act—one that celebrated freely chosen romantic love and bound a couple together for life. The promise of a lifetime's conjugal devotion differentiated the Song dynasty culture of romance from that of the Tang era's conception of temporary union. In the Song, we have the happy ever-after.

Pre- and extramarital sexual intercourse was, however, considered immoral by society at large and was, therefore, criminalized. Accordingly, something was needed to sanitize its subversive nature. As was the case in Victorian England and many societies up until the sexual revolution of the 1960s, premarital sex could be reclaimed by marriage, especially in cases whereby the woman became pregnant. In love stories of eleventh-century China, marriage could similarly salvage a woman's fallen virtue, as we also saw with Tan Yige. In the words of a fourteenth-century courtesan heroine: "Thanks to your condescending to marry me as a first wife, I could cast aside my former grime and cut away my previous indiscretions."[53] While Miss Li is no ex-courtesan, her insistence on marrying Zhang is premised on the Confucian ideal that, in imperial China, a woman should not know two husbands. Her verbal suicide "note" makes this clear—that is, only death or marriage could expunge her misdemeanor. This reminds us of how Yingying considered herself unworthy of marrying anybody but her lover, even though she eventually did so. In Victorian England, a similar idea motivated the action of the heroine in Thomas Hardy's *Tess of the d'Urbervilles* who, having been coerced into casual sex by a womanizer whom she grew to dislike, thereafter "could never conscientiously allow any man to marry her" despite her fervent love of the hero, Angel Clare.[54] As we will see, marriage as a means to reclaim compromised female virtue and neutralize the subversive nature of illicit sex was an innovative theme that would be further developed throughout the Song period and beyond.

When we compare "Zhang Hao" to Tang dynasty love stories, gone is the erotic triangle whereby the protagonist competed with another male for the heroine. It is, rather, the heroine who competes with another woman. This device complements other aspects of the plot that play to the male's sense of physical and intellectual superiority, such as when Miss

Li first expressed her desire for matrimony. Indeed, her attempted suicide is a substantial encomium to male self-esteem. Her speech, furthermore, is extremely flattering to Zhang and, through him, male readers. Besides her professed intention to marry, on receipt of his poem she also says, "You, sir, are truly talented. I would wish to spend my life at your side. Please keep this in mind!" Miss Li's urgent desire to marry Zhang illustrates the type of marriage market described above in which successful examination candidates could expect marriage proposals from illustrious families. Zhang's conversation with his friend at the story's outset also alludes to this. Such was the need for members of the upper classes to marry well that many similar cases may be found in short stories, *zhiguai*, and anecdotal accounts of the Song period.

One intriguing aspect of this story is the possibility that Miss Li had not seen Zhang prior to the meeting in the garden. Had she not done so, she is in effect arranging her own marriage. Her choice, accordingly, is based on male intellectual talent and reputation rather than physical attraction. Alternatively, her having spied Zhang "though cracks" or from across the wall may have been taken for granted by contemporary readers and, therefore, treated elliptically by the storyteller as important narrative details were similarly handled in other stories. While the latter is more in keeping with the love story's conventions, the former would constitute a significant innovation vis-à-vis the culture of romance's premises—that is, scholastic ability, possibly a reputation for good character, family connections, and the like could form the basis of a freely chosen, self-arranged marriage. Accordingly, the spirit of romantic love could be honored without recourse to illicit sex, as was the case in other Song-period stories.

The parallels between "Zhang Hao" and "Yingying's Story," discernable early in the narrative, are also intriguing. Although we cannot be sure if the storyteller of this particular version was cognizant of the Tang precursor, those who circulated another version of the story during the Song period undoubtedly were. In a parallel text from the Southern Song collection titled *New Stories from a Green Lattice Window*, Miss Li is accorded the name Yingying, written with the same characters as the Tang dynasty heroine.[55] As Yingying's lover, Zhang, was a demure youth at the outset, so was Zhang Hao. Hao enjoyed studying and, by his own confession, was not of a lustful nature. Yet his desire for Miss Li led to illicit sex despite the fact that, as his friend put it, marrying her would have been "as easy as flipping one's hand" in view of his wealth, good looks, and social standing. Indeed, Zhang Hao justifies his ardor with the same idiom used by Yingying's lover—that is, waiting for the marriage would reduce him to a dried fish in a shop—a well-established metaphor denoting one's demise. Unlike "Yingying's Story," Zhang Hao's narrator does not portray Miss Li as a *femme fatale*. Such intertextual references to the ninth-century masterpiece point to its popularity in the late eleventh century.

Although Zhang takes the initiative, albeit at his friend's suggestion, Miss Li not only encourages him but is extremely bold. Given her especially young age—thirteen (*sui*), which would have been as young as twelve or perhaps even eleven by Western reckoning—her sexual forwardness appears highly improbable, especially since social custom dictated that women of elite families dwell within the inner confines of their spacious houses most of the year. One wonders from where Miss Li would have learned such sexual aggressiveness. Even by Chinese standards of the period, the minimum marriageable age for a girl was fifteen (*sui*). Hence the gulf between the girl's portrayal and almost certain social reality suggests literary creativity, even wish fulfillment. In this respect, the story's heroine and others like her might remind the modern reader of Nabokov's "nymphet" (i.e., an almost pubescent girl), especially in view of the numerous stories that compare such young women and girls to fairies or goddesses, as was also the case here.[56] Hence, while sexual aggressiveness on the part of a young girl may stretch the modern reader's credulity, it may be understood as an elite male's constructed image of an ideal marriage partner—that is, young, beautiful, bright-eyed with a slim waist, fair skinned, and, moreover, a virgin. When we consider the importance placed on protecting patrilineal purity throughout the imperial period, the emphasis on virgins as ideal lovers and life partners is readily understandable.[57] In any case, Miss Li's forwardness conveniently relieves the male protagonist—representative of a morally upright, Confucian-trained scholar-official—from charges of lust, even though she constituted the object of both his gaze and verbally articulated desire.[58]

Miss Li's audacity in lodging a legal suit also begs credulity, and not simply due to her young age. Outside the pages of a love story, this would have created a scandal ruinous to both her own reputation and that of her family. Indeed, her confession to having engaged in sexual intercourse was no less than a confession to criminal behavior—that is, that of consensual illicit sex. In view of this, the magistrate's favorable verdict strains belief, particularly his premise that premarital sex equates to an informal engagement. Furthermore, since Zhang's formal betrothal would have been considered legally binding according to Song dynasty law, his fiancé's family could have enforced their legal rights.[59] Nevertheless, unusual events constituted the stock-and-trade of the love story, whether or not they were the product of elaborated gossip or outright fabrication. Such extraordinary conclusions and legal rulings evidently held a fascination for readers throughout the imperial period.[60]

The trial that resolves the lover's difficulties is also integral to the short-story category known as "legal cases" (gong'an). Both similar and dissimilar to modern detective stories, their plots involve the solving of a crime, usually by a provincial magistrate, or else the proceedings of a legal trial. First emerging during the Song dynasty, such stories evolved into a highly sophisticated form by the end of the Ming.[61] The blending of the legal-case prototype and that of romance was common during the Song, and even more so during the Ming. In the Tang love story, when a dispute arose over a woman, it was almost always a senior male who arbitrated. In the Song, although this earlier plot resolution was not abandoned, the adjudicating senior male began to take the form of a magistrate, if not the protagonist's parents. This may well reflect contemporary elite male interest in the judicial system given the large number of them who served as metropolitan or provincial magistrates during their civil service careers. The frequently favorable verdicts handed down in regard to cases of illicit sex in the context of the love story may also indicate the confidence that some elite men paced in the judiciary.

Finally, "Zhang Hao" is perhaps the earliest extant love story featuring a lover's meeting that occurs in a garden setting. From the twelfth century, an increasing number of literary romances occur in similar settings. Large, private gardens would have been ideal venues for real-life romantic trysts between both members of the upper classes and their servants alike. Furthermore, the garden's profuse flora provided a storehouse of romantic symbolism such as is found in love poetry. Indeed, the peony, a bunch of which Zhang gives to Miss Li and to which he compared her, in some contexts symbolized female genitalia, if not beautiful women. Other symbols of romance, such as the moon and breeze, could be readily enjoyed in garden settings. In the pages of a love story, gardens often become liminal spaces in which patriarchal authority could be held at bay—ideal settings with which to demarcate private spaces in the pursuit of private, romantic desires. This new motif might be related to an increased interest in horticulture on the part of Northern Song elites as may be seen from the increasing production of specialized works, such as Li Gefei's (fl. late eleventh/early twelfth century) *Famous Gardens of Luoyang* (*Luoyang mingyuan ji*) and Sima Guang's account of his Garden of Solitary Joy (*Dule yuan*).[62] The popularity of this motif grew considerably, as may be seen from Ming and Qing dynasty novels and short stories, notably the famous *Dream of Red Mansions* and *Plum in a Golden Vase*. That this geographic setting was first developed by Song-period storytellers indicates their considerable contribution to Chinese literary history.

Another instructive example of illicit sex, "Story of Twin Peaches" (*Shuangtao ji*, early twelfth century), presents an alternate solution to the dilemma of an unwelcome arranged marriage. The title is derived from a love token, twin peaches—themselves a symbol of romantic love—growing on a single stem, that the adulterous male gives the heroine. Reminiscent of unofficial biographies, such as Qiongnu and Tan Yige, the narrative commences with an extended description of the heroine's physical beauty while establishing her pedigree. Wang Xiaoniang (Miss Xiao) is the unmarried daughter of a well-to-do family from Taiyuan. Given the coincidence of both surname and place name, her family may have claimed descent from one of the Tang dynasty's aristocratic clans. Before she had come of age, we are told how her beauty surpassed that of the madding crowd (*se yi guan zhong*): "Her eyebrows evoked the verdure of mountains in springtime, her eyes embodied the brilliance of water in autumn. Her body was fragrant, her skin soft, and her curls as were dark as is kohl. Indeed, past beauties could not hold a light to her radiance." This image of feminine beauty is fairly generic and not unlike that of Miss Li in "Zhang Hao." Although the narrator proceeds to describe the hero, commencing with the heroine anticipates her role as a moral paragon. Rather than act as a narrative subject, however, she remains an object of the male articulating subject. As Miss Xiao is her childhood name, the storyteller half-heartedly attempts to conceal her identity. He furthermore professes reluctance to provide the male's name and simply refers to him as Master Li, given the scandalous nature of the affair. Since stories such as these were read literally and—at least loosely—based on actual events, the story likely circulated orally as gossip before having been recorded. It supposedly occurred in 1102.

Master Li is Miss Xiao's neighbor. He is descended from a prominent family and is married, although this latter detail does not emerge until midway through the story. He is described as "[n]aturally unrestrained and of handsome appearance, of open temperament, able to write in an ornate style, and of a heroic disposition; in sum, he was not of the mundane world." Li falls instantly in love when, one day, he sees Miss Xiao emerging from her house. On another occasion during a calendrical festival, he is able to flirt mildly with her as they pass on the street. Following this encounter, he manages to communicate his feelings through an old lady who has dealings with the Wang household. In an attestation of Miss Xiao's moral rectitude, the old lady initially doubts the heroine's amenability to Li's advances: "Miss Xiao is of a serious disposition and is not given to laughter and banter. How might I dare directly broach the matter? I'll wait for a convenient occasion to probe her on your lordship's behalf. Success is by no means assured, though." Yet, when the she is able to raise the subject, Miss Xiao openly declares her love for Li:

> Some time ago I went to the Western Garden due to the Cold Food Festival and I happened to meet him on the street. I must confess, I do like him. He spoke to me and I replied, but we were unable to speak at leisure as the traffic was busy. Since then my heart has not been able to let him go. When faced with the moon and breeze, I am unable to utter a sound. Who would have thought it? I only broach the subject now since you are such a discreet person.

Although this may merely articulate wishful thinking on the part of the male storyteller, Miss Xiao's speech clearly establishes her own free choice. At her suggestion, a tryst is soon arranged. Li scales a low wall to reach her, after which the couple engage in sexual intercourse. Unlike Tang-era stories, this is described through comparatively explicit metaphors, such as: "her brows knitted together as the flower's heart was penetrated." Driven by sexual desire, the couple continue to meet over an extended period so that everyone knew about the affair except Miss Xiao's parents.

At this juncture, Li becomes so besotted that he suggests divorcing his wife so as to marry her, but she refuses on moral grounds. The attention given to this incident, in the form of lengthy dialogue, asserts the heroine's good character while apologizing for her immoral conduct.

> One day, the young man said to Miss Xiao, "I wish to divorce my wife and marry you. What do you think?" She replied, "You cannot! It would be lacking in gentlemanly behavior were a

man to divorce his wife without cause. And for a woman to steal another's husband through illicit means would be remiss in terms of womanly virtue. We would be spurned by society and ghosts alike. You shouldn't talk like this! I would have you take stock of yourself and not mention it again."

The lover's private space is soon disturbed when Miss Xiao's parents arrange a marriage for her. Wishing to remain faithful to Li, she weighs her choices in a lengthy monologue.

> [Zhuo] Wenjun was a widow. Admiring [Sima] Xiangru's high-minded principles, she eventually eloped with him, yet by doing so she alienated herself from her parents and was disparaged and laughed at generations thereafter. This is something I could not do. Green Pearl, on the other hand, was a debased concubine. Having been favored by Shi Chong, when the Prince of Zhao[63] would have ravished her, she was faithful to her former master at the cost of her life. Her honor was not compromised and she garnered the world's admiration. Since I cannot elope as did Wenjun, I am willing to emulate Green Pearl's example so as to repay Mr. Li's consideration.

Green Pearl, as noted in the previous chapter, supposedly committed suicide by jumping from a window to avoid another man's attentions, thereby becoming a byword for a loyal mistress. The "Story of Twin Peaches" concludes tragically with Miss Xiao's own suicide by hanging. The recorder comments, "Alas! That one should be possessed of such deep feeling (*you qing*)! Given that she initially carried on with (*luan*) Li yet eventually died for him, we can see that her determination and moral integrity did not alter. Had she not met Master Li and, instead, married Mr. Liu, she clearly would have been a chaste woman."[64]

It is unusual in surviving Song-period love stories for married men to seduce unmarried daughters of comparable social class; normally male protagonists were unmarried. Had Mr. Li wished to marry Miss Xiao without divorcing his wife, he would have needed to take her as a concubine, an arrangement to which her parents would have likely objected given the high status placed on wives throughout the imperial period. Malicious gossip may also have ensued from such an arrangement.[65] Therefore, unlike Zhang Hao who married his lover despite his initial intention, and unlike

Yingying's lover who might have married her had he chosen to, Li and Miss Xiao's adulterous relationship could never amount to more than a transitory, illicit affair.

The end commentary addresses the criminality and immorality associated with illicit sex by contemporary readers, the likes of whom Bu Feiyan's morally orthodox, ninth-century critic affords a glimpse. Nonetheless, Miss Xiao is not portrayed as a *femme fatale*, unlike Yingying and Ouyang Zhan's courtesan lover. On the contrary, the recorder recognizes her inability to suppress romantic feelings (*qing*). While tacitly acknowledging her immoral conduct ("Had she not met Master Li and, instead, married Mr. Liu, she clearly would have been a chaste woman"), he nonetheless praises her steadfastness and, indeed, loyalty.

Miss Xiao's loyalty to her self-chosen lover at the cost of her own life is construed as a virtue given the Confucian ideal of female fidelity to one husband. Her suicide salvages her compromised chastity and mitigates the subversive nature of illicit sex. Unlike the above stories in which premarital sex was redeemed by marriage, suicide achieves the same result. The commentator therefore stops short of calling her a "chaste woman" (*zhenfu*) and compares her with a well-established historical exemplar. The theme of a woman committing suicide so as to maintain chastity was developed with increasing frequency throughout the Song period and was to become a popular form of denouement in short stories of the Yuan and Ming dynasties. Therefore this story, along with other eleventh-century examples we have seen, represents an early treatment of the theme.

Although historical precedents existed for heroine lovers who committed suicide, heroines of mid-Tang dynasty love stories did not do so over a lover. As an alternate means of demonstrating romantic loyalty, many died after separation from their man, as already noted. Indeed, there was no need for a mid-Tang heroine to commit suicide since literary romances of that period tended to construct love as a transitory relationship. The subversive nature of illicit sex was contained within the bounds of a discreet, fleeting affair to which society would generally turn a blind eye. Moreover, the courtesan lovers who frequently appear in these stories, being of debased social status, were not held to the same rigorous sexual standards as were the upper-class heroines of the Song dynasty stories. In rare instances whereby romance leads to marriage, the utopian denouement signals optimism in the patriarchal social structure. Conversely, that a Northern Song heroine must commit suicide to reclaim fallen virtue strikes a stringent moralistic tone in regard to sexuality and romance. Even though our storyteller is sympathetic, he evidently feels it necessary to weigh Miss Xiao's actions in light of moralistically conservative standards. The storyteller's increased emphasis on female chastity speaks to the growing influence of morally conservative attitudes in regard to female fidelity that was gaining greater acceptance by the educated elite of the era—the same type of attitude that eventually coalesced into Neo-Confucian thought. Indeed, we may see a similar emphasis in Madam Sun's and other stories.

Such emphasis on female chastity may be further elucidated by comparison with similar stories of the mid-Tang period. There are, however, few extant examples in which an upper-class, unmarried daughter has an affair with a married man. "Miss Ren's Story" is superficially close as Miss Ren is unmarried and she becomes a married man's mistress and is upheld as a paragon. Unlike the upper-class Miss Xiao, however, she is both an ontological and social "other" and is celebrated for her general loyalty and obedience. Although she demonstrated her faithfulness to one man by resisting rape, suicide was not required to accomplish this. She was eventually killed because she reluctantly obeyed her lover's command to undertake a journey. The "Story of Yingying" also bears limited comparison to "Story of Twin Peaches" given the social status of the lovers, although Yingying's lover was not married while Yingying herself was cast as a *femme fatale*. Nonetheless, Yingying freely chose her lover. Moreover, her idea that sexual promiscuity rendered her unworthy to marry him defers to the same orthodox principle that motivated Miss Xiao's suicide. The story's denouement, conversely, saw both protagonists marry other partners. Nowhere did Yingying entertain thoughts of suicide, nor did the male storyteller consider it necessary for her to do so. The ninth-century heroine Bu Feiyan, like Miss Xiao, was similarly contrasted to Green Pearl, although she was another man's concubine and her lover was unmarried; in a sarcastic articulation from an orthodox, moralistic viewpoint, an anonymous commentator criticizes her inability to match Green Pearl's conjugal fidelity. Despite this dissenting voice, Bu Feiyan— like Miss Xiao—died so as to pay the price for infidelity, while her lover escaped unscathed. Nevertheless, had her husband not caught and beat her, there is no suggestion that she would have committed suicide so as to redeem lost virtue. In contrast, Miss Xiao, as a promiscuous, unmarried daughter, was singled out in our late Northern Song story due to the increased valorization of female chastity that began during this period. Had she not committed suicide to salvage her fallen virtue, she may well have been portrayed as a *femme fatale* rather than a paragon.

As noted above, assuming a factual basis for this story, it would have initially circulated as oral gossip. Indeed, Miss Xiao articulates her fear of gossip and social disapproval. Nevertheless, the storyteller evidently harbored a particular motive for selecting and recording it. To be sure, the extended—albeit metaphoric—description of the couple's lovemaking, the detailed manner in which the tryst was arranged, the poetry Li gave Miss Xiao (not addressed above), as well as their tender dialogue all clearly aestheticize the story's romantic elements while undermining the immoral overtones that many contemporaries would have attached to it. This aestheticization of illicit sex establishes an alternate voice within the story that conflicts with the moralizing nature of both the dialogue and end commentary. This was also the case in some Tang dynasty stories previously discussed, particularly the postface to Ouyang Zhan's story and its inclusion of (supposedly) contemporary readers' reception through the device of the two anonymous interlocutors, one who sympathized with the tragic heroine and another who took the moral high ground. No doubt many contemporary readers of "Story of Twin Peaches" would have been similarly torn between a moralistic reading and one more sympathetic to the story's romantic aspects. Indeed, had the storyteller been of an overly moralistic disposition, he would have had no reason to record the story. That he did so indicates a tacit interest in the romantic, hence the celebratory tone of the lover's meeting, their illicit lovemaking, and the like. Nonetheless, he evidently felt it necessary to present the story within a moralistic framework that honors the heroine's fidelity to one man. Accordingly, the end commentary may be understood as a token apology to conservative readers.

The "Story of Twin Peaches," therefore, affords readers a sense of a society beyond the pages of the love story *per se*. As may be seen from her monologue toward the conclusion, social expectations from both Miss Xiao's parents as well as unnamed others weighed heavily on her decision against elopement. The heroine is so afraid of gossip that suicide is preferable to risking alienation from her parents and loss of reputation. The scandalous nature of such a socially unsanctioned liaison becomes almost palpable as we are granted a window into the psychology of a romantically inclined young woman of the period, even though her speech and actions are mediated through a male storyteller's consciousness, assuming they are not outright constructions thereof. Living in the twenty-first century, we may more easily imagine Miss Xiao's suicide to have been motivated by depression rather than compulsion to reclaim fallen virtue. Nonetheless, assuming the story has a grain of factual basis, the early twelfth-century storyteller overinterprets her action so as to bolster androcentric interests. Her suicide acts as both a model of virtuous behavior and a warning against the dangers of adulterous affairs.

"Four-Fold Blended Incense" (*Sihe xiang*, early twelfth century) is another story featuring illicit sex, yet surprisingly, unlike those discussed above, no moralistic apology is discernable. The male protagonist, Sun Min, is a National University student. The day prior to the Lantern Festival, his uncle, a member of the imperial clan, invites him to a private banquet where he sees several beautiful concubines and serving women. The narrator tells how he "dared not look" at them, implying both sexual attraction and mild competition with the uncle. As he returns to the University after the banquet, he stops at a Zen Buddhist temple where he meets a woman accompanied by a maid servant. Although somewhat plainly dressed, she is of "unsurpassed beauty" the likes of which "he had not seen." He believes her to have been one of the banquet guests. Sun's modesty prevents him from directly conversing with her, even when she buys him tea from a passing vendor. When he proceeds to visit the nearby Temple of State Minsters (*Xiangguo si*), she dispatches her servant to summon him. He follows the servant "both surprised and joyful." Having finally engaged him in conversation, the woman says, "We happened to meet just now by chance. I thoroughly admire your bearing and have it in mind to show you a good time even though you've given me no encouragement. What do you say, sir?" She then invites him to join her at another Buddhist temple: "Sir, you may go to the south side of the western cloister of the Chongxia temple on the morrow. You will find Old Sister Li in the second courtyard. I will be there and we can meet each other. I do hope you won't miss the appointed hour." The "western cloister" or "gallery" is likely an intertextual allusion to the "Story of Yingying." Sun keeps the rendezvous during which time he and the woman partake of a sumptuous repast and, as is usual for the love story, wine foreshadows a sexual encounter. "Late that night, once the wine had run dry, the beauty pressed Sun to sleep with her. When he reached her boudoir, [he saw] red candles flickering brilliantly, verdigris incense rising in a pure plume, flowers embroidered on the bed curtains and a quilt embroidered with phoenixes. The young man's senses were even more dazzled. He then lay with her on the pillow and the clouds and rain they enjoyed cannot be fully described." "Clouds and rain," as previously noted, was a ubiquitous euphemism for sexual intercourse. Nevertheless, the woman is evasive when Sun asks about her name and family background. Dawn breaks and, before they part, she tells him to contact her via a fruit seller who keeps a stall in front of the Huangjian Temple: "Whatever you do, sir, don't shillyshally."

After this the pair meet at least four times within the following month. On one occasion, the woman sends a box of blended incense (from which the story derives its title) to Sun at the University. As he receives it in the presence of his peers, the others correctly guess that he is having an affair. Sun unsuccessfully tries to discover the woman's identity from the delivery boy. Come midsummer, however, he suddenly falls ill: "His appearance became sickly and his appetite decreased. His peers urged his to return post-haste to his parents and, although he feigned agreement, he eventually failed to depart." His father, tipped off by one of his classmates, sends a servant to bring him home. Unable to refuse the patriarch's wishes, he arranges a simple farewell meal with his lover at an inn.

> My father has bidden me to return and convalesce. We must, therefore, temporarily separate. It is not my wish to do so." After a moment's hesitation, the beauty replied, "Your journey, sir, cannot be prevented. If you would not forget me, we can meet again if you are able to return to the capital on the day of mid-Autumn. If, by chance, you miss the date, I will not be able to see you again. By all means, take care of yourself! This is my humble wish.

Sun's parents, nevertheless, prevent him from returning in time. When he finally does, he is shocked to learn that the Huangjian Temple has burned to the ground; nor can he locate the fruit seller. When he proceeds to the Chongxia Temple, he is told that Sister Li left more than twenty days previously; as she was a nun from another Temple, she merely rented the courtyard. While loitering in the room where the beauty had previously entertained him, he finds a love poem written on a wall in his lover's handwriting. Having read the poem, he becomes "distraught," (*yinghuo*) or severely confused, for an entire year but eventually recovers with no lasting ill effects.[66]

The most unusual and tantalizing aspect of this story is its narrative ambiguity. Who was the woman and what exactly was the nature of the lovers' affair? As the story's recorder speculates in his end commentary:

> As for Master Sun's lover, in the end we do not know who she was, nor do we know where she resided. Once Sun returned home, he never saw her after mid-autumn had passed. When he reached the capital on the day of the Double Ninth festival, Master Zhang was missing, Sister Li had left and the beauty's whereabouts could no longer be traced. How accurate was her prophesy! Yet Sun's lover: was she a person? Was she a ghost? Was she an immortal? This cannot be known. Is it not strange?

While the plot closely resembles a prototypical story of union followed by permanent separation, the woman's identity is necessary to guide our interpretation. As Sun thought when she first approached him, she may have been a banquet guest. In a Southern Song story titled "The Tryst of Crimson Silk," the young concubine of an aging official arranges a rendezvous with a young man at a Buddhist temple after which the pair abscond. In fact, sexual encounters in cloisters attached to Buddhist temples are not uncommon in short stories of the period. According to prevailing social conditions, it was permissible for upper-class concubines and wives to participate in religious ceremonies held at public temples. Storytellers sometimes exploit the possibility that, during such occasions and with the connivance of a nun, they might conceivably have met lovers. There were salacious stories in which monks lured women to temples where they might sexually exploit them. If Sun's lover was the wife or concubine of an influential man, her hiding her identity and acting through intermediaries makes sense.

Sun's having met with her in a public space, unaccompanied by a male relative, is however unusual. In real life, women traveling alone were considered suspect, although in the story this is neutralized by the occasion of the *Shangsi* festival during which time it was common for both men and women to be out and about enjoying the spring air. Nevertheless, a chance meeting with a woman was a well-established motif in *zhiguai* and love stories alike. In the former, during a calendrical festival, a man might meet with a woman who proves to be a ghost or were-creature. Sun's deteriorating health after a month of sexual intimacy suggests she was a ghost, according to the narrative conventions of the *zhiguai* genre. Prolonged contact with *yin* energy was thought to dissipate the male's lifeforce and cause illness, which, without a Daoist exorcist's timely intervention, may have led to death. Yet Sun's illness leaves him little worse for wear and merely acts as a plot device to separate the lovers. His prolonged "distress" at the narrative's conclusion is perfunctorily treated and may be explained without recourse to the anomalous. Nonetheless, the woman's prediction and its fulfillment that they could not meet again were Sun to miss the appointed date was an established element found in many *zhiguai* accounts, suggesting that something anomalous is afoot.

The third possibility raised by the author-compiler that the woman may have been an immortal (or a goddess) also must be considered. During the banquet Sun enjoys with the beauty prior to their first sexual encounter, we are told that the food and fruit provided came from rare and distant places; the serving ware, furthermore, is described as far from that commonly used (*jiong yuan chensu*). The ambiguous term, *chensu*, can mean "common." Alternatively, as a binary opposition to something from the immortal realm, it can mean "of this earth." Therefore, the term could mean "far from that of the mortal realm," thus hinting that the woman was an immortal. If this was the case, Sun's several sexual encounters with her would not have caused illness or death, as would be expected had she been a ghost. It would also explain the woman's accurate prediction toward the narrative's conclusion. Furthermore, her inexplicable disappearance resembles the denouement of many prototypical encounters with the goddess. On the other hand, such stories normally reveal the immortal's identity and the benefits she brought to her mortal lover by the conclusion, if not earlier, suggesting that she was not immortal. Still, the storyteller may have suppressed such detail to achieve ambiguity and thereby add mystique to an otherwise straightforward narrative. Therefore, the heroine's ontological status remains elusive. Narrative ambiguity was certainly innovative for the period and is, lamentably, only found in a handful of Song-period stories.[67]

The fact that no attempt is made to apologize or redeem the illicit sex depicted here is rare, even in the context of the culture of romance. As we saw in "Zhang Hao," sex is mitigated and reclaimed by marriage. In the "Story of Twin Peaches," the heroine must die so as to recover her lost virtue and pay for her lover's adultery. On the contrary, this story maintains a neutral tone throughout, neither condemning nor overtly celebrating the romantic aspects. Besides telling the reader that the lovers met four times within a month, the narrator pays little attention to the sexual encounters. "He then lay with her on the pillow and the clouds and rain they enjoyed cannot be fully described" is the only description offered. Such terse attention to illicit sex certainly helps contain its salacious nature. No moralistic tone is discernable, unlike other Song dynasty stories we have seen. The story's narrative ambiguity masterfully diffuses the subversive nature of illicit sex. To be sure, before readers can pass judgment, the woman's identity requires resolution. This intriguing story reminds us that not all love stories of the Song period were presented within moralistic frameworks.

What Red Thread Has Joined Together, Let None Put Asunder: Conjugal Sanctity

Another important theme relating to conjugal love is the sanctity of marriage, related to which is the importance of honoring marriage contracts. As social values, such ideas had long been enshrined in the Confucian canon. Nonetheless, as many eleventh-century love stories began to foreground marriage, the sanctity of this institution became a natural secondary theme, as can be seen in "Madam Sun's Story." The theme comes to the fore in "Story of Distant Mist" (*Yuanyan ji*, late eleventh, early twelfth century). With a simplistic plot bereft of extended description, this somewhat terse narrative tells of a young merchant's son named Dai Fu. Merchants were generally despised by the educated elite since their pursuit of monetary gain ran counter to Confucius's admonition against profit-seeking. Despite his humble background, Dai gains entry to the prestigious Imperial University. After arriving in the capital, he marries Miss Wang, a tavern keeper's daughter. Unfortunately, Dai's father dies while away from home, which presumably terminates his material support. This misfortune is compounded by Dai's keeping the wrong company. When his meager wealth is dissipated and he is unable to support his wife, the enraged father-in-law reclaims his daughter. Madame Wang, however, wishing to remain faithful to her husband, refuses her father's demand that she remarry. "If you don't grant my request [to return to Dai], I won't set foot in another's house. I'm prepared to die so as to repay Fu." She subsequently falls ill and becomes bedridden. Her father, an extremely stubborn man, is adamant that she will not return to her dissolute husband, despite sympathetic intervention by relatives: "You can cut off my head, but my daughter will not go back to Dai." Prolonged separation from her husband exacerbates her illness, which eventually proves fatal. After her death, acting on instructions delivered through a maidservant, Dai surreptitiously removes her remains to his native place where poverty forces him to become a for-hire boatman. He also resorts to fishing. His continues to be disconsolate about his deceased wife and, consequently, is often depressed. One day while fishing, he notices someone watching him through distant autumn mist.

> Indistinctly, amidst the misty waves, there was someone watching him. A few days elapsed and he had not caught any fish; he only saw the person in the mist. After a year the figure appeared to grow closer. After another half year, it was closer still. Within another month it was not 50 [double-] paces away. He looked closely a realized that it was his wife, Madam Wang. He broke down as did she and they related to each other their regret at having parted. After another ten days, she was no more than a few [double-] paces distant.

Dai reported this anomaly to his landlord as he bade him goodbye. The incredulous landlord dispatched his son to follow and, from the son's point of view, the narrator describes what he saw:

> Dai moved his boat onto the lake. After a short while, a woman approached. Holding Dai's hand, she said, "I have followed you on the road ever since you brought my bones back to Yun [Prefecture]. Your *yang* energy was strong and so I didn't dare materialize before you. I have watched you fishing on the lake for two years, now. I couldn't reach you as the [fated] time had not arrived. Now is the time!" Embracing Dai, she disappeared into the waters of the lake taking him with her. The landlord's son returned home, terrified.

Dai's corpse was found a few days later.[68]

This story is instructive for several reasons. First is the importance attached to conjugal loyalty, as manifested in the argument between father and daughter. Madam Wang's determination is seen in her declaration not to remarry. She therefore conforms to the orthodox Confucian maxim that a woman should not marry two husbands, thus establishing herself as a chaste female. Such conjugal loyalty, however, problematizes the binary between filial piety and wifely loyalty, both of which were cornerstones of orthodox morality. The imperative for both sons and daughters to obey their parents throughout the imperial era was extremely strong. Indeed, we have seen its importance in the stories discussed above as protagonists showed great deference to their parents' wishes. Nevertheless, once married, a wife was considered part of her husband's household and primarily beholden to him. In many similar Song-era stories, therefore, a wife's duty to her husband trumped that owed to her parents. By refusing to divorce her husband and remarry, Madame Wang displayed an impeccably high standard of conjugal loyalty, albeit it at the expense of filial piety. The hardship she must have suffered, elliptically passed over by the narrator, only intensifies this aspect of her virtue. Yet there were conservative thinkers, Zhu Xi among them, who considered a husband's inability to support his wife sufficient grounds for annulment.[69] Zhu's stance is somewhat extreme for his time when we remember that there were no legal grounds for a wife to initiate divorce proceedings throughout the imperial period. To be sure, Neo-Confucian thought proselytized by Zhu Xi may be discerned in the father's portrayal, which is further evidence that such ideas were gaining acceptance during the period. The story, however, valorizes wifely loyalty in regard to this contentious issue.

The valorization of female fidelity over filial piety is corroborated by a quasi-biography written by the Northern Song courtier Zhao Dingchen (1070–early twelfth c.). In his *Bamboo-Dwelling Maverick's Collection* (*Zhuyin jishi ji*), Zhao tells of a cousin who had been deceived into marrying a gambler and a drunkard. When the husband eventually landed himself into legal strife, her parents pressured her to divorce him, yet the cousin insisted on remaining faithful regardless of her husband's shortcomings.[70] Zhao's testimony about his own cousin further attests to the increased importance of female fidelity during the late Northern Song, although how widespread it was is unclear.

Second, the social mobility theme resurfaces. The young protagonist, as a merchant's son, was considered lowest ranked among the commoner class. Consequently, his becoming a student at the prestigious Imperial University promised possible membership to the elite scholar-official class. This reflects contemporaries' faith in the examination system as an egalitarian vehicle of upward social mobility, despite the improbability that disadvantaged outsiders could successfully compete against their privileged peers, as Hartwell has shown. Yet, as in other stories, the death of a parent leaves the offspring in financial need, which, together with Dai's dissolute lifestyle, led to a rapid decline in socioeconomic status. Furthermore, in light of Hartwell's data pointing to examination success *following* marriage into an influential family, Dai Fu's having married a mere tavern keeper's daughter was another factor against success. Even so, the expectation that stories like these were based on reality indicates contemporary readers' expectation that young men outside of privileged, elite circles might beat the odds and improve their lot.

The socially marginal, non-elite status of the protagonists also helps distinguish the story from earlier ones. To be sure, it was unusual in stories recorded by the scholarly elite to focus on non-elite protagonists before the late Northern Song period.[71] Besides the merchant's son, the tavern keeper and his daughter were also from humble backgrounds. Moreover, the image of a female innkeeper would have reminded contemporary readers of the famous elopement between Sima Xiangru and Zhuo Wenjun since the latter was reduced to serving in a tavern before reconciliation with her wealthy father. Nevertheless, unmarried, tavern-keeping women were undoubtedly much more accessible to men from a variety of class backgrounds, which may explain their not infrequent appearance in love stories. Conversely, merchant's sons rarely functioned as male protagonists before the eleventh century. This story marks a growing trend throughout the Song dynasty whereby elite storytellers turned attention to those from inferior social classes. Hitherto unprecedented commercial development of urban centers is invariably cited to explain this phenomenon.[72] Contingent with commercial growth was the rise of townspeople (*shimin*) who, as a kind of urban-dwelling "middle class," supposedly influenced the art and literature produced by the cultural elite. Such an easy explanation, however, fails to account for the flourishing commercialization during the Tang dynasty when goods flowed in and out of China across both land and sea. As this literary trend is more pronounced in Southern Song stories, I will return to it in the next chapter—suffice to note its emergence here.

This story is also an early example in which both lovers die. Although this occurred in a handful of tersely narrated Tang dynasty stories and poems, the main narrative interest lies in their extraordinary conclusions—that is, occurrences that ran contrary to normality.[73] Hence the *zhiguai* element overshadows that of the romantic. While this element is decidedly strong in "Story of Distant Mist," conjugal love is equally important. In fact, given the lovers' circumstances, death seems the only means by which they may reunite. Since this double-tragic element became ubiquitous in love stories of late-imperial China, its first appearance in a prototypical eleventh-century narrative, one that downplays the paranormal aspect, is significant. I will return to this theme in the next chapter.

Widow and *de Facto* Widow Fidelity

As noted above, it was not uncommon for widows to remarry during the Song period. Madam Sun, for example, was married no fewer than three times. Large dowries and the ability to control them, in addition to unprecedentedly generous apportioning of family property to daughters, gave upper-class women considerable assets that they could retain control of in the event of remarriage. Moreover, many women, even among the upper class, could ill afford to live independent of a husband's financial support and protection regardless, it seems, of their dowries, or perhaps due to insufficient dowries. Not surprisingly, numerous love stories, anecdotal narratives, and *zhiguai* accounts bear witness to widow remarriage. Nevertheless, based on the longstanding Confucian proscription against women having sexual relations with more than one husband, the Confucian canon had long enshrined widowhood as an ideal female virtue. The *Book of Rites* states: "Faithfulness is the basis of serving others, and is the virtue of a wife. When her husband dies, a woman does not remarry; to the end of her life she does not change."[74] The importance of widow chastity as an ideal feminine virtue began to gain acceptance throughout the eleventh and twelfth centuries. Indeed, some women were reluctant to remarry despite advice from close natal relatives to do so.[75] Similarly, letters of the period sometimes noted the desirability of widow fidelity in regard to a woman's second marriage.[76] This ideal was further proselytized by paintings of the period depicting King Shun's two widows who, according to the popular legend, drowned themselves, after which they became the two goddesses of the Xiang River. To be sure, Ebrey has surveyed a diverse range of Song-period literary sources praising faithful widows (see figure 2.2).[77]

This trend coincided with the reassessment of the Confucian tradition by thinkers such as the Cheng brothers. Cheng Yi's rejection of widow remarriage proved extremely influential on later thinkers who identified with the Zhu Xi School of Learning (later termed "Neo-Confucianism"). Cheng states:

> [Someone] asked, "If a widow is alone and poor with no one to depend on, is it alright for her to remarry?"
>
> [Cheng Yi] replied, "This theory arose only because in later ages people fear freezing or starving to death. But starving to death is a mere minor matter; losing one's integrity is a matter of the gravest importance."[78]

Figure 2.2. Goddess of the Xiang River.

Zhu Xi's inclusion of this quote in his influential *Reflection of Things at Hand* indicates his endorsement of Cheng Yi's sentiment and ensured that widow fidelity and Neo-Confucian thought would thereafter go hand in hand. For example, the Confucian thinker Zhang Zai optimistically notes, "Today, that women should not remarry after the death of their husbands is considered a fundamental moral principle."[79] Accordingly, widows—even young ones—were increasingly praised when remaining chaste so as to honor a deceased husband. Reflecting this slowly growing albeit still tentative trend, widow chastity as a literary theme appeared with increasing frequency in love stories of the eleventh and twelfth centuries, certainly more so than in the previous centuries. The valorization of widow chastity/fidelity furthermore complements the increasing moralistic tone already noted in stories of the period.

In regard to the love story, one important early example is "Preface to the Ballad of Ai'ai," attributed to the eleventh-century statesman Su Shunqing (1008–1048). Based on internal evidence, Li Jianguo dates its recording to 1034.[80] Unfortunately, neither the original preface nor its ballad is extant. The earliest reference is given by Xu Ji (1028–1103) in his anecdotal *Collection of the Filial and Chaste* (*Jiexiao ji*, eleventh century). Xu gives his own edited version of Su's preface along with a commentary.[81] A summary has been preserved in *Redacted Record of Housemaids* (*Shi'er xiaoming lu shiyi*, early twelfth century) and *New Stories from a Green Lattice Window* (*Lüchuang xinhua*, likely mid- to late twelfth or thirteenth century). This story is also unusual given both its first-person narrative voice and its focus on Yang Ai'ai as its main protagonist. Her lover, Zhang Cheng, however, remains a shadowy figure throughout. According to Xu Ji, Su claimed to have taken Ai'ai as his "subject" (*zhu*). Although we cannot be sure how Su originally portrayed his heroine, the Ai'ai that appears in extant summarized versions has been rendered yet another interpellated paragon of female virtue. Little wonder, therefore, that Tao Zongyi (active 1360–1368), writing in the fourteenth century, includes her in a brief list of chaste females—Green Pearl among them—that he compares with those of his own era.[82]

The preface's introduction, not unlike that of a biography, tells how Ai'ai was a talented musician from childhood, having been born to a courtesan family in Hangzhou. She was only fifteen (*sui*) at the story's outset; again the virginal "nymphet" stereotype reemerges, as this was the minimum—even prime—marriageable age for a girl of the period. She met Zhang during a boating excursion on West Lake (near Hangzhou), after which the pair journeyed to the "capital"—that is, Bianliang. There they led a life of pleasure. The narrative ignores the sexual aspect of their relationship, but this may be assumed given the couple's frequent and sustained sightseeing. They are separated when Zhang's father "apprehended" (*bu*) and removed his son. Su Shunqing came to hear about Ai'ai when she moved to the same laneway as his mother. Admiring her good character, the mother often visited her. When news arrived of Zhang's death, Ai'ai vowed never to marry, despite pressure from several would-be suitors. She henceforth ate vegetarian fare and gave up music. The heartbreak she suffered was said to have eventually caused her death (see figure 2.3).[83]

This straightforward plot conforms to a prototypical story of union that is followed by permanent separation. One wonders, however, what romantic details have been lost in its re-recording, as its interest for Xu Ji and his readers evidently lay in Ai'ai's chastity and unshakable resolve. Her youth and beauty combined with her self-imposed poverty would have added to the story's piquancy for upper-class male readers; here again is Martin Huang's idea of a "languishing beauty."

Although Ai'ai and her lover were not formally wed, they may be considered a *de facto* married couple based on her celibacy after Zhang's removal and subsequent death. Indeed, her decision to remain faithful to his memory conforms to the ideal of widow chastity. Contemporary readers' valorization of this feminine virtue may be seen from Xu Ji's commentary. "When Ai'ai resided in the capital, she conducted herself as would a widow with the certain intention to die. Therefore, although rich and powerful men went to great lengths to tempt her, they could never

Figure 2.3. West Lake, Hangzhou.

change her mind even unto her death. Such behavior cannot be called minor chastity; she is none other than a remarkable woman. Those who have been called female martyrs in the past have shared her mind even though their actions have differed."[84] Xu Ji praises Ai'ai's ability to rise above her courtesan background. In fact, he over-interprets her decision to elope as a means to escape the moral turpitude that he associates with a courtesan's profession. Her determination to die upholding her feminine virtue rendered her, in Xu's eyes, not merely a "chaste woman" but a "remarkable woman" (*qi nüzi*). For Xu Ji, Ai'ai's death redeems her moral iniquity (courtesan background, elopement, and illicit sex) and transforms her into a flag-bearer of orthodox patriarchal values. His choice of a former courtesan is, however, strange; were there not similar moral exemplars within the ranks of upper-class women? Conversely, Xu reserves scathing criticism for Zhang, who he condemns as unfilial for eloping with a courtesan against his parents' knowledge. Interestingly, he does not portray Ai'ai as a *femme fatale*, and her part in the elopement is overlooked. Given the historical, albeit unofficial, nature of Ai'ai's story, here then is evidence of how illicit sex could be salvaged by fidelity to one man. We saw this in the Tang-era "Huo Xiaoyu's Story," whose heroine was also a courtesan. It resurfaced in Tan Yige's story. In Huo Xiaoyu's case, fidelity took the form of female chastity, whereas in Tan Yige's story and elsewhere marriage to one's lover had the same result, although Tan was prepared to remain celibate failing reunion with Zhang.

Ai'ai's story is furthermore instructive as to how love stories were received and circulated. As I have noted, the story must have been initially told by Su Shunqing's mother and Ai'ai's other female neighbors. Here, then, is rare, indirect evidence of female collaboration in regard to the circulation of love stories, albeit in their oral form. Su, a young examination graduate at the time, subsequently recorded the story. Xu Ji's association with the story's recorder and protagonist is, nonetheless, unclear. The details of his edited version differ when compared to the other aforementioned versions. Xu's reasons for editing the original reveal a trenchantly orthodox moral stance. He states: "Su Zimei's 'Ballad of Ai'ai' is no longer extant. Its diction is, however, indecent and the preface fails to portray Ai'ai's true mind. Consequently, there is nothing that would edify posterity. I therefore wish to replace the content of Su's written piece with this ballad so as to resolve any scholarly confusion."[85] Li Jianguo surmises that Su Shunqing's original preface may have taken the form of a short story (*chuanqi*). This was the case for several Tang- and Song-period ballads, as we have seen with "Preface to the Ballad of Eternal Sorrow" and the like. As Li Jianguo observes, Xu Ji's criteria for editing and choosing not to circulate the original was based on orthodox moral grounds—that is, indecent diction and nothing that would edify future readers.[86] Given that Ai'ai's story almost certainly involved illicit sex, we may assume this was a major reason for Xu's objection. His moralistic professions suggests that he may well have excised any elements celebrating romantic love, including metaphorical description of sexual intercourse. In any case, he has lamentably robbed posterity of Su Shunqing's original. This, therefore, is evidence that the surviving corpus of love stories, or any type of stories for that matter, represent a highly selective group based on the divergent agendas and personalities of their author-recorders. As this phenomenon is reminiscent of Darwinian natural selection, we might label it "moralistic selection" according to the extent to which editors, recorders, and storytellers of the Song and Yuan dynasties may be considered orthodoxly "conservative."

A handful of pre–Song dynasty anecdotes about chaste widows may be found scatted throughout the chapters titled "women" in the *Comprehensive Record*.[87] For example, a story attributed to Zhang Zhuo (c. 660–c. 740) focuses on a young widow of six or seven years' duration. She repeatedly dreams of a ghost who presses her for sex. After unsuccessfully attempting to exorcise the ghost with Daoist spells, she finally repels him by cutting her hair, not making up her face, and refraining to bathe. In recognition of her chastity, the local authorities granted her household a laudatory banner.[88] In a story from the Five Dynasties period (907–60), a songstress commits suicide after failing to avenge the murder of her husband; the murderer had hired thugs to kill the husband and abduct the woman.[89] Therefore, as noted above, while the valorization of widow chastity was not new to the Song dynasty, it certainly gained popularity during this period until reaching a virtual "cult" status in late-imperial China.

Candidates Borrowing from Courtesans

Another prominent Northern Song motif was that of a young examination candidate or low-ranking civil servant who borrowed money from a courtesan to study or cover travel expenses.[90] This remained popular given the increased importance of examination culture throughout the Song. As with Tang dynasty stories in which young candidates lodge with courtesans, these Song stories also occur in impersonal, urban settings.

Unlike their Tang precursors, they address the financial reality of romance and its intersection with social mobility. If we can believe the image of a high-class, wealthy courtesan as portrayed in loves stories themselves or anecdotal collections such as *Record of the Northern Quarter*, such women and their procuresses evidently amassed enormous sums. For the courtesans' part, lending money to promising candidates presented a means of escaping their debased status and entering the upper-class. Although scholar-officials were not legally permitted to marry women of courtesan and servant status, either as wives or concubines, such things did occur.[91] No doubt the illegality of doing so added piquancy to related gossip. This motif, therefore, reflects the increasingly fluid class boundaries for women of debased social status while hinting at the financial constraints confronting many less-wealthy scholar-officials.[92]

In the "Story of Li Wa," we saw how the financially successful heroine retires from her trade and, with accumulated wealth, paves the way for her aristocratic lover's examination success. Compared to other extant Tang dynasty stories, this was a notable exceptional, though. It was not until the Northern Song that the theme assumes prominence. Among the earliest extant examples is that of "Chen Shuwen" (late eleventh, early twelfth century) whose eponymous protagonist was a resident of the capital, Bianliang. He passed the civil service examinations and received a provincial posting in Chang Prefecture, over 600 kilometers away on the Grand Canal. The narrator tells of how:

> He had not the means to support himself for two or three days together and so was unable to proceed to his posting. He had a commanding physique and was handsome, yet he was given to depression. He would often idle in the house of a courtesan, Cui Lanying. There Chen spoke of his posting but explained that poverty prevented him from going. Lanying said to him, "Although I am no relation to you, I have over a thousand strings of cash in my purse. I have long wished to marry and if you don't have a wife, then I'll marry you!" Chen replied, "I have not yet married. If this be the case, then it would be a beautiful thing." They made a vow there and then.

The duplicitous Chen returned home to his wife and suggested that he travel alone while she remain in the capital, promising to remit money. She agreed, and so Chen took his courtesan-lover to his posting.

Three years later, when returning by boat upon the expiration of his appointment, Chen decided to murder her so as to avoid possible legal trouble when his true marital status emerged. Accordingly, he got Lanying drunk one night and pushed both her and her maid into the river, where they drowned. To cover his crime, Chen, "in tears, called out, 'My wife has fallen into the Bian River. Her maid tried to save her and fell in with her.' As it was dark at the time and the river was as swift as an arrow, even though the boatman moored by the margin while trying to fish her out, they could not see her." Chen returned home, we are told, with several thousand stings of cash, a handsome profit for the mere thousand that Lanying had provided. He used this to open a warehouse and, within the space of a year, had become "notably wealthy."

On the day of the winter solstice festival, Chen and his wife were strolling by Bianliang's Xiangguo Temple when he noticed his former lover and her maid following behind. Using a pretext to send his wife on ahead, he managed to speak with the pair, who claimed to have been rescued. "Last time we fell into your trap. After we tumbled into the water, we drifted for several [Chinese] miles. We found a piece of flotsam that prevented us sinking again. Then, calling out, we were rescued." Chen's reply shows him unrepentant. "You were drunk and, standing on the deck, you lost your footing and fell into the water. The maid tried to rescue you and so fell in as well." Lanying appears not to believe him, as she replies: "We need not talk about the past again. It brings nothing but hate." She then invited him to her lodgings. Anticipating unwillingness, she threatened to lodge a legal suit should he not comply. Therefore, on the advice of an acquaintance, he visited her accompanied by a man-servant who waited outside all day. Neighbors asked what he was waiting for, and so he explained. When the neighbor replied that the house was empty, both proceeded to investigate. Inside they found drinking cups strewn on the ground. "Chen's face was turned upwards, his hands tied behind his back. He appeared like one who had been judicially executed." The storyteller comments: "This story was commonly known throughout the capital. In cases when men cannot exact punishment for cases of wrong-doing, ghosts will surely do so. This principle is crystal clear, yet how strange."[93]

Chen's likely motive for murder was the possibility that his wife, concubine, or a third party might accuse him of illegally marrying a courtesan, not to mention bigamy. As Beverly Bossler has noted, a high-ranking official, Lai Zhishao, was demoted for taking a courtesan as his concubine in the 1080s. A decade later, an imperial clansman, Zhao Shixian, was demoted and removed from the line of succession for the same crime.[94]

Although "Chen Shuwen" lacks a specific temporal setting, events on which it was based likely occurred around the same time as these two cases.

"Chen Shuwen" blends prototypes of both the—then fledgling—crime story with that of the *zhiguai*. The considerable volume of extant stories from this period focusing on crime without necessarily including anomalous content indicates contemporary readers' interest in crime as a literary type. Understanding the women to have survived based on their reemergence at the temple would, nonetheless, be a misreading. As indicated by the end commentary, the author-recorder understood them to be ghosts, even though this is not made explicit in the narrative itself.

The theme of social mobility also comes to the fore. The fact that Chen was able to pass the examinations despite straightened financial circumstances portrays the examination system as a meritocratic vehicle for social mobility. Both Chen and his courtesan-lover's rise and fall in fortunes also illustrate the somewhat fluid boundary between the scholar-official and commoner classes. Chen was initially an educated commoner. Overnight he was elevated to the scholar-official class while, by the conclusion, he had turned to commerce. Despite having become a merchant, he would still have been considered of scholar-official stature due to having passed the examinations, yet he could straddle both classes. Nonetheless, given the salacious and gossipy nature of this account, the storyteller may have intended to slander Chen by linking him with the despised merchant class, not to mention his financial dependency on a courtesan. Without corroborating evidence, it is difficult to ascertain the extent of this story's verisimilitude in this respect.

As with other stories of this prototype, this one addresses the monetary resources commanded by courtesans despite their debased social class. While courtesans could amass large amounts through sexual labor, some—represented by Lanying—were willing to exchange money for improved social status. A debased courtesan could utilize amassed wealth to buy her way out of servitude through the support of a scholar-official. Although Chen's having taken her as a concubine or passing her off as a wedded wife was illegal, it vividly depicts how laws could be flouted. The story, therefore, is further evidence for Bossler's contention that the Song was a period in which traditional social barriers for lower-class women began to break down.[95] Well-off courtesans evidently presented a potential source of financial support to impoverished scholars.

The narrator comments how this story circulated as local gossip. To be sure, had a scholar-official—albeit a low-ranking one—been found murdered in a disused house, we can well imagine the gossip it would have engendered.

Half-truths and straight-out fabrications may well have embellished whatever kernel of truth existed, yet contemporaries, used to reading literally as they labored under the "tyranny of history," would have largely taken much for face value. Liu Fu's comment about ghostly retribution certainly foregrounds contemporary belief in ghosts as manifestations of deceased humans and their ability to exact justice for crimes undetected in the mortal realm. Indeed, widespread belief in otherworldly retribution fueled many revenge prototypes as ghosts of wronged lovers returned for vengeance.

A more widely circulated and lengthier example of scholars borrowing from courtesans is the "Story of Wang Kui" (mid- to late eleventh century).[96] Given the story's defamatory nature and the prominent scholar-official status of the protagonist's father and brother, the storyteller suppresses the hero's name. The term *kui* refers to Wang's valedictorian status in the imperial examinations. Hence, the story could be alternatively titled "Valedictorian Wang."

The story tells of how Wang failed a metropolitan examination for having used a taboo word in his essay. He soon after journeys to Shandong, where, in the company of acquaintances, he meets a beautiful courtesan, Guiying. Guiying entertains the group with wine and song while praising Wang's scholastic talent. After he extemporizes a poem for her, she invites him to stay overnight. During the night, the following conversation takes place:

> "What's your surname, sweet lady? With a face like yours, yet still you engage in such a profession! Why is this?" "My surname is Wang and I come from a good family," she replied. "You, sir, are a single gentleman. Yet you have not a scrap of gold in your purse and you tire yourself by travelling throughout the countryside. If, sir, you would but rouse yourself to study daily, I would undertake to provide the cost of your brushes and paper as well as your clothing." From that time on, Wang remained as a guest in Guiying's bordello.

A year later, when another metropolitan examination is announced, she offers him traveling and related costs to go to the capital.

> "All my assets," she said, "amount to no less than several hundred thousand. You may take half to use on your trip west."
> "I've been a guest here for more than a year," replied Wang

with a long sigh. "I'm deeply sensible of your having provided me with food and clothing, yet now I'm obliged to take your wealth to cover the cost of my journey west. If I don't find honor, then that will be an end to it. If, however, I do claim honor, then I swear that I won't forsake you."

Despite Wang's promise, Guiying is evidently suspicious as she has him accompany her to a local temple. There, before the deity's image, she makes him swear that he will return and marry her. He leaves the following day.

Having passed the examination as its valedictorian, however, Wang regrets his promise. His father, furthermore, makes a match for him with a daughter of the Cui family. "'My ranking is such as this,' he thought to himself. 'I've caught the public eye no sooner than passing the exam. Yet now I've been sullied by a common prostitute. Besides, my father is exceedingly strict. Surely he won't accept her.'" Consequently, Wang reneges on his promise and ceases communication with Guiying. Unaware of this, she continues to send him poetry and letters. When Wang journeys to Xu Prefecture to undertake a government posting, Guiying dispatches her own messenger with a letter and a gift of clothing. Nevertheless, the angry Wang throws the letter on the ground and rebuffs the messenger. With the messenger's return, Guiying finally learns the true state of affairs. "Guiying, meanwhile, in joyful expectancy, came out to greet him [her messenger] and to ask what had transpired. When she heard what he had to say, she fell to the ground howling. After a long time, she said to her attendant, 'Today Wang Kui has broken his vow to me. I'll kill him. Only then will I be at ease. I may be a woman, but I'll die to avenge myself.'" She then goes to the local temple where she and Wang had previously made their vows. After informing the deity of what had occurred, she returns home and commits suicide with a razor. The plot is resolved as the courtesan's vengeful spirit proceeds to claim Wang's life.

> Wang happened to be in the examination hall. The hour was late and he was perusing exam papers. Then, all of a sudden, someone appeared from the sky. It was Guiying. Her hair hanging loosely and sword in hand, she pointed at him, cursing. "Wang Kui, you treacherous villain! I've scoured the high heavens and plumbed the Yellow Springs below looking for you without result. Yet you were here all along."

She argued her cause eloquently and Wang, knowing that he could not overcome her, said with a sigh, "It's my fault. I'll hire some monks for you this very day. They can recite sutras and recommend your rebirth. They can burn reams of paper money; surely that will be enough." "The only thing I want is your life," replied Guiying. "What use would I have for Buddhist writing and paper money?"

All those present heard him speaking with Guiying but did not see her form. Therefore, as though he were suffering from a fit, Wang seized a cutting knife and attempted to stab himself but those around him came to the rescue and he was not seriously harmed.

After returning home, even a Daoist exorcist hired by his mother was powerless to intervene. It was not long, therefore, before he successfully committed suicide.[97]

The manner in which Wang meets Guiying (in a group of, presumably, young men who visit the local brothel district), the banter during their initial meeting, in addition to her encouraging him to study is reminiscent of "Li Wa's Story." Unlike Li Wa, Guiying's offer is not made as reparation for having wronged him. She evidently admires his talent and wishes to financially invest in him as a means of raising her social status. Therefore, similar to other Song-era stories we have seen, social mobility comes to the fore.

Unlike Li Wa's story, Wang Kui follows the retribution prototype first developed during the mid- to late Tang dynasty of which "Huo Xiaoyu's Story" is a fine example.[98] In Wang Kui's case, the supernatural element is much stronger. Yet unlike *zhiguai* accounts in which illicit sex usually embodies negative connotations, the reason for Wang's demise lies in his own moral shortcomings vis-à-vis the culture of romance. Specifically, his broken promise to marry Guiying despite the fact that he was both emotionally and financially in her debt. Verbal agreements were considered serious matters in imperial China. And, to be sure, Wang's solemn vow before a local deity sanctified his promise. His initial untrustworthiness, therefore, takes on a sacrilegious tone and the consequent retribution he receives echoes numerous *zhiguai* stories in which broken promises to deities are punished. Wang's vow to marry Guiying furthermore echoes Li Yi's pledge to live with Huo Xiaoyu for an agreed period of time. Since

Wang's promise was not legally binding, however, paranormal means are necessary to serve justice and thereby assuage the righteous indignation undoubtedly felt by many contemporary readers "of feeling" (*you qingzhe*, my own use of the term). The importance attached to marriage contracts during the Song dynasty that we saw in other narratives is, furthermore, clearly discernable here.

Besides its development of distinctive Song-period themes and narrative elements, the manner in which the story circulated widely as gossip is also instructive. This is elucidated by the famous scholar and book collector Zhou Mi (1232–1308) who, writing in the late thirteenth century, quotes from a lost eleventh-century work compiled by Wang Kui's classmate, Chu Yushi (fl. eleventh century). Chu contends that the "Story of Wang Kui" is a scurrilous attempt to slander his friend, Wang Xianmin (1036–1063).[99] He gives the names of Wang's father and brother, their native place, as well as the father's career rotations prior to Wang's scholastic success. He furthermore attests to the basic facts of the story; that is, Wang passed the examination in 1061 having initially failed, the location, as well as the nature of his official posting. He furthermore attests to Wang's serious and studious nature. Rather than die at the hands of an avenging spirit, Chu tells how Wang died of poisoning after taking a dangerous medicinal concoction, Golden Tiger/Azure Haze (*Jinhu bixia*). Chu explains Wang's demise as stemming from a mental illness that led to hallucinations during his final posting. This, he contends, was the reason for Wang's premature return home. Chu visited Wang shortly before his death, at which time he had largely recovered but remained somewhat depressed.[100] In light of this testimony, the hallucinations that Wang reportedly suffered may have been misinterpreted by superstitious colleagues and underlings who readily subscribed to ghostly apparitions. Furthermore, based on Chu's information about Wang's social status, it seems unlikely that he would have had "not a scrap of gold" in his purse, as the courtesan avers. Chu's attestation to Wang's studious character similarly contradicts the courtesan's admonition for him to "rouse" himself to study. These details, therefore, appear fictitious and were likely meant to slander Wang.

Chu's information is corroborated by Zhang Shizheng's (?–after 1073) mid- to late eleventh-century *zhiguai* account. After giving Wang's basic biographical facts and the year in which he passed the examination, Zhang described firsthand the hallucinations that Wang experienced since he himself was one of Wang's colleagues in Nanjing.

> He [Wang] suddenly said to his fellow examiners, "The candidates are yelling and berating me outside. Why don't you stop them?" He sent someone to see to it, but there was no one there. This occurred on three or four occasions. Shortly after this, he said, "Someone holding a warrant has come to arrest me." Wang appeared terrified. He took a small knife from the table and slashed himself. Those around prevented him and he was not seriously injured. After that he returned to his native place to receive treatment.

Zhang proceeds to offer alternate explanations for Wang's behavior. Besides the avenging courtesan's ghost, he suggests the alleged suicide of a wronged housemaid who threw herself into a well.[101]

In light of Chu and Zhang's alternate versions of the Wang Kui story, we may readily see how inexplicable occurrences were easily interpreted as ghostly or otherworldly phenomena. Undoubtedly numerous *zhiguai* accounts arose in a similar fashion. It also reminds us of the salacious nature inherent in the culture of romance—that is, the potential for love stories to discredit one's enemies by portraying them as wastrels, betrayers of women, and the like. While some readers celebrated life's romantic aspects, others maintained considerably more conservative attitudes toward sexuality. Yuan Cai, for example, a magistrate whose rulings are recorded in the *Enlightened Judgments of Famous Magistrates* (*Minggong shupan qingming ji*), opines that, "Those who are literati [scholar-officials] but marry government courtesans, are they not criminal against propriety? Are they not a disgrace to their literati friends? It is not permissible! It is not permissible! It is absolutely not permissible!"[102] Undoubtedly there would have been many more who entertained similarly views. Yuan Cai was, after all, simply expressing what was enshrined in the law of the period. In regard to our story, it would not have been unusual for Wang to have occasionally visited a courtesan for a drink and witty conversation as numerous, if not most, examination candidates and scholar-officials did. Nonetheless, it would have been easy for an ill-wisher to fabricate a story about Wang Kui's having cohabited with a courtesan then withdrawing an offer of marriage. Chu Yushi professes ignorance about who slandered Wang, although he surmises that the author wished to make a profit from sales to despicable youths (*yu shili yu nianshao xiaxie bei*).[103] The term *shili*, making profit through sales or the marketplace, strongly suggests that an unnamed storyteller or printer-publisher was profiting monetarily from the story. If so, the term "despicable youths" is a rare—

albeit derogatory—reference to an eleventh-century consumer market for love and paranormal stories.

"The Story of Wang Kui" is generally attributed to the statesman, Xia E (fl. eleventh century). Chu Yushi, however, rejects this. Alternatively, he may have been unwilling to humiliate Xia and so outwardly professed not to accept his authorship while castigating the "anonymous" culprit. Li Xianmin, compiler of the *Extensive Records of the Cloud Studio*, cites and endorses Xia's authorship. In fact, Li accepts the ghost story's validity and laments the demise of such a promising intellect as Wang, blaming his death on *yaoxin*.[104] What he means by this term is unclear as *yao* could refer to ghosts and monsters but, in this context, it could alternately refer to a *femme fatale* or else might simply modify the graph *xin*—that is, scurrilous rumors. Similarly, Li Jianguo accepts Xia E's authorship given that (1) Xia E wrote sympathetically about the courtesan Wang Youyu, mentioned above, and (2) Li Xianmin, he claims, personally *saw* Xia's written account (nowhere, however, does Li Xianmin state this, at least not in the 1997 reprint).[105] Nevertheless, the popularity enjoyed by stories such as Wang Kui's point to the many readers and raconteurs of the period who would have sympathized with the jilted courtesan.

Although the motif of candidates borrowing from courtesans is intimately connected with examination culture, it appears to have evolved from an earlier tradition of the *faji* story, as may be seen from a few surviving examples. Ouyang Bin (894–951), protagonist of an anecdote titled "Ruiqing," was a grand councilor of the Kingdom of Shu (Sichuan) during the Five dynasties period. According to the anecdote, money borrowed from a courtesan, Ruiqing, whom he knew while seeking employment in the Kingdom of Chu (927–963), enabled him to travel to Shu where he attained a position that led to high honors.[106] In a Tang story titled "The Woman who Sold Hammers," the famous statesman, Ma Zhou (601–648), befriended a female innkeeper when he first arrived in the capital as a minor functionary. At his request, she arranged employment for him as scribe to an influential courtier. Ma came to prominence when a memorial he drafted gained the Taizong emperor's admiration. After this he married the humble innkeeper.[107] While Ma was neither an examination candidate nor did he borrow money from the woman, the idea of gaining prominence thanks to a woman is clearly similar to that of examination candidates profiting from courtesans.

As may be seen from this brief survey, groundbreaking new themes reflect demographic and socioeconomic changes that had occurred by the end of the Tang-Song transition. Given the its importance to a newly arisen ruling elite, marriage emerged as an key new theme. Whereas Tang-era storytellers often recounted fleeting affairs between educated men and women of inferior status, under the Song storyteller's writing brush, more often than not, such interclass liaisons resulted in marriage. More frequently, though, marriage between partners of equal status became a favorite narrative topic. Even arranged marriage was reconciled with the culture of romance so long as it coincided with the young couple's wishes. Love stories of the period also reveal a deep-rooted concern with social mobility, particularly anxiety over downward mobility. This corresponds to what social historians have demonstrated in terms of increasingly blurred class boundaries, particularly those relating to lower-class women. The Northern Song also marked a time when the Confucian tradition was being reevaluated and, during the Southern Song, would coalesce into the philosophical school known as Neo-Confucianism. Yet there were many who were not considered Neo-Confucian thinkers whose ideas coincided with those of this influential movement. Given the widespread acceptance of Neo-Confucianism's increasingly strong influence on daily life, it was natural for its fundamental tenets to find their way into the literature of the day. Hence, it should not be surprising to discern didactic notions in love stories of the period when compared with those of the Tang.

Chapter 3

The Southern Song Dynasty (1127–1279)

The Song dynasty was almost extinguished by its powerful northern neighbor, the Jurchen, to whom the conquering Manchus of the seventeenth century traced their ancestry. The fall of Bianliang to Jurchen troops in early 1127 marked the end of the Northern Song. The reigning emperor and his retired father, the imperial family and their retainers—including thousands of palace women, countless art treasures, and other booty were removed to the Jurchen capital in the far north. The dynasty was soon after reestablished in the south by a prince of the blood, Zhao Gou (1107–1187, r. 1127–1162), known posthumously as the Gaozong emperor. After a brief stay in present-day Nanjing, Gaozong designated the relatively small city of Hangzhou as his capital in 1129. It was renamed "Provisional Safety" (Lin'an) in view of the court's initial intention to prosecute the war and regain the northern plains, which constituted China's cultural heartland. Bitter fighting ensued for several years. At one time the new emperor and his retinue narrowly avoided capture by taking to sea. Fearful of army loyalty after an entire Song army rebelled, Gaozong concluded a treaty with the Jurchen in 1142, largely brokered by pacifist bureaucrat Qin Gui (1090–1155). Qin henceforth became Gaozong's all-powerful chief minister and ruled with an iron fist until his death in 1155. This treaty brought a lengthy period of peace until 1161 when hostilities once again erupted. The Song court soon concluded another peace treaty that lasted until the early thirteenth century when yet another short-lived campaign ended in disaster for the Song court. The Song Empire never recovered its lost northern territories. China was not reunited until a new steppe enemy, the Mongols, captured the Southern Song capital in 1276 after having destroyed the Jurchen state.[1]

Although the educated elite of the Southern Song continued to value public life and spared no effort to educate and prepare their offspring for bureaucratic careers, they no longer attempted to specialize in government service. As noted in the previous chapter, the Northern Song professional bureaucracy tended to marry into local gentry clans as the eleventh century progressed, thereby trading social prestige for pecuniary gain. This resulted in a blurring of boundaries between the two until, in Hartwell's words, "their families became indistinguishable from those of the local gentry."[2] This phenomenon coincided with a widespread tendency to diversify as members of the upper classes pursued careers in commerce or as local teachers. Accordingly, much energy was spent on local, even lineage-oriented projects, such as community granaries, charitable estates, private academies, and the like.[3] Furthermore, as the dynasty progressed, an exponentially increasing number of examination candidates competed for a limited number of vacancies. Hence, a prestigious bureaucratic career became inaccessible for many well-educated men of letters who, thereafter, had little choice but to direct their energies elsewhere.

Activity on the local level went hand in glove with the spreading influence of the Zhu Xi School of Learning. Zhu Xi's vision of self-cultivation through a mastery of the Four Books with the aim of attaining sagehood gained widespread acceptance and, in 1241, was recognized as the official state cult. Henceforth its core curriculum would coincide with that of the imperial examinations, which thereafter spread its influence further. From this period onward, Zhu Xi inspired moral transformation as a marker of elite status, which, to a certain extent, came to replace the ideal of government service. Accordingly, the importance of one's place within the local community grew as bureaucratic service became both irrelevant to self-cultivation and inaccessible for the majority of educated men.[4]

Reunion Stories

As Jurchen armies captured Kaifeng and overran the northern provinces, many ethnic Chinese refugees migrated south. Among them were numerous members of the upper classes. Sandwiched between West Lake and the Qiantang River, the relatively small city of Lin'an was soon swamped with refugees even before its designation as the new dynastic capital. Given the ensuing political chaos and social upheaval, it is not surprising that reunion stories attracted widespread interest during the earliest decades of the dynasty, judging from numerous extant narratives and anecdotes of the period. These typically told of couples who were separated during the fall of the Northern Song and its aftermath or during one of several rebellions that plagued its final years.

A lengthy reunion story may be found in *Miscellaneous Stories from the Green* (mentioned in the introduction), compiled by Wang Mingqing (1127–after 1214).[5] The fact that the story was anthologized several times and used as a basis for several operas attests to its popularity.[6] "A Husband and Wife Honor Their Old Pledge" (*Fuqi fu jiu yue*) tells of two upper-class families, the Xings and the Dans, who lived next door to each other in the Northern Song capital in 1126, just prior to dynastic collapse. Xing's sister is, coincidentally, Dan's wife. Their names, nevertheless, are disguised; Xing is ambiguously referred to as District Magistrate Xing and Dan as Judge Dan. The Xing's have a daughter named Chunniang, while the Dan's have a son called Fulang. As the boy is slightly older than the girl, both children are well matched according to the traditional dictum that the husband be older than his wife. In their infancy, their families agree to marry them when they come of age, something not uncommon for the period.[7] Some sixteen or so years later, when District Magistrate Xing takes up a provincial posting and his family accompany him, it is agreed to conduct the wedding ceremony once they return. Unfortunately, the Xings are murdered by rebels and Chunniang is sold to a Quanzhou brothel. The Dans, naturally, are unaware of this. The plot's forward momentum is then suspended for a static description of Chunniang's accomplishments as a courtesan—accomplishments made possible due to her upper-class background.

> When Chunniang was 10 years (*sui*) old, she was able to read the *Analects of Confucius*, the *Book of Mencius*, the *Classic of Poetry* and the *Book of Documents*. She could, furthermore, compose short lyrics. Hence, when the brothel madam taught her music and performing arts, there was not one in which she did not excel. Whenever she served at a state banquet, she was able to extemporize lyrics based on old ones while paying attention to the particular context. She could relate readily with others. Her complexion was clear and delicate, while her

> mannerisms were elegant. She did not carry on with saucy talk and kissing. She had the air of inherent gentility.

Such attention to the heroine's talent and knowledge, particularly pertaining to the Confucian classics, reminds us of other heroines, such as Tan Yige. When Fulang comes of age and inherits scholar-official status from his father (due to the *yin* privilege mentioned earlier), he is appointed a fiscal commissioner to—coincidentally—Quanzhou. There he happens to meet Chunniang who is now a celebrated courtesan known as Yang Yu. Having been separated since childhood, the pair do not recognize each other. Nevertheless, deep attraction is born. During a banquet attended by his unnamed friend, the local judiciary administrator, Fulang manages to speak with her semi-privately. As he inquires about her past, he realizes that she is none other than his lost fiancé.

> Praising Yang Yu's beauty while expressing admiration for her artistic accomplishments, he therefore said, "You are also the descendent of an illustrious family, but I can't determine exactly who they might be." Embarrassed, Yang replied, "I was originally from a family of scholar-officials and have fallen far in the world. Madam Yang is not my real mother." The fiscal commissioner (Fulang) then asked about her father's name and rank. In tears, she replied, "My original surname is Xing. We lived in the Filial Resonance District of the capital next door to my uncle. I was betrothed to his son. My father received the posting of magistrate in Shunyang County, Deng Prefecture. Unfortunately, both my parents were murdered by bandits. I was kidnapped and sold here." The fiscal commissioner continued his questions. "What was the name of your uncle and who was his son?" "My uncle's surname is Dan. At the present time he is a judge in Yangzhou. His son was called Fulang. I do not know if he's dead or alive." She thereupon broke down.

Suspicious that she might enjoy her lot as a courtesan, Fulang conceals his identity and attempts to console her by citing the respect she enjoys from the local officials and her comfortable lifestyle. Chunniang retorts by pointing out the impropriety involved in entertaining a succession of men. "I have heard tell that a woman is naturally disposed to having a family and a home. I wish to be someone's wife, even were he an unimportant commoner who wears short gowns made from cloth, no matter had we nothing but beans to eat and water to drink."

Confident of Chunniang's distaste for the *demimonde*, on another occasion Fulang proposes marriage. Chunniang accepts while reiterating her wish to escape the ranks of courtesans. Fulang, therefore, writes to his parents explaining the situation. Much ink is spilled describing the manner in which the elite males rescue the languishing heroine. Fulang's father, then a serving official in the prestigious Secretariat, has Chunniang's uncle petition the imperial court to have her released from the register of state-owned courtesans. When approved, the uncle personally takes the petition to Quanzhou. Nevertheless, as with many a Tang dynasty love story, a rival appears in no less a person that Quanzhou's prefect. Instead of promptly approving Chunniang's release, he calls her to a private banquet where he hugs her, demanding a reward. Rebuked by the local controller-general who is also present, he apologizes and swiftly completes the arrangements; Chunniang is to be married from his house with the judicial administrator acting as matchmaker, while Fulang's uncle is to give her away.

The narrative, surprisingly, does not terminate there. Sometime after the ceremony, when Fulang's tenure in Quanzhou is about to conclude, at his wife's request he agrees to hold a farewell dinner for ten of Chunniang's former co-workers and the brothel owners. In Chunniang's words, "When I ended up in the world of courtesans, I was cared for by this husband and wife and am very close to my sister-courtesans. Now that I'll be going far away, I'll never see them again. I'd like to arrange a small banquet to say goodbye to them. What do you think?" At this dinner a young courtesan, Li Ying, who addresses Chunniang as "aunt," bursts into tears at the prospect of separation. Li Ying, we are told, was especially close to Chunniang because they shared a room where Chunniang taught her music. "Overcome by emotion, she [Li Ying] suddenly rose and, holding Chunniang's hand, said, 'Auntie, now you'll escape and be on top of the world, while I have fallen into the dung heap. I'll never be able to get out.' She then broke down." Chunniang therefore persuades her husband to accept Li Ying as a seamstress (cum-concubine), prompting a sarcastic comment from the prefect about Fulang wishing to catch two birds with one arrow. Fulang's subsequent homecoming is poignant, albeit briefly sketched. Although his parents are initially reluctant to accept Li Ying, they later relent, having been won over by her thoughtfulness and pliancy. The story concludes in 1155. By then, the family has moved to Wuling (modern Changde) where Chunniang and Li Ying are recognized as first and secondary wives, respectively. Li Ying, moreover, has born a son.[8]

Among the narrative's several themes, the idea of honoring a marriage contract and its intersection with downward social mobility is prominent. We saw in the previous chapter how Qiongnu's engagement was broken due to financial ruin. This undoubtedly was common practice.[9] In Chunniang's story, the possible disgrace of accepting a former courtesan as a bride/daughter-in-law would have been all the more reason to spurn the betrothal. Nonetheless, numerous stories and anecdotes bespeak of the moral obligation to honor agreements which, in the wish-fulfilling world of the short story, they often did. This story is a poignant example of this theme, which would be frequently developed in love stories throughout the dynasty. The fulfillment of Fulang and Chunniang's betrothal despite murder, abduction, judicially sanctioned sexual slavery, and gossip would certainly have attracted many contemporary readers.

Much narrative interest is engendered as elite males rescue an upper-class daughter who languishes in sexual servitude. Gratuitous attention given to the mechanics of Chunniang's release from the courtesan's register (not fully summarized above) and the prefect's wonton behavior intensify this aspect of the story. Here, again, we find the image of what Martin Huang terms a "languishing beauty." Chunniang, for her part, upholds orthodox morality with her twice-professed desire to quit the ranks of courtesans and marry a commoner. As with Northern Song–era stories, the heroine becomes a spokeswoman for moral orthodoxy even though she is not upheld as a paragon. Moreover, upper-class anxiety over downward social mobility is intensified by Chunniang's Confucian education and poetic talent—that is, her childhood knowledge of Confucian classics, such as the *Book of Songs* and *Book of Documents*. While reference to these texts is a well-established formula indicating superior education, the addition of *Mencius* and the *Analects* strongly suggests the influence of Neo-Confucian thought as these became cornerstones of Zhu Xi's curriculum for self-cultivation. Her understanding of the classics and her upper-class lineage and upbringing enable Chunniang to master every performing art she is taught, including the ability to extemporize lyric poetry. Her appearance and manner similarly distinguish her from the common herd. Here, therefore, is an upper-class notion that breeding and family background could prevail over environmental disadvantage. Despite being sold into prostitution, the daughter of a Confucian-trained gentleman could rise above her "sordid" environment while, at the same time, excel in that environment. Nevertheless, Chunniang's embodiment of an upper-class woman and Confucian values are sullied by her status as a courtesan. Read synecdochally, the cherished Confucian values she embodies are tarnished by association with prostitution. Accordingly, orthodox male-constructed morality is displaced onto the female body. No doubt contemporary male readers would have felt a compulsion to save both the female body and its conflation with Confucian learning. By doing so, they could also reaffirm their own cultural values.

Nevertheless, Fulang's test of Chunniang's resolve to relinquish a courtesan's lifestyle reveals anxiety that she may enjoy entertaining multiple partners rather than upholding wifely virtues such as chastity, fidelity, and obedience. No doubt he also hesitated to marry a serving courtesan given the social disgrace it would have entailed. Chunniang's virtue is further tested by the prefect's sexual advances. From this we may see how the upper-class male articulating subject, while investing cultural superiority in a female of his own rank, concurrently portrays her as potentially promiscuous and disloyal. We saw in chapter 1 how Tang-era storytellers betrayed similar anxiety. The idea of woman as a *femme fatale*, then, was never far from the minds of elite male storytellers even while they extolled female virtue. This is another reminder of how the love story's celebration of romantic freedom of choice provided a testing ground for female loyalty.

Circumventing the legal prohibition against scholar-officials marrying courtesans is problematic. To be sure, Fulang's father and Chunniang's uncle petitioned no less an authority than the imperial court to have her released from the register of state courtesans. When the prefect hands Fulang his father's letter and the imperial decree to release Chunniang, he remarks, "This is a beautiful thing." I understand this to mean fulfillment of the couple's childhood engagement, which no doubt proved a decisive factor in her release. Nonetheless, the story twice alludes to the immoral nature of a scholar-official's marrying a courtesan and its ensuing gossip. When Chunniang suggests fare-welling her former co-workers and the brothel owners, Fulang replies, "There is not a person in the whole prefecture who doesn't know about your previous doings. Moreover, it can't be concealed. Then what's the harm in it." Furthermore, a metatextual end commentary tells how Fulang, after his retirement from public service, would tell the story to other scholar-officials "without concealment." The fact that Fulang may have wished to conceal Chunniang's past had it not been common knowledge indicates the scandalous nature of events. Nevertheless, as the end commentary makes clear, the scholar officials who heard the story considered Fulang's actions a righteousness act; hence we return to the idea of ethics vis-à-vis fulfillment of a marriage vow.

Although not specifically marked, contemporary readers would have almost certainly viewed the couple's remarkable reunion as an example of marital predestiny. This expectation is established at the outset in view of the children's comparable ages, their betrothal as infants, and the fact that Xing's wife was Dan's sister. The betrothal of infants or very young children was not uncommon during the Song period and, in love stories, was invariably viewed as predestined.[10] Intermarriage between upper-class families, as noted in the previous chapter, was a common strategy used by the professional elite to perpetuate their superiority.[11] Indeed, interfamilial marriage over two or more generations was not uncommon during the Song dynasty and, in love stories, is often a sign of conjugal predestiny. The intermarriage of the royal houses of Qin and Jin during the Warring States period provided a historical precedent, and this became another frequently cited intertextual marker of the corpus. Marriage between cousins was permissible as long as the couple's surname did not coincide. Hence, while this enabled first cousins to marry, it ironically prevented unrelated couples from doing so were they to have shared a surname. Contrary to expectation, this was not used as an obstacle to marriage by Song dynasty storytellers.

Another of Wang Mingqing's reunion stories (untitled) is set during a rebellion instigated by Fan Ruwei, a Fujian rebel who died in 1132. It tells of a provincial official, Lü Zhongyi, whose unmarried daughter was kidnapped by Fan Ruwei's bandits and compelled to marry a relation of the rebel leader, Fan Xizhou. Fan, we are told, was a scholar and a gentleman who was compelled to join the rebellion given his kinship with its leader. Despite the marriage's coerced nature, it was conducted according to ritual and Madam Lü was recognized as Fan's primary wife, as opposed to a concubine. This is significant as it legitimized the marriage according to a strict interpretation of Confucian precepts. The new bride accepts her situation and, so it is implied, finds happiness with her husband; undoubtedly his education distinguishes him from a common rebel while resonating with upper-class readers. When government troops are about to recapture the rebel-occupied city, Madam Lü urges him to flee.

"I have heard that a chaste woman does not serve two husbands. Since you have reported our marriage to your ancestors and thus completed our marriage ritual, I am now a woman of your family. The city is hard pressed, cut-off and will soon fall. You are the rebel's clansman and will not escape. I cannot bare to see you die." So saying, she took hold of a knife and was about to slit her throat. Fan stopped her, saying, "I fell in with the rebels, but it wasn't my intention to do so. If I can't exonerate myself, then death by execution will be my lot. But you are the daughter of a scholar-official. Your having been kidnapped and brought here was ill fated, but the [government] army commander and officers are all northerners. Since you're a northerner, perhaps you can find your father since you speak their language. You may then have another chance to live." Madam Lü responded, "In that case, I won't remarry for the rest of my life. But I'm afraid of being captured by the soldiers. I vow I will not to be dishonored again. So there is only death for me." Fan replied, "If, by chance, I manage to escape, I won't remarry either so as to repay your feelings this day."

Madam Lü remains in the city and unsuccessfully attempts suicide so as to maintain her chastity amidst the chaos following its fall. She is rescued by her father who, coincidentally, happens to be serving with the victorious army as a military attaché. He urges her to remarry after their return to Lin'an, but she refuses. The father tells her,

"I'm not sure if you could marry a civil official, but there's bound to be a military officer we could find. Yet you're not content to become a titled lady. You'd prefer to be the wife of a bandit and won't let him go!" Madam Lü replied, "Although he may be called a 'bandit,' he is actually a gentleman. He is a scholar. It was because he was forced by his clansmen that he had no choice but to follow them. He often helped people when he was in the city. He surely won't die if there's a guiding principle in the universe. From henceforth, I will serve my family at home. I will be an old woman who serves her two parents. That will make me happy. Where is the need to remarry?"

At this the father relents. Fan Xizhou's education clearly underscores the importance that the educated, elite storyteller placed on social status in relation to marriage. Had Fan been an illiterate rebel, the story may well have ended differently or may not have been recorded.

The couple is eventually reunited when Fan, a newly appointed civil servant with an assumed name, visits his wife's father on official business. "Madam Lü asked her father, 'Who was that who came just now?' 'An envoy from Guang Prefecture,' he replied. 'His speech and his manner,' she replied, 'are just like Mr. Fan of Jian Prefecture [Fujian].' Lü laughed. 'Your Mr. Fan died at the hands of rebel soldiers. His bones are rotten by now. This man says his surname is Her. He is not the slightest relation to your Mr. Fan.'" Nevertheless, when "Mr. Her" pays a second visit to Madam Lü's father, the latter asks about his background. He confesses his true name and how he was forced to rebel. After the recapture of the besieged city, he surrendered and changed his name when the rebels where defeated, after which he fought in Yue Fei's (fl. twelfth c.) army; Yue Fei was a highly successful commander who fought for the Southern Song court. When Lü asks whether he is married, he tells of his vow not to do so. "'Later I found my mother in Xin Prefecture. Until this day I have not remarried. There is only mother and I, the two of us, and a kitchen concubine.' When he finished speaking, he broke down and cried until his voice was hoarse." On this note, the story rapidly concludes happily as the father reunites Fan with his daughter.[12]

The father's doubts as to whether his daughter could remarry a civil official, as opposed to a military officer, reflects the general snobbery that civil officials reserved for the military throughout the imperial period. This prejudice was especially strong during the Song dynasty. Here, again, is the importance of class background in regard to marriage. Related to this is downward social mobility—that is, the daughter of a high-ranking scholar-official not only being forced to marry but to do so beneath her station. This aspect would have enabled twelfth-century readers to derive pleasure from the image of a languishing beauty while desiring her release. Part of the story's sophistication lies in its nuanced portrayal of social status; the husband may be a rebel, albeit a reluctant one, but he is also an educated "gentleman." Regardless of his financial position, it was unlikely to have been comparable to that of the Lü's. To be sure, the heightened attention to class background help distinguish this story from others of the period that ignore socioeconomic intricacies.

As with the "Story of Distant Mist," this one foregrounds the tension between a woman's filial and marital duties. In view of the importance of filial piety, the daughter was obliged to obey her father's wish that she remarry. Yet, based on the same system of social values, the daughter is correct to assert the immorality of marrying two husbands, particularly while the first is still living. Nonetheless, in a society in which widows routinely remarried, this seems a scrupulously point to carry. Furthermore, marriages were sometimes judicially annulled when husbands had committed certain crimes or were unable to support their wives. Rebellion against the imperium would certainly have justified this, as the father points out. Actually, this was the only way in which Madam Lü could cleanse the shame of being a rebel's wife, a state tantamount to treason, despite her having been married under duress. The daughter's defiance of her father, therefore, affirms the Confucian maxim that a woman should not know two husbands regardless of external circumstances, which in this case were strongly in favor of remarriage. This affirms the importance that Neo-Confucian thinkers, such as Cheng Yi and Zhang Zai, attached to widow and female chastity. Her unwavering resolve is comparable to that of chaste paragons extolled in other short stories of the period. Hence the story prioritizes conjugal fidelity over filial piety.

Married couples promising not to remarry as a sign of mutual loyalty is another important theme here. Little wonder, therefore, that the narrative appears first in a subsection labeled "virtuous couples" in the "chastity/fidelity" section of the *History of Affection*.[13] As may be seen from the struggle between father and daughter, her oath not to remarry proves vital for reunion with her husband. The husband's vow is equally important. Had Fan remarried, the daughter may well have agreed to remarry. Therefore, Fan's regaining his wife through fidelity may partly be understood in light of the women-as-reward theme that we first saw in mid-Tang dynasty stories. Unlike Tang-era precursors, the husband's meritorious deed is loyalty to his wife. He did, however, keep a concubine, although her main duties were culinary. If modern readers view this as a double standard, it must be remembered that social status was of crucial importance in twelfth-century Chinese society; concubines of the period were increasingly compared to bought goods and, therefore, dispensable. A first wife, on the other hand, obliged to assist in her husband's ancestral sacrifices, was of primary importance.[14] Fan's acquisition of a concubine was, furthermore, justified by filial piety—to serve not only him but, more importantly, his mother. Hence contemporary readers would likely have viewed her as a kind of maid.

The theme of married couples pledging not to remarry reoccurs in many stories of the Southern Song dynasty. This indicates the increasing importance of *mutual* marital fidelity during this period. Hong Mai, for example, recorded a story titled "Madame Zheng" in which the male meets with other-worldly punishment for failing to observe such a promise.[15]

> Zhang Zineng's wife, Zheng, was stunningly beautiful. Zhang held the position of an erudite in the Court of Imperial Sacrifices when she fell ill and died. Just before she died, she bade him farewell. "You must marry another, my lord. Think of me no longer." In tears, Zhang replied, "How could I bear such a thing?" "How can a person's words be relied on?" backtracked the wife. "You should swear before heaven." Zhang swore. "Should I break my word, let me become a eunuch and meet with a horrible end."

The wife then died. True to the *zhiguai* genre, the story focuses on how her corpse reanimated and walked on the night of her death, explainable by Daoist belief about spirit-possession of the recently deceased. Three years later, Zhang was persuaded to marry the daughter of an influential bureaucrat.

> Yet, from then on, Zhang was often given to melancholy and unhappiness. He was once taking an afternoon nap when he saw Zheng enter through the window. "What of your old promise?" she railed. "How could you bear break it? I was fortunate to have borne two daughters. But since we never had a son, why did you not buy a concubine? You were bent on taking a new wife? Why? Calamity is about to strike." She then mounted the bed and reached for his private parts. Racked with pain, Zhang urgently called out to his household. But by the time they arrived there was nothing to be seen. From then on he was like a eunuch and met with a bizarre end.

Although this story is marginal to the love story prototype, the husband's promise not to remarry corresponds to that of Fan Xizhou. The reader is not told why the promise was made but, presumably once given, the husband appears obliged to observe it. The fact that Zhang had no sons to maintain his patrilineal line may have rendered the wife's demand both bewildering and unreasonable to contemporary readers, especially when she herself initially urged him to remarry. Nor is a reason given for her change of heart. Nevertheless, her final question as to why he did not take a concubine indicates how he may have navigated these difficulties.

The detail about the wife reaching for Zhang's "private parts," in view of his consequent eunuch-like state, is a clear yet rare reference to male castration anxiety. This detail, alongside the fact that the wife destroyed Zhang's posterity, tacitly casts her as a *femme fatale* figure or, at least, an early example of the type of shrewish wife that Keith McMahon has studied in literary works of late-imperial China.[16] In another of Hong Mai's accounts, "Zheng Jun's Wife," the husband similarly promises not to remarry. When he later does so, however, the wife's ghost forgives him. Nevertheless, he too dies unnaturally ten years later.[17]

Writing in the early thirteenth century, Li Changling (fl. 1233) discusses Zhang Zineng's vow not to remarry. After summarizing the narrative, he comments: "The term 'wife' denotes 'an equal.' Once [a wife is on] equal [terms with her husband], it is not easy to replace her. This is the foundation for interpersonal ethics and the rule for married couples. For harmony in the home, this comes first. . . . Nowadays people only know that the other has died; they do not know that although the body is destroyed, the spirit has not disappeared and must surely harbor perceptions even more intense than in life."[18] Hence, for Li Changling, the marital bond extended beyond death of the body, as premised on the religious beliefs of the era. The idea that men should not remarry represents a wider trend. The Neo-Confucian thinker Zhang Zai opined that men should not remarry. He did, however, concede that second marriages were sometimes unavoidable due to consideration of household management. After asserting that women should not remarry on the grounds of moral principle, he goes on to say, "Surely men should not remarry either. Still, if one analyzes the situation according to degree of importance, [a wife] is essential to care for parents, manage the family, perform sacrifices, and continue [the descent line]. Therefore there is the principle of taking a second wife."[19] Such sentiments were related to the distaste for keeping concubines that gained traction among Neo-Confucian adherents during the eleventh, twelfth, and thirteenth centuries. Li Kezhuang, for example, admired how Ao Taoshun and his wife prepared their own meals rather than keep concubines to do so. Yang Shi (1053–1135) praised Zhang Fu (1045–1106) for pursuing scholarship rather than concubines. Zhu Xi extoled the famous general, Zhang Jun (1097–1164), for not having taken a concubine his entire life. Similarly, Liu Zai praised the "old-style virtue" of Lu Jun (1155–1216), who never took concubines, opining that,

"Ritual begins with care in the relationship between husband and wife."[20] Thus did many such morally conservative thinkers emphasize the wife's role since, unlike a concubine, only a wife could participate in the family ancestral cult and properly serve her in-laws according to time-honored Confucian ritual.

By the thirteenth century, such thinking had coalesced into what Bossler terms "a new model of the virtuous married couple." In his collected writings, Yuan Xie (1144–1224), a follower of the Neo-Confucian scholar, Lu Jiuyuan, discussed his friend who, while on active bureaucratic duty away from home, had no concubine to cook for him. This was despite the fact that his wife had chosen one to follow him as she, herself, chose not to travel far from home. When asked, his friend responded that, in antiquity, "When the wife was not present, concubines did not dare to spend the night." Lu's end commentary is telling: For a woman to be without jealousy, for a man to be without desire [for a concubine]: since ancient times, this has been difficult. Now milord's wife has chosen a concubine to serve him—clearly she is without jealousy. Milord himself is calm and self-composed, untroubled by desire, austere like an ascetic of the wilderness. They can be called a true husband and wife: how far beyond vulgar custom they are!"[21]

Therefore, the idea that Fan Xizhou, Zhang Zineng and other literary characters remained faithful to their separated or deceased wives reflects this growing intellectual trend, related to that which valorized chaste widows as previously discussed. And although we may be tempted to understand this as a mark of marital equality, such ideas, first and foremost, supported traditional Confucian social values.

A longer story, titled "Yiniang of Taiyuan," concludes in a similar manner as "Madame Zheng." It narrates the reunion of a married couple who was separated during the invasion that overthrew the Northern Song dynasty. Considerable attention to conjugal love invites a reading as a love story, although it more resembles a *zhiguai* account. Although the main protagonist is Han Shihou, the narration commences from the point of view of his cousin, Yang Congshan. During Yang's captivity in the Jurchen capital of Yanjing (modern Beijing), he located Han's missing wife, Madam Wang (Yiniang). While reading poetry written on the wall of a tavern, Yang recognized one written by Madam Wang about her missing husband. When he caught up with her outside the tavern, she explained how she and Han were separated. "My husband and I once escaped to Huaisi but were captured by the Jurchen. Their leader, General Saba, wanted to force himself on me. I couldn't allow myself to be the subject of such humiliation. And so, taking a dagger, I cut my own throat yet did not die. The leader's wife, Lady Hanguo, heard of what had happened and took pity on me. She promptly ordered me saved and treated, and then bade me follow her."

On another occasion when Yang was admiring calligraphy and poetry written on the same tavern wall, he was surprised to see a poem written by his cousin, Han Shihou, who had come north as a diplomat. Yang, therefore, hurried to meet him and told him of his wife's whereabouts. Han, however, was shocked. " 'Recalling the time of her capture, I personally saw her die by cutting her own throat,' he recounted. 'How could she be alive?' " Yang took him to Madam Wang's residence. Nonetheless, what on his last visit had been an imposing edifice was now desolate and overgrown with weeds. They received an explanation from a local lady. " 'Yiniang is indeed here, but she is not living,' replied the woman. 'Lady Hanguo admired her virtue and so brought the remains here to be cremated. When Lady Hanguo passed away, she had the ashes buried together with her.' " The two men entered the deserted building and spoke with Madam Wang's ghost, who materialized before them. When Han proposed removing her ashes back home, Madam Wang conditionally agreed.

> "Because of my love for you, my lord, my soul resides here in solitude," she said. "How could I not be willing to return? But if I follow you south, you must frequently visit and console my loneliness in the nether regions. Should you re-marry and cease your care of me, it would be better not to return." Han was moved to tears and swore never to re-marry. . . . After several years, Han had no posterity and so he re-married. And, for this reason, he neglected the grave of his former wife. Then he dreamed that she came to him, frightfully indignant and acrimonious. "I was perfectly at peace over there, yet your lordship forcibly removed me," she railed. "And now you have reneged on your promise. I cannot bear such solitude myself; soon you too will share this feeling." Han, both regretful and frightened, became ill. Knowing he could not avoid it, he passed away within a few days.[22]

Again, a husband promises not to remarry—that is, ritually receive a woman into his home and accord her the status of a "first" wife (as opposed to that of a concubine). Honoring such a promise enables Fan Xizhou to reunite with his wife in the previous narrative, whereas in Hong Mai's *zhiguai* accounts failure to do so results in the protagonists' deaths. Read as a love story, Yiniang's story develops as a broken promise/revenge prototype following Han's remarriage. These stories' drastic denouements demonstrate the seriousness with which contemporaries viewed pledges not to remarry. Yiniang's request that Han not remarry nicely illustrates Li Changling's idea about deceased wives' postmortem sentience. As female fidelity and widow chastity were accorded increasing importance over the course of the Song dynasty, a concomitant trend was afoot for men to remain faithful to deceased wives, although they could fulfill such a pledge while still keeping a concubine or two.

"Resolute Lady of Taiyuan" is furthermore a noteworthy example of the patriotic literature that flourished during the first decades of the Southern Song dynasty, circulated by the generation for whom the humiliation of near dynastic overthrow remained an unhealed wound. Indeed, bitter faction fighting ensued at court between pacifists who advocated peace with the Jurchen and irredentists who argued for military recovery of the conquered territories. As mentioned above, Qin Gui eventually persuaded the Gaozong emperor to conclude a peace treaty, after which Qin became a supremely powerful chief minister until his death in 1155. Hong Mai, as one who would have continued the war, recorded many such patriotic stories in which spirited females were martyred by the Jurchen. "Villagers Kill Barbarian Horsemen," for example, records several stories under the one title. One tells of how several women attacked and killed a "barbarian" as he tried to kidnap two women. On another occasion, a woman forced to perform menial chores for an invader pushes her persecutor down a well. A third anecdote tells of a family who successfully attacked and killed two "barbarians" who were about to burn their house.[23] Similarly, the statesman and poet Zhou Zizhi (1082–1155) wrote a biography titled "The Maiden of Huyin," which recounted how an unmarried daughter offered herself to a Jurchen commander who was about to execute her father. After the father's release, while walking with her captor beside a river, she drowned herself rather than submit to rape and subjugation.[24] These accounts illustrate a persistent pattern: in order to save family members, a young woman sacrifices her life while preserving her virtue—that is, sexual purity. Unlike moral exemplars we have seen in love stories so far, these women are upheld as paragons not merely because they preserve their chastity but because they resisted an alien invader. Defense of the dynasty, patriotism, and sexual purity are, therefore, conflated. Hence the women are honored as torch-bearers of Chinese and Confucian cultural superiority. As Beverly Bossler has noted, however, such writing was intended to shame men rather than to truly valorize female subjectivity.[25] While writers extolled members of the "weaker sex" as brave resistance fighters, they tacitly criticized powerful male bureaucrats and pacifist ministers, exemplified by Qin Gui, who were willing to surrender and even collaborate with the enemy. This rhetoric was again evoked toward the end of the dynasty in the face of the Mongol conquest, and again toward the fall of the Yuan dynasty.

Yiniang's suicide preserves her chastity and, given that her attackers were alien invaders, by doing so she joins the ranks of female martyrs in a patriotic struggle. Her action demonstrates her loyalty to both her husband and the dynasty. Although this is largely overshadowed by more important narrative strands, its irredentist propaganda value remains powerful. The projecting of patriotic values onto a love story, albeit one that manifests a greater resemblance to the *zhiguai* genre, is extremely rare. In view of the tumultuous nature of the Jurchen invasion, extant love stories of the period are surprisingly silent on the horrific events that must have psychologically scarred many survivors. On the contrary, they maintain a spirit of optimism. Reunion stories with happy endings were selected and recorded, while darker ones about death, rape, and permanent separation were largely ignored. Perhaps the dearth of such topics implies the extent of the trauma felt by those who suffered firsthand as they preferred to forget rather than relive the experience in literature. Nonetheless, in light of the growing value attached to female and widow chastity that began in the Southern Song, a significant number of anecdotes and short stories set during the chaos of the Song-Yuan and, later, the Yuan-Ming transition depict virtuous/patriotic widows who choose suicide instead of capitulation and sexual servitude to conquering aliens.

Suicide Pacts

As noted above, "Story of Distant Mist" is perhaps the earliest extant love story in which *both* protagonists die, besides the *zhiguai* accounts discussed above in which widowers' "infidelity" to deceased wives results in death. Such a tragic element vis-à-vis the love story was comparatively rare for the Song period. A handful of extant stories, however, focus on couples who carried out suicide pacts. Rather than detailed narratives in the *chuanqi* form, extant versions of these stories are all tersely related, probably summaries of what were originally much longer—possibly oral—narratives. The male protagonist is usually of indeterminate social status or else of liminal membership to the upper class, such as the wastrel son of an elite family. Female protagonists are invariably courtesans, singing girls, or prostitutes. Having fallen in love, external forces prevent the couple's elopement and, unable to bear separation, they commit suicide.

Hong Mai records an instance of double suicide titled "Miss Fu Jiulin" that supposedly occurred in 1174. The suicide was precipitated by the stringent vigilance of the woman's mother; even though the heroine was a musical courtesan, her mother exhibited considerable control over her daughter's sexuality.[26] Zhou Mi records a similar story titled "Master Wang and Miss Pei Both Hang Themselves" in which the couple drown themselves in West Lake.[27] Although Zhou's work was compiled in the mid–thirteenth century, the temporal setting is given as the late 1170's. The story could, therefore, be of twelfth-century origin. The (probably) mid- to late twelfth-century *New Stories from a Green Lattice Window* includes three stories of double suicide.[28] In two of these, titled "Master Yang Accompanies Xiunu on a Journey" and "The Love between Zhang Dao and Liang Chu," suicide is committed when the young men's families send letters urging their return. Both stories include poetry. In one poem, the composer hopes to reunite with his lover in his next incarnation. Dating is problematic for both stories as neither includes any internal date. Wei Chishu's (dates uncertain) *Nanchu xinwen* is cited as a source for one. As Wei supposedly lived during either the Tang or Five Dynasties, the story may be much earlier than the twelfth century, but this is far from certain.[29] In another item from the *New Stories*, the male reneges on his side of a suicide pact and eventually dissuades his lover from doing so.[30]

Stories of suicide pacts first appearing in both these twelfth-century collections, as well as Zhou Mi's thirteenth-century work, indicate the theme's continuity across these centuries. For the first time in the love story's history, double suicide emerges as an alternate—albeit tragic—resolution for obstacles that lovers faced. This idea developed into an extremely popular concluding device for love stories of late-imperial China as storytellers explored love's tragic dimensions.[31] To be sure, although numerous heroines died for their lovers, it had been hitherto rare for the *male* protagonist to die. If the death of male protagonists in later narrative works became increasingly popular, this trend may be traced to the Southern Song.

As extant stories do not address the couple's motives for committing suicide, we can only guess what they may have been. One of Luo Ye's narratives, however, includes a scene in which the protagonists contemplate suicide. The heroine is a young concubine of an aging bureaucrat. After having spent the night together at a temple, they are faced with permanent separation the following morning. When she declares her intention to commit suicide rather than return to her master, her young lover agrees to join her. The couple are, nevertheless, rescued by the timely intervention of an eavesdropping nun. Her speech is worth quoting verbatim as it reveals the couple's motive:

> "Once I bid you goodbye," said the woman, "it will be for all eternity. I'm held a solitary prisoner deep inside the inner courtyard and we won't be able to see each other again. All I can do is miss you and nurse my grievance . . . Oh, there is no life; there is only death . . . better to die for you. Don't forget the things I said today and I'll be grateful to you . . . in the underworld."
>
> As she finished speaking, her fragrant cheeks were awash with tears and her brows creased themselves into furrows.
>
> "I wouldn't have known that last night's pure bliss could turn into today's sweet sorrow," he said. "This may be your nature, but *I'm* not made of wood or clay. How could I bear to live without you? So that both of us need not endure separation's wretchedness, I'd rather die with you."
>
> "I'm glad you feel this way," said the woman. "Since we can't share the same bed in life, we may share the same grave in death."
>
> She then undid her girdle and tied it into a joined-heart knot. Fastening the other end to the rafter, she implored the young man to die with her."[32]

A nun intervenes at this point and suggests they elope. As the heroine remarks, the couple was unlikely to meet again. Hence, on the spur of the moment, they are so overcome emotionally that they cannot endure impending separation. The sexually frustrated concubine, unhappy with her restricted life serving an old man, instigates the idea. In light of the paragons surveyed above and in the previous chapter, however, she (and, through her, the male storyteller) may have viewed suicide as her only option to reclaim lapsed chastity. Similar to the adulterous Bu Feiyan, who died at her husband/master's hands, the concubine must redeem her fallen virtue through suicide. And the male, caught up in the moment, agrees to join her. Although this couple's decision is made on the spur of the moment, the couple who drowned themselves in Zhou Mi's account planned their suicide. What is innovative here is the male's willingness to die for his lover, rather than the old paradigm whereby it was invariably only the female who died.

It is unclear how contemporary readers would have reacted to stories of double suicide. Those sympathetic to the love story's romantic aspects may have considered the motif an indictment of an overly conservative society unwilling to accommodate romantic love. Alternatively, the possibility that their sons would die after having become entangled with prostitutes may well have been an anathema to moderate or conservative, upper-class fathers, not to mention the challenge male suicide posed to patriarchal control. In a commentary to "Fifth Brother Sun" (discussed below), the story of a young man who died of illness caused by unrequited love, Hong Mai cites the protagonist's death so as to warn his readers about the younger generation's lack of self-control. Hence stories concluding in suicide may well reflect, among other things, upper-class male anxiety. Moreover, suicide would have violated the Confucian idea of preserving the body given by one's parents and, therefore, undermines filial piety. It would also have violated the Buddhist idea about killing life. Furthermore, given the extremely negative value placed on death in Chinese societies even today, it is likely that these stories would have been read negatively.

Languishing and Dying Males

From examples previously surveyed, we have seen how heroines often grew ill or died due to unrequited love. Particularly prevalent in Tang-period stories, this motif frequently reoccurs in those of the Song. If the stories contain a shred of verisimilitude, such was the inordinate number of heroines who died for their lovers that graveyards in Tang and Song China must have overflowed with their corpses.

The idea that a woman's health could deteriorate due to romantic longing was thought to have a physiological basis. Song dynasty medical treatises posit that unregulated sexual impulses could cause irregularities of a woman's blood and thereby lead to illness. Xu Shuwei (1080–1154) appears to be the first to link women's sexual frustration and illness in his *Treatise on Ninety Manifestations of Cold Damage* (*Shanghan jiushi lun*). This stands in contrast to earlier medical works that simply conflated female sexuality with reproduction, such as Chu Cheng's *Chu Cheng's Posthumous Work* (late fifth century).[33] There is, however, no comparable theory in relation to male physiology. Despite this, a few extant Southern Song dynasty love stories portray male protagonists who fall ill due to unrequited love. Moreover, their illness significantly affects the plot. The only earlier example of this motif is found in the Northern Song story, "Wang Youyu." When the eponymous heroine and her lover must separate, she cuts a lock of her hair as a love token. Her lover, Liu Fu, "brooded that he cannot see her [Youyu's] face and so took to his bed. Worrying over him during the night, Youyu sent someone to nurse him. Once he recovered, he sent a long poem."[34] As this excerpt shows, the male protagonist quickly recovered and his brief illness had no bearing on the plot. It was rather the heroine's later fatal illness that brought it to a close. On the contrary, in Southern Song–period stories, the male's illness—or, in one instance, death—is integral to plot resolution. This new development reversed the well-established motif of the grief-stricken or dying heroine, although the "Wang Youyu" story suggests that its origin may lie in the eleventh century. As it became a frequently utilized plot device from the fourteenth century onward, the Southern Song–period examples surveyed below are significant milestones (see figure 3.1).

Set during the mid-thirteenth century, the eponymous protagonist of "Pan Yongzhong" was staying with his father in Lin'an while the latter awaited a provincial appointment. Pan was only sixteen (*sui*). He would often amuse himself by playing the flute beside his upper-story balcony. "In the building next door, separated by twenty or so yards, behind a damask-dressed window replete with a red blind and green curtains, a girl would listen to the sound of his flute, gazing at him through her lowered blind. As time passed, she would sometimes roll up her blind and expose [the lower] half of her face." This alluring description of the heroine's bedroom window and the female Gaze evokes a semi-erotic atmosphere while establishing an expectation of romance. Given the cramped living

182 | The Chinese Love Story from the Tenth to the Fourteenth Century

Figure 3.1. The female Gaze.

conditions suffered by residents of Lin'an, it is easy to imagine the pair occupying second- or third-story rooms facing each other over a crowded street below. Unusual for the love story, there is no description of the girl; this is displaced by the description of her sumptuous, silk-framed window. The reader must gauge her beauty from Pan's reaction when he saw her riding a sedan chair in the street. "The sedan's windows were all half open. Two pairs of eyes beheld each other at a distance of no more than one [Chinese] foot. Pan's soul took flight. It was as though something had been lost." That night, when he again plays his flute beneath bright moonlight, the girl rolls up her blind and leans on her balcony, thereby passively encouraging him in a manner not unlike other heroines. When Pan visits a friend of the girl's family the following day, he and the reader finally receive a verbal description, albeit terse, of her appearance and talent. "She is the master's grand-daughter. She studied under my father when she was young. She is exceedingly clever and her appearance is comely. She also writes poetry." The knowledge of her talent and wit coupled with beauty increases Pan's infatuation. As the pair grow more familiar, they exchange poems written on silk wrapped around a pecan (*hutao*) that they throw between their windows. When the pecan-wrapped poem misses its target and falls to the street below, the couple must rely on the assistance of a middle-aged female shopkeeper who found it. This woman subsequently assumes the role of a go-between. After the young man is obliged to follow his father to a provincial posting, his pining for the girl leads to illness.

> Pan suddenly became unhappy and the ensuing depression led to illness. His father had him treated yet, having consulted over ten different doctors, two months passed and he was still no better. He said to Peng, an upper-classman at the Imperial University, "I have come to the end of my road. My illness is not something that medicine and plaster will cure." He then told him the reason, adding, "She was the one I saw that day out on the outing." Peng told the father who remained worried.

At this juncture, the go-between arrives with news that the girl's mother has agreed to marry her daughter to Pan. "Since your lordship left, the girl has fallen ill and is on death's doorstep. Her mother was able to ascertain the cause having found a handkerchief in her pillow. She is now willing to marry her daughter to your son. What is your pleasure?" Pan's father finally consents and the narrative is brought to a happy conclusion. In a quasi–end commentary, we are told how the couple's poetry circulated throughout the capital and eventually reached the emperor's attention.[35]

Here, then, is a further indication of how love stories—and related poetry—may have circulated, perhaps even in the form of the aforementioned *benshi shi* genre.

When contrasted to the androcentric idea that women would fall ill over a man, the idea that males could pine after inaccessible women suggests a heightened importance of the female in and of herself. Rather than simply act as foils for male competition or mirrors with which to affirm male identity, from at least the late twelfth century, the story's temporal setting, women sometimes become an idyll worth falling ill for. This reaffirms the heightened concern for women in Song dynasty narratives, as previously noted, although women are still not accorded genuine narrative agency. Nonetheless, the shift away from purely androcentric issues redefines the premises of the culture of romance compared to the mid-Tang period.

Although the female's falling ill helps resolve the plot, greater emphasis is placed on the male's illness as events are consistently filtered from his point of view. The narration's terseness, particularly toward the conclusion, prevents us from understanding how sickness brought about a resolution. The reader must assume that the boy's illness induces his father to finally consent, as was the case with the girl's mother. The narrative does not directly articulate parental opposition on either side, although the secretive nature of the love affair and hints in the lover's exchanged poetry implies possible opposition. Given that twenty (*sui*) was considered the minimum marriageable age for a male, the boy's father likely considered him too young for marriage. As in other Song-period stories, both the young lovers' parents play a pivotal role as arbiters of the young couple's conjugal felicity.

Despite the story's terse form, two significant intertextual markers are conspicuous. First, the young man's flute playing is reminiscent of Sima Xiangru's zither playing and, to be sure, there is an allusion to Sima in one of the poems. Similarly, the girl's watching him from her balcony evokes how Zhuo Wenjun peeked at Sima while he was a guest in her father's house. Indeed, both the male and female Gaze play an important role in this story as the young couple use their gaze to convey mutual affection as a prelude to exchanging poetry. For contemporary readers, Pan's flute playing surely evoked the myth of Xiao Shi and Nongyu who eventually attained immortality by flying into the sky astride phoenixes. Xiao Shi was renowned for playing the pipes, while both he and Nongyu (daughter of King Mu of the state of Qin) were symbolic of a loving couple.[36] Along with the story of Sima Xiangru and Zhuo Wenjun, the myth of Xiao Shi and Nongyu were frequently cited in both love stories and poetry.

Related to the motif of lovesick men are a handful of twelfth-century stories in which males fall ill and actually die for their lovers; "Shen Zhenzhen Marries Zheng Huaigu," found in *New Stories from a Green Lattice Window*, is a good example. As with other items in *New Stories*, this one's succinct style precludes detail. The story features a well-known Tang dynasty scholar-official and cites Zhang Junfang's eleventh-century *Collected Love Stories* as a source, although it is not found in extant editions of *Collected Love Stories*. Whether the device of the dying male was included in Zhang's eleventh-century work or whether it represents a twelfth-century elaboration is therefore uncertain.

The story narrates events leading up to Zheng Huaigu's (fl. early ninth-century) death. Its plot follows the Tang-period prototype in which a social senior bestows a beautiful concubine on a protégé. In this case, Zheng's mentor, General Liu, gives him a beautiful concubine just prior to Zheng's accepting a bureaucratic appointment in Chang'an. In a display of power, Liu arrayed several concubines in his banquet hall. Noticing Zheng's attraction to one of them, Liu introduces her as Shen Zhenzhen and promises to give her to Zheng once the latter receives his new posting. He then prevails on Zheng to compose a poem as Zhenzhen's unofficial betrothal gift. Once Zheng arrives in Chang'an and receives his new position, as good as his word, Liu sends the concubine to him. When she arrives, she bows before him and he helps her rise. As he holds her hands, he inexplicably releases a sigh and dies.[37]

Two earlier versions of the text exhibit significantly different denouements. In an item titled "Zheng Huaigu" from *Extensive Records* (*Taiping guangji*, compiled in 998), Zheng often visits General Liu in the latter's sumptuous Luoyang mansion. During these visits, he is allowed contact with Liu's concubines, indicating the close social bond between mentor and protégé. Availing himself of such access, Zheng flirts with the concubines. They report his misconduct to Liu, who, pitying Zheng's poverty while admiring his talent, takes no action. During a farewell dinner that Liu throws for Zheng, who is about to *seek* a bureaucratic position in Chang'an (in the *New Stories*' version, Zheng is already a bureaucrat), Liu asks him to compose a poem as a compliment to an unnamed concubine. Liu is so pleased with the completed poem that he promises to send the concubine to Zheng once he attains a posting. He does so half a year later, when Zheng attained the position of erudite in the National

University. When the concubine stops at the Joyous-Auspicious Hostelry prior to reaching her final destination, news reaches her of Zheng's death. After this, Liu marries her to another. The *Extensive Record* cites *Mr. Lu's Miscellaneous Records* (*Lushi zashuo*), compiled by Lu Yan (739–99), as its source.[38] Another Tang-period version from *Tang Poems and Their Narrative Context* (*Tang shi jishi*) corroborates *Mr. Lu's* version.[39] The plot is very similar and it does not name the concubine. In the versions from *Mr. Lu's Records* and *Tang Poems*, Zheng was already dead before Zhenzhen could join him.

Therefore, unlike the *New Stories* version, Zheng's death in these earlier ones was unrelated to romance. This explains why the *Extensive Record*'s editors catalogued the story in a chapter focusing on "righteous conduct" (*qiyi*) rather than the "transformation through love" (*qinggan*) section where it may otherwise have been placed. Hence, to the tenth-century editors, this was a story extolling General's Liu's generosity in bestowing a concubine to a protégé. It is only in the hands of the *New Stories*' author-compiler, or his source, that Zheng's death is linked to romance. It is therefore reasonable to consider the motif of a dying male as a Southern Song invention, the likely period of the *New Stories* compilation. Furthermore, the heroine's name is likely a twelfth-century elaboration as earlier versions maintain her anonymity.

The *New Stories*' recorder makes no attempt to explain the reason for Zheng's sudden death. As a plot device, it certainly differs from Pan Yongzhong's illness as it does not overcome any obstacle to romantic bliss—quite the contrary. It is more reminiscent of how Ouyang Zhan died after receiving his deceased lover's *memento mori*. Yet Ouyang's heroine was portrayed as a *femme fatale* and predeceased him, whereas Zheng Huiagu's lover stood before his eyes. These inconsistencies are likely the result of an anecdote about righteous behavior having been recycled as a love story. Given the unfortunate lack of contemporary documentary evidence, further light cannot be thrown on this question. Indeed, the terseness of the *New Stories* account prevents detailed analysis.

Coincidentally, the *New Stories*' mysterious denouement coincides with other twelfth-century short stories and anecdotes in which males die just before their romantic desires are fulfilled. "The Nun from West Lake Convent," for example (mid- to late twelfth century), found in Hong Mai's *zhiguai* collection, tells of a wealthy young man who was infatuated with another's wife. Acting through a Buddhist nun as an intermediary, he eventually lures the woman to the nun's temple on the pretext of participating in a celebratory meal. There she is plied with so much wine as to necessitate her lying down. When she wakes, she is shocked to find the young man's corpse lying beside her. The narrative concludes with a trial after the youth's body was found concealed on the temple grounds. The storyteller explains the youth's demise as, "[t]he overly happy youth had probably been lying in the room, waiting. And, as soon as his wish had been fulfilled, he was ecstatic to the point that it killed him."[40] The prominent crime elements render the story marginal to the love story's prototypes, yet the motif of the dying male closely resembles that of Zheng Huaigu in *New Stories*. Here is further evidence suggesting that the motif is a Southern Song invention.

"Fifth Brother Sun" is a significant example of this motif as it more closely resembles a love story prototype. Recorded by Hong Mai during the twelfth century, it recounts the tragic story of Sun Yu, who fell in love with his cousin, Zhenzhen, on a visit to his uncle's house in Lin'an. Hong does not describe Sun's positive personal traits; he simply notes that he was eighteen or nineteen, somewhat young for marriage by contemporary standards. Similarly, the lovers' mutual attraction is tersely rendered; Hong simply tells us how "the two of them would gaze at each other and in their eyes was a promise of love and devotion." Shortly after Sun returned home, a matchmaker called and so his mother asked his preference. "Someone like Zhenzhen would do," he replied. When the mother approached her brother on the subject, he agreed providing that Sun could pass the provincial examination. Given his love of study, Sun set about his task enthusiastically yet, despite several attempts, he remained unsuccessful. After several years had elapsed, Zhenzhen's marriage could no longer be postponed and so she was betrothed to the son of a minor official. Sun, as may be imagined, grew greatly despondent at the news. A further meeting with Zhenzhen did not help matters.

> [Sun] Yu went to visit his elder brother Su in Lin'an, and so went to drink at his uncle's place. Zhenzhen took advantage of the occasion to speak with him. In tears, she said, "I have already been promised to another. What we had is now lost." Yu remained no longer and journeyed to the old family home in Kunshan (in modern Jiangsu). On the road he met his nephew, Ge, whom he invited to journey with him on the same boat. "Do I have what is commonly called love sickness (*xiangsi bing*)?" he asked his nephew. "I have been listless for some

time now and am losing my direction. My intestines hurt all over, like tiny pin-pricks. Surely I will die of this?"

After arriving home, Sun experiences a strange vision that he relates to his nephew. "Just then I had not fully fallen asleep when I heard someone calling 'Fifth Brother.' I looked and it was Zhenzhen. So I hurriedly climbed out of bed but there was nothing to be seen. What does this portend?" After ten days the cousin returned to Lin'an, where he attended Zhenzhen's wedding banquet. It was there that, miraculously, Zhenzhen saw Sun standing beside her. After this she became ill for about a month. It was later ascertained that "Sun was already sick by this time. He was thin and weak, and his bones had begun to protrude from his flesh. Accompanied by his mother, he went to consult a physician in Suzhou." It was during this consultation that Sun died after vomiting blood. He was, however, still alive at the time of Zhenzhen's wedding banquet. Hong Mai surmises that some or all of his souls may have prematurely left his body prior to his actual death.[41] Hong's comment about the story demonstrates his unsympathetic attitude in regard to young love: "The younger generation is prone to unbridled thoughts and they know nothing of good or bad. This was a particularly pernicious case and so I have recorded it as a warning."[42]

As Hong Mai included the story in his *zhiguai* collection, his interest evidently lay in the incident of astral travel, but he also wished to warn others about the dangers of uncontrolled and unsanctioned love between young people. Accordingly, his rendition suppresses prototypical love story elements as he foregrounds those of the paranormal. As the heroine's name coincides with that of Zhang Huaigu's lover, including its written form, one wonders if the story was retold or elaborated based on the Tang precursor.

The death of the male, as a plot device, is more significant than in Zheng Huaigu. Although the protagonist's death in the Tang story constitutes its central core, there is no apparent link between it and the romantic aspects. Zheng's sudden and unexpected death grants the story its impact. On the contrary, Sun Fu's death is due to unrequited love and develops gradually. It furthermore frustrates the love story's characteristic plot trajectory while engendering a tragic conclusion. Such a denouement certainly deprives male readers of any possible pleasure derived from seeing a languishing female die for love of a male. To be sure, contrary to the culture of romance, she marries another. More typical of the love story, it was Zhenzhen who should have grown ill while pining for her cousin. Her illness could have prompted her father to relent or, alternatively, could have resulted in her death in which case the conclusion might have taken one of several formulaic courses. Hong Mai's rendition as a *zhiguai* account renders it marginal to a love story prototype. Nonetheless, given the increased evocation of this motif in later literature, its emergence in the twelfth century is significant.

Before turning to other themes, one extremely famous instance of the dying male motif should be addressed: the legend of Liang Shanbo and Zhu Yingtai, mentioned in the introduction. According to popular (oral) tradition, these lovers died and, true to the *zhiguai* genre, transformed themselves into butterflies. Such was the legend's popularity during late-imperial times that it spawned numerous operas, songs, and prosimetric ballads. The earliest documentary evidence dates to the Song period, although one text cites a Tang dynasty source; hence the story might predate the Song. One of the Song commentators even argues that the protagonists were fourth-century personages. Unfortunately, as none of the Song-period sources provide a coherent narrative, we cannot be certain in what form it circulated during that time. The received version developed over several centuries, embellished by countless raconteurs and playwrights.

The purportedly "earliest" version of the story is found in *Records of the Heated Room* (*Xuanshi zhi*), compiled by Zhang Du (fl. ninth century).

> Yingtai was the daughter of the Zhu family in Shangyu. She disguised herself as a man in order to travel and study, and she devoted herself to her work together with a certain Liang Shanbo of Guiji. Shanbo's style name was Churen. Zhu returned home first, and only when, two years later, Shanbo paid her a visit did he realize that she was a girl. He was greatly disappointed as if he had lost something. He told his father and mother to ask for her hand, but she had already been promised in marriage to the son of the Ma family.
>
> Later Shanbo served as magistrate of Yin county. When he died of an illness, he was buried on the west side of the city of Yin. When Zhu was on her way to marry Ma, her boat passed by his grave. Wind and waves prohibited the boat from going on. When she learned that this was the location of

his grave, she left the boat and wept for him. The earth then suddenly split asunder and swallowed her. This was the way she was buried together with him.

The chancellor of the Jin, Xie An (320–385), reported this to the throne, which bestowed upon it the title "Grave of the Loyal Wife."[43]

Despite its purported ninth-century provenance, this account is found in an eighteenth-century compilation. Moreover, it does not appear in extant editions of *Records from a Heated Room*, nor is it included in the *Extensive Records*. Since the *Extensive Records* cites many items from the *Records from a Heated Room*, one would expect this story to have also been included. All this strongly suggests that the ninth-century attribution is a later fabrication. Since no document from the Song exists that would corroborate the narrative strands found above, the plot elements and themes conveyed in this version cannot be considered of authentic Song dynasty provenance.[44]

A twelfth-century excerpt from Zhang Jin's (ca. 1130–ca. 1180) *Maps and Facts of Siming in the Qiandao Reign* (*Qiandao Siming tujing*) alleges that Liang Shanbo and Zhu Yingtai studied together. Although it states that Liang did not realize Zhu was a woman (due to his "guileless simplicity"), it does not specify her "disguising" herself as a man. It does, however, mention a double grave honoring a loyal wife.[45] Why she would be honored in this way is unclear as she never married Liang according to the received tradition. The idea that a woman would die for an unwedded lover, nonetheless, corresponds to the eleventh-century courtesan, Aiai's, faithful demise. An excerpt from a regional gazetteer dated 1268 mentions the existence of a grave and an inscribed rock purportedly marking Zhu Yingtai's place of study. It refers to the legend of the butterflies as well as a local oral tradition that Zhu Yingtai was a woman. The author disputes this as he attempts to establish a historically factual basis for the story. Based on temple records, he contends that the Shanjuan Temple was built by Emperor Wu of the Southern Qi dynasty (r. 483–93) after having bought real estate that once belonged to Zhu Yingtai. He concludes that a woman was unlikely to have sold land for temple construction.[46] It seems that the legend's alleged pre-Tang provenance might be based on this account.

These excerpts confirm several key aspects of the Liang Shanbo and Zhu Yingtai legend, while the motif of the couple studying together corresponds to several love stories of the thirteenth and fourteenth centuries (e.g., see "Zhang Youqian," discussed below). Furthermore, if Liang Shanbo's death was caused by unrequited love, it would nicely fit with the stories discussed above. Unfortunately, lack of further detail prevents us from drawing conclusions. The idea that deceased souls could be transformed into butterflies dates to at least the late Tang dynasty[47] and was evoked in many Song-period stories. Hong Mai, for example, recorded a story titled "The Little Ghost Wife" (*Gui xiao niang*) in which a maid was possessed by the spirit of a deceased wife. Significantly, when mourners had gathered nearby the graveside following the burial, a butterfly was seen. Resembling a cicada, its prolonged flying around caused the husband to consider it the soul of his deceased wife. After this, the maid began to speak like and adopt the wife's mannerisms.[48] Therefore, the Liang and Zhu story might have been no more than an intriguing *zhiguai* account during the twelfth and thirteenth centuries. Since the literary theme of cross-dressing women was not consistently developed until the mid-Ming dynasty, this aspect of the Liang Shanbo and Zhu Yingtai story may be a Ming-era elaboration.

Cross-Dressing Males

Although cross-dressing as a literary theme was not consistently developed until the Ming dynasty, one of Luo Ye's stories tells about a young man who, at his parents' request, masqueraded as his sister and, consequently, attained a bride. If the twelfth- or thirteenth-century provenance of Luo Ye's *Drunken Man's Talk* can be trusted, the theme of cross-dressing males hence stems from the Southern Song period, mindful that the compilation may have been compiled during the Yuan dynasty. "They Become a Couple Thanks to Their Brother and Sister" tells of twin siblings from a weaver's family. The sister, Yanggu, was betrothed to a son of the Gao family. Gao's son happened to see Yanggu on a springtime outing. The sight enflamed him so much that he wished to marry her immediately (reminiscent of the protagonists of "Zhang Hao" and "Yingying's Story"), but he was refused due to her young age. He consequently grew ill. Thinking that marriage would cure him, his father requested that the ceremony be brought forward. Yanggu's father declined. He did, however, send his son, Yisun, dressed as a girl so as to console the lovesick groom-to-be. Yisun was warned not to "stay on as would a wife." During his sojourn with the Gao's, the disguised Yisun slept with the sick male's sister while waiting for the illness to subside. A month or so later, when his father recalled him, Yisun was "sorely reluctant to leave." When the matter was exposed, Gao wished to sue. " 'If you take the matter to court,' everyone told him, 'both parties are guilty. Better to have them marry.' " The story concludes with a short ditty observing how the brother received a wife thanks to his sister and vice versa.[49]

This somewhat brief account reads more like an anecdote and is, therefore, marginal to the prototypical love stories discussed in chapter 1. Luo Ye categorized it as a humorous story about women. To my knowledge, it is the only such story extant from the Song or Yuan period featuring a cross-dressing male. Secondary themes, such as lovesick males, focus on non-elite protagonists, and illicit sex mitigated by marriage, are consistent with other stories of the same period. Contemporary readers may furthermore have understood it as a story of conjugal predestiny given the extraordinary circumstances that led to marriage. The fact that a similar story was retold in several Ming-era collections attest to the motif's popularity hundreds of years later.[50] Why it does not appear in other anthologies of the Song or Yuan period, or why the theme was not exploited during this time, is unclear. Similar stories likely circulated, possibly in oral form, that are no longer extant.

Marital Predestiny Revisited

In chapter 2, I discussed how Northern Song stories, such as "Zhang Hao," often neutralized the dangers of illicit sex through marriage. Indeed, in Yanggu's story, related above, the storyteller offers explicit reasons for marrying erring couples. Several of Luo Ye's stories in his *Drunken Man's Talk* develop this theme while breaking new thematic ground. As mentioned earlier, marriage was considered to be premised on individual fate according to popular religious belief. This idea inspired many Tang dynasty stories about marriage, such as Wei Gu, who attempted to murder his predestined bride-to-be. Similarly, the characters in several of the *Drunken Man's* stories speak of marriages "made in Heaven," karmic affinity, or else remark how a chance meeting could not have been accidental, thereby implying the workings of fate. Although such ideas *per se* were nothing new, several of the *Drunken Man's* stories evoke the universal belief in conjugal predestiny to advocate freedom of choice in marriage and justify sexual intercourse. In the story of "Liang Yiniang," for example, the narrator speaks through the heroine's parents to excuse their daughter's fornication. As the introductory narrative was intended to frame several of the heroine's poems, it is comparatively brief and, as such, lacks detail or narrative flourish. Indeed, more so than a prototypical love story, it resembles the *benshi shi* genre. The story's inclusion in another anthology, *New Stories from a Green Lattice Window*, indicates its popularity throughout the late twelfth and thirteenth centuries.

Yiniang, the narrator tells us, was the educated daughter of a scholar-official's family. "At the age of fifteen she could compose both poetry and prose, besides which she possessed a graceful demeanor." Many had unsuccessfully proposed marriage, including the protagonist, Mr. Li, who was Yiniang's maternal cousin. Although Yiniang's mother rejected Li's suit for unspecified reasons, he and Yiniang thereafter developed a mutual attraction. This was consummated one day while Yiniang's parents were, coincidentally, attending a family wedding. "As they had long since conveyed their mutual desire on a regular basis, from henceforth they truly became *a match made in Heaven*." Their unguarded looks led to discovery, after which they were separated for a year. During this time, Yiniang wrote several poems and letters reproduced by the storyteller. Her parents eventually allowed the couple to marry. Their reasoning is explained in a brief but important monologue:

> When heaven and earth coalesced, everything in the natural world was born; when man and the Way are matched, merit is thereby perfected. That men and women should live together is but a basic human desire. Destroying their love (*en'ai*) because they committed an impropriety isn't as good as allowing them to marry. This would stifle idle gossip. And, such being the case, only he who bends to the will of heaven will survive. Furthermore, did not the Liu's and the Fan's intermarry for generations, as well as the Zhu's and the Chen's, not to mention the royal houses of Qin and Jin? Is it therefore not improper for us?[51]

Evoking the authority of the Confucian tradition, this brief speech embodies considerable authorial commentary. First, the line about basic human desire is derived from the *Book of Mencius* which, as already noted, became a core Confucian text especially revered by Zhu Xi and his followers.[52] The preceding lines are derived from *Exemplary Sayings of Master Yang* (*Yangzi fayan*), another Confucian classic completed around

9 CE by the famous Confucian thinker Yang Xiong.[53] Hence, the revered Confucian tradition is evoked to help naturalize sexual desire and, to be sure, its physical expression. Second, the parents consider practicality; marriage will salvage their initial misdemeanor while, at the same time, stifle gossip. We have seen this in other stories. Third, several historical precedents are cited. As I have already mentioned, the royal houses of Qin and Jin during the Warring States period had, by the Song era, become a by-word for interfamilial marriage, which was by no means uncommon. The mention of the Zhus and the Chens alludes to a Tang dynasty poem by Bai Juyi about multiple marriages between two villages, while the allusion to the Lius and the Fans points to the Confucian historical classic, the *Zuozhuan*.[54] These three references appeal to the authority of tradition vis-à-vis interfamilial marriage. Perhaps, then, the cousins' kinship was the reason for the mother's initial objection, although this was not unusual for the period. Given the reverence reserved for the Confucian classics as well as history in general throughout the imperial period, the parents' monologue articulates a powerful justification for illicit sex and human desire.

When the narrator tells of the couple's sexual encounter, he remarks how from that time on they became "like a match made in Heaven." This clearly alludes to conjugal predestiny. What is innovative, compared to earlier stories, is its correlation with sexual intercourse; that is, when sanctioned by destiny, illicit sex betokens an informal engagement or marriage that may be later ratified by orthodox Confucian ritual. Hence both the freely chosen marriage and the illicit sex that precedes it are both justified according to the widely held belief in conjugal predestiny. The author-compiler seems to ask: if marriage is predestined, then what does it matter if a couple agrees to marry with neither go-betweens nor parental consent, even if premarital sex is involved? Although this remains a strategy to apologize for and neutralize the subversive nature of premarital sex, it goes a step further than previous stories by evoking revered folkloristic tenets that, in other contexts, reconciled young couples to the necessity of arranged marriages. In other words, what was a tool to support an orthodox patriarchal institution is utilized to circumvent that institution in the interests of conjugal free choice. This idea must have been no less subversive to conservative-minded contemporaries as it must have been scandalous. It would certainly have been a serious affront to traditional Confucian mores, particularly when we consider that arranged marriage was the norm up to and including the early twentieth century.

By this we may appreciate the idea's groundbreaking magnitude and the storytellers' "emancipated" worldview. Evoking marital predestiny to justify illicit sex, in this manner, is a consistently reoccurring theme throughout the *Drunken Man's Talk*.

Another of Luo Ye's narratives develops this idea yet, unlike Yiniang's story, its protagonists refrain from illicit sex. "Miss Zhang Elopes with Star Brother at Night" is a story of two eponymous lovers, both children of scholar-official families, whose names allude to the myth of the Oxherd and the Weaver Maid discussed in the introduction. Star Brother's mother, Jade (Qiongniang), had married Weaver Maid's father. Hence the young protagonists were first cousins. Moreover, they were born at the same time of the same day with the boy being slightly older. Their mothers betrothed their children before birth: "Since we are close relatives and no barrier divides our mutual affection, should we give birth to a boy and a girl, let's pledge them in marriage so as to enhance our good will." Jade reaffirmed their intention as the children grew older. Indeed, she often had the pair sit together during family festivities, remarking how they were "a match made in Heaven!" The pair welcomed this attention and they "exchanged marriage vows with their eyes and embraced each other in spirit." At the age of six they attended school together. Star Brother eventually went to live with the Zhang's, not unlike an uxorilocal son-in-law. When the pair were sixteen (*sui*), prime marriageable age for the girl albeit a little young for the boy, their grandfather journeyed to the dynastic capital to receive a new civil service posting. During this time, he was approached by a matchmaker acting on behalf of a powerful government minister who proposed marriage between Weaver Maid and the minister's son. In awe of the minister's political influence, the grandfather readily agreed. This news devastated the lovers. A despondent Star Brother was about to relinquish his hopes when Weaver Maid promised to elope.

> That night, once people had settled and all was quiet, he had just retired when suddenly he heard the sound of footsteps in the western gallery. A short while later brought a tiny knock at the door. Remembering Qingluan's (Weaver Maid's servant) promise, he rose to open the door and indeed saw that Weaver Maid had arrived, supported by Qingluan. They entered and at once Weaver Maid bade him close the door.
>
> "Since our parents promised me to you before we were born," she said in a low, trembling voice, "I've looked forward

to when I would serve you as a wife. The love between us is eternally enduring. Even though our bodies die and our bones decay, it cannot wash away this promise. Now that my grandfather is a thousand miles away, he wishes to renounce his intention and pledge me to another. Therefore I've come to you. I'm prepared to elope with you this night so as to fulfill the happiness of a hundred years."

They left home that night and hired a boat to Sichuan, where they married and settled down. En route, however, Star Brother "sought the pleasure that [only] married couples enjoy." Weaver Maid's response was scathing: "Women," she retorted, "invariably hold themselves chaste. I'm eloping with you this day not for lust but for righteousness. How could I face the world were I to lose my righteousness for lust? Such matters should wait until after we've settled into a home, selected an auspicious day and completed our nuptials. The feeling between a husband and wife should be one of mutual respect. This is what I would expect from a gentleman." Once settled in Sichuan, however, the powerful minister heard of their elopement and, having traced their whereabouts, prosecuted them. In a *gong'an*-type (legal case) conclusion, the judge sides with the young couple, thereby bringing the narrative to a happy conclusion. The couple's legal depositions are also included. These documents allow an intimate understanding of the protagonists' psychology while recounting events from different viewpoints.[55]

Similar to other Song dynasty stories we have seen, this one harmonizes arranged marriage with conjugal free choice. Predestiny is foregrounded as the couple successfully marry despite considerable obstacles. In this respect, it is reminiscent of Wei Gu's story in "Inn of Betrothal." Of equal importance is honoring betrothal agreements. And, since this coincides with their mothers' wish, the lovers are simultaneously fulfilling their filial duty to obey their parents.

The mother's verbal agreement was, nevertheless, informal. The exchange of betrothal gifts, a crucial ritual among the six matrimonial rites, did not occur, nor was any written contract drafted.[56] Moreover, no matchmaker was engaged. Since the role of matchmaker had been enshrined in Confucian classics dating back to the ancient *Rites of Zhou* (*Zhouli*), their involvement in wedding arrangements was considered another crucial part of the marriage ritual.[57] Despite such irregularities, the storyteller endorses the mother's informal arrangement over the formal one made for sociopolitical reasons by the family patriarch. This valorizes the spirit of Confucian ritual over its form. Nonetheless, in order to uphold their mothers' wish and fulfill their destinies, the young couple must defy social norms, patriarchal authority, expose themselves to gossip and, by their elopement, engage in a morally questionable undertaking that was also construed as a criminal act—that is, engaging in illicit sex without a marriage ceremony arranged by a matchmaker.

These crimes and misdemeanors are largely condoned by evoking belief in marital predestiny. Several strong hints, given at the narrative's outset, are nicely summarized in the protagonists' legal depositions. Weaver maid submits:

> Ever since my mother and aunt conceived Star Brother and myself, with one heart and mind did they promise us in matrimony for the second generation in our family. Heaven's mind silently assented to human minds and the boy was actually born before the girl. Star Brother and Weaver Maid: how could these names have been chosen randomly? Henceforth between the Lü's and the Zhang's, a marriage of their second generation was ordained. . . . Although our two families had not exchanged betrothal gifts, there was the expectation that we were sure to become man and wife.

As she points out, their names evoke the longstanding legend of the Oxherd and the Weaver Maid, indicating both their mothers' verbal betrothal and the expectation that they would marry. Contemporary readers would have viewed the close timing of their births as further evidence of predestiny. Their parents' interfamilial marriage and the mothers' intention to repeat it further affirm the workings of fate. In the words of Star Brother's deposition, "Respectfully I submit it is not a lie that our two families were close-knit and that our mothers betrothed us while pointing to their newly conceived wombs, as a couple destined from before birth to enjoy a long and happy life together." He also argues that the coincidence of their gender betokens predestiny, especially since he was born before Weaver Maid: "When the hour of our birth arrived, indeed there was a boy and a girl. And, since no great time had elapsed between our births, we were of the same age. Thanks to Heaven's gifts and the oath takers' firmness . . ." He furthermore reiterates the general expectation that they would marry: "During our childhood, people would point out what a handsome couple we would later make and, before we had shed our swaddling clothes, everyone looked forward to the day we would join in happy matrimony." This recalls his mother, Jade's remark about how the pair was "a match made in Heaven."

Having weighed the evidence, the magistrate agrees with the couple:

> According to the testimony, prior to the man and woman's having been born, their aunts and uncles concluded a matrimonial agreement. When vows are honored, one's dependability may be commended. Although people in the past have found it necessary to wait for the completion of a ceremony before taking a wife, there have been those among the ancients who did so without proclamation. Star Brother and Weaver Maid are as though long married. The right honorable Commissioner for Military Affairs must seek a new spouse and relinquish . . .

His assertion that those among the ancients married without go-betweens likely refers to the legend of the sage-king Shun to whom the legendary King Yao married his two daughters. The magistrate's granting priority to the earlier betrothal echoes other stories, such as "Zhang Hao," and makes explicit the importance placed on the integrity of marriage agreements.

In contrast to Li Yiniang's story, no illicit sex is portrayed. On the contrary, it is repudiated through Weaver Maid's monologue on the night of their elopement. The couple presumably refrain from sexual intercourse until they undergo a marriage ceremony on an auspicious day chosen by a diviner, although this is left for readers to surmise given the storyteller's avoidance of references to illicit sex. All this certainly helps the lovers at the trial. As we have seen in other stories from both sides of the Northern and Southern Song divide, expunging overtly immoral elements may well reflect the growing influence of Neo-Confucian thought. The storyteller's impeccably correct stance vis-à-vis orthodox morality renders it, therefore, a "chaste" love story long before the advent of chaste scholar-beauty romances during the Ming and Qing dynasties.

Evoking destiny to justify both marital free choice and illicit sex may be found in several other works of both Southern Song and Yuan dynasty provenance. *New Stories from a Green Lattice Window* contains many, although the *New Stories*' terse style seldom specifies fatalistic elements, which require the reader's own judgment. A particularly valuable example, titled "Zhang Youqian," is found in *Recorded Stories from a Green*

Lattice Window (*Lüchuang jishi*). Although *Recorded Stories* was likely compiled in the fourteenth century, the story itself purportedly occurred during the 1250s and exhibits several themes typical of Song dynasty love stories; hence I tentatively consider it of thirteenth-century origin. Even if its fourteenth-century recorder-compiler added later embellishments, its illustration of the conjugal predestiny theme renders it worthy of attention, mindful of its possible later provenance.

It is a story of neighbors, the Zhangs and the Luos. The Zhangs' son is called Youqian, while the Luos' daughter is named Xixi. Their shared birthday, sometime between 1234 and 1236, foreshadows a story of marital predestiny. The head of the Zhang household, Zhang Zhongfu, is an impoverished scholar-official, while "newly rich" (*quxing er fu*) Luo Renqing is probably of the merchant class. As a child, Miss Luo is sent to study at the Zhang household, where unidentified "people" (classmates?) tease her and Youqian with a folk belief that, "People born on the same day will become husband and wife." Both children, however, welcome this idea and, unbeknownst to their parents, secretly devise a contract to its effect. On reaching puberty, they engage in sex beneath a pomegranate tree.[58] The following year, Miss Luo ceases her studies, while Zhang Youqian accompanies his father to stay with the prefect of Yue prefecture. After his return, Miss Luo gives him ten gold coins and a "pill of longing" (*xiangsi zi*, possibly a kidney bean) as love tokens. "He once tossed the coins in a game. His mother saw him and when she asked about it, he replied, 'I received them from Miss Luo.' The mother guessed what was on his mind. She then sent a local woman to propose marriage." Luo's father, however, initially refuses in view of the Zhangs' relative poverty, but then agrees providing the young protagonist passes the imperial examinations and becomes an official. Two years elapse as Zhang once again accompanies his father to wait on the prefect of Yue. Unfortunately, by the time he returns, Miss Luo has been betrothed to the son of a wealthy family surnamed Xin. Zhang was "greatly despondent" at the news. He then sends a local woman with a lyric poem accusing Miss Luo of infidelity to their mutual vow. She retorts, "Accepting the betrothal gifts was my parents' idea. If only I could see you! I'd rather die with you than live forever with someone else." She then arranges for Zhang to scale the wall separating their two households with the help of a ladder and a camellia tree, after which they continue to meet clandestinely. Lamps are used as a signal: one for "no" and three for "yes." A month later, Zhang is again compelled to follow his father, this time to Hubei. Typical of a love story, tearful leave-taking ensues during which Miss Luo gives him gold and a brocade as parting gifts. She tells him, "I hope that I will not be married soon so that, by the time you return from the north, we can meet again. Otherwise you may look for me at the bottom of a well. We then must fulfill our destiny in the next lifetime." During his time in Hubei, Zhang undertakes a provincial examination and returns shortly before Miss Luo's marriage. She promptly sends a go-between with a request to meet along with a lyric poem about "conjugal destiny" (*yinyuan*). When Zhang comes to her, she says,

> "We're lucky to have this meeting! It's a shame you had to go to Hubei and didn't come back earlier. From now on we must see each other every night, as there is only two months [left before I am to be married]. If I can [during this time,] fully enjoy myself with you, I could die with no regrets. You're young, you're talented and handsome. You've a bright future ahead. I dare not be like those common people (*shisu ernü*) and ask you to die with me." They faced each other, in tears . . . From then on, there was not a night on which he did not come to her.

At this point, the Luos catch them, presumably *en flagrante*, and have Zhang arrested. Miss Luo unsuccessfully attempts suicide by throwing herself into a well. Zhang confesses to the magistrate who, admiring the young man's talent, wishes to release him. The Xins, however, are unwilling to let matters rest. Zhang's mother informs his father who attempts to secure his son's release. Precisely at that juncture, young Zhang is announced as valedictorian in the recent examination. On the strength of this, the magistrate is able to resolve the case in his favor. To be sure, as a successful candidate, Zhang has partially fulfilled Luo's condition that he pass the examinations and become a bureaucrat (he passes the metropolitan round the following year). So as to demonstrate the lovers' predestined good fortune, the story tells of how Zhang eventually attained a directorship and how he and his wife "grew old together."[59]

This story exhibits a number of important themes already discussed. Conjugal freedom of choice is again celebrated and illicit sex is integral to plot development. Not only does it go unpunished, the narrator's tone is decidedly sympathetic. Furthermore, the criminality and immorality associated with it are salvaged both by Zhang's scholastic success and the lovers' subsequent marriage. In the words of Feng Menglong's commentary, "a scandalous business, contrary to expectation, becomes a beautiful yarn."[60]

Strong hints point to marital predestiny. As in the story of Star Brother and Weaver Maid, Miss Luo and Zhang Youqian are born on the same day. The storyteller specifically draws attention to the fatalistic import of this when he mentions the children's teasing. Also similar to Star Brother and Weaver Maid is their studying in school together. This is a common motif that first emerged during the Southern Song period and, in this context, reinforces the destiny theme. The written agreement drawn up by the lovers as children, while not legally binding, establishes an informal engagement predating that of the Xins. We also saw this in "Zhang Hao," whose heroine defeated a rival betrothal by claiming a prior engagement, albeit without written agreement. Furthermore, Miss Luo expresses her wish to fulfill conjugal predestiny in the next lifetime, premised on the Buddhist idea of reincarnation. Hence, as with Luo Ye's stories discussed above, widespread belief in marital destiny is evoked to justify both illicit sex and marital self-determination.

As previously mentioned, the blending of love story and *gong'an* prototypes is an increasingly common feature of Southern Song love stories, a trend that would intensify throughout the Ming dynasty. Zhang Youqian, more so than the average protagonist, faced the seemingly insurmountable problem of (1) being charged with consensual illicit sex, and (2) his lover's imminent marriage to a rival. Fortunately during his trial, "the magistrate empathized with him on account of his [literary] talent. He wished to forgive his crime, but the Xins commanded enormous wealth and were determined to carry their point." Nevertheless, Zhang's having escaped scot-free may have surprised contemporary readers. Little wonder, therefore, that the storyteller carefully explains the machinations behind his release. Once official notification of Zhang's examination success arrived, the magistrate released him. This prompted Xin to appeal to the prefecture. Yet the sympathetic prefect persuaded Xin to relinquish his suit: " 'Miss Luo is not a virtuous girl. Of all the beautiful girls in the world, why should you wish to have her?' He [the magistrate] bade Mr. Luo return the bride price to Xin, who then dropped the case. He then ordered the clerks to draw up a divorce document on Xin's behalf. This was circulated throughout the prefecture, after which the bride price was returned. He then secretly wrote to the magistrate directing him to resolve Zhang's matrimonial entanglement."[61] The magistrate subsequently persuaded

Luo Renqing to accept Zhang as a son-in-law. The sympathetic prefect and magistrate, with perhaps the help of Zhang Zhongfu's string-pulling, exerted themselves to assist our young protagonist. Had the strict letter of the law been enforced, both Zhang and Miss Luo would have been liable for one and a half years' hard labor for engaging in illicit sex. Luo would have faced further penalties for breaking the betrothal agreement. Nonetheless, this aspect of judicial proceedings is perhaps not as incredible as may first appear. Based on numerous legal rulings recorded in *Enlightened Judgements*, McKnight and Liu note how thirteenth-century magistrates exercised considerable leeway, often applying the spirit rather than the letter of the law as they attempted to reach a consensus between litigants.[62] Zhang's having passed the prefectural round of examinations evidently helped his case, although only candidates who qualified for bureaucratic rank by passing the metropolitan round could have expected judicial privileges, such as reduction of punishment.

Miss Luo's attempted suicide is reminiscent of Miss Li in "Zhang Hao." Although the narrator does not explain her reasons or the aftermath of her action, it is reasonable to assume that she was reserving her sexual favor for one "husband," thereby salvaging lost chastity. While she is not hailed as a paragon as in other stories, her attempted suicide conforms to orthodox morality and largely redeems her character in regard to prevailing social expectations, even though the prefect feels obliged to describe her as "not virtuous." Her initial suggestion of a suicide pact is also significant. As noted above, this is first broached in the letter she sends to Zhang soon after her betrothal to Xin: "I'd rather die with you than live forever with someone else." Her subsequent change of heart is articulated in a speech to Zhang just prior to their discovery: "I wouldn't dare to be like those common couples and ask you to die with me" (*bugan yi shisu ernü tai, yao jun ju si ye*). Her word choice of "common couples" (*shisu ernü*) corresponds with that of Luo Ye's aforementioned heroine and presumably alludes to such suicide pacts as previously discussed. Nevertheless, based on extant sources, such stories invariably featured a woman of lower-class background. Had Miss Luo and Zhang fulfilled such a pact, they would have been the first upper-class lovers to do so, hence her reference to class: *common* couples. Nonetheless, as I will discuss in the following chapter, tragic denouements featuring the death of upper-class lovers became an extremely popular feature of Yuan dynasty love stories. This story's near-tragedy appears to anticipate this later trend.

The interclass aspects of the characters' social backgrounds also contribute to the social mobility theme discussed in chapter 2. The Zhangs were members of the Song ruling elite by dint of their scholar-official status. Yet, as previously discussed, not every member of such families need have been serving officials and, as competition for scarce civil-service positions intensified, it became increasingly difficult for all educated men to serve. Even when a bureaucratic posting *was* obtained, it may not necessarily have been generously compensated. In this story, the Zhangs were not considered financially well-off despite their elite status. From Luo's perspective, this made them undesirable in-laws, notwithstanding the prestige he would have gained through a matrimonial alliance to a family of the educated elite. This affords a glimpse into the complexity and fluidity of social boundaries during the period; nominal membership to the upper classes was tempered by financial considerations in a burgeoning protocapitalist economy. Luo's insistence that the young Zhang pass the examinations and become a bureaucrat points to the importance placed on this ideal even at a time when the chances of doing so were diminishing. That Miss Luo's father, not a member of the educated upper class, would value examination success furthermore indicates the widespread prestige commanded by the imperial examinations.

More so than other Song period–stories discussed, androcentric values articulated within the narrative are comparatively prominent. Most noticeable is how the bureaucratic establishment unites to assist the beleaguered young protagonist. This is reminiscent of the help received by the Tang dynasty protagonist, Han Hong, to recover his abducted concubine, Miss Liu. Unlike the Tang story in which mostly military officers perform martial feats to rescue the languishing heroine and petition the court to shield the lovers from subsequent retaliation, here cultured men of letters and power-wielding bureaucrats effect the protagonist's release from prison while paving the way for him to marry his predestined life-partner. These scholar-officials, the magistrate, and the protagonist's parents replace the senior male figure, prominent in Tang-era stories, as arbiter of the lover's felicity. Besides class solidarity, their willingness to help largely stems from admiration of the protagonist's poetic talent. Hence, Zhang's successful marriage to Miss Luo may partly be understood in light of the woman-as-reward theme developed during the Tang period. Furthermore, the fact that Zhang's mother initiated the marriage proposal—albeit unsuccessfully—illustrates Patricia Ebrey's observation about the active role of mothers in arranging their children's marriages.[63]

In erotic triangles of Tang-era stories, the rival male is typically visible. On the contrary, here the protagonist's rival, Xin, remains a shadowy figure. His suit simply presents another obstacle that the lovers must surmount. Moreover, focus on the story's romantic aspects diminish the importance of the erotic triangle. Not only is a large portion of the plot devoted to clandestine meetings, illicit sex, and lovers' dialogue, several exchanges of love poetry solicit the reader's sympathy for the lovers while creating a romantic mood. The socioeconomic considerations of interclass marriage and the marital predestiny theme attract the main narrative focus.

A comparison of the above three stories with those from the Northern Song that condoned illicit sex—"Story of Twin Peaches," "Zhang Hao," and "Four-Fold Blended Incense"—reveals notable thematic similarities. The first two valorize the sanctity of marriage. "Story of Twin Peaches" is the most moralistically orthodox, as its heroine redeemed her lost chastity through suicide. The heroine of "Zhang Hao" attempts suicide for the same reason, although the subversive nature of illicit sex is ultimately effaced through marriage. "Four-Fold Blended Incense" is highly unusual as no attempt is made to apologize or atone for illicit sex. On the contrary, although these three Southern Song stories—"Liang Yiniang," "Miss Zhang Elopes with Star Brother at Night," and "Zhang Youqian—negate the subversive nature of illicit sex through marriage, they also evoke conjugal destiny to sanctify the former while endorsing matrimonial freedom of choice. The combination of these ideas as an apologetic strategy was highly innovative for the period. Such was its influence that love stories of the Yuan and Ming dynasties would frequently return to it.

Seafaring Stories

Since at least the Tang dynasty, maritime trade routes had existed between China and the outside world, notably via Arab traders. Together with commerce in general, maritime trade expanded exponentially throughout the Song period. The imperial Court increasingly relied on taxes generated by trade in order to replace diminished revenue after the Jurchen conquest of the central plains and fund its reparations according to the terms of the peace treaty. Thanks to monopolies on specialized items, such as tea and salt, the Court's revenue soon surpassed that of the Northern Song. Southern ports, such as Wenzhou and Quanzhou, rapidly developed into thriving commercial hubs crucial to the trade links between the Song Empire and her southeast Asian neighbors. Given the growing importance of maritime trade throughout this period, a considerable number of extant accounts, anecdotes and short stories tell of sea-going merchants who are sometimes marooned in unknown lands. This motif is not found in earlier love stories.

Although seafaring stories were largely unconnected to the love story's prototypes, two recorded by Hong Mai adapt established themes and plot devices to narrate an affair between a marooned mariner and an "island woman" of unspecified ethnicity. These accounts are almost certainly different versions of the same story given their common plots, slight variations notwithstanding, and Hong Mai himself notes their similarity. They were first published in 1161 and 1194, respectively.[64] The earlier one was told by a Quanzhou monk who claimed that his cousin was its protagonist, while the latter's source is unclear. The earlier one tells of a merchant who embarked from the port of Quanzhou on a voyage to Srivijaya, an ancient Sumatran kingdom. The merchant was the only survivor when the ship sunk. Saved by flotsam, he eventually drifted to an island inhabited by a single woman who sheltered him in her cave-home, feeding him and granting him sexual favors. Initially she was unwilling for him to wander freely. In the earlier version, she blocks the entrance with a large stone, while in the latter she simply cautions him not to come and go at will. During this time, the pair have children. He fathers three children with her in the earlier version, and one in the latter. The story approaches its climax when, one day, while walking near the shore, he saw a boat moored below a rocky outcrop. The boat was from Quanzhou and on it were people he knew. The two versions offer significantly different denouements. In the latter, when the merchant saw the Quanzhou boat, he, "rushed back to the cave, took hold of his son and carried him straight to the boat. The woman followed. Realizing that he could not return, she called his name, cursing him. She wailed pitifully before falling to the ground as though her breath would fail her. Beneath the sail, Wang raised his hands in thanks as he, also, wiped away his tears." In the earlier version, her reaction is markedly different. "The woman rushed over, calling out passionately. Realizing that he could not return, she fetched their three children and slaughtered them before his eyes."[65]

It is not difficult to see how a story such as this drew from both the plot and stock characters of a prototypical Tang love story. The cultural center has been replaced with an unknown periphery beyond the sea. Instead of an educated young gentleman, a young merchant acts as protagonist. The courtesan has been replaced by a south sea island woman whom the storyteller's writing brush has rendered exotic. In both versions the reader is told that she wears "not a stitch of clothing." In the earlier version, the merchant could not understand her language yet, in the latter, he unbelievably not only understands but converses with her. Although the earlier version does not depict the woman beyond her nakedness, the other describes her as exquisite and lovely (*xiumei*) with unbound hair extending to the ground. Long hair was a common cliché used to describe beautiful women in both Tang- and Song-period stories. In Hong's account, therefore, Han Chinese feminine beauty is mapped onto that of ethnic Others. Nevertheless, such hyperbolic description—"not a stitch of clothing"—begs belief and is clearly a construction of the storyteller's imagination. While until recent times it was customary for indigenous southeast Asian jungle-dwelling women to appear bare-breasted, it is highly unlikely they would have been completely naked. Similarly, it would have been unlikely that such women would not have tied their hair during the day. That she alone inhabits the island and promptly gives herself to the merchant sexually is clearly a male Chinese fantasy about the ready availability of indigenous women and the civilized storyteller's ability to possess them, just as urban courtesans were sexually and emotionally available to educated, upper-class protagonists.

In the love story's typical plot, as we have seen, it is usual for public business to intrude into the lovers' private space. In this story, the private world is shattered by the arrival of a boat from the civilized center. Moreover, onboard are males of the protagonist's acquaintance. In the face of public recognition, the male is virtually compelled to leave his exotic lover. Accordingly, the superiority of civilized Chinese culture exerts irresistible power over its members.

Hong Mai's fascinating yarn demonstrates how the love story could be adapted to accommodate new motifs and settings. The sea-faring story did not, however, spawn a sub-branch of the love story. And the combination of the love story and seafaring prototypes was not unique to the Southern Song period. A Northern Song story from Liu Fu's *High-Minded Conversations* titled "Wang Xie" (late eleventh century) tells of a Tang dynasty traveler who reached a country known as the Kingdom of Black Apparel (*Wuyi guo*; *wu* also denotes "crow") after having been shipwrecked.[66] The story largely follows an animal-bride prototype common in the *zhiguai* genre as the male protagonist marries a girl who eventually proves to be a were-bird—that is, one who could change shape between a human and a bird. Given the marriage and the freely chosen love affair, the romantic elements are strong. As with Hong Mai's protagonist, so too does this story's young male return to the Middle Kingdom, this time by means of superhuman magic.

Themes and trends found in Northern Song love stories continued into the Southern Song. Anxiety over social mobility and moral orthodoxy are particularly noticeable, while heightened focus on non-elite protagonists assumed greater prominence. Marital predestiny, cross-dressing, along with lovelorn males, themes that would receive considerable attention in later periods, were first developed by Southern Song storytellers. The theme of lovesick males marks a significant departure from that of the languishing female that appeared often in earlier stories. That a male would grow ill for unrequited love indicates a heightened respect for women. It also complements anecdotal narratives of the period that focused on a female paragon, regardless of her social status. Likewise, the morally orthodox ideal of mutual marital fidelity, whereby both husband and wife should remain faithful to each other, is first discernable in love stories of the period. It was ideas such as these that extended the culture of romance far beyond the parameters laid down by pioneering author-recorders of the Tang era.

Chapter 4

The Yuan Dynasty (1279–1368)

The Mongol conquest and consequent reunification of China ushered in unparalleled social change. The imposition of power, achieved by military might, was brutal. Invading armies, using terror as a means to encourage prompt surrender, sometimes massacred entire cities that resisted. Numerous Chinese bureaucrats, loyal to the fallen dynasty, refused to collaborate with the invaders who, in their eyes, were culturally inferior. Many chose retirement from public life as an honorable alternative. Others committed suicide. Indeed, numerous historical records attest to widespread suicide as the Mongols completed their conquest of Song territory. Some did so in family groups, reminiscent of the mass suicides by Okinawan civilians as the islands fell to American forces toward the close of World War II.[1]

The Mongol conquest, ironically, achieved what the military-weak Southern Song Empire failed to do: reunite China's central plains with the fertile south. Moreover, for the first time in Chinese history, traditional Chinese territories were politically united with the western steppe regions in a vast pan-Asian empire. Consequently, ethnic Chinese men of letters could freely travel to hitherto inaccessible areas and learn about customs they may have only read or heard about, notably the central plains that were under Jurchen control for much of the twelfth and thirteenth centuries. Demographically, the conquest created an unprecedentedly pluralistic society given a multicultural influx of the Mongols and their allies. Interethnic marriage between indigenous Chinese and other ethnicities was not uncommon. The fourteenth-century diarist Kong Qi (c. 1315–late fourteenth c.), for example, speaks of his Uighur sister-in-law who ruffled his conservative family's feathers by her pleasure-seeking predilections.[2]

Despite the multiculturalism engendered by the Mongol rulers, society was far from equitable. During and following the conquest, the Kublai khan (1215–1294) appointed military commanders, administrators, and advisors from ethnically diverse backgrounds that included Uighurs, Tanguts, and Tibetans, as well as Mongolians. Appointment of lesser functionaries were based on recommendation. A quota limited ethnic Chinese to no more than one-third of bureaucratic positions. At the same time, Kublai suspended the time-honored examination system as a means of bureaucratic recruitment. Consequently, the majority of indigenous Chinese found themselves disenfranchised from the central administration, notwithstanding a minority of collaborators, such as the celebrated artist and scion of the Song imperial family, Zhao Mengfu (1254–1322). It was not until 1314, during the reign of the Ayurbarwada Buyantu khan (r. 1311–1320), that the examination system was reinstated. Throughout the short-lived dynasty, Kublai and successive Mongol emperors abrogated central authority to corrupt local magnates who tended to grossly abuse their power. This situation was exacerbated by the selling of bureaucratic posts, particularly in the latter half of the dynasty. The resulting systemic weaknesses in the Mongol system of government and increasing corruption led to the breakdown of central authority as early as 1330.[3]

The Yuan government attempted a far-reaching mechanism of social control with their household registration system according to which households were categorized based on professional specialization. Military households, of great importance to the Mongol armies, were obliged to provide military service to the state. Similarly, entertainment households would contribute to calendrical and other festivities. Other groups included artisans, merchants, intellectuals (Confucian), agricultural laborers, and so on. Membership of such categories was considered hereditary and, at least in theory, members were tied to these fixed categories. In practice, however, mobility was possible as the boundaries between debased and commoner, elite and non-elite, became increasingly blurred. Unfortunately, the system's hereditary nature saw the reemergence of large-scale enslavement of the disenfranchised in conquered territories.

Thanks to the Mongol emperors' predilection for dramatic entertainment, the Yuan dynasty was a golden age of operatic and performing arts. As early as 1274, Kublai virtually doubled the size of the Entertainment Bureau, whose members routinely performed in state-sponsored productions. Besides this, numerous other entertainers were organized into private troupes and were available for hire. During a time in which the erstwhile educated elite were largely barred from government service, it was only natural for them to channel their literary and cultural talents into alternate areas. Hence, many men of letters embraced the new genres with enthusiasm. And, to be sure, the rise of fully developed, narrative dramas was intimately connected with courtesans who, through their professional household registration, provided labor for the burgeoning entertain market. Given the heightened prestige of the dramatic arts brought by court patronage, performers, male and female alike, often attained considerable fame, not unlike today's Hollywood stars. Many educated, Confucian-trained scholars who enjoyed opera and drama sought to legitimize what some others considered a somewhat disreputable art form, despite the genres' popularity. Several writers, accordingly, extolled the performers' skills and wrote about female performers in unprecedentedly glowing terms.[4]

The Mongols' marriage customs, based on the socioeconomic needs of a nomadic steppe culture, were vastly different from those of the sedentary Chinese. When introduced to China, such was their impact that they helped change the very social status of Han Chinese women. During the Song dynasty, as previously discussed, upper-class women may have commanded substantial dowries that possibly included land. From the Yuan period, however, increasingly exorbitant bride prices (money paid by the groom's family to that of the bride) began to significantly outweigh a woman's dowry. As was customary with nomadic people, Mongols paid enormous sums for a bride. Accordingly, if the groom were to die young, the family could generally not afford to have his wife's labor (along with her dowry assets) withdrawn through remarriage elsewhere. In Mongol society, therefore, levirate marriages were the norm according to which a widow, especially a young one, would be married to an eligible relative—perhaps even a brother—of her deceased husband. To ethnic Chinese, however, this was tantamount to incest given the importance of proper social distinctions; from a wife's perspective, a husband's brother was considered equivalent to a blood brother. Although the levirate was initially applied universally, it was later restricted to those who observed the custom, after which Chinese were allowed to marry according to their indigenous practices. Nevertheless, the bride price grew increasingly important and Chinese marriage practices were not the same thereafter.[5]

Surprisingly, none of these radical social changes are discernable in love stories of the period. It was as if no such thing had occurred. Han Chinese culture and all its trappings continued, such as examination culture, poetry exchange, arranged and freely chosen marriage, et cetera.

Given documented cases of interracial marriage, one would expect such cases to have been worthy of a storyteller's brush, yet this is not the case. This itself raises intriguing questions about the writing and preservation of texts; that is, which narratives have been preserved and why? Did Han Chinese storytellers simply retreat into a cultural cocoon vis-à-vis the recording of love stories?

Comparatively few short stories written in classical Chinese during the Yuan period survive, prompting some literary historians to conclude that this was a period of decline for the short story.[6] It is, however, difficult to imagine why men of letters would have ceased circulating and recording short stories, particularly when the imperial examinations as a bureaucratic recruitment tool were suspended for the dynasty's first forty or so years. As an alternative means of employing their time, numerous members of the educated elite must surely have continued to circulate and record new stories while compiling old ones. This was, to be sure, a time-honored practice based on oral circulation of gossip and newsworthy events.[7] Furthermore, if the recording and compiling of short stories had indeed experienced a decline, one would expect a similar trend regarding the printing and publishing of *xiaoshuo*. This was not the case. As Lucille Chia observes—at least in relation to the vibrant publishing center of Fujian, book printing suffered no noticeable deterioration across the Song-Yuan transition.[8] Rather than indicating decline, the dearth of extant stories is far more likely due to the hazards of textual preservation. Nevertheless, compared to the Song dynasty, the comparative scarcity of extant love stories impedes a more comprehensive understanding of relevant developments during the hundred or so years of Mongol rule. There are two main compilations containing love stories for the period.

Completed in 1378, barely eleven years after the fall of Mongol rule, Qu You's (1341–1427) *New Stories Written while Trimming the Lampwick* (hereafter *Trimming the Lampwick*) is a milestone of the classical language short story and inspired several copycat compilations. Qu was an accomplished poet and spent much of his life as a school teacher. Despite its eclectic subject matter, *Trimming the Lampwick* preserves no less than eight well-written love stories. Although completed within the very first years of Ming rule, almost all its stories are much earlier. Given the strong, traditional tendency to read narratives as based on actual events, it is reasonable to attribute Yuan dynasty provenance to these stories and, even if Qu You embellished somewhat, he did so shortly after the dynasty's collapse. In this respect, the work resembles the late tenth-century *Extensive Records,* compiled during the early Song dynasty, to which thousands of Tang dynasty and earlier stories owe their survival. This makes *Trimming the Lampwick* an extremely valuable repository of Yuan dynasty stories worthy of attention.

Man of letters Tao Zongyi (1316–1403) pursued a reclusive lifestyle, having repeatedly declined offers to join the bureaucracy. Given the treacherous political climate, this proved a wise decision.[9] Tao, consequently, devoted much of his life to study and literary pursuits. He is best known for his massive compilation of short stories titled *Unverifiable Stories* (*Shuofu*). Like the tenth-century editors of the *Extensive Records*, Tao collected, categorized, and compiled abridged passages from perhaps up to a thousand sources from diverse genres, including classics, history, miscellaneous writing, and, to be sure, short stories.[10] He is also known for his valuable anecdotal collection, *Recorded after Ploughing* (*Chuogeng lu*), comprising contemporary stories and matters recorded during his lifetime. With a preface dated 1366, the collection was completed just prior to the Mongol dynastic collapse. Several short love stories are included, although narrative terseness reduces their literary value. Nonetheless, some offer unique insights while corroborating themes found elsewhere.

Double-Tragedies, Separated Lovers, and Faithful Men

Conspicuous among extant fourteenth-century stories is *Bella and Scarlett* (*Jiao Hong ji*, alternatively titled *Jiao Hong zhuan*).[11] Although it takes the *xuanhe* reign period (1119–25) of the Northern Song as its temporal setting, it is generally thought to have been written around the turn of the fourteenth century.[12] Twelfth-century historical details, nonetheless, appear accurate.[13] Its eponymous title alludes to the main female protagonists, Miss Jiaoniang and her maid, Feihong. In this respect, it appears to have influenced the title of *Plum in the Golden Vase* (*Jin Ping Mei*), whose author also named his work after its three main heroines, as well as several medium-length prose narratives that later adopted the same device. No extant Yuan dynasty imprints are known to exist. Authorship is generally attributed to Song Yuan—that is, Song Meidong (fl. 1280).[14] Unfortunately, very little is known about his biography.

At around 17,000 characters, its ponderous length distinguishes the work from the short-story (*chuanqi*) genre.[15] Rather, it is considered the earliest extant example of the medium-length short story (*zhongpian chuanqi xiaoshuo*). Such works were especially popular from the Ming dynasty onward, and most, if not all, took romantic love as their central theme. Strictly speaking, the extensive scholarly attention they have attracted and their generic distinction from the short story place them outside the parameters of the present study. Nonetheless, given the paucity of Yuan dynasty prose narratives, in addition to *Bella and Scarlett*'s close thematic correspondence to the short, classical language love story, I include it in my survey of fourteenth-century love stories. If we disregard literary aspects made possible by its unusual length and concentrate on prototypical themes, it may profitably be compared and contrasted to earlier love stories to which it owes a considerable debt.

Bella and Scarlett narrates the tragic romance of two cousins, Shen Chun and Jiaoniang (hereafter Miss Jiao). Having failed the metropolitan examination, Shen pays an extended visit to his uncle's house, where he meets and falls in love with his young cousin. Her reluctance to greet him reminds us of Yingying's initial behavior toward Mr. Zhang in the ninth-century story. When Miss Jiao finally emerges, the reader is given their first description of the young woman's physical appearance: "Her glossy, raven locks were made up into twin buns; her beauty would have stolen a march on a lady's portrait. Although she had not applied rouge, her complexion was naturally radiant. As the young man rose to look at her, he was lost without realizing it."

The story may be divided into several episodes. The first follows Shen Chun's attempts to win his cousin's affection. Miss Jiao's behavior during this part of the story is characterized by rebuttal of Shen's mild advances and silence when pressed to reveal her feelings. Her demure behavior contrasts sharply with the comparatively brazen heroines of Song dynasty stories. Static plot development in the form of set dialogues slows the plot's forward momentum, while an astonishing degree of attention is given to details. The storyteller's manner of narrating action sometimes evokes a visual quality, akin to the type of woodblock print often used to illustrate novels of the late-imperial period. For example: "Late one evening, Miss Jiao was embroidering beneath her red [gauze] window. Leaning on the sill, she beheld the roseleaf brambles, not taking her eyes from them for quite some time. Unbeknown to her, the young man softly directed his steps behind them. She gave a long sigh and he knew that something was on her mind." The pictorial nature of this vignette vividly portrays a languid beauty inside her boudoir while, outside, her lover creeps about undetected; the action of both protagonists is simultaneously laid before the reader's view.

As she has not yet articulated her feelings for Shen, he can only guess what her sigh denotes. Their subsequent mutual yet hidden affection is similarly developed in several subsequent scenes. Love stories of former centuries were never so subtle. Even in "Yingying's Story," the heroine's abrupt transformation from impeccably correct maiden to ardent lover may appear unconvincing given lack of authorial explanation or more detailed plot development. In this and other respects, *Bella and Scarlett* is closer to the eighteenth-century masterpiece, *Dream of Red Mansions*.

Besides verbal hints, Shen Chun conveys his feelings through several poems he gives to his cousin. Once, when he accompanies his uncle on an outing, Miss Jiao enters his room where she sees a poem written about herself on the wall. She responds with a matching rhyme, thus expressing in verse what she cannot do in direct dialogue.

> 'Tis hard to wake when springtime sorrow weighs upon one's dreams,
> The sun is distant, the breeze high, while the water-clock is flat.
> My broken soul cannot bear that, at the place where I first arise,
> On a branch bereft of blossom, an oriole bursts forth in song.[16]

Traditional Chinese poets often used the oriole as a symbol of conjugal affection, hence Miss Jiao's final line contrasts this happy symbol with her lonely state. The phrase about her "broken soul" in the penultimate line reveals her loneliness. This is but one example of numerous poetry exchanges that occur throughout the narrative, typical of Yuan and—especially—Ming dynasty narratives.[17]

Frustrated by Miss Jiao's sustained reticence, Shen Chun finally confronts her.

> One late spring day, the day of Little Cold,[18] Miss Jiao happened to be sitting alone beside a stove. When Shen entered from outside bearing a sprig of pear blossom, Miss Jiao simply looked at him without getting up. He then threw the blossom on the ground. Rising slowly, she picked up the blossoms and asked, "Why did you throw this away, brother?" (Given their kinship, the cousins address each other as would brother and

sister according to established custom.) "The flowers brim with tears," he replied, "and I don't know what they're thinking. That's why I got rid of them." Miss Jiao replied, "The Emperor of the East has things well in hand. It's enough to provide amusement during the night. Why should my brother seek any deeper meaning?" "You have made me a promise. Don't go back on it!" "What promise?" she asked with a smile. "Think about it," he responded. She did not answer, but said, "The wind is a little strong. You may sit here and share the fire." The young man eagerly accepted and, coming to the mat, sat down beside her. Only a foot or so separated them. Miss Jiao therefore placed her hand on his back, saying, "Are your clothes warm enough? I'm afraid the cold may oppress you." The young man abruptly replied, "How is it that you think of my being cold but not that my heart is broken?" "What makes you heart-broken?" she asked with a smile. "I'll try to think of a solution." He explained, "Don't mess around with me! Ever since I met you, my soul has taken flight and can no longer remain in my body. My nights are bitterly long and I can't get a wink of sleep. Your teasing me just now is enough to show your heart. I see that your words and manner toward me are not without feeling, yet when I express my deep emotions, you angrily repel me . . ." For a long while, Miss Jiao remained deeply affected. Then she said, "You distrust me. How can I refrain from speaking out? I have known about your heart for a long time, so how could I hold myself so high as to play with your affections? I'm deeply afraid of what evils might follow if it doesn't work out. For several months now, I haven't been able to concentrate on anything. I have found no peace in my dreams, nor can I eat or drink. It's just that you don't know about it." With a long sigh, she added, "You distrust me deeply. Let future matters take their course and, if things don't work out, I'll die in deference to you."

This pivotal episode illustrates several key points. Up until this juncture, Miss Jiao has been blowing hot and cold to Shen Chun's hints of love. As he observes, she consistently takes a moralistic stance, although this reaction arguably exhibits greater verisimilitude than do earlier love stories. The promise he mentions alludes to Miss Jiao's aforementioned poem. In this intimate, fireside scene, she articulates her reason for holding back and openly expresses her love. As we will see, her fears foreshadow the tragic denouement. The narrative detail is also striking. Unlike shorter Tang and Song stories in which important aspects of the plot were treated elliptically, here the protagonists' motives are articulated explicitly. The author's use of a pear blossom is also significant. It not only starts their conversation but, moreover, clearly acts as a figure for their feelings. Although allegorical meaning was routinely entrusted to natural images—particularly flowers—in Chinese poetry and painting, it was seldom, if at all, used as a narrative device during this period, aside from clichéd phrases such as "clouds and rain" for sexual intercourse, or when women's faces were compared to flowers and the like. Such use of naturalistic symbolism and double-entendre reoccurs in other parts of the narrative. Indeed, the setting's very *mise en scène* embodies a secondary level of meaning—that is, the lovers' sitting beside a stove on a cold day symbolizes the state of their relationship, perhaps in addition to the private space they attempt to demarcate against external social pressures. That the story's author-recorder draws on poetic devices to write a narrative enhances both the story's depth of meaning and aesthetic charm while further distinguishing it from its predecessors.

After this scene, the plot focuses on the protagonists' attempts to arrange a romantic tryst. Unlike earlier love stories, several unsuccessful attempts build tension as mundane obstacles prevent their meeting. On one occasion, rain prevents Shen Chun from reaching his beloved. On another, Miss Jiao enters his room at night only to find him drunk. Shen also falls ill due to separation from his beloved, but soon recovers. Even on the night of their first tryst, he is initially unable to find her door. This affords the reader a further description of Miss Jiao from Shen's point of view, albeit in formulaic language: "The young man beheld Miss Jiao's alluring body and bewitching manner, her radiant, flawless skin, and how she seemed to float on air, as though Heng E, Goddess of the Moon, had alighted to purvey the mortal world." Although the description of their lovemaking differs somewhat to other stories, it still evokes well-established metaphors: "Not waiting for more to be said, their feelings fused. Miss Jiao moaned seductively and murmured weakly, as though her body could not withstand [Shen's vigor]. They gave full reign to their passion, like mandarin ducks with necks entwined or else phoenixes that called to each other. None could surpass them." During this episode, Miss Jiao asks Shen to be gentle in view of her sexual inexperience. Although the pain experienced by a virgin was frequently addressed in erotic novellas of the Ming and Qing dynasties, its appearance here is unprecedented, again attesting to the story's verisimilitude. The lovers continue to meet frequently after this initial tryst.

It is not long, however, until Shen Chun's father calls him home, after which the young man cannot stop thinking about Miss Jiao. When his parents agree to accept her as their daughter-in-law, a matchmaker is dispatched to propose marriage. Unfortunately, although Uncle Wang is well disposed to having Shen as a son-in-law, he refuses in view of a law prohibiting first cousins to marry. The consequent disappointment causes a relapse of Shen's illness. Given ineffectual treatment, an exorcist is engaged who diagnoses a malevolent haunting, having been first bribed by Shen to do so. Also on the hero's instructions, the exorcist recommends Shen be removed from his natal home. This conveniently enables the young protagonist to convalesce in his uncle's house.

Prior to his illness, though, his friend takes him to visit a local courtesan, Lianlian. When, after a night of pleasure, she asks the reason for Shen's melancholy manner, he explains about his relationship with Miss Jiao. To his surprise, Lianlian has heard of her reputation for beauty, having seen a portrait painted for the purpose of matchmaking. When asked, Shen naively agrees to bring her one of Miss Jiao's personal effects. Fulfillment of this promise will cause future trouble for the lovers.

Shortly after Shen's return to Uncle Wang's, the narrator introduces the supporting heroine, Feihong (flying red [petal]), a senior family maid. Due to the aunt's jealousy, she "had not been favored" by Uncle Wang—that is, she had not slept with him, as frequently occurred in wealthy households vis-à-vis masters and their female servants. "Although she was attractive, she paled in comparison with Miss Jiao. Only her eyebrows were comparable." She could also compose poetry and, reminiscent of a courtesan, she was skilled at witty repartee. Although Shen does not actively seek her company, he cannot help occasionally conversing with her. Feihong, for her part, sometimes invents excuses to engage him in conversation, thereby eliciting Miss Jiao's jealousy. At one time Miss Jiao berates Feihong after seeing her and Shen Chun together in the garden. Soon after this, Shen steals one of Miss Jiao's slippers so as to fulfill his promise to the courtesan. Following on his heels, Feihong finds it and carries it away. When she later wears them at a family gathering, pretending that Shen had given them to her, Miss Jiao suspects an affair between her and Shen Chun. An anonymous poem left in the garden for Shen that later proves of Feihong's composition engenders further suspicion. Miss Jiao's consequent distrust prompts her to shun the young man, and considerable time passes before he vindicates himself. As is sometimes done in other love stories, he makes a vow before a local god. One day soon after, a jealous and resentful Feihong sees the lovers strolling in the garden. Persuading the aunt to visit the garden on the pretext of flower viewing, she engineers their discovery. Given his embarrassment at having been seen walking with Miss Jiao unchaperoned, Shen decides to return home. Thus ends the first part.

The second part sees Uncle Wang, accompanied by his family, travel to a new bureaucratic posting and, en route, he visits the Shen's. During a briefly snatched conversation with Shen Chun, Miss Jiao reaffirms her intention to die if they cannot be together. After she leaves, Shen is predictably disconsolate. He "returned to his study where he spent the endless days, crying constantly. [Sitting] beside the window in the morning or the lamp in the evenings, he all but relinquished his studies. He would sometimes write poetry, none without allusion to Miss Jiao or Feihong." While teary farewells on the part of both sexes were well-established conventions in the love story, the image of a crying, disconsolate male, moping for an absent lover, is rare as it projects female behavior onto the male body.

Encouraged by his brother, Shen Chun recommences exam preparation, not long after which the pair travel to the capital to sit for the metropolitan examination. Both top the lists, after which they return home in glory where the pair are toasted by their local community and family. Success in a further examination secures them bureaucratic appointments. While the brother is appointed a recorder of documents, Shen is made a revenue manager "in view of his skill with a bow and arrow." It is significant that martial prowess is added to his poetic and scholastic talent as well as good looks. This is consistent with similar references in other Yuan-period love stories, although it is rare or nonexistent during the Song dynasty. When Uncle Wang learns of the brothers' success, he invites them to stay. Only Shen, however, can go because the elder is duty-bound to care for their parents and manage the household.

Given the aunt's suspicion of Shen due to the garden incident, on this visit he is quartered in an apartment some distance from the main hall. To further complicate matters, rancor between Miss Jiao and Feihong prevent the lovers from meeting lest the maid discover and report them. Feihong, Miss Jiao explains, has been given charge of the housekeeping in view of her mother's frequent indisposition. Hence she wields greater power that before. Time elapses and Shen eventually decides to leave, given his inability to be with his beloved. Then, one night, she comes to him and shares his bed with a promise to return every night thereafter. So as to avoid suspicion, she instructs him to avoid conversation with her during the day when they meet in the main hall. Unbeknown to Shen, "Miss Jiao" is actually the ghost of a previous tenant's daughter who died in the same room. The elated Shen, believing her to be real, consequently all but ignores Miss Jiao during the day, sometimes not bothering to enter the main hall for several days.

Miss Jiao, meanwhile, is busy bribing Feihong with her most treasured possessions so as to regain the maid's favor. "As for rare and exquisite items that Feihong would daily admire, she had but to open her mouth and Miss Jiao would give them to her, whether it be brocade, embroidery, gossamer, silk, gold, silver, pearls, or jade; Feihong had but to desire them. She also addressed her as 'Miss Feihong.' In view of this deferential treatment, Feihong eventually relents." Nevertheless, given Shen's disregard of her, Miss Jiao grows increasingly disconsolate, unable to understand why he would snub her. She confides to Feihong: "I have been parted with Shen Chun for over a year. Now only inches and feet separate us, yet we are as far apart as ever. How can I bear it?" She concludes this monologue in a swoon that signals the beginning of an illness. Informing Mrs. Wang that her daughter is suffering from a springtime chill, Feihong conceals the reason for the malady. The narrator describes how Miss Jiao "grew thin and emaciated" and, when Feihong went to see her, she "had just wiped her tears and was sitting alone on the bed, utterly unable to control her feelings." This poignant vignette compares nicely with Shen Chun, who sat alone in his room on an earlier visit when Miss Jiao, suspecting his motives, withheld her affection. It may also remind readers of the languishing Huo Xiaoyu from the ninth-century story, after her lover had abandoned her. The empathetic Feihong, eager to help, suspects that Shen is seeing a prostitute given that some live in the vicinity. She then dispatches junior maids to spy on him.

The servants, understandably, create considerable confusion when they report that Shen is sitting and talking to their mistress. The clever Feihong guesses the truth. Miss Jiao summons Shen to the main hall the following day where she convinces him that he is being haunted. The fearful Shen is initially reluctant to return to his apartment but agrees so that Aunt Wang may intervene. Therefore, when Feihong, accompanied by two of the younger servants, brings the aunt outside his window, the same sight confronts them as did the servants the previous night. The ghost disappears as a servant raps on the window. When Shen pleads with the aunt to save him, she has him lodged in the main hall. The uncle orders Shen nursed because his health has declined through prolonged exposure to the ghost's *yin* vapor. Thus, convalescing in close proximity to Miss Jiao's room, the lovers are able to visit each other unbeknownst to the parents.

Soon after, however, the aunt dies of an illness, so Shen returns home for the mourning period. After this, Uncle Wang visits the Shens. Now that he is free of a jealous wife, he has made Feihong his concubine. At her suggestion, he asks Shen to accompany them home to undertake the management of his household as he is about to leave for another bureaucratic posting. This enables Shen and Miss Jiao to continue their romance almost openly. They bribe all the servants to ensure loyalty and suppress potential gossip. Therefore, when Uncle Wang returns, he is none the wiser about his daughter's indiscretions. On the contrary, he is so pleased with his nephew's household management, as well as his talent and good looks, that he relinquishes his opposition to their marriage. The elated Feihong conveys the news to the lovers.

> "If you please, Miss, your and the young master's long-standing wish has been granted. Dare I not congratulate you both?" Miss Jiao questioned her. "Your father has it in mind to arrange an alliance," she responded. "He has sent me to inquire as to your consent. He fears that the young master will not agree." Miss Jiao replied, "So Heaven does not hinder people after all." They consequently kept the lamps burning all night and forgot to sleep.

The uncle's fear that Shen would refuse lays bare his disconnection with the young people's lives. Nonetheless, a matchmaker is sent to Shen's father, who agrees. He then sets about selecting an auspicious day to deliver the betrothal gifts.

Unfortunately for our lovers, the son of an influential man decides to marry Miss Jiao, having seen her portrait. This decision is taken when he happens to be in the company of the courtesan Lianlian, who had previously admired Miss Jiao and for whom Shen Chun had stolen a slipper. Lianlian extols Miss Jiao's beauty: "The portrait has not done her the least justice. Her feet are exquisitely tiny,[19] her brow is incredibly delicate and, as for poetry and letters, none can touch her." Lianlian's praise evidently inflames the young man; there and then, he announces his intention to marry her. Lianlian attempts to dissuade him, citing gossip that Miss Jiao "has had a lover for some time. I'm afraid that her virginity is not . . . intact." The son replies, "To have such a wife would be happiness indeed. There would be no need to inquire about this." Accordingly, he presses his father to pressure Uncle Wang, who, in the face of hefty gifts and repeated threats, reluctantly agrees.

The lovers are, naturally, thrown into despondency. Although Miss Jiao has a reputation for singing sad songs, she has never done so for Shen Chun. She does so now. Her emotions, however, prevent her from finishing. This poignant scene calls to mind Yingying's emotionally charged zither performance for her lover toward the conclusion of the ninth-century story, just prior to their breaking up. It is also reminiscent of the song that King Xiang of Chu composed and sang with his consort, Lady Yu, on the eve of his final battle during which Lady Yu took her own life. Hence, Miss Jiao's song signals tragedy to come. She falls ill again and, for two months sees Shen only once when lifted from a sickbed to do so.

When Shen's father also succumbs to illness, Shen is obliged to bid farewell to Uncle Wang and return home. After he leaves, Miss Jiao's illness worsens.

> She cried disconsolately both day and night, not bothering to look into her mirror. The radiance of her countenance became dull while her subtle beauty faded. [She was like] a willow lost in mist or a pear blossom drowned in rain. If she happened to see swallows flying in pairs from the rafters or a lone goose calling on its way, her melancholy became uncontrollable.[20] Her illness intensified within the space of a fortnight; soon she would be unable to rise again.

In view of Miss Jiao's imminent demise, Feihong sends a letter urging Shen to see her. Fearing his parents' disapproval, he arrives surreptitiously on a boat that he moors nearby the Wang family compound. Feihong secretly brings Miss Jiao to the boat, where they bid each other a tearful goodbye.

> Having boarded the young man's boat, Miss Jiao took his hand and wept uncontrollably. "I cannot come again. I regret that there's nothing I can do to repay your love. Unhappily, having been obliged to obey my parents, I am unable to spend the

rest of my life with you. You, on the other hand, have a successful career ahead. You will choose a good spouse who will share your honors; this is something I myself can no longer hope for. When we sat beside the stove that time, I told you that, 'If it doesn't work out for us, I will die for you.' Would I dare turn my back on these words now? Yet, you have a weak constitution and are often sick. Take care of yourself! Don't trouble yourself thinking of me!" She took out the cut-off sleeve (that was stained with her blood on the night of their initial lovemaking), saying, "I thank you for your generous affection. When I think of the time we had, [I wonder] how it could ever come again?" She cried even more bitterly, as did Feihong.

Fearful of discovery, Feihong hastens her return. She disembarks and, when Shen's boat sets sail, she watches it disappear into the far distance. Here, again, the narrator fuses both scene and narrative content as occurs in poetry.

After his departure, Miss Jiao disfigures herself and feigns madness in a futile attempt to avoid her imminent marriage. Although her father is sympathetic, under social and legal pressure to honor his agreement, he presses her to marry. She attempts suicide with a knife, but she is saved. Feihong reasons with her, but to no avail. "After a few months, Miss Jiao indeed died of melancholy" (*yi you zu*).

Poems and letters that she wrote for Shen Chun arrive just prior to the news of her death. On their receipt, Shen "in a daze, lost his wits. He would face a [lovely] scene heartbroken, or else would sit alone writing characters in the air. At times he would murmur as if conversing with someone." He attempts to hang himself with her scented scarf, but he is rescued. His brother unsuccessfully tries to reason with him. After saying goodbye to both his parents and brother, he refuses food and frequently loses consciousness. He dies soon after.

The story does not conclude here, though. When Uncle Wang learns of his death, in an act of contrition for keeping them apart, he decides to send Miss Jiao's coffin to the Shen family cemetery so that the lovers may be buried together. Having the lovers buried together in this way evokes the legend of Han Ping and his wife, discussed in chapter 2, where branches planted over the separated couple's graves miraculously joined together. The story of the butterfly lovers, Liang Shanbo and Zhu Yingtai, also comes to mind. After Feihong returns from the funeral with Uncle

Wang, she sees the lovers' ghosts. They speak of a happy existence on the legendary immortal isles and request that she and the uncle attend the ritual sweeping of ancestral graves the following spring. When they do so, twin mandarin ducks, a symbol of romantic happiness, are seen flying around the grave. The ducks disappear once the ritual libation and offering for the dead conclude. Contemporary readers would have understood the ducks to be manifestations of the lovers' souls, not unlike the butterflies that appear at the conclusion of the Zhu Yingtai story.[21]

Contemporary readers may have understood the story's conclusion as illustrative of a line from the *Classic of Poetry*: "While living, we may have to occupy different apartments; but when dead, we shall share the same grave."[22] Meng Chengshun (1599–1684), libretto-writer of a dramatic version of the story, regards both Miss Jiao and Shen Chun as people of chaste integrity (*jieyi*) in view of their willingness to die for romantic fidelity.[23] Miss Jiao's death is foreshadowed several times and, therefore, is perhaps not wholly unexpected. When she finally agrees to become Shen Chun's lover after initial resistance, during the pivotal episode beside the stove, she says: "Let future matters take their course and, if things don't work out, I'll die in deference to you." This speech reveals her unspoken hope to marry while remaining pessimistic about its outcome. She reaffirms this intention during a family visit to Shen's household later in the story, and also during their final farewell. Although her attempted suicide is unsuccessful, she eventually dies of self-imposed starvation exacerbated by melancholy. Conveniently, it enables her to avoid an unwanted marriage. More significantly, it enables her to reclaim lost chastity by demonstrating fidelity to one man. Unable to marry the man to whom she had given herself, death is the only way she may satisfy both prevailing social expectation and the culture of romance. Hence she joins the ranks of faithful, Northern Song–era heroines, such as Miss Xiao in the "Story of Twin Peaches," Madam Wang in "Story of Distant Mist," and the courtesan Ai'ai.

Shen Chun's death, on the other hand, is neither predictable according to generic conventions, nor is it necessary to redeem lost chastity or apologize for illicit sex; Miss Jiao's demise already achieves this. His death may be understood as intense love for and fidelity to his beloved. Such is his devotion that, as Richard Wang observes, he banishes sociopolitical advancement for Miss Jiao's sake.[24] This is made clear when his brother lectures him after her demise: "A man should have lofty ambitions. You, little brother, have achieved high scholastic success and a great career is at your feet. Yet you would rather die at a woman's hands?" To this Shen responds, "I will never get another such as her."

As a literary motif, the death of both upper-class lovers represents a milestone in the love story's development. The male protagonist of a Song dynasty story may have fallen ill because of a woman, but only in rare instances would he have died. And, to be sure, male protagonists who did die were not socially successful members of the upper class. Having attained examination success, Song dynasty protagonists would not have sacrificed public honor and career for romantic attachment. More often than not, stories of the period concluded with them attaining both career/scholastic and romantic fulfillment. Indeed, as we have seen, examination success often provided the key to plot resolution.

On the contrary, *Bella and Scarlett* values romance over sociopolitical advancement, thus subverting orthodox social values.[25] One cannot help but wonder if this would not have been possible had it not been for suspension of the imperial examinations over the first forty or so years of the Yuan dynasty.[26] Disenfranchised elite men, unable to serve the emperor according to traditional cultural norms, had little choice but to undertake alternate pursuits to government service. In any case, this groundbreaking theme of educated men spurning scholastic success and bureaucratic careers frequently reoccurred in Ming dynasty stories, both of the short- and medium-length varieties.[27] During an era when, compared to previous periods, civil service careers were often ruined by capricious political machinations and competition for bureaucratic placement became exponentially intense, the theme gained considerable currency and almost certainly reflects contemporary social sentiment. Shen Chun's unswerving devotion to Miss Jiao anticipates the character of Jia Baoyu in the renowned novel *Dream of Red Mansions*, who remained devoted to his beloved cousin, Lin Daiyu, even after her untimely death.[28] For Xiao Chi, Baoyu's rejection of a bureaucratic career "epitomizes the syndrome of the cynical high Qing literati."[29] It is significant that a central theme of the famous eighteenth-century novel was first explored in *Bella and Scarlett*, for it points to the heights of thematic innovation attained by the early fourteenth-century love story.

Shen Chun's devotion to Miss Jiao clearly owes a debt to Southern Song love stories in which males refused to remarry in deference to the heroine, such as "Fan Xizhou," as well as sundry *zhiguai* accounts. These stories coincide with Zhang Zai's idea that, in the context of widow chastity,

"Surely men should not remarry either." Unlike the protagonists of *Bella and Scarlett*, Fan Xizhou did not participate in a tragic conclusion, and the husbands of the *zhiguai* accounts did not live up to their resolve. More so than such accounts, the extent of Shen's fidelity resembles that of Fifth Brother Sun, who died of, in his own words, "lovesickness" after his beloved was married to another. Unlike *Bella and Scarlett*, "Fifth Brother Sun" lacks a double tragedy; his beloved continues living as a married woman by the story's conclusion. Nor did Fifth Brother Sun forsake public service. On the contrary, he tried repeatedly to enter the bureaucracy through scholastic means. Indeed, in this twelfth-century story, the possibility of romantic felicity, academic success, and a bureaucratic career were conflated. Moreover, the storyteller intended his story as a warning about the dangers of romantic attachment, which is incompatible with the spirit of romance. In contrast to this, Shen Chun's death denotes single-minded devotion to one woman and, therefore, breathes new life into the culture of romance.

Thematically closer to *Bella and Scarlett* are Southern Song stories about couples who enacted suicide pacts, at least in regard to the shared double-tragic conclusion. As previously noted, the small number of extant examples and the brevity of their narration, however, hampers an understanding of the couples' motives. Faced with insurmountable social pressure, they evidently considered suicide the only viable way to avoid separation in this life and unite in the hereafter. The same idea is evident in the paranormal denouement of *Bella and Scarlett*, as Miss Jiao's and Shen Chun's spirits speak of a felicitous existence on the immortal isles. Although *Bella and Scarlett* and the suicide-pact stories share the motif of both lovers dying for love, Miss Jiao and Shen Chun do not commit suicide, although they attempted to do so. Furthermore, the protagonists of suicide pact accounts—at least based on extant material—invariably comprised a lower-class woman and a young man with marginal ties to the educated elite. On the contrary, both protagonists in *Bella and Scarlett* hailed from decidedly upper-class backgrounds. Moreover, the reasons for their demise, the naturalistic manner of their deaths, in addition to the narrative's gradual build-up to its tragic conclusion, help distinguish *Bella and Scarlett* from previous narratives. To be sure, the courtesan-class heroines of the suicide-pact stories need not have committed suicide to reclaim lost chastity or fulfill social expectations; the same sexual morality applied to both the upper classes and commoners alike did not apply to the debased classes. In regard to its double-tragic conclusion, *Bella and*

Scarlett story paves the way for similar denouements involving upper-class protagonists frequently found in Ming dynasty literature.

As Itō Sōhei and Cheng Yizhong observe, the protagonists' deaths imply authorial criticism of the overly strict patriarchy that barred their love.[30] Miss Jiao herself points to her parents' role in their frustrated love. When farewelling Shen Chun for the last time, she says, "I regret that I have no way to repay you. Unhappily, compelled by 'one's parents' command,' I am unable to follow you for the rest of my days." The phrase "one's parent's command" (*fumu zhi ming*), found in the revered Confucian philosophical work the *Book of Mencius*, provided unquestioned authority for the institution of arranged marriage and the parents' role therein.[31] Miss Jiao's father's explanation that burying her together with Shen Chun is to make amends for having kept them apart admits his culpability in their demise. Even more telling is contemporary censure. After the lovers' joint burial, the author of an anonymous postface opines: "It must have been because of their parents' inability to understand their hearts and aspirations that such young people could meet with such a catastrophe."[32] Even without such explicit guidance, by contemporary standards Uncle Wang compromised his integrity by agreeing to the Shuai's marriage proposal having already offered Miss Jiao to Shen Chun. This certainly flouts the earlier theme to honor betrothals no matter the cost. Therefore, unlike many Song dynasty love stories, Miss Jiao's parents no longer act as benevolent arbitrators of the lovers' conjugal destiny. On the contrary, they create an insurmountable roadblock to romantic felicity. This itself was not new; Miss Wang's father in "Story of Distant Mist," for example, broke up his daughter's marriage given his adamant opposition to his son-in-law. Some Song-period parents initially refused their consent, only to later change their minds or have them changed by intervening magistrates. Nonetheless, parents as a romantic obstacle became an increasingly reoccurring theme of other Yuan and Ming dynasty love stories. Once more, *Bella and Scarlett* anticipates future trends.

If Miss Jiao's death conforms to moralistic expectations that women should avoid sexual intimacy with anyone besides her husband, the author does not overtly portray her as a paragon of feminine virtue in the mold of many Song dynasty heroines. The lack of moralizing soliloquys spoken through her character or metatextual commentary precludes explicit didactic content. Rather, emphasis is placed on the progression of the lovers' mutual love and psychological state. Romantic aspects of the story are aestheticized and celebrated, while unsavory ones are suppressed, such as the lovers carrying on a carnal relationship behind Uncle Wang's back. If Miss Jiao's death is partly due to social pressure, her devotion to Shen Chun is equally, if not more, important.

Besides the death of both protagonists, the characters' mutual suspicion further distinguishes the story from its precursors. Before Miss Jiao's declares her feelings, Shen Chun's uncertainty is addressed several times, and we only later learn how Miss Jiao's misgivings about a successful outcome prevent her from being more open. Such initial suspicion culminates in the stove-side scene discussed above. The misunderstanding surrounding Shen's having made off with Miss Jiao's slippers causes serious and protracted alienation. And, after its resolution, Shen's deliberate avoidance of Feihong causes the latter's rancor, which is not resolved until much later. Prior to the slipper incident, the narrator relates, "Although the young man did not engage Feihong in conversation, she would search for matters to discuss with him. Miss Jiao would feel uncomfortable whenever she saw this. Now that the young man had come again, Feihong became even more solicitous of him and Miss Jiao grew suspicious." Little wonder, then, that Miss Jiao castigated Feihong when she saw the pair catching butterflies in the garden. Such narrative strands are accorded considerable detail, resulting in a highly convincing plot. For the first time in a love story, female jealousy acts as an obstacle to romantic happiness. Although female jealousy, as a literary theme, had occasionally arisen in Tang and Song dynasty stories, it typically focused on feminine rivalry and only rarely affected the male protagonist. Here, several characters are involved.

Another episode of protracted suspicion arises during Shen Chun's affair with the ghost. Mistaking it for Miss Jiao and acting on its instructions not to address the real heroine when in the company of others, Shen inadvertently causes his lover considerable emotional pain. His unintended heartlessness is compounded by his prior vow of fidelity made before the local god. To be sure, a sacred vow made to a woman was a clichéd element of the betrayal prototype, harking back to "Li Wa's Story." Such a vow clearly foregrounds the male's callousness and establishes an expectation of disloyalty. In *Bella and Scarlett,* the author almost satirizes these prototypical elements. Shen Chun's inadvertent betrayal of his beloved engenders a biting irony highly unusual for the love story of the period.

While some Song dynasty love stories featured garden settings, this is given greater significance in *Bella and Scarlett*. The garden is where Miss Jiao's mother "catches" her and Shen as they walk unchaperoned. The garden is also home to Shen's living quarters during the ghostly haunting and, indeed, enables the haunting to occur. Glimpses of the garden also form the backdrop of picturesque vignettes such as when Shen Chun, while tip-toeing through the roseleaf bramble blossoms, overhears Miss Jiao's sigh. To be sure, Shen's extended sojourn in the garden anticipates that of Jia Baoyu and the young female characters in *Dream of Red Mansions*; in this respect, too, it may well have acted as a model for the celebrated novel. Similarly, the importance of the Ximen Qing's sumptuous garden in *Plum in a Golden Vase* also comes to mind. And, to be sure, the adaptation of Shen's having stolen Miss Jiao's shoes in the sixteenth-century novel, along with other shared elements, demonstrates a direct link between the two works. The author's extended treatment of the garden setting in *Bella and Scarlett* surpasses its comparatively simplistic portrayal in the hands of Song dynasty storytellers. Given that *Bella and Scarlett* developed a geographic setting that was to become so important to prose literature of late-imperial China further attests to the groundbreaking nature of this fourteenth-century story.

Although the basic plot of *Bella and Scarlett* may have been based on earlier sources, as Itō Sōhei speculates,[33] it is unlikely based on oral circulation or, indeed, prior written versions from which many of the stories surveyed in this study evidently evolved. The degree of narrative detail, the ponderously lengthy plot, the build-up to pivotal scenes, the extensive dialogue, the psychological depth given to the main protagonists, the poetic sensibility with which several scenes are narrated, are far too sophisticated to have been the product of orally circulated gossip. Some poems extemporized immediately following the lovers' first sexual encounter, for example, could not have been collected for posterity. The traditional poetic device whereby scene and emotion are fused, or where secondary levels of meaning are entrusted to imagery, all point to conscious creation on the part of a single author. In regard to poetic devices, Cyril Birch touches on this issue when speaking of a Ming dynasty operatic version. For Birch, the lampblack shared by the lovers early in the story symbolizes both Miss Jiao and Shen Chun as a pair of lovers (*caizi jiaren*) as well as two users of the brush; she uses the lampblack to adorn her features and he to express his poetic talent. "Calligraphy, painting, poetry and feminine beauty are inextricably linked." Furthermore, shared lampblack prefigures shared bodies.[34] There are several similar instances of this poetic device throughout the story. Since this is irrelevant to a thematic study such as this one, I will refrain from reviewing them here. Suffice to note that such poetic sensibility indicates conscious literary craft on the part of the storyteller. Therefore, in contrast to stories based on gossip or historical factuality, *Bella and Scarlett* constitutes a landmark of Chinese protofiction.

Recorded shortly after the fall of the Yuan dynasty, Qu You's "Story of Cuicui" tells of two childhood sweethearts, Liu Cuicui and her lover, Jin Ding. Cuicui is the daughter of a wealthy commoner family (*minjia*), while Jin's family comprise impoverished scholars. Hence, the class disparity often explored in Southern Song love stories continued into the late fourteenth century, while downward social mobility vis-à-vis scholar-official families once more resurfaces. Although Cuicui's physical appearance is not described, we are told, "she was born intelligent and could understand the *Classic of Poetry* and the *Book of Documents*. Her parents, therefore, did not impede her aspirations and so enrolled her in school." As with several stories from the Southern Song period, Cuicui and Jin Ding meet and fall in love as schoolchildren. Their comparable age elicits teasing that they will eventually marry, as was the case with Zhang Youqian and Miss Luo of the Southern Song story. Delighted at this prospect, they exchange love poems. After Cuicui grows up and is removed from school, her parents proceed to arrange her marriage. She, however, cries and refuses to eat. After ascertaining the reason, her parents decide to marry her to Jin Ding, which is surprising given the socioeconomic disparity. Nonetheless, as her father later observes, "haggling over money in regard to marriage is the way of barbarians." This monologue openly satirizes pecuniary motivation in regard to marriage, often only implied in earlier stories. Jin's parents, however, are initially unwilling given their relative poverty. Nonetheless, the Lius' matchmaker prevails, and the lovers are married with none of the obstacles that stimulated plot development in most other stories. In view of Jin's poverty, Cuicui's father accepts him as an uxorilocal son-in-law lest his daughter suffer from want of material comfort. They exchange love poetry on their wedding night and, in formulaic metaphor, the narrator compares their lovemaking to mandarin ducks, peacocks, and kingfishers.

The first obstacle arrives when Zhang Shicheng (1321–1367), an unsuccessful claimant to the throne during the fall of the Yuan dynasty, raises troops who sweep through the locality. Cuicui is abducted by one of his generals, yet the circumstance surrounding her kidnapping and the effect of the rebel occupation on her family are not specified. The plot jumps to when Zhang Shicheng has eliminated all rivals except for Zhu Yuanzhang (1328–1398), founding emperor of the Ming dynasty. By then the chaos caused by the military situation has—at least locally—subsided.

This enables Jin Ding to leave home in search of his wife. "I vow that if I cannot see her, I will not return." Although he knows the identity of Cuicui's kidnapper, he is forced to follow the general's circuitous troop movements for a considerable period. By the time he finally catches up with him, he has been reduced to begging. He is granted an interview with the general after an unusually lengthy inquisition by the latter's gatekeeper. So as to gain access to Cuicui, Jin pretends to be her brother. When the general calls her out to greet him, contradistinction between the lovers' physical proximity and their ability to communicate freely is made apparent as, in the general's presence, they may only greet each other as would brother and sister. The general then invites Jin to stay. Given a change of clothes, he is assigned the task of managing the general's library, in view of his literacy. Although book-loving readers may vicariously delight in this situation, Jin is unable to see his wife let alone rescue her given her strict confinement in the women's quarters. Time elapses, and autumn soon arrives. In traditional art and poetry, autumn—the season prior to winter and death—frequently symbolizes decline. The narrator vividly illustrates this idea with such description as, "The west wind (itself symbolic of autumn and decline) rose in the evening while the white dew turned to frost. Jin stayed alone in the empty room, unable to sleep the whole night." As with the poetic technique found in *Bella and Scarlett*, here too emotion and scene are fused. Jin manages to smuggle a poem concealed inside his robe that he requests be taken to Cuicui for mending. Jin's heartbreaking poetic imagery and tone deeply affect her as she "soundlessly swallows her tears." She responds with a poem of her own in which she affirms her intention to die for him: "Unable to follow you in life, I will do so in death."

"Having received the poem, Jin understood that she had promised to die, and so he gave up hope." Unable to reach or rescue his wife, increased melancholy causes terminal illness. In a theatrical manner, he dies just as his "sister" cradles his languishing head in her arms. Cuicui herself dies soon after. Before she dies, she persuades the general to bury her next to Jin. "The general, not standing in the way of her wish, actually buried her to the left side of Jin's grave. In this way the two grave mounds stood side by side."

The story does not conclude here, however. Filial piety must be propitiated. This is achieved through a former family servant who had become a traveling merchant. When he passes by the lovers' graves, he sees a magnificent house and grounds. Cuicui and Jin invite him inside, where they regale him with a sumptuous banquet. When he asks how they came to be there, Cuicui recounts how Jin came looking for her. She claims that they have taken up temporary residence there, having been released by the general. She then gives the servant a letter for her parents. Written in beautiful parallel prose that showcase Qu You's literary prowess, this letter reiterates the events surrounding her capture and hints at her fear of physical punishment were she to have disobeyed her captor. Although she expresses her wish to have escaped, she does not specify what prevented her from doing so. She repeats the lie about having been released, evoking several literary precedents, including the famous story of how the early Tang general, Yang Su, returned a princess to her husband. She also alludes to a Tang story of a servant girl who died before her upper-class lover could marry her; they were reunited only after she was reborn. This subtly hints at her own ghostly status. Given the numerous allusions to famous love stories, the letter appears unlike that which a daughter would write to her parents under the circumstances. Here, then, is a rent exposing dissonance between verisimilitude and literary creativity.

On receipt of this letter, the delighted father, with the former servant as a guide, travels to collect the couple but is shocked to see a wasteland of weeds where the imposing mansion had formerly stood. The true state of affairs is explained to them by an obliging local monk. That night, the couple's ghosts visit the father for a final farewell. Cuicui reiterates the story of her capture and her feelings on being forced to serve a new master. In this respect, she compares herself to the ninth-century heroine, Miss Liu, who was abducted by the Turkic general, Shazhali. She then explains her and Jin Ding's demise. When the father proposes returning their bones to their homeland, she pleads that they be allowed to remain in peace surrounded by the tranquil, picturesque landscape, protected by benevolent local deities. The father then wakes, "as if from a dream." The next day, he makes a ritual offering of food and drink before returning home.[35]

The "Story of Cuicui" differs from many earlier reunion stories. In those of the Tang or Song dynasties, sagacious social seniors frequently—but not always—detected the lovers' affection and, unselfishly, returned the captured wife or else gave their own concubine to the hero. Indeed, the allusion to Yang Su recalls the reunion story in which the separated couple used a broken mirror as a means to reunite. Accordingly, had Southern Song readers been able to read "Story of Cuicui," they may well have expected the plot to follow the reunion prototype given the motif of children studying together, the expectation that they would marry, as well as several allusions to famous antecedents sprinkled liberally throughout the narrative. The plot, however, subverts any such expectation. No less than seven years elapse before Jin Ding finally relocates Cuicui following her abduction, during which time she would have almost certainly been sexually possessed by her captor, although this is treated elliptically. Once Jin Ding gained acceptance into the general's household, albeit deceptively, a reader informed by previous reunion stories may have expected the senior male to return the wife. Nonetheless, not only are the couple kept apart, the story concludes with a double tragedy. As with *Bella and Scarlett* and other Yuan-period love stories, this taste for tragedy marks a new trend. Although a handful of extant Tang dynasty anecdotes tell of senior males who refuse to return abducted women, or else duplicitously commandeer wives or concubines, reunion stories were much more common throughout the Tang and Song periods, particularly after the fall of the Northern Song. From the Yuan dynasty onward, however, both protagonists were frequently held apart and/or died under tragic circumstances.

A comparison with the ninth-century "Miss Liu's Story" nicely illustrates key differences. Both stories use the erotic triangle as the male protagonist must compete with another man for his wife's fidelity and affection. As previously noted, "Miss Liu's Story" features two such triangles. Moreover, Miss Liu's abduction engenders male bonding as various men collaborate to successfully assist the protagonist. Such androcentric values are largely absent in "Story of Cuicui." No male helpers emerge to support Jin or to rescue the languishing Cuicui. Overshadowing male sexual rivalry is the poignancy surrounding the lovers' separation, their mutual love, and their beleaguered hopes of reunion. Rather than endure permanent separation, the couple choose death as an ultimate expression of fidelity. Hence, not unlike Song-period stories, our late fourteenth-century storyteller emphasizes romantic love over the male-centered values ubiquitous in Tang-period stories.

Cuicui's initial failure to commit suicide so as to avoid knowing two husbands prevents any authorial impulse to portray her as a torchbearer of orthodox morality. Her reason for remaining alive—the threat of domestic violence—touches a realistic note rarely addressed in the short story. Yet her death, as with other heroines we have seen, reclaims fallen virtue. Such wifely devotion, to the point of death, certainly affirms orthodox Confucian values that had been gaining increasing acceptance since the eleventh century. Nevertheless, the didactic tone of many Song dynasty stories—although still discernable—is largely overshadowed by those of romantic love and realistic touches.

The fact that Jin did not even attempt to plead for his wife's return suggests its futility vis-à-vis the narrative world. Indeed, a feeling of sadness and hopelessness pervades the story's later stage. This may well reflect the near social collapse and violence wrought by the Yuan-Ming transition, particularly in the region where our story occurs. While the Tang-Song and Northern-Southern Song transitions often witnessed violent periods, as previously noted, Song dynasty storytellers generally ignored numerous instances whereby wives and daughters would have been abducted and raped. Instead they focus on hopeful stories of reunion under unlikely circumstances. Such wish fulfillment is noticeably lacking in the "Story of Cuicui," as indeed in many other Yuan dynasty love stories. In its place, one often finds a pervasive pessimistic tone.

The fact that Jin Ding died before his wife is another innovative aspect of the story. In *Bella and Scarlett*, it was the heroine who died first, which is certainly more common. Jin's dying first valorizes the female as it renders the male effeminate, and brings to mind Southern Song male protagonists who fell ill for their lovers. Besides stories of suicide pacts, the only other instance of a protagonist dying for a lover is that of "Fifth Brother Sun." Yet Sun was a very young man who died having been unable to marry his cousin. Moreover, his story was written as a warning, not as a celebration of romantic love. His death is qualitatively different from that of Jin, who died unable to rescue his wife.

Early in the story, Jin gives Cuicui a poem in which he indirectly expresses his love. Cuicui's rejoining poem is of particular interest as it includes a rare early reference to the famous legend of Zhu Yingtai. This is all the more important given that the plot details of the Zhu Yingtai story at that time are unclear. The poem is as follows:

> All my life, I have regretted Zhu Yingtai;
> For what reason did she not open her heart? (*huaibao*)
> I would have the Lord of Spring diligently undertake
> To move the flowering trees so they may grow in the sunlight.

In apparent contrast to herself, Cuicui implies that Zhu Yingtai was reticent in the face of her lover's advances. Furthermore, the conclusion of "Story of Cuicui" shares similar elements to that of both Zhu Yingtai and *Bella and Scarlett*: the tragic deaths of both protagonists, the shared graves, and the related paranormal events. Considering these commonalities, in addition to the shared narrative convention of two lovers held apart, the mature form of the Liang Shangbo and Zhu Yingtai story may well be a product of the fourteenth century.

Another of Qu You's stories, titled "The Lady in Green," set in the *yanyou* reign period (1314–1320), tells of a love affair involving a ghost. The story commences when the protagonist, Zhang Yuan, sojourns to West Lake (near the former Southern Song capital, Lin'an, modern Hangzhou), where his lodgings happen to abut the former residence of the famous chief minister, Jia Sidao (1213–1275). The plot initially develops conventionally. Early one evening, he meets a beautiful green-clad young girl, fifteen or sixteen years [*sui*] old, who claims to be his neighbor. She "readily responds" when he flirts with her and, after their first sexual encounter, she visits him every night while departing at dawn. When she eventually reveals her true form—that is, the ghost of Jia Sidao's concubine, she evokes unfulfilled karmic destiny to justify their carnal affair. She explains that, during Zhao's previous lifetime, they were both Jia Sidao's servants. Their mutual attraction led to an affair which, once discovered, was punished with their deaths. Hence the story narrates the aftermath of a double tragedy, while fulfillment of romantic destiny stimulates the remaining plot development. Nonetheless, similar to fleeting affairs with immortal women, this too must eventually end. Rather than disappear into the ether, as was usual, the ghost woman simply collapses into an unresponsive state. Zhao buries her remains, which are reduced to clothes and jewelry after she is encoffined. Significantly, "affected by her love," Zhao vows never to remarry. He enters a temple and lives the remainder of his days as a Buddhist monk.[36]

The structure and plot trajectory resemble more an encounter with a goddess than with a ghost. As with immortal women, it is the woman who mysteriously appears to the man and initiates the liaison. She exhibits superior knowledge about the workings of fate. She also recounts several stories about the past—that is, Jia Sidao and his self-serving cruelty. Also like goddesses, she is the one who must leave the male, tearfully announcing the expiration of their allotted time together.

Several themes and motifs we have seen reoccur here. As opposed to the conventional premise of the *zhiguai* genre whereby ghosts are harmful, this story's protagonist knowingly, even if not initially, enters into an affair with an ontological other that leaves him none the worse. "Miss

Ren's Story" was an early exploration of such an idea, which during the Song dynasty reoccurred much more frequently. Traditional Chinese folk belief in destiny is evoked as a means that enables the lovers to fulfill their unrequited romantic fate. This combines with popular Buddhist belief in reincarnation, while the woman's spirit having remained in the vicinity of her murder reflects the idea that a person's ten souls may not dissipate after death. Marriage between ghosts and humans in several Tang-era stories is similarly premised on conjugal destiny, so this is nothing new.

What is new is the male protagonist's fidelity to a ghost woman. We saw how, during the Southern Song period, an expectation arose whereby widowers would refrain from remarriage, even though many protagonists fell short of this ideal. In this story, the male not only lives up to it but remains faithful to a ghost whose earthly and heavenly souls have finally dispersed and, according to the story's logic, is soon to be reincarnated. Throughout imperial China and well into the twentieth century, living people were sometimes married to deceased partners according to a phenomenon known as spirit marriage (*minghun*).[37] "The Green Lady" possibly reflects such folklore. In any case, such a denouement certainly takes the old theme of the faithful male a step farther. Yet romantic loyalty ignores the male's filial duty to perpetuate his ancestral lineage. The fact that both his parents were deceased at the story's outset compounds neglect of such an important social expectation. Even though protagonists who attain Daoist enlightenment in many earlier stories frequently exchanged their home for a mountain hermitage in pursuit of immortality, they usually left children behind to carry on ancestral sacrifices and a wife to care for the children. Hence, their social obligations had been fulfilled, whereas this is not the case here. The denouement is, furthermore, strikingly similar to *Dream of Red Mansions*, which concludes with Jia Baoyu's disappearance in search of religious enlightenment. Hence, the conclusion is unique for stories of the period. And while not every faithful male turned to the Buddhist or Daoist church, the theme of the faithful male reoccurred in several other extant love stories of the Yuan dynasty.

Several themes noted above—a taste for tragic denouement, male fidelity, and sustained separation of both protagonists, are also found in Zheng Xi's (fl. 1324) *Dream of Spring* (*Chun meng lu*), completed in 1318. Its form resembles the *ben shi shi* genre, made popular during the Tang dynasty, in which a poem is prefaced with an explanatory introduction. Nevertheless, containing over five and a half thousand characters, *Dream of Spring* is considerably longer than any of its precursors, notwithstanding the late seventh-century *Dalliance in the Immortal's Den* (*Youxian ku*), which it resembles in some respects. In view of the numerous poems and letters that largely comprise the work, it might be considered China's first epistolary narrative. Indeed, its form, content, and denouement brings to mind Richardson's *Clarissa*. As Cheng Yizhong notes, the use of personal letters to replace third-person narration differentiates *Dream of Spring* from the *ben shi shi* genre and renders it unique among its forerunners.[38] These poems and letters were purportedly exchanged between the author and a young lady to whom he unsuccessfully proposed marriage. The preface's first-person voice, unusual for prose narratives, also helps distinguish it from other works. As the preface succinctly provides key details, I will present it in lieu of my own summary.

> West of the city lived a daughter of the Wu family, raised in a family of scholars, exquisite in both talent and beauty. She was an expert player of the zither and of chess, as well as an accomplished poet and calligrapher. Literati praised her one and all. When her father passed away, at an early age, his final wish had been that she should become the spouse of a scholar. The girl herself, too, believed that she was possessed of uncommon attainments.
>
> When earlier this year I was a guest at the Hong residence, a matchmaker arrived one day, saying that she had been much put upon by the family's long search for a suitable groom. By way of a joke, the son of Mr. Hong Zhongming had suggested that she approach me. I declined, saying that I was already married. Yet unexpectedly the matchmaker requested that I write a poem anyway, to be transmitted to the girl. On a whim I composed a song lyric to the melody "Mulanhua man." By the following day, the girl had written a reply to my poem, using the same melody and rhyme, and she had entrusted this to the matchmaker. "When Miss Wu read your lyric," said the matchmaker, "she fervently praised its author's grace, but her mother objected to the matter, saying that your Excellency was already married. The girl, however, is enamored entirely of your talent and composed a lyric to harmonize with yours." In addition, she sent her old wet-nurse to have a look at me, and to tell me of her intentions. Even if she could only be a secondary wife, she would not refuse. She asked me to prevail

on an intimate acquaintance to persuade her mother to allow her marriage to me. Since I had been in town only briefly, however, I had but few acquaintances. At a loss, I asked a certain Wu Huaipo, the Dean of the local academy, to go and persuade the mother, but in the end she would not consent. A son of the Zhou family, fearful that I should succeed, had brought over a betrothal sum to coax the mother. The mother succumbed to the offer, consenting to follow the Zhou and accepting the betrothal gifts. In tears, the girl shouted, "My father commanded on his deathbed that I should marry a scholar. This son of the Zhou has no learning and no attainments. He only knows how to play the lute. I vow that I shall never marry into the Zhou family." In a fit of feigned madness, she threw her cap on the ground. Her mother lost her temper and beat her. The girl thereupon became so angry that she fell ill. The illness was serious enough that her mother repented. To avoid thwarting her daughter's wishes, she entrusted the betrothal gifts to the matchmaker, to be returned to the Zhou family.

The girl's illness, however, showed no sign of improving. In that realization, the girl wrote me a letter: "My illness is in truth due to you. If my life cannot be saved, I shall bear my regret into the underworld. Knowing how much you love me, how will I ever forget?" Moreover, just before she died, she cried and told her maid, whose name was Meirui, "I am in love with Mr. Zheng. I have lived for Mr. Zheng, and I shall die for Mr. Zheng. After I die, you must take Zheng's poems and other writings and hide them in my coffin. That is my wish." Before long, she indeed passed away.[39]

This preface summarizes the arc of events from Zheng Xi's biased viewpoint, while the poems, letters, and elegies that follow provide nuanced psychological and emotional detail. Before concluding, Zheng Xi tells of how Miss Wu's mother, grief-stricken at her daughter's demise, also died. He presents further poems extolling Miss Wu and his affair, purportedly composed by friends. Elegizing a deceased beauty in this way brings to mind the poems and dirges written by male admirers for the deceased ninth-century courtesan Yan Lingbin, documented in *Record of the Northern Quarter*.[40] For Christian de Pee, such literary production equates to the "lurid fascination with beautiful, virtuous dead women in biographies of chaste widows" during the period.⁴¹ That male authors and readers appeared to derive pleasure from languishing deceased beauties takes Martin Huang's observation about "languishing beauties" a step further.

Dream of Spring defies neat classification in regard to love story prototypes. Its plot resembles the union followed by permanent separation prototype given the tragic denouement, yet the lack of physical contact between the protagonists is highly unusual. In *Dream of Spring*, romantic "union" may be understood as metaphysical union—a union of minds brought together in poetry and letters. As Zheng Xi remarks: "After I read the two song lyrics she had written in response to mine, I realized that their talent, emotions and beauty were of a rare kind. That is why I am utterly unable to forget her."⁴² For the author, therefore, the woman's inner beauty and intellect overrides her physical appearance although, presumably guided by second-hand reports, he mentions her somatic beauty several times. Replacing the male Gaze of other stories is an interior Gaze under which the heroine's physical attractiveness and literary talent must be imagined from the beauty of her verse and prose, as well as the gift of her handmade, embroidered collar, omitted from the above summary. The metaphysical nature of *Dream of Spring* and its lack of sexual consummation distinguishes it from virtually every love story previously analyzed. Even while Star Brother and Weaver Maid of the chaste Southern Song story refrained from sexual intercourse during their elopement, it may be assumed that they eventually did so after having arranged their own wedding ceremony. Zheng Xi may not have intended to record a love story; nonetheless, it is easily read as such, albeit one that might be considered prototypically marginal.

In regard to the would-be lovers' social status—an unmarried daughter of the educated elite and a married scholar-official, only one other comparable precedent comes to mind—that is, "Story of Twin Peaches," the Northern Song dynasty account of illicit sexual congress between Mr. Li and Wang Xiaoniang, both members of the upper class. As in *Dream of Spring*, Li's married status is the chief obstacle to the couple's romantic happiness. The reader will remember how Li hoped to overcome this hurdle by offering to divorce his wife. True to the form of a virtuous paragon, Xiaoniang dissuades him with a moralistic argument. After a protracted affair during which the lovers exchange poems and love tokens, Xiaoniang is betrothed to another. So as to avoid this unwanted marriage while remaining faithful to her lover, Xiaoniang salvages her lost chastity by committing suicide, thereby conforming to the Confucian principle for a woman to have only one husband. Similarly, Miss Wu is mindful of Zheng's wife as she repeatedly chides him for want of devotion to both wife and children. For example, in a brief message attached to some poems, she writes, "The plum blossom in your hometown still depends on you as her husband."[43] The plum blossom became a reoccurring symbol for Zheng's wife based on his use of it in an earlier poem:

> The plum blossom in the old garden is desolate and worn,
> Allowing the eastern wind to accost the apricot.
> How much more when the plum blossom hath no speech,
> While the apricot blossom kindly invites to linger.[44]

Here, Zheng juxtaposes the image of a plum blossom with that of an apricot, which symbolizes Miss Wu. Zheng, unlike Li, does not offer to divorce his wife. He simply expresses his gratitude at Miss Wu's willingness to accept the inferior position of a concubine and, in his letters and elegy, repeatedly cites this in an apparent apology for his role in her demise. Unlike Xiaoniang, Miss Wu is not portrayed as a virtuous paragon. The imagistic metaphor of a plum blossom for Zheng's wife lacks the moralistic tone of Xiaoniang's speech. Moreover, as no illicit sexual intercourse occurs, Miss Wu has no need to reclaim fallen chastity through death. Nonetheless, both these heroines pay the price for male sexual gratification, or, in this case, would-be gratification. Whereas Xiaoniang welcomed Li's advances from the outset, Miss Wu initially resisted. Her resolve was broken only after, what Christian de Pee terms, a protracted "literary assault."[45]

As already noted, numerous literary heroines died for their lovers from at least the eighth century. The reader will remember how the ninth-century adulterous concubine Bu Feiyan died by her master's hand when caught virtually *en flagrante*. While her lover may be partly or largely to blame for her death, she herself bears significant guilt, and as her dying confession reveals, she had no regrets given the romantic fulfillment thereby derived. Miss Wu, in contrast, is guilty of little more that entering into an unauthorized correspondence with a married man and resisting her mother's arranged marriage. While moralistically minded, contemporary readers may have considered these serious offenses (filial impiety and violation of social expectation), because, as the anonymous commentator argues, Zheng Xi is largely to blame given his instigation of the literary affair.

Another past heroine who died due to unrequited love is the tenth-century Wang Youyu and, indeed, Miss Wu alludes to her in one of her letters. Wang Youyu was a concubine-heroine who, being unhappy with the immorality associated with a courtesan's profession, wished to quit and marry. When the bureaucrat Liu Fu arrived in her district (Hengyang), she immediately marked him as her future husband. Although Liu returned her affections and the couple enjoyed a brief love affair, Liu was eventually recalled home by his father. Family business prevented him from honoring his promised reunion with Youyu, after which prolonged separation caused her to contract a fatal illness.[46] Although Miss Wu never saw Zheng Xi and the couple never experienced physical love, her death and its cause is similar to that of Wang Youyu insofar that both heroines died pining for absent lovers. True, Wang Youyu had sexual intercourse with Liu Fu, but given her courtesan status, this was not illicit; moreover, her affair with Liu was an attempt to extricate herself from what contemporaries considered a morally dubious profession. Hence, unlike Wang Xiaoniang, Wang Youyu's death does not salvage fallen chastity. Given the metaphysical nature of Miss Wu's "union" with Zheng, no precursor text in which the heroine dies quite lends itself to comparison with *Dream of Spring*. Despite this, the futility of her death intensifies its tragic nature. Ironically, it occurred at the very point when her mother had relented by returning the betrothal gifts to the Zhou's. This should have paved the way for a felicitous ending, as it did in many previous stories, such as Pan Yongzhong's, in which the illness of both protagonists prompted their parents to withdraw their objections.

Zheng's motive for publishing both his and Miss Wu's correspondence is unclear. At the conclusion of his preface, he surmises that readers will understand his sadness. In view of the sporadic apologetic tone, it is reasonable to assume that he wished to partly, if not largely, exculpate himself regarding her death and shift the blame to the mother and uncle. In a second elegy, he writes, "Who bears the guilt for having reduced that soul [i.e., the deceased Miss Wu] to this state? The mother's lack of clear vision, and the uncle's unreasonable words."[47] To be sure, this statement implies that Miss Wu's death was undesirable and avoidable. Elsewhere he repeatedly points to the deceased father's wish that his daughter marry a gentleman, apparently to counter the mother's acceptance of the unscholarly Mr. Zhou. Despite Zheng Xi's protestations and the largely first-person voice that controls the story, the reader is left with the distinct impression that Zheng himself is largely to blame for Miss Wu's demise. To be sure, Zheng's attempts to denounce others invite the reader's judgment. In this respect, the first-person voice that narrates purportedly autobiographic experience in regard an illicit affair resembles that found in "Yingying's Story," whose protagonist's apology invites the reader's censure despite Zheng Xi's attempt to exculpate himself of wrongdoing.

A postface penned by an pseudonymous author, possibly not Zheng Xi, styled Zhen Zishu (or Jia Zishu, depending on which edition one reads), foregrounds Zheng's role in Miss Wu's death. Commencing with quotes from Confucian classics so as to establish an ideal Confucian gentleman's character and behavior, the author proceeds to demonstrate how Zheng fell short of this ideal. Quoting from Zheng's poetry and letters, he argues that Zheng intended to seduce Miss Wu. "As for the girl's perturbed heart and stricken mind, the mess of her actions, the disobedience of her mother's orders, and her refusal to marry a common man to the point of wasting away her health without regret, in all this she was guided by Tianqu [i.e., Zheng Xi]. He cannot hide his guilty face."[48] Considering the postface's vitriolic tone and the clear intention to vilify Zheng, one wonders whether it was not written by the uncle, or perhaps the spurned fiancé. Cheng Yizhong speculates that it was written by Zheng Xi himself.[49] Regardless of its actual author, the postface highlights the notions of blame and guilt inherent to the plot while articulating the type of orthodox, moralistic standpoint that we have seen in many Song dynasty stories.

When compared to the Yuan-period stories analyzed above, several points of commonality are discernable. Perhaps most prominent is the pathos engendered by death and tragedy. Although the heroine's death is clearly construed in a negative light, the "lurid fascination"[50] exhibited by Zheng Xi's acquaintances provides an opportunity for eulogistic composition, while the manner in which death acts as a climax for romantic correspondence constitutes the work's *raison d'être*. This strikes a chord with the sad demise of Miss Jiao in *Bella and Scarlett* along with several famous Tang dynasty heroines, such as Huo Xiaoyu, Bu Feiyan, and the aforementioned Ling Yanbin, among others. Besides Miss Jiao, however, none of these heroines' deaths feel as tragic or senseless as that of Miss Wu. The denouement, furthermore, contrasts sharply with the majority of Song dynasty stories in which conjugal bliss was threatened by rival marriage proposals. Regardless of what staunch opposition was offered by stubborn mothers or aggressive suitors, such stories almost always concluded felicitously. And, if the heroine died, it was deemed necessary to salvage lost chastity. Hence the taste for tragedy and the pessimistic tone it engenders may be considered a distinctive marker of Yuan period stories.

I have noted above how enforced separation of lovers emerges as a trend in extant Yuan dynasty stories. In *Dream of Spring*, not only are the lovers kept apart, they do not even lay eyes on each other. Although unable to clandestinely meet as is usual in the love story, Zheng Xi and Miss Wu manage to engage in an imagined, literary-constructed sexual union. In one of Zheng's poems, he writes, "Night after night, I long for you, a dream of fluttering butterflies; the eastern wind accosts the apricot blossom in spring." In this context, butterflies are to a flower as males are to a lover, hence the imagery alludes to a sexual encounter. In the ultimate line, Zheng likens himself to the eastern wind that captures Miss Wu, who in turn is likened to an apricot blossom. Miss Wu replies in kind: "On the pillow with the mandarin ducks I think of you every night; in the dream of butterflies I encounter you each time." As already noted, mandarin ducks were a ubiquitous symbols of conjugal felicity and were often used as a metaphor describing sexual intercourse. Deprived of a real-life encounter, the lovers must entrust their sexual fantasies to poetic imagery. While this was nothing new in poetry, a similar narrative device was used some 300 or so years later by the famous Ming dynasty playwright Tang Xianzu (1550–1617). In his renowned play *Peony Pavilion*, the lovers make love in a dream, which mitigates the play's sexual content during an era of stringent moral conservatism. In *Dream of Spring*, such imagined intimacy merely accentuates the physical gulf that divides the lovers.

I have already discussed the significance of male fidelity in both Southern Song and Yuan dynasty stories. Although Zheng Xi does not fall ill or die to demonstrate his loyalty, and does not leave his wife in response to Miss Wu's death, the question of his demise is addressed. When discussing the possibility of her death in her final letter, Miss Wu urges Zheng to take care for the sake of his wife and children: "My death is not burdened by anyone I shall leave behind. If you should fall ill, the plum blossom in your hometown, and its blue-green plums [i.e., the young children], will have no one to rely on."[51] In one of Zheng's elegies, he considers death, and then rejects it based on this exhortation. After imagining her as an immortal in Heaven, he writes: "Then I knew that her soul was of a heart with me. Why would I refuse even going with her? Then suddenly my soul returned to my hometown, and I worried that my nest of children would be without support. Since in her letters the deceased told me to take care of myself, how could I die and leave everything behind? Alas, her mother died of her worries. Sincere were her regrets, but to what end? Duty prevents me from seeking death, and thus I trust that sooner or later my time will come."[52] These lines demonstrate that Zheng, even if insincere, at least felt the need to address the idea that he, too, should die for loyalty to his beloved. This is further evidence of death as a demonstration of male fidelity vis-à-vis the culture of romance during the era.

The social disparity between the educated and talented scholar-official and his rival, the son of the Zhou family, is also noteworthy. Zheng's charge that he beguiled Miss Wu's mother with money suggests a wealthy commoner, perhaps someone belonging to the despised merchant class. Indeed, the anonymous author of the postface confirms that Zhou was a "common (status) man." Moreover, as Miss Wu observes, "Of the scriptures and the histories he has never learned; the music of his lute is not worth hearing."[53] Therefore, male sexual rivalry is again conflated with both class rivalry and education level. Given unprecedented commercial expansion throughout the Yuan and, notably, the Ming dynasty, rivalry between literate yet impoverished members of scholar-official families and wealthy yet culturally inferior merchants and townspeople became more commonly depicted in love stories than previously.

Besides the blending of poetic and prose genres, *Dream of Spring* is also unusual given its deceptively simple, even mundane, storyline that lacks the remarkable turn of events typical of the love story. Static plot devices predominate as narrative interest is invested in the lovers' (or would-be lovers') emotions, hopes, and fears. Moreover, its focus on arranged marriage is also unusual. To be sure, given its epistolary form, it's purportedly historical, first-person narrative voice, and the conflicting voices within the text, the story resists comparison with prototypical love stories based on the analytical parameters of this study.

Uxorial Fidelity

The previous two chapters discussed Song dynasty storytellers' increasing emphasis on widow chastity and wifely fidelity. This trend intensified in stories and anecdotal narratives of the Yuan dynasty.

Set in Jiaxing (modern Zhejiang), another of Qu You's stories, "Story of Aiqing," tells of a wife who, during the last chaotic years of the dynasty, committed suicide to avoid rape by the commander of a Mongol army. Before her marriage to a Mr. Zhao, Luo Ai'ai (also known as Aiqing) was a celebrated courtesan renowned for both beauty and wit, as well as poetic and artistic talent. Zhao commanded enormous wealth and hailed from a family of scholar-officials, although he does not appear to have been a serving bureaucrat at the time of his marriage. Aiqing became an ideal wife. The narrator tells how she "[d]iligently undertook her wifely duties, strictly administered the family rules, chose her words carefully before speaking, and did not act without attention to ritual. Zhao valued her highly." Domestic happiness is interrupted when Zhao's paternal relation offers him a post in the central government. Unwilling to leave home for fear of his mother (his father is already deceased) and wife's safety, he is hesitant to accept. The selfless Aiqing persuades him otherwise: "I have heard that a man makes his mark in the world with martial prowess. A man, being of strong constitution, should stand tall. He should establish a name for himself so as to glorify his parents. How can you allow romantic love (*enqing*) to stand in the way of success and reputation? It will be more than enough for me to take care of your mother's needs." Thus relieved of his filial obligation, Zhao chooses an auspicious day to leave. By the time he arrives in the capital, Dadu (modern Beijing), however, illness has forced his relative to leave office. Without means to support himself, Zhao is stranded and unable to immediately return.

During his absence, the mother falls ill over excessive worry about her son. "Aiqing would diligently administer her medicine and personally prepare all her meals. So as to avert disaster, she would worship the Buddha and other divinities; in order to allay the mother's fears, she would sooth[e] her with white lies." Despite such solicitous treatment, the mother's condition persisted and, six months later, she died. Aiqing's devotion at this time equaled her nursing. She "mourned according to the prescribed ritual, even making the coffin herself. She buried her mother-in-law in White Ramie Village. After the burial, she would weep before the spirit tablet day and night. Her excessive sadness was such that she grew quite thin."

It is then that rival claimant to the throne Zhang Shicheng raises troops and sweeps through Jiaxing. The central government dispatch forces to oppose the rebels but, suffering defeat, they plunder the area, Jiaxing included. One of the commanders attempts to force Aiqing to become his mistress. Feigning compliance, she buys time to bathe (in preparation for burial), after which she hangs herself with a silk scarf. The commander then wraps her body in an embroidered quilt and buries her beneath ginkgo trees in the back garden.

After the fighting subsides and the rebel armies disperse, Zhao finally manages to return home. All that greets his eyes, however, are "rats running over the rafters and owls hooting in the trees." Having learned of his mother and wife's demise from an old servant, he exhumes his wife's body. When he uncovered her corpse, "her face was as though still alive as her skin had not corrupted." He then washes her body, dresses her in fine clothes, and reburies her in a coffin adjacent to his mother's grave. He then prays to her spirit: "My lady, you were intelligent and talented in life, so much that none could equal you. Although you have died, how could you mingle with the madding crowd and lose touch with me. If you can hear me in the underworld, I ask that you allow me to see you just once. Although the living and the dead tread separate roads and people fear to go against this, the love that I have for you is intense; of this you can have no doubt."

That night, Aiqing's ghost materializes before Zhao: "It was as if someone were approaching. Slowly, slowly and they were there. At a distance of five or six (double) paces, one could recognize the features; it truly was Aiqing. She was sparingly made up and wore everyday clothes. She looked just as before except that a silk scarf was wound around her neck." When she speaks, rather than address their mutual love, she recounts the mayhem she experienced. She thanks him for marrying her and thereby raising her from the debased status of a courtesan, which she denigrates with formulaic clichés. She predicts her rebirth as the son of a family named Song; this has been delayed until she could say goodbye thanks to their "powerful romantic affection." The couple then "enjoy each other's company as in former times." The next day, Zhao travels to verify Aiqing's prediction. When he locates the Song household, Mrs. Song has indeed given birth to a baby boy after having been pregnant for twenty months; the exact duration since Aiqing's death. The story concludes with Zhao's request to adopt the child and his ongoing social bond with the family.[54]

We have previously seen a wife's attempted suicide so as to prevent rape by marauding soldiers—that is, the twelfth-century Madam Lü, wife of the reluctant rebel, Fan Xizhou. And, indeed, the ideal that a woman would die rather than suffer sexual humiliation was enshrined in the Confucian tradition. Nonetheless, compared to the Song period, a far greater number of stories and anecdotes survive from the fourteenth century that idealize this feminine virtue, despite the paucity of extant Yuan-period short stories. This new trend demonstrates the increased importance placed on wifely fidelity during the period. From the fourteenth century on, this idea would only grow stronger throughout the remainder of the imperial period. Also significant here is the story's neglect of class disparity in regard to marriage. As we saw in the previous two chapters, earlier narratives were more likely to problematize marriage between upper-class men and former courtesans. That a former courtesan could marry into an elite family of scholar-officials, albeit an impoverished one, reflects the increased opportunities for lower-class women to better themselves as class boundaries became increasingly blurred throughout the period.

Coinciding with the didactic theme of wifely virtue is the heroine's role as a virtuous paragon, not unlike many Song dynasty stories that we have seen. In fact, the manner in which the narrative initially focuses on the female as well as her courtesan status is reminiscent of earlier heroines, such as Tan Yige and Wang Youyu. Unlike Tan's story, which lovingly foregrounds romantic aspects, "Story of Aiqing" diminishes romantic love while highlighting the heroine's filial devotion to her mother-in-law. When the matriarch is sick, Aiqing personally prepares meals instead of delegating the task to a servant. After the mother-in-law dies, Aiqing punctiliously discharges her duty to mourn the deceased not in order to fulfill social expectations but, it appears, due to genuine human affection. Furthermore, Aiqing supports social norms by persuading her husband to undertake—albeit unsuccessfully—a bureaucratic career and thereby serve the emperor. To be sure, the storyteller does not address the couple's romantic life. Ironically, it is only after Aiqing dies that the narrative acknowledges the physical side of their love and, even then, it is tersely addressed. Aiqing's virtue does not go unrewarded: as she tells Zhao in her goodbye speech, her reincarnation as a male is due to preservation of chastity (*zhenlie*) in the face of death.

Significantly, all this filial piety and wifely fidelity is specifically projected onto the national polity. At the conclusion of her farewell speech, Aiqing opines: "Wives and concubines who turn their backs on their masters and cast aside their families are no less shameful to their husbands than those who betray their sovereign and country, having partaken of his bounty." Evoking the well-established conflation of family management and national governance, the author—speaking through Aiqing—invites a secondary level of interpretation. Although readers may consider her story as based on historical events, this speech invites them to contrast Aiqing's fidelity to the treachery of unnamed others external to the narrative. In such social critique, one may discern widespread frustration with the corruption and political turmoil that attended the dynasty's collapse. The same sentiment is echoed in Aiqing's farewell song performed prior to her husband's leaving for the capital when she speaks of the "three honorable character-types" (*san zhen*)—that is, the filial child, the dutiful minister, and the faithful wife. All were considered different manifestations of the same virtue. Indeed, the plot exemplifies all three. First is Aiqing's devotion to her mother-in-law. Furthermore, to relieve Zhao's obligation to care for his mother, she persuades him to serve the sovereign, hence valorizing the second virtue. Finally, Aiqing's suicide to preserve her chastity completes the triangle. Moreover, in regard to her own speech about wives and concubines forsaking their masters, Aiqing herself is the embodiment of both a wife and concubine. Hence, a similar didactic tone found in many Song dynasty short stories reemerges during the Yuan with narratives such as this.

This story furthermore poignantly illustrates Li Changling's idea, cited in the previous chapter, that the love between a husband and wife survives physical death. When arguing that widowers should remain faithful to their deceased wives' memories by refraining from remarriage, he posits that the deceased wife's spirit would still have sentience and would, therefore, be hurt should a husband replace her with another.[55] Although we do not know whether Zhao remarried in this story, the sexual intimacy he shares with his deceased wife toward the conclusion is premised on such a belief. We saw how this reoccurred in other stories of the period, such as the "Lady in Green." Hence Bossler's idea of "a new model of the virtuous married couple" nicely encapsulates the relationship between Zhao and Aiqing.[56]

A story titled "The Martyr's Grave," recorded by Tao Zongyi after 1346, recounts the demise of a faithful wife who committed suicide to avoid an enforced second marriage. Madam Guo was the wife of an unnamed soldier under the command of a certain Commander Li stationed in Tiantai. Her beauty was praised by whoever saw her. As she was a common soldier's wife, presumably she was more subject to the male Gaze than her upper-class counterparts. Later in the narrative, we are told how she relied on weaving for her livelihood during her husband's incarceration. Commander Li was particularly impressed with her charms and so, when he dispatched troops to arrest some provincial thieves, he included Madam

Guo's husband in their company. He then availed himself of the husband's absence to visit the lady and flirt with her. She, however, staunchly resisted and informed her husband after his return. One day, when the commander was passing by their house, the soldier invited him inside for a cup of tea. Suddenly remembering his superior's affront to his wife, he seized a sword and attacked him. The commander, nonetheless, escaped, after which the husband was arrested. He was then arraigned for attempted murder of a commanding officer, an offense punishable by death.

During the husband's time in jail, he was befriended by an especially solicitous jailor. Unbeknownst to the husband, the jailor also coveted his wife. When a high-ranking official arrived with the power to execute criminals and it seemed as though the husband's days were numbered, the jailor sought the husband's blessing to marry his wife. When the husband suggested this to her, she replied: "Your [impending] death is down to my good looks. Do you think I would marry twice so as to save my skin?" After she returned home that day, she summoned her children and explained her intention to sell them.

> In tears, she said, "Your father will soon die. Your mother's death is also near. There's no one to look after you, my little ones. In the end, you must surely die from hunger and cold. I'll have to sell you. How can mother bare do this? Given the situation, there's nothing else I can do. When you live in someone else's house, it won't be like being at your parents' knees. You mustn't persist in being high and mighty or silly. If there is sentience in Heaven and you both grow up, you can make calendrical libations to your mother and father. In this way we will have survived [into the next generation]."

People in the street sympathized with the woman as she took her children to the marketplace. She used a third of the proceeds to prepare a meal for her husband. When she saw him, her grief initially prevented her from speaking. She suggested he share the meal with the jailor as repayment for the man's kindness. The remaining money, she said, could later be used for living expenses. She then told him that she would not be able to see him for some days as she had accepted work as a hired servant.

Following this final farewell, she went to a local river where the current was notoriously swift. Although she waded into its waters, inexplicably she was not washed away. In a manner befitting the *zhiguai* tradition, she "sat in a lotus position and died." This extraordinary occurrence evidently sanctifies her self-sacrifice. When news of her death reached the local government, they buried her nearby. After having successfully petitioned higher authorities, the official title of "Chaste Martyr, Madam Guo's Tomb" was carved in stone over her grave. Ironically, the husband was released after a high-ranking military official visited the locality and learned the truth of the case. Finally, the locals returned his children. In response to his wife's fidelity, the husband vowed never to remarry.[57]

Unlike the educated elite protagonists of numerous short stories, these are commoners—members of a military family subject to men of letters' prejudice throughout the imperial era. Focusing on commoners was not unique to the Yuan; as previously observed, numerous Song dynasty storytellers did so and, not infrequently, merchants acted as main protagonists of Tang dynasty stories. Nevertheless, it is the cultural values of the educated elite that prevail in such stories. To be sure, the purpose of Madam Guo's unswerving resolve and ultimate sacrifice was to avoid forced remarriage, which coincided with orthodox Confucian morality. Her sacrifice is rendered all the more poignant by the sale of her children, but, as she pointed out, it was also a practical measure that would ensure the perpetuity of ancestral sacrifices to both herself and her husband. Again, this satisfies orthodox Confucian practice. If social values of townspeople (*shimin*) and the lower classes differed from those of the ruling elite—which must have been the case to some extent—there is no evidence of it in this and other such narratives.

Madam Guo's setting aside the remaining two thirds of the proceeds that could later "be reclaimed and used for self-subsistence" is, in this light, curious as it implies foreknowledge that her husband would survive his incarceration. Perhaps embellishment after the fact was responsible for this inconsistency. That she died before her husband is, furthermore, unusual in this story type. More typical was the suicide of a faithful wife shortly after her husband's death or murder. Finally, as we have seen, the husband's vow not to remarry echoes many other thirteenth- and fourteenth-century stories. Hence, even military couples could aspire to the ideal of mutual conjugal fidelity.

This example is, admittedly, somewhat marginal to the prototypical love story. Nevertheless, it nicely illustrates the theme of wifely fidelity and its inclusion in the "chaste affection" section of the *History of Affection* attests to its generic affiliation with the category.[58] It also resembles anecdotes of female martyrs who committed suicide to avoid rape and enforced second marriages. Numerous such accounts were produced over the course of the Yuan dynasty. The earliest recount the suicide of loyal subjects of the fallen Song Empire—men, women, and children who, as noted above, chose death rather than surrender to an alien regime. Some tell of consorts and palace women who, having served the last Song dynasty emperors, preferred death when threatened with rape by Mongol soldiers.[59] Among these, that of Madam Wang is among the most widely circulated. She was captured by a Mongol commander during the fighting around 1276. Indeed, Mongol law permitted warriors to attain wives as war booty. Having persuaded him to postpone consummation of their "marriage" until her murdered husband's mourning period had elapsed, she was force-marched through mountainous terrain. En route, she threw herself from a cliff, but not before having written a patriotic suicide poem in her own blood on the cliff face. According to the legend that consequently arose, the passage of years and rain could not efface her handwritten testament. Decades after, the authorities erected a shrine commemorating her unswerving integrity.[60] Toward the fall of the dynasty, as social order disintegrated into corruption and lawlessness, many more such stories of female martyrs were recorded. Although they bear little generic resemblance to love stories, both story types share the increasingly important theme of wifely fidelity.

It is perhaps no surprise that Yuan-period narratives would often develop this theme given the increasing prominence placed on widow chastity at the time. To be sure, the idea of faithful wives and chaste widows is closely related. The Yuan government was so concerned about widow chastity that it eventually formulated a legal definition of a "chaste widow," in view of the numerous petitions it received for recognition as the dynasty progressed.[61] Households officially recognized as having produced a chaste widow were rewarded with reduced taxes and corvee labor obligations, not to mention social prestige. Hence, powerful incentives were given that contributed to the pressure placed on widows to remain unmarried. Yet widow chastity as a cultural value was nothing new, as we have seen in several other stories. Nonetheless, in regard to widows of the previous two dynasties, especially upper-class ones, remarriage was the norm, whereas the Yuan period marked a turning point against this trend.[62] From this period onward, more and more narratives would extol faithful wives and chaste widows. This growing social trend enables us to understand the actions of faithful heroines, such as Miss Jiao, who atoned for their sexual indiscretions with death.

A Turn of the Courtship Screw: Threesomes

In several erotic novellas (or, more precisely, medium-length short stories) of the Ming and Qing dynasties, the male protagonist simultaneously woos and wins not one but two or more wives. This significant new trend was an idea first developed during the Yuan dynasty. Although few such examples of what I will term the "erotic threesome" survive from the fourteenth century, this is likely due to poor textual preservation.

One of Qu You's stories, titled "Palace of Twin Fragrance," is a tale of two sisters, Lanying and Huiying, daughters of a wealthy Suzhou rice-seller. The story is set early in the *zhizheng* reign period (1341–70) of the Shun emperor (Borjigin Toghan-Temür, r. 1333–70) and commences with a lengthy focus on the sisters' living arrangements and cultural accomplishments. Their father installed them in a "palace" (a building at least two stories high, known as a *lou*; in this context, an Italian Renaissance-era *palazzo* comes to mind) named Lanying and Huiying's Palace of Twin Fragrance, from which the story takes its title. Unusually, the reader receives no description of the sister's physical charms; the narrator simply states that they "are both intelligent and beautiful." Their talent is particularly noticeable in their poetry. A short anthology of their poems, ten of which Qu You includes in the narrative, supposedly so impressed the famous Yuan dynasty poet Yang Weizhen (1296–1370) that he composed two poems in response. The love story proper commences when a young Master Zheng pays an extended visit. The sisters' father treats him as he would a family member given his friendship with Zheng's father. Zheng is described as "youthful, of a gentle disposition and in possession of elegant manners." Rather than stay within the family compound, as is more usual, he sleeps on his boat, which is moored below the tower, presumably on one of the canals for which Suzhou is famous. The two sisters direct their female Gaze on his—presumably—naked body as he bathes. On one such occasion, they toss a pair of lychees to him in a gesture of romantic affection; given the fruit's red outer kernel (the bridal color), it often symbolizes romantic love in traditional painting and poetry, while a pair symbolize fertility. Following this, on a moonlit night when all is still, the sisters lower a swing supported by silken chains to the level of his boat on which they hoist him up into their boudoir. "Face-to-face, their intense joy was such that they could not speak." Nonetheless, they entered the bedroom, hand in hand, where they "took full measure of intimacy." Several poems are exchanged following this initial encounter, after which all three meet every night (see figure 4.1).

Time elapses and Zheng worries about discovery and the social disgrace it would entail. In a pivotal monologue, the sisters propose a plan.

> We are deeply aware of our unworthiness and, although we live secluded in our women's quarters, we have a little knowledge of the classics and histories. We are, therefore, not unaware of voyeurism's shame and the merits of preserving ourselves [for our future husband]. Yet, when faced with [the beauty of] an autumn moon or spring flowers, we regret that such times may pass us by in vain. And so, given our weak natures, we're apt to lose control. We've been guilty of voyeuristic pleasures and have willingly given ourselves to you. We are grateful for the condescension you've showed us and that you have not rejected us. Although the six rites of marriage have not been performed, one word will be enough to seal our sincerity so that we may enjoy the pleasures of the bedroom and be your

Figure 4.1. Houses facing a canal in Suzhou. (Photograph courtesy of Alison Inglis)

> wives forever and ever. Why do we say this all of a sudden and invite suspicion? Mr. Zheng! Mr. Zheng! Although we're mere women, we are capable of careful planning. On some future day, if and when our affair comes to light and our parents reprimand us, just do as we say and eventually we can marry into your family. If you don't follow this plan, then you can look for us in the underworld. In any case, we won't marry another.

Immediately after, Zheng's father writes to press his return, yet his reluctance to leave raises his host's suspicions. During a search of his daughters' apartments, the girls' father discovers Zheng's love poetry. He then decides to marry them for practical considerations—that is, the irreversibility of their sexual indiscretions in addition to Zheng's good looks and first-rate family pedigree. Zheng's father readily agrees when a matchmaker is sent to propose marriage. After this the young man lives with his in-laws in an uxorilocal marriage, which was not infrequent during the imperial period. The narrative concludes with information that locals knew about the affair and circulated it as a written account.[63]

This is perhaps the first time a protagonist engaged in a threesome with two women whom he later married. Dan Fulang, protagonist of the Southern Song story "A Husband and Wife Honor their Old Pledge," discussed in chapter 3, also married two wives within a short timeframe. Yet the circumstances under which Dan came to marry his predestined childhood sweetheart and then acquire her fellow courtesan, as well as the authorial concerns, differ vastly from that of Master Zheng and the twin sisters. He certainly did not sleep with them simultaneously, as was the case here. Dan's second wife, Li Ying, was of humble courtesan status and became his servant-concubine only through the intercession of his first wife, Xing Chunniang, whom had been recently rescued from sexual servitude. Unlike Zheng, Dan did not have a clandestine affair with the two women. Besides this, the only other comparable example is a Tang dynasty story in which the protagonist sleeps simultaneously with two goddesses.[64] Yet this "fairy" story was exceptional, and the protagonist kept faith with his original goddess. Protagonists invariably wooed one woman at a time. Even in the racy seventh-century story, the *Immortal's Grotto*, the two goddesses refused the protagonist's proposal that all three sleep together. The turn of the screw found in "Palace of Twin Fragrance" anticipates the later trend of scholar-beauty romances and erotic works in which male protagonists have affairs with several women, sometimes simultaneously—what Martin Huang terms "polygamous desire."[65]

The manner in which the sisters take the initiative conforms to a well-established pattern, even if the device of the swing to afford their lover access is unique. Yet the throwing of the lychees reminds us of how Pan Yongzhong and his lover tossed a pecan between their second-story rooms. As they express their willingness to marry none other than Master Zhang, the sisters' monologue is laced with the same type of orthodox morality as we have seen in other stories. The subsequent marriage reclaims their fallen chastity. Their father's response to their indiscretion further echoes Liang Yiniang's parents who, for similar reasons, allowed their daughter to marry her self-chosen lover. Unlike the Liang Yiniang story, the sisters' monologue sharply focuses on the immorality associated with illicit sex. Phrases such as not being "not unaware of voyeurism's shame" and having "willingly given ourselves to you" indicate *mens rea*. Such ideas place the story firmly within the moralistically orthodox intellectual milieu of the thirteenth and fourteenth centuries, although this undermines the story's otherwise celebration of romantic love.

As may be seen from this chapter, several themes and trends discernable in the Southern Song dynasty came to fruition during the brief hundred or so years of Mongol rule. Among these is the degree to which female fidelity was developed in not only love stories but also the anecdotal literature of the period. Hand in glove with the valorization of faithful widows, heroines unable to marry their self-chosen lover often chose death so as to reclaim lost chastity. The same ideas used to justify widow chastity were applied equally to males and, in the pages of the love story, mutual conjugal fidelity expanded the culture of romance beyond the straightforward celebration of men's romantic life, as was the case during the mid- and late Tang era. Accordingly, male protagonists remained faithful to deceased spouses and lovers, even at the cost of their lives. Lovers were often held apart. To be sure, such was the pessimistic tone of many love stories during this period that double-tragic conclusions became quite popular. It was also during the Yuan dynasty that the love story in its short, classical language form transformed into the medium-length short story. The significance of this development can hardly be underestimated as it paved the way for new genres, such as the scholar-beauty story, the erotic short story, and the erotic novel.

Conclusion

As may be seen from this study, social, economic, and political shifts across the Tang-Song transition are reflected in groundbreaking new themes and motifs. Northern Song storytellers exhibited a deep concern with social mobility, something largely ignored by their eighth- and ninth-century predecessors. Unlike tersely narrated Tang dynasty stories of marriage that largely illustrated the workings of conjugal predestiny, or else told of utopian marriages with immortal women, marriage between human protagonists became a major concern for eleventh- and early twelfth-century storytellers. Marriage and transitory affairs between humans and nonhumans, such as ghosts and foxes, also became more frequent as the ontological Other became less threatening, at least in the pages of a love story.[1] Furthermore, greater detailed—albeit metaphoric—description of sexual intercourse further distinguished stories of this period from earlier ones that tended to depict such acts more sparingly. Nevertheless, many Song-period stories were narrated within a moralistic framework even though this countermines the story's overall valorization of romance. While female chastity, particularly widow chastity, had always been revered in the Confucian tradition, this ideal began to receive greater emphasis on the other side of the Tang-Song transition.

As already noted, social attitudes toward romance and sexuality did not fundamentally change over the Tang-Song transition. Both remained politically and morally subversive. So as to defuse the threat romance posed to authority, Song storytellers continued to utilize the same strategies as their Tang predecessors while developing new ones. So as to demonstrate loyalty, many heroines—particularly courtesans—continued to die for their lovers. By far the most common strategy, nonetheless, was to neutralize the criminal and immoral nature of premarital sex through marriage. And, given the importance of social mobility, marriage became the endgame for many a love story. In a society that enshrined arranged marriage as an institution, love stories envisaged the ideal of freely chosen marriage based on romantic attachment rather than sociomonetary considerations. Occasionally, narrative interest centered on events that occurred *after* the marriage. Some stories portray an arranged marriage in which the couple enjoys a loving relationship. Judging from the pleasure couples found in their mutual poetic and cultural pursuits, love seemed to encompass more than mere physical coupling. Indeed, it is significant that the vast majority of Song-period love stories involved poetry exchange. Hence for the first time in the love story's development, romantic love, admiration of another's cultural attainments, sex, marriage, and parentally sanctioned marriage were all harmonized; one element did not preclude another as tended to be the case in earlier stories. While Mr. Zhang and Yingying's ninth-century romance was but a transitory affair, such a pair tended to marry in the pages of Song-period stories. Parents tended to replace the senior male as arbitrators of romantic felicity, although the senior male as a character type did not completely disappear. Consequently, domestic and garden settings were added to those of metropolitan streets. If the parents were unwilling to agree to a match, a sympathetic magistrate might overrule them. Hence many love stories of this period were closely affiliated with the newly emerging *gong'an* story type in which magistrates solved crimes and passed judgment on wrongdoers.

One wonders what led to this new concern about marriage and why Tang dynasty storytellers largely ignored it. In stories from both sides of the Tang-Song transition, romance acted as a testing ground for loyalty; would a woman freely choose a man were social obligation and pecuniary necessity laid aside? In both periods marriage was inextricably tied to social obligation. Bound by the time-honored dictum of "one's parents command and the words of a matchmaker" found in the *Book of Mencius*,[2] betrothed couples were expected to obey their parents' will. It was only in the case of a second marriage that they might choose themselves. Indeed, arranged marriage was considered an alliance between two families. Rather than an expression of romantic love, its purpose was to forge and strengthen sociopolitical power and was, theoretically, irrelevant to or incompatible with romance. Furthermore, in premodern China, marriage was considered predestined. Perhaps, for Tang dynasty storytellers, something predestined could not constitute a testing ground for freely given loyalty. And although this still applied to Song society, other factors engendered change.

To be sure, the comparatively fluid social boundaries that developed during the Song dynasty led to considerable anxiety over social mobility. As I have already observed, membership to the upper echelons of society, the scholar-official class, was not guaranteed as it largely depended on scholastic success measured by an increasingly competitive examination system. Although every male member of a family need not have attained the presented scholar degree or held office, this was the main way in which a family could establish and maintain elite status. Even so, office-holding was not particularly well remunerated and it was possible for a modest family's fortunes to decline after the death of its (male) head of household, as numerous narratives bear witness. Hence, households that relied primarily on bureaucratic service alone without substantial financial backup would have been particularly vulnerable to life's vicissitudes, especially in a period with a comparatively high mortality rate. Little wonder that eminent northern families began to marry into more affluent southern gentry clans by the Southern Song period. Illustrious aristocratic clans of the Tang dynasty, by contrast, did not generally experience such a degree of financial instability, politically instability notwithstanding. I would, therefore, argue that Song-era scholar-official families' relatively uncertain socioeconomic base contributed to considerable anxiety on the part of educated male storytellers, many of whom hailed from such families.

Furthermore, faction fighting among the ruling elite became increasingly bitter as the eleventh century progressed. Although the bureaucratic reforms of the *qingli* reign period (1041–1048) caused the first serious fissures, an extremely rancorous and protracted struggle was triggered by the chief minister, Wang Anshi's, economic reforms, first implemented in 1167.[3] As two major factions vied for supremacy over many decades, those on the losing side frequently found themselves exiled to the malarial south where many died of disease. Many victims of banishment lamented their fate in their poetry and prose writing. Such power struggles may have contributed to anxiety over the type of downward mobility that we perceive in love stories even though faction fighting *per se* was irrelevant to the plot.

Given the increased anxiety that the Northern Song elite evidently felt over downward social mobility, it follows that marriage would have become an important mechanism to avoid this, more so than previously.

Marriage, as a means of improving a family's socioeconomic position, took on considerable importance for the upper classes, whose lives and interests are often portrayed in short stories of the period. For the first time in the love story's development, therefore, stories told of marriage between couples of comparatively equitable class background. Others focused on interclass marriage between educated, elite men and women of inferior status, especially courtesans, taking the Tang prototype of the temporary liaison between the two groups a step further. Yet other narratives took townspeople as their subjects, such as the merchant's son and tavern keeper's daughter in the "Story of Distant Mist."

Unlike Jane Austen and many eighteenth- and nineteenth-century English authors who plumbed the intricacies of marriage and its interconnection with inheritance and property ownership, Song dynasty storytellers frequently neglected such finer considerations. The minute details of financial disparity, such as who stands to gain how much by marrying whom, the size of the woman's dowry or the bride price paid by the groom's parents, are all taken for granted. Class disparity, when addressed, is often reduced to stereotypical labels. Hence, Owen's observation about the "repression" of financial reality in Tang-era stories may also be observed in those of the Song. Nonetheless, Owen sees this as a gauge to detect the gulf between social realty and what he understands as "fictions" of romance. For many Song-Yuan period storytellers, socioeconomic reality was generally an unspoken binary opposition against which the culture of romance could develop. This is because their interests lay elsewhere.

For many such storytellers, individual agency in regard to marriage became the primary focus. In union stories culminating in marriage between partners of disparate social status and/or wealth, often the ethical imperative to honor a betrothal despite such inequality carried the main narrative burden. In the story of Zhang Youqian, the son of an elite yet impoverished family, although class disparity is addressed, it is the importance of honoring a betrothal that is stressed. This is the central theme that holds a variety of secondary ones together. In the "Story of Fan Xizhou and Madam Lü," the importance of remaining faithful to one's spouse in the face of separation and intense social pressure to remarry overrides both class differentiation and even disloyalty to the state. In this case, marital fidelity was mutual. Hence, moral imperatives and ethical principles were valorized over socioeconomic reality of which the storytellers and their readers took for granted. It was the storytellers' ingenuity that enabled them to harmonize romantic love, time-honored folklore, and orthodox ethical principles.

Nonetheless, this emphasis and its consequent disregard of socioeconomic disparity saw many Song period protagonists make imprudent, certainly inequitable, marriages. Hence, some stories ironically trivialized the compulsion to marry well. Many stories may therefore be understood as wish fulfillment on the part of the male articulating subject—that is, to choose a poetically talented, physically attractive, and morally upright wife who requites the young man's love despite social and financial imperatives against such a match. This is not to say that the stories were works of fiction in the modern, Western sense. Since many were based on fact and circulated orally as gossip before being recorded, they almost certainly caught public attention due to their newsworthiness or their extraordinary nature. If, supposing, a Miss Li ever actually brought a legal suit to nullify a rival betrothal, as we saw in "Zhang Hao," this would have undoubtedly been the exception, not the rule. To be sure, the newsworthiness attached to a well-circulated story and its exceptional nature implies the opposite, as selected end commentaries make explicit. Therefore, wish fulfillment discernable in many stories was thought to be grounded in historical precedent and not simply a fictitious fantasy. One's wish to win the lottery is a good analogy; the hope to do so is based on real-life occurrences, even though the chances are slim.

As many scholars have noted, orthodox Confucian morality, more so than before, may be discerned in numerous short stories from the eleventh century onward. The love story is no exception to this general trend. Even while a storyteller often valorizes an illicit affair, his exuberance is tempered with didactic apologies. The male storyteller's moralistic agenda is frequently projected onto the heroine. In this way, some love stories attempted to contain romance within morally acceptable boundaries. This often resulted in a tension between moral conservative and more permissive voices that competed within the same text. This pattern undoubtedly reflects the ascendency of stringently orthodox Confucian principles as exemplified by Zhu Xi and his followers that began in the eleventh century. This trend would only intensify throughout the Southern Song and would hold sway for the remainder of the imperial period. While many scholars have linked such moral orthodoxy—particularly in regard to women's social status—to the rise of Neo-Confucianism, Beverley Bossler has demonstrated how "Neo-Confucian scholars were not so much leading changes in gender ideology as providing post-facto justifications for those changes."[4] In other words, the gradual acceptance of Neo-Confucian thought was part of a wider intellectual trend. As Zhuge Yibing argues, many major Northern Song statesmen and thinkers sought to reassert Confucian moral standards that were neglected during the period of disunity prior to the dynasty's establishment. The reaffirmation of such cardinal Confucian virtues may be seen in the forthright opinions offered to the emperor by luminaries such as Tian Xi, Wang Yuran, Fan Zhongyan (989–1052), Ouyang Xiu (1007–72), and the like.[5] Such a trend certainly makes sense in light of the socioeconomic changes relating to women's property rights during the Yuan dynasty, as studies by Birge and others have shown. Regardless of causes, it should be no surprise to see such an important intellectual shift reflected in stories of the period. Significant for this study is that such moralistic thought acts as a period marker for love stories of the era, distinguishing them from earlier ones.

More so than Tang-era heroines, Song-Yuan period women were constructed as virtuous paragons who upheld aspects of orthodox Confucian morality. In the Northern Song, the courtesan Ai'ai exemplified "widow" chastity. Tan Yi'ge, Miss Xiao, and others hold firm to the Confucian notion that a woman should not know two husbands, while the latter's decision not to elope was based partly in deference to her parents, thus honoring filial piety. Madame Sun repels adulterous advances and, after her remarriage, teaches her new husband financial integrity. Madame Wang in "Story of Distant Mist" resists her father's attempt to remarry her after having been forcibly separated from an insolvent husband. Stories such as these display a heightened emphasis on female fidelity and filial piety, both of which formed cornerstones of Confucian social regulation. As Bossler notes, though, in regard to intellectual trends, while this theme was not overly prominent during the eleventh century, it would take on much greater importance after the fall of the Northern Song in 1127.[6] Hand in hand with orthodox morality, the construction of female characters as virtuous paragons would continue throughout the imperial period.

Related to this is the increased use of a narrative form that focused on female subjects. Akin to a biography, the narrative commences with the heroine and tells of her social background and early life. Such an introduction provides the foundation for one or two salient events developed in anecdotal form. Alternatively, a fully developed narrative may follow. Ensuing events are largely narrated from the heroine's point of view, albeit in a third-person voice. Often the reader is allowed considerable access to the heroine's thoughts and feelings through monologue, dialogue, or poetry. The same device also justifies dubious moral aspects of her story, such as Tan Yi'ge's courtesan status. As I have noted, however, this focus on the female does not achieve, or even attempt to achieve, genuine female agency. The heroine remains an object of the male narrator's brush, often his Gaze. The female is interpellated in the Althusian sense. In other words, she is upheld as a paragon of virtue and sometimes, in an end commentary, she is favorably contrasted with those of dubious morality. While this favorable portrayal of women may evince heightened respect on the part of male storytellers and readers, such constructed paragons were, according to the recorders themselves, exceptions rather than representative of the norm.

We saw in chapter 1 how romantic aspects of numerous eighth- and ninth-century love stories were virtually overshadowed by androcentric considerations. Accordingly, women were frequently reduced to tokens of exchange in a male world of sociopolitical and sexual competition. Although male-centered themes do not entirely disappear in Song dynasty love stories, their importance is largely diminished because storytellers tended to focus on other matters. Hence, from the Northern Song onward, the love story's plots are often more "intimate" and small scale as they focus on two lovers along with the arbitrator of their happiness, be it a parent or magistrate. Erotic triangles are still occasionally found but, rather than overshadow romantic love, they tend to present a trivial obstacle that the lovers must overcome in order to marry. In such cases, the third point of the triangle frequently remains a shadowy figure unworthy of the storyteller's attention. Therefore, many Song dynasty stories do not lend themselves to the type of analysis that foregrounds androcentric relationships in Tang-era narratives—certainly not to the same degree. As noted earlier, it may be problematic to characterize these earlier love stories as "celebrations" of romantic love since literary romantic liaisons of the period were frequently overshadowed by male social relationships. In view of this, I would argue that the culture of romance did not fully come to fruition until storytellers of the Northern Song period freed humanistic love from the shackles of androcentric concerns. As Wang Yi-pei notes, "The scope of Song men's concern for women appears more broad and deep [compared with their Tang dynasty predecessors]."[7] If, therefore, Tang dynasty writers became more interested in women, as Rouzer observes, this trend was maintained and refined by their Song-era counterparts.[8]

Compared to the groundbreaking themes pioneered by Northern Song storytellers, those of the Southern Song seem somewhat modest. Nonetheless, thematic innovations that emerged during this period evidently influenced storytellers, writers, and playwrights of the Yuan and Ming dynasties. Lovesick males, the death of both main protagonists, cross-dressing, chaste widows, and the like were to become staple themes of late imperial literature.

The upsurge of reunion stories throughout the twelfth century, not only in regard to the love story but also the *zhiguai* genre, are easily understandable in light of the catastrophic changes wrought by near-dynastic collapse. Countless people perished during the invasion while large numbers of refugees fled the Jurchen armies to settle in the south. Although no statistical data exists, it is reasonable to assume that numerous married couples would have been permanently separated in the chaos following the fall of Bianliang (modern Kaifeng). In this respect, the short stories of the period bear witness to a phenomenon on which many historians and anecdotalists remained silent. If short stories generally represent remarkable, newsworthy exceptions to the norm, extant reunion stories may therefore be read as wish fulfillment that at least some separated couples may have reunited.

An important and innovative idea found in Southern Song love stories is the evocation of marital predestiny to condone illicit sex and marital free choice. This often reoccurs in Luo Ye's *Drunken Man's Talk*. As we saw in chapter 1, many Tang-era short stories illustrate the workings of conjugal predestiny, which no doubt reflects widespread belief in fatalism and encouraged conformity to the institution of arranged marriage. Author-compilers such as Luo Ye, however, utilized this idea to subvert traditional norms in support of the culture of romance; if marriage is truly predestined, what does it matter whether the couple arranges their own marriage by selecting a partner of their choice? They will still be destined to marry, in any case. Accordingly, any illicit sex involved becomes akin to an informal consummation of a marriage vow. This new approach to marital predestiny must certainly have represented a considerable challenge to tradition orthodoxy, especially given the ascendency of moral conservatism as exemplified by Neo-Confucian thought. To be sure, the institution of arranged marriage was so entrenched that it continued until the early decades of the twentieth century when it was finally swept aside by the May Fourth intellectuals. The longstanding nature of the institution indicates the foresightedness of Southern Song storytellers who opposed it.

The phenomenon of husbands remaining faithful to absent or deceased wives constitutes another significant new theme that we first see in stories of the Southern Song. Its reoccurrence in several stories complements the heightened importance of writing about women during the period. It also reflects the increasingly influential idea of marital equality as the basis for interpersonal ethics—that is, husband and wife as equal partners supporting patrilineal values. Behind such ideas is the moral conservatism that defined the period, according to which widow chastity was extended to widowers. Its proponents also disdained the spread of concubinage during a period in which class boundaries were being increasingly eroded. Hence, arguments for conjugal parity were often made with the iniquities of concubinage and its consequent effacing of proper class distinction in mind. We know that wealthy, upper-class women, the type often portrayed in the stories, often commanded large dowries that assured a degree of financial independence. Through such financial resources, they likely secured the respect of not only their husbands but also that of their in-laws. Large dowries, therefore, may have partly fostered a heightened respect for upper-class women. Nonetheless, in the pages of the love story, the theme of marital equality significantly redefines the culture of romance's parameters while undermining whatever androcentric values we may find.

While many heroines of the love story continued to fall ill or die due to unrequited love, that the male protagonists of Southern Song stories also did so marks another thematic innovation of the period. Although this first appeared in the Tang dynasty story "Ouyang Zhan," an isolated example and marginal to the love story's prototypes, Southern Song storytellers developed the motif more seriously. If a woman's falling ill or dying for a man foregrounded androcentric values by bolstering men's self-esteem, as was seen in earlier stories, lovesick men imply a reversal of this logic. This suggests increased importance of women, gender parity, and complements the motif of faithful husbands. Related to this are stories of suicide pacts in which young, disenfranchised lovers preferred death given overwhelming social pressure to separate. Premised on belief in reincarnation, some couples made this choice hoping for romantic fulfillment in the next lifetime. As a plot device, the idea provided a new resolution to the typical obstacles that lovers faced in order to marry, albeit a tragic one. Such a denouement would have been inconceivable to Tang dynasty storytellers, whose literary love affairs were generally fleeting in nature. Indeed, much pathos was engendered by the lovers' eventual separation, or else the heroine's death. As it became increasingly common for both lovers to die in Yuan and Ming dynasty short stories and opera, we may appreciate the influence Southern Song storytellers exerted on later generations.

By the Yuan dynasty, female fidelity had assumed even greater importance than before. Numerous stories and anecdotes recount instances of suicide or heroic deaths whereby wives resist rape or enforced remarriage. Tao Zongyi's anecdotal collection, *Record Completed after Ploughing*, exhibits a particularly strong predilection for this theme. As already noted, the theme complements the literary valorization of female martyrs who died resisting bandits and invading men-at-arms. Given the growing value placed on widow chastity throughout the Yuan that developed hand in hand with the rise of Confucian orthodoxy, this should not surprise us. Nonetheless, the very frequency with which the theme reoccurs in narrative, historical, and anecdotal collections is striking.

Related to female fidelity are doubly tragic conclusions whereby upper-class protagonists of both gender die. *Bella and Scarlett* was a first in this regard. We saw how some heroines of Northern Song stories died in order to uphold moral orthodoxy. The adulterous heroine of "Story of Twin Peaches" commits suicide to restore her fallen virtue, having entered into a scandalous affair with a married man. Similarly, the courtesan Ai'ai died as would a chaste widow after the death of her *de facto* husband. Having indulged their romantic passions, both these women atoned for illicit sex with their deaths. The heroine of *Bella and Scarlett* died for the same reason; unable to marry the man to whom she had given herself, in the face of a coercive arranged marriage, death was the only available means of remaining sexually faithful to one man according to both prevailing social expectations and the culture of romance. The reason her lover, Shen Chun, also chose to die is more difficult to explain. Presumably, his dying for an unattainable lover was an extension of the Southern Song idea that a husband and wife were equal and that a wife, in Li Changling's words, "is not easy to replace."[9] Indeed, Shen makes the same remark to his brother toward the story's conclusion. Although he and Miss Jiao were not formally married, their marriage may easily be considered a *de facto* one. As already noted, the notion of gender equality in regard to marriage is consistent with the heightened importance placed on women during the period, while extending the culture of romance's parameters beyond what was previously expected. Death, however, in Chinese culture is almost always viewed in a negative light. To be sure, this was the way in which the anonymous author of *Bella and Scarlett*'s preface understood the conclusion. When discussing how the lovers were "hounded to death," he remarks "truly, it is grievous."[10] Furthermore, the story's narrator opines, "that those so young should have met with such misfortune seems to have stemmed from the parents not having examined their hearts and inclinations. Is it not sorrowful? Is it not sad?"[11] If male readers derived pleasure from the pathos generated by tragic conclusions in which the heroine died, it may have been more difficult to stomach the hero's death. Were double tragedies, then, intended as indictments of the growing moral conservatism of the period vis-à-vis the culture of romance? One would be justified to think so.

Even so, it is interesting to note how tragic conclusions are embellished with paranormal phenomena. In *Bella and Scarlett*, both lovers' ghosts attest to a happy afterlife on the immortal isles. The deceased married couple in "Story of Cuicui" similarly profess contentment and resist a father's intention to remove their remains from their grave. And the spirits of Liang Shanbo and Zhu Yingtai return as butterflies. Far from frightening and inexplicable phenomena, these manifestations of the dead are portrayed as miraculous. They enable the living to communicate directly with the deceased and receive assurance of their happiness. Perhaps, then, paranormal elements grafted onto double-tragic conclusion were intended to lighten the story's tone? If so, they certainly undermine whatever pathos might be felt given the protagonists' death and, with it, much of the negativity we might attach to it. In this light, the couple's death may alternatively be understood as a further indication of the type of wish fulfillment we have seen in earlier stories. In this case, the articulating subject projects a wish for a happy ever-after, even in the face of permanent separation by death. I am not, however, endorsing this as the preferred interpretation; I am merely exploring an alternative.

Even when both lovers/spouses of Yuan-period stories do not die, prolonged and repeated separation is a reoccurring theme. A surprising number of extant union stories conclude with permanent loss, while failure to reunite subverts the prototypical conventions necessary for what would otherwise constitute reunion stories. To be sure, out of eight love stories found in *New Stories while Trimming the Lampwick*, six follow this pattern. Therefore, if Song dynasty stories offer overly optimistic resolutions to obstacles, those of the Yuan period are marked by pessimistic sentiment—one that generally precludes a happy ever-after. Although marriage remains the goal of our literary couples, tragic circumstances are such that they rarely realize or attain their conjugal bliss. According to this trend, the culture of romance becomes an elusive ideal—one much sought-after but rarely found. In this respect, Yuan dynasty stories resemble some famous Tang-period ones that concluded with the death of the heroine and the lovers' permanent separation. Unlike these eighth- and ninth-century stories, matrimony was the expected outcome. Under the Yuan dynasty storyteller's writing brush, the poignancy of the tragic denouement is intensified with the demise or permanent separation of both protagonists.

The cult of *qing* (love, affection, feeling, sentiment, empathy—it is difficult to find an exact English equivalent for this particularly ambiguous term) during the late Ming dynasty has attracted much scholarly attention, and rightly so.[12] Wang Yangming (1472–1529), Li Zhi (1527–1602), and other proponents of *qing* as a natural and legitimate human emotion exerted a significant influence on Chinese philosophy while laying the foundation for an equally profound reevaluation of *qing* in the field of literature. Groundbreaking works, such as the *Peony Pavilion* (*Mudan ting*), *Peach Blossom Fan* (*Taohua shan*), *Palace of Everlasting Youth* (*Changhen dian*), and *Plum in a Golden Vase* all explored the nature of *qing* in a positive light. This trend eventually culminated in the late-imperial masterpiece *Dream of Red Mansions*, which, according to its author, is "largely about *qing*." Daniel Hsieh, for one, has recognized the importance of *qing* as a theme of Tang-era love stories that arose many centuries prior to the literary and philosophical debates of the late Ming dynasty.[13] Significantly, *qing* as a cultural concept did not disappear only to reemerge hundreds of years later. As this study shows, *qing* was a crucial theme underlying most, if not all, love stories of the Song and Yuan periods. Frequent evocation of the term *qing* as an intertextual marker contributed to the corpus' generic identity. References to "those of feeling" (*you qing zhe*) embedded in the narrative implied a constructed, if not actual, readership for the love story. *Qing*, when conceptualized as a legitimate human emotion, was applied to evaluate male protagonists' behavior toward women, particularly those who had committed themselves emotionally. Sometimes this was made explicit, but more often than not it remained an unspoken criteria. Such consistent use of the concept throughout the Song-Yuan era attests to the concept's literary and, no doubt, social importance during this period. Compared to its usage during the Tang period, it had clearly reached a considerable level of sophistication, particularly when we consider women's heightened focus in Song-Yuan narrative literature and the correspondingly diminished emphasis on androcentric concerns. Therefore, the love story of the Song-Yuan period paved the way for the more thorough exploration of *qing* that was to occur in late-imperial China.

Based on the present study, key aspects of Song dynasty short stories are difficult to correlate with Zhou Shuren's disparagement. Notwithstanding some that are set in the pre–Song period, the vast majority narrate contemporary events, despite Zhou's assertion to the contrary. Many Song-era stories were didactic, as Zhou and others have observed, but given the increasing influence of orthodox moralistic thought that coalesced into and was represented by Neo-Confucian, such influence on contemporary narrative literature was inevitable. Yet, moralistic exhortations do not detract from the interest and aesthetic beauty of the best-written stories any more than didactic content marred Zhou's own writing. To be sure, his fiction doggedly satirized traditional society and encouraged the overthrow of numerous established customs. Both Zhou's and traditional narrative conform to the age-old Confucian dictum that literature serve moralistic purposes, no matter how we define "moralistic." Zhou's charge that Song dynasty stories were poor "imitations" (*mofang*) of Tang dynasty precursors, likewise, appears inaccurate. The love story's quasi-generic nature ensured that later storytellers would work within the boundaries of received prototypes, borrowing elements from earlier works while developing new ones. "Tan Yige," for example, while resembling a fleeting romance between a scholar-official and a courtesan that was so typical of the Tang dynasty, was developed into an innovative account thanks to its emphasis on social mobility and freely chosen marriage. If we discard an artificial divide between "Tang" as opposed to "Song" and think of the love story as one continuous literary tradition, artificial boundaries and labels dissolve. Accordingly, it is not so much a question of which is better, but rather how the same literary corpus developed over time. Within the same tradition, it was inevitable that storytellers would borrow earlier elements while breathing new life into the corpus based on their own cultural and intellectual *weltanschauung*. Therefore, if we look beyond purely formalistic innovation, assertions that narrative literature of the Song and Yuan fell short are reduced to opinion and personal preference. The same may be said of other Song-era short-story types.

Nevertheless, if Zhou Shuren did not appreciate short stories of the Song and Yuan, contemporaries and their successors did. I have observed how short classical language stories were frequently adapted for other genres, such as the vernacular short story, the medium-length short story, and the scholar-beauty romance. Moreover, numerous operas of the Ming and Qing dynasties were based on these older sources. The large-scale adaptation of short, classical language stories for groundbreaking new literary genres speaks volumes about the importance of the source. Likewise, the fact that they were repeatedly anthologized throughout the late-imperial period attests to their enduring popularity. Therefore, as stated in the introduction, without the classical language love stories of the Song and Yuan period, operas of the Yuan and Ming era may not have existed, or certainly not in their current form. Similarly, as previously discussed, several great novels of the Ming and Qing dynasties drew inspiration from the short love story, which further bears witness to the latter's importance.

The vast majority of Tang-era short stories feature upper-class protagonists. From the Song and Yuan dynasty, however, many non-elite characters came to the attention of the storyteller's writing brush. Although a Tang story may have occasionally taken a merchant as its hero, merchants-protagonists were far more common from the eleventh and twelfth centuries onward. Similarly, courtesans, soldiers and their wives, farmers, local magnates, impoverished students without strong connections, and unspecified commoners not infrequently became the *dramatis personae* of stories from this period onward. Moreover, many stories originated from non-elite tellers. In the preface to the fourth installment of his *Record of the Listener*, for example, Hong Mai tells of having accepted stories from rural monks, the down-and-out, guests, Daoists, blind "shamans," village women, debased servants, and itinerant soldiers.[14] As previously noted, this trend has led numerous scholars—particularly in China and Taiwan—to consider Song dynasty *xiaoshuo* as having been influenced by the taste and culture of townspeople (*shimin*).[15] Nonetheless, as this study has demonstrated, even in stories that follow the fortunes of ordinary folk, it is elite values that predominate. Even when non-elite tellers recounted stories to educated author-compilers, it is through the consciousness of these men of letters that the stories in question are mediated. Hence, upper-class values controlled the narration and, equally importantly, upper-class storytellers selected the stories. Moreover, many author-compilers of the Song and Yuan periods were comparatively famous insofar that their names are still known today. Even those to whom Hu Yinglin referred disparagingly as "village scholars and elderly countryfolk,"[16] whose biographies are not extant were, nevertheless, members of the educated elite by dint of their literacy during a period of extremely low literacy. We cannot simply assume that they were professional storytellers or some other member of the commoner class simply because their names have not survived. Hence *xiaoshuo* production was largely controlled by the educated upper classes and mediated through their worldview. Furthermore, we do not know whether common people's values differed from those of the ruling elite. One would expect a degree of difference, given diverging economic factors. Yet, for all we know, common people may have largely adhered to elite Confucian values, just as commoners in European societies largely supported ruling-class values up until—and even after—the rise of the proletariat. Nevertheless, the argument that classical language stories of the period cater to the tastes of the common classes assumes a clear differentiation in social and moral values. While this might hold true to an extent, thanks to the elite's domination of literary production we know so little about the non-elite values of this period that any generalization or assumption about a distinctive set of commoners' values must be fraught with danger.

Notes

Introduction

1. Feng Menglong, *Stories Old and New*, trans. Shuhui Yang and Yunqin Yang (Seattle: University of Washington Press, 2000), 490–92.

2. *Wikipedia*, https://en.wikipedia.org/wiki/Butterfly_Lovers.

3. Roland Altenburger, "Is it Clothes that Make the Man? Cross-Dressing, Gender and Sex in Pre–Twentieth Century Zhu Yingtai Lore," *Asian Folklore Studies* 64, no. 2 (2005): 173.

4. I follow Stephen Owen's definition of the mid-Tang as approximately spanning 791 to 825. See Owen's *End of the Chinese Middle-Ages: Essays in Mid-Tang Literary Culture* (Stanford, CA: Stanford University Press, 1996), 2.

5. Richard Wang, "The Cult of *Qing*: Romanticism in the Late Ming Period and the Novel *Jiao Hong Ji*," *Ming Studies* 33 (1994): 42.

6. Daniel Hsieh, *Love and Women in Early Chinese Fiction* (Hong Kong: The Chinese University Press, 2008), 3.

7. Lu Xun, "Zhongguo xiaoshuo shilüe," in *Lu Xun quanji*, vol. 9 (Beijing: Renmin wenxue, 2005), 115.

8. Lu Xun, "Zhongguo xiaoshuode lishi yanbian," in *Lu Xun quanji*, vol. 9 (Beijing: Renmin wenxue, 2005), 323.

9. Ibid., 329.

10. Zheng Zhenduo, *Chatuben Zhongguo wenxue shi* (Taipei: Zhuangyan, 1991).

11. On this dichotomy, see Li Jianguo, *Song Yuan zhiguai chuanqi xulu* (Tianjin: Nankai daxue, 1997), 1–7.

12. On the neglect of Song dynasty prose narrative, see Yu Shiu-yun, *Songdai chuanqi xiaoshuo yanjiu* (Taipei: Huamulan wenhua, 2007), 1–3.

13. Li Shiren, "Songdai lishi wenhua yu wenyan duanpian xiaoshuo de liubian," *Qiushi xuekan* 38, no. 2 (2011): 127.

14. Regarding the direct influence of Song-period short stories on Ming and Qing dynasty opera, see Chen Yiyuan, *Yuan Ming zhongpian chuanqi xiaoshuo yanjiu* (Hong Kong: Xuefeng wenhua shiye, 1997); Fu Xihua, *Mingdai chuanqi quanmu* (Beijing: Renmin wenxue, 1959); and Zhuang Yifu, *Gudian xiqu cunmu huikao* (Shanghai: Shanghai guji, 1982).

15. Cheng Yizhong, "Songdaide chuanqi xiaoshuo," *Wenshi zhishi* 2 (1990): 10. The translated title appearing here is Judith Zeitlin's. See her *Historian of the Strange: Pu Songling and the Chinese Classical Tale* (Stanford, CA: Stanford University Press, 1993), 1.

16. Yu Shiu-yun, *Songdai chuanqi xiaoshuo yanjiu*.

17. Although the term "storyteller" often evokes the sense of a professional oral teller, following Manling Luo's example, I apply the term to actual narrators of written stories. Given that most Song and Yuan dynasty stories were conveyed orally, often in a gossipy, informal manner prior to being recorded, ascribing a single "author" in the post-Romantic sense is inappropriate. See Manling Luo, "Remembering Kaiyuan and Tianbao: The Construction of Mosaic Memory in Medieval History Miscellanies," *T'oung Pao* 97 (2011): 263–300, especially p. 272n27.

18. Paul Rouzer, *Articulated Ladies* (Cambridge, MA: Harvard University Asia Center, 2001), 202.

19. Gu Shi ed., *Mu Tianzi zhuan xizheng jiangshu* (Shanghai, Shangwu, 1934).

20. In Song Yu's "Gaotang fu" ("Rhapsody of Gaotang"), King Huai of Chu (r. 328–299 BCE) dreamed of sexual union with a goddess while visiting Mount Wu (Witch's Mountain). As David Roy has pointed out, King Huai is often confused for King Xiang (298–265 BCE). See *Plum in the Golden Vase*, vol. 1, trans. David Roy(Princeton, NJ: Princeton University Press, 1993), 479n47. The translated term "Witch's Mountain" is Roy's. For a study and translation of the poem, see Lois Fusek, "The K'ao-t'ang fu," *Monumenta Serica* 30 (1972–73): 392–425.

21. Xiao Tong, *Wen Xuan* (Beijing: Zhonghua, 1977), 270.

22. On sexual hygiene, see Robert van Gulik, *Sexual Life in Ancient China: A Preliminary Survey of Chinese Sex and Society from ca. 1500 B.C. until 1644 A.D.* (Leiden: Brill, 1974); also see Donald Harper, "The Sexual Arts of Ancient China as Described in a Manuscript of the Second Century B.C.," *Harvard Journal of Asiatic Studies* 47, no. 2 (1987): 539–93.

23. For an early reference to Sima Xiangru's elopement, see chapter 117 of Sima Qian, *Shiji*, in *Ershiwu shi*, vol. 1 (Taipei: Yiwen, no date), 3000–3001. For the story's evolution, see Idema, "The Story of Ssu-ma Hsiang-ju and Cho Wen-chün in Vernacular Literature of the Yuan and Early Ming Dynasties," *T'oung Pao* 70 (1984): 60–109. For Han Shou, see the *huoni* chapter in Liu Yiqing, *Shishuo xinyu* (Taipei: Pingping, 1975), 690.

24. Given the traditional Chinese cosmological concept that the universe was composed of essential vapor (*qi*) from which all things spontaneously came into being, referring to paranormal entities with the term "supernatural" fails to fit

this paradigm because it implies an ontological hierarchy. The traditional Chinese schemata conceptualizes all things as existing on the same level. I therefore use the term "paranormal" throughout this study as this more closely approximates the Chinese term *guai*. For a discussion of the traditional Chinese concept in English, see Andrew Plaks, *Archetype and Allegory in* Dream of the Red Chamber (Princeton, NJ: Princeton University Press, 1977), 146.

25. Owen, *End of the Chinese Middle-Ages*, 130–48. Howard Levy also recognized this shift. See his "Love Themes in T'ang Literature," *Orient/West* 7, no. 1 (1962): 67–79.

26. Owen, *End of the Chinese Middle-Ages*, 130–48. I use the term "romantic love" throughout this study in a general sense, conscious of the complexities in defining the concept and that "love" has been understood differently in diverse cultures and historical periods. As my interest lies in literary history, it is beyond the scope of this study to define the concept or discuss it as a cultural artifact. In stories of the Song and Yuan, romantic love seems to have entailed a combination of both physical and metaphysical attraction—that is, appreciation of the beloved's poetic or cultural talent, or their personal integrity. For a concise overview of love in a literary context, see Lynn Pan, *When True Love Came to China* (Hong Kong: Hong Kong University Press, 2015), 26–71.

27. Hong Yue, "Romantic identity in the Funerary Inscriptions (muzhi) of Tang China," *Asia Major* 21, no. 1 (2012): 33–62. Beverly Bossler also documents cases whereby famous men of letters celebrated their concubine-lovers in writing. See Bossler, *Courtesans, Concubines and the Cult of Female Fidelity* (Cambridge, MA: Harvard University Asia Center, 2013), 63.

28. Hong Yue, "The Discourse of Romantic Love in Ninth Century China" (PhD diss., Harvard University, Cambridge, Massachusetts, 2010), 3.

29. Rouzer, *Articulated Ladies*, 201–2.

30. Levy, "Love Themes in T'ang Literature," 67–68. On the ban against aristocratic intermarriage, see Liu Kairong, *Tangdai xiaoshuo yanjiu* (Taipei: Shangwu, 1966, rpt. 2005), 65.

31. See, for example, "Zhang Guo's Daughter" and "Clerk Liu's Daughter" in chapters 330 and 386 of *Taiping guangji*, vol. 3, ed. Li Fang et al. (Shanghai: Shanghai guji, 1990), 395 and 729–30.

32. One notable exception is "The Powder Seller" (*Mai fen er*), purportedly from the *Youming lu* (*Records of the Hidden and Visible Worlds*), compiled by Liu Yiqing (403–44). This tells of a young man who, enamored over a girl who sold face powder, buys her wares every day as an excuse to see her. When the pair eventually meet for sexual intercourse, the young man is so ecstatic that he drops dead. At the story's conclusion, he returns to life when his beloved comes to mourn him. This narrative is highly unusual for *zhiguai* accounts of the early period and, as demonstrated by this study, bears hallmarks of both Tang and Song love stories. Therefore, given that the extant *Youming lu* is an eighteenth-century

redaction based on a sixteenth-century redaction of supposedly Tang-era sources, the story may have been erroneously attributed to the fifth-century compilation. See chapter 274 of the *Taiping guangji* vol. 3, 1045–65.

33. Yu Ji, *Daoyuan xuegu lu*, cited in Zhao Weiguo, "Lun Liqing yu Songdai liqing xiaoshuo chuangzuo," *Henan daxue xuebao* (*shehui kexue ban*) 43, no. 1 (2003): 57.

34. Lu Xun, *Zhongguo xiaoshuo shilüe*, 70.

35. For a concise discussion of *chuanqi* as a genre, see Sarah Yim, "Chuanqi," in *The Indiana Companion to Traditional Chinese Literature*, ed. William Nienhauser et al. (Taipei: SMC Publishing, 1986), 356–60. For detailed treatment, see Sarah Yim, "Structure, Theme and Narrator in T'ang "*ch'uan-ch'i*" (PhD diss., Yale University, New Haven, Connecticut, 1979); Li Zongwei, *Tangren chuanqi* (Beijing: Zhonghua, 2003); Wu Zhida, *Tangren chuanqi* (Shanghai: Shanghai guji, 1983); Liu Ying, *Tangdai chuanqi yanjiu* (Taipei: Zhengzhong, 1982); Liu Kairong, *Tangdai xiaoshuo yanjiu* (Shanghai, Shangwu, 1955). On the generic link between *zhiguai* and *chuanqi*, see Lu Xun, *Zhongguo xiaoshuo shilüe*, 70.

36. Lu Xun, *Zhongguo xiaoshuo shilüe*, passim.

37. Levy, "Love Themes in T'ang Literature," 68. Li Jianguo also acknowledges hearsay (*wenjian*) as a source for stories recorded by the educated elite. See Li Jianguo, *Song dai zhiguai chuanqi xulu*, 164.

38. For example, in an end commentary to an item from his *Chicken Rib Collection* (*Jile bian*), Zhuang Chuo (1070s–1140s) explains how he re-recorded a story some decades after the written version was destroyed in a fire. See Zhuang Chuo, *Jilei bian* (Beijing: Zhonghua shuju, 1983), xia. 98–99.

39. Wang Zhi, *Mo ji*, cited in Cheng Yizhong, *Song Yuan xiaoshuo yanjiu* (Nanjing: Jiangsu guji, 1998), 53.

40. According to historical documents, the famous scholar and calligrapher Ouyang Xun's (557–641) physical appearance resembled that of an ape. The short story slanders his parentage by claiming that his mother gave birth to him after having been raped by a paranormal ape. See *Taiping guangji*, vol. 4, 294–95. For an introduction and translation in English, see Jue Chen, "A Supplement to Jiang Zong's *Biography of a White Ape*," *Renditions*, Spring (1998): 74–85.

41. Hong Mai, *Yijian zhi*, vol. 4 (Taipei: Mingwen, 1994), 1818.

42. Hong Mai, *Yijian zhi*, 363. The translating appearing here is that of Inglis, *Hong Mai's Record of the Listener and Its Song Dynasty Context*, 28.

43. On this, see Inglis, *Hong Mai's Record of the Listener and Its Song Dynasty Context*, xi, 2, 26–29, 31, 40–41, 46, 48–49, 88, 123–24, 128.

44. Li Jianguo also notes this tendency in regard to Song dynasty author-compilers. See his *Zhiguai chuanqi xulu*, 5. Li Changqi, author of the influential *Jiandeng yuhua* (*Further Stories after Trimming the Lampwick*), states at the very end of his preface: "Interested parties may simply get a laugh out of reading it [the *Jiandeng yuhua*]; wherefore lies the necessity of getting caught up in the historical veracity

of a story?" Li Changqi, *Jiandeng yuhua*, in Qu You, *Jiandeng xinhua* (Taipei: Shijie, 2010), 51. Similarly, Leo Tak-hung Chan discusses how readers of Ji Yun's (1724–1805) *Random Jottings at the Cottage of Close Scrutiny* (*Yueweicao tang biji*) generally understood his stories literally. See his *The Discourse on Foxes and Ghosts: Ji Yun and Eighteenth Century Literati Storytelling* (Hong Kong: Chinese University of Hong Kong, 1998), 193–97.

45. On this, see Dong Guoyan, *Dangzi, Rouqing, Tongxin: Mingdai xiaoshuo sichao* (Taiyuan: Beiyue wenyi, 1992), 151.

46. Ming Dong Gu, *Chinese Theories of Fiction: A Non-Western Narrative System* (Albany, NY: SUNY Press, 2006), 5.

47. Sarah M. Allen, *Shifting Stories: History, Gossip and Lore in Narratives from Tang Dynasty China* (Cambridge, MA: Harvard University Asia Center, 2014), 7. Lee Yu-hwa understands the "Story of Li Wa" as the rewriting of a popular story and not one created by its nominal author, Bai Xingjian. See Lee Yu-hwa, *Fantasy and Realism in Chinese Fiction* (San Francisco: Chinese Materials Center Publications, 1984), 25.

48. Lee Yu-hwa, *Fantasy and Realism in Chinese Fiction*, 8.

49. For a discussion of this in English, see James Hightower, "Yuan Chen and the 'Story of Ying-ying,' " *Harvard Journal of Asiatic Studies* 33 (1973): 106–19.

50. Su Chen, *Song chuanqi xiaoshuo xuan* (Taipei: Sanmin, 2010), 228. The Tao Gu story is retold in several Song-era sources among which Shen Liao's version is but one, thereby attesting to the story's enduring popularity. For a concise summary of these sources, see Li Jianguo, *Songdai zhiguai chuanqi xulu*, 141–42.

51. Hu Yinglin, *Shanshi shaofang bicong* (Beijing, Zhonghua, 1958), 475–77. Knowledge of Xu Xuan's supposed gullibility comes from several Song dynasty sources. For example, Chen Zhensun, *Zhizhai shuli jieti* (Taipei: Shangwu, 1978), 324–25; Jiang Shaoyu, *Shishi leiyuan*, cited in Ting Ch'uan-ching, *Songren yishi huibian* (Beijing: Zhonghua, 1981), 127–28.

52. Lu Xun, "Zhongguo xiaoshuo shi lüe," 73; Lu Xun, "Zhongguo xiaoshuode lishi bianqian," 232.

53. Private conversation with Professor Idema in Cambridge, Massachusetts.

54. See Alister Inglis, "Hong Mai's Informants for the *Yijian zhi*," *Journal of Song-Yuan Studies* 32 (2002): 83–125.

55. Luo Ye, *Xinbian zuiweng tanlu* (Shanghai: Shanghai gudian wenxue, 1957), 3.

56. This is also the approach that Sarah M. Allen has taken in *Shifting Stories*.

57. On this point, see Alister Inglis, *Hong Mai's* Record of the Listener *and Its Song Dynasty Context* (Albany, NY: SUNY Press, 2006), 3.

58. Anne McLaren, *Chinese Popular Culture and Ming Cantefables* (Leiden: Brill, 1998), 46–47.

59. Zhao Weiguo also recognizes this fact and dates the work's completion to shortly after 1044, the completion year of its most recent datable narrative.

See his "Lun *Liqing ji* yu Songdai liqing xiaoshuo chuangzuo," 58. Also see Li Jianguo, *Songdai chuanqi xulu*, 84.

60. Chao Gongwu, *Junzhai dushu zhi*, vol. 4 (Taipei: Shangwu, 1978), 838.

61. Other scholars have also noted *Collected Love Stories*' contribution to literary classification. See Sun Xun and Zhao Weiguo, "Chuanqi ti xiaoshuo de yanbian zhi bianzhe," *Shanghai shifan daxue xuebao* (*shehui kexue ban*) 30, no. 1 (2001): 89; Zhao Wei, "Mingdai liqing chuanqi xiaoshuo yanjiu" (MA dissertation, Hebei Normal University, 2006), 10.

62. Chao Gongwu, *Junzhai dushu zhi*, vol. 2 (Taipei: Shangwu, 1978), 261.

63. Luo Ye, *Xinbian zuiweng tanlu*, 1–5. For a complete translation in English, see Alister Inglis, *The Drunken Man's Talk* (Seattle: University of Washington Press, 2015). The translated story titles that appear here are modified from the above.

64. Because ten out of the fourteen *chuanqi* titles given in Luo Ye's *Drunken Man's Talk*, as well as all four of the Ming dynasty bibliophile, Hu Yinglin's, *chuanqi* samples (see note 66) are identifiable love stories, in addition to peripheral evidence, Sun Xun and Zhao Weiguo argue that *chuanqi* replaced *liqing* as a generic classifier for love stories after the twelfth century. They further argue that *chuanqi* did not refer to a broad range of story types until recent times. This argument is, however, problematic for several reasons. As several *chuanqi* stories in Luo Ye's list are no longer extant, nor are they summarized in other sources, these may not have been love stories. Furthermore, Hu Yinglin's citation of four examples is hardly sufficient to define a generic classifier. Besides this, Luo Ye's list of *yanfen* stories, which contains identifiable love stories between humans and ghosts, also included romantic love between human protagonists—see "Lin Shumao Elopes with Miss Chu," "Jingnü has an Affair with Chen Yanchen," and the story of Liang Yiniang's love affair in the *Drunken Man's Talk*—none of which feature romance between humans and ghosts. Hence, *yanfen* apparently referred to love stories between humans and was not restricted to those that transgressed ontological boundaries. Even if the *Drunken Man's Talk*'s author intended *chuanqi* to refer to love stories, such usage is uncorroborated by other writers. Furthermore, the dating of the *Drunken Man's Talk* is problematic; some argue for a Southern Song dynasty provenance while others consider it to have been compiled during the Yuan dynasty. For an overview of the dating controversy, see Alister Inglis, "Luo Ye's *Zuiweng tanlu* and the Culture of Romance," *Chinese Literature: Essays, Articles Reviews* 35 (2013): 99–100; Sun Xun and Zhao Weiguo, "Chuanqi ti xiaoshuo de yanbian zhi bianzhe," 84–93.

65. Tan Zhengbi, *Huaben yu guju* (Shanghai: Shanghai gudian wenxue, 1956), 18. Scholars from the People's Republic of China generally follow Tan's assumption. See, for example, *Zhongguo xiaoshuo tongshi*, vol. 2, ed. Li Jianguo and Chen Hong (Beijing: Gaodeng jiaoyu, 2007), 841; Ye Dejun, "Xiqu xiaoshuo congkao," in *Xiaoshuo suotan* (Beijing: Zhonghua, 1979), 596; Xiao Xiangkai, *Song Yuan xiaoshuo shi* (Zhejiang: Zhejiang guji, 1997), 104–5; Sun Xun and Zhao Weiguo, "Chuanqi ti xiaoshuo de yanbian zhi bianzhe," 92.

66. Meng Yuanlao, *Dongjing menghua lu* (Beijing: Wenhua yishu, 1998), 86–87, 306.

67. The translated list presented here follows that of Hua-yuan Li Mowry. See Feng Menglong, *Chinese Love Stories from "Ch'ing-shih*," trans. Hua-yuan Li Mowry (Hamden, CT: Archon Books, 1983), *passim*.

68. Hu Yinglin, *Shaoshi shanfang bicong*, 474–86 *passim*. His sample love stories are those of Zhao Feiyan, Yang Guifei, Cui Yingying, and Huo Xiaoyu.

69. Li Jianguo make a similar point about Hu's fuzzy generic delineation. See his *Zhongguo xiaoshuo tongshi*, vol. 2, 403–4.

70. On this matter in relation to Hu Yinglin's work, see Laura Hua Wu, "From *Xiaoshuo* to Fiction: Hu Yinglin's Genre Study of *Xiaoshuo*," *Harvard Journal of Asiatic Studies* 55, no. 2 (1995): 353.

71. The translated list follows that of Alister Inglis, *The Drunken Man's Talk*, unpaginated table of contents.

72. Owen, *End of the Chinese Middle Ages*, 131.

73. Glen Dudbridge, *Books, Tales and Vernacular Culture: Selected Papers on China* (Leiden: Brill, 2005), 207.

74. Dirk de Geest and Hendrik van Gorp, "Literary Genres from a Systemic-Functionalist Perspective," *European Journal of English Studies* 3, no. 1 (1999): 33–50; Eleanor Rosch, "Human Categorization," in *Studies in Cross-Cultural Psychology 1*, ed. N. Warren (London & New York: Academic Press, 1977), 1–49. De Geest and van Gorp's theory is also based on the cognitive psychology of Eleanor Rosch. See "Principles of Categorization," in *Cognition and Categorization*, ed. Eleanor Rosch and B. B. Loyd (Hillsdale, NJ: Lawrence Erlbaum, 1978), 22–48.

75. L. A. Zadeh, "Fuzzy Sets," *Information and Control* 8 (1965): 338–53.

76. Ludwig Wittgenstien, *Philosophical Investigations* (Oxford: Blackwell, 1978).

77. Robert Ford Campany, *Strange Writing: Anomaly Accounts in Early Medieval China* (Albany, NY: SUNY Press, 1996), 24.

78. As storytellers of the Song and Yuan period did not address same-sex love, we may discount it from the definition for this period.

Chapter 1

1. Hsieh, *Love and Women in Early Chinese Fiction*, 3.

2. Denis Twitchett, "The Composition of the T'ang Ruling Class: New Evidence from Tunhuang," in *Perspectives on the Tang*, ed. Arthur Wright and Denis Twitchett (New Haven, CT: Yale University Press, 1973), 50–51.

3. Twitchett's term "super-elite" is used to delineate a core of supremely powerful aristocrats at the apex of the political spectrum and a larger group of "scholar-officials" who were more influential at the local level. See ibid., 56–57.

4. Liu Su, *Sui Tang jiahua*, cited in Liu Kairong, *Tangdai xiaoshuo yanjiu*, 64

5. Chapter 119 of the *Xin Tang shu*, cited in Liu Kairong, *Tangdai xiaoshuo yanjiu*, 65.

6. Ouyang Xiu, *Xin Tang shu*, in *Ershiwu shi*, vol. 26 (Taipei: Yiwen, no date given), 95.1324.

7. Liu Su, *Sui Tang jiahua*, cited in Liu Kairong, *Tangdai xiaoshuo yanjiu*, 64.

8. These means are entry on the grounds of one's father or grandfather's noble title, entry through hereditary privilege due to one's father or grandfather having been a bureaucrat of or above the fifth rank, entry through service in the guards, entry through management of public funds, promotion from the clerical service, or entry based on imperial favor. See Denis Twitchett, *The Birth of the Chinese Meritocracy: Bureaucrats and Examinations in T'ang China* (London: China Society, 1976), 8.

9. On this and other aspects of supervision, see Yang Bo, *Chang'an de chuntian: Tangdai keju yu jinshi shenghuo* (Beijing: Zhonghua, 2007), 21–30.

10. Twitchett, *The Birth of the Chinese Meritocracy*, 12.

11. Cited in Yang Bo, *Chang'ande chuntian*, 82.

12. Sun Qi, *Beili zhi*, in *Jiaofang ji, Beili zhi, Qinglou ji* (Beijing: Zhonghua, 1959), 22. The translation is Rouzer's from *Articulated Ladies*, 249. For further analysis on the *Beili zhi*, see Linda Rui Feng, "Unmasking *Fengliu* in Urban Chang'an: Rereading *Beili zhi* (Anecdotes from the Northern Ward)," *Chinese Literature: Essays, Articles, Reviews* 32 (2010): 1–21.

13. Sun Qi, *Beili zhi*, 33.

14. Sun Qi, *Beili zhi*, 32. The translation is Rouzer's from *Articulated Ladies*, 274.

15. Sun Qi, *Beili zhi*, 33.

16. Hsieh, *Love and Women in Early Chinese Fiction*, 13, 26.

17. Rouzer, *Articulated Ladies*, 201.

18. C. P. Fitzgerald, "The Consequences of the Rebellion of An Lu-shan upon the Population of the T'ang Dynasty," *Philobiblon* 2 (1947): 4–11, cited in Earl Pritchard, "Thoughts on the Historical Development of the Population of China," *The Journal of Asian Studies* 23, vol. 1 (1963): 11. Also see Edwin G. Pullyblank, *Background of the Rebellion of An Lu-shan* (London: Oxford University Press, 1955), 172–77.

19. Dennis Twitchett and John K. Fairbank, *The Cambridge History of China*, vol. 3 (Cambridge: Cambridge University Press, 1978), 333–463. See also Paul Kroll, "The Flight from the Capital and the Death of Precious Consort Yang," *Tang Studies* 3 (1985): 25–53.

20. *Quan Tangshi*, ed. Wang Shizhen and Wang Yunwu (Taipei: Shangwu, 1966), 309.3496.

21. Ibid., 217.2276.

22. Bai Juyi, *Bai Juyi ji* (Beijing: Zhonghua, 1979), 12.239.

23. Manling Luo, *Literati Storytelling in Late Medieval China* (Seattle: University of Washington Press, 2017), 27–28.

24. Luo, *Literati Storytelling in Late Medieval China*, 28.

25. Originally found in Gan Bao, *Soushen ji* (Taipei: Guji, no date given), 12.399–400.

26. Liu Fu devotes an entire chapter (*Qianji* 6) to this topic in his *Qingsuo gaoyi*. The stories he includes are "Story of Mt. Li" (*Lishan ji*), "Story of the Hot Springs" (*Wenquan ji*), "The Precious Consort's Stocking" (*Guifei washi*), and "Ballad of Mawei" (*Mawei xing*). See Liu Fu, *Qingsuo gaoyi*, in *Songdai biji xiaoshuo daguan*, vol. 24, ed. Zhou Guangpei (Shijiazhuang: Hebei jiaoyu, 1995), 404–15.

27. Cited in Fung Yu-lan, *A History of Chinese Philosophy*, vol. 2, trans. Derke Bodde (Princeton, NJ: Princeton University Press, 1953), 42–43.

28. Fox-fairies vis-à-vis the *zhiguai* tradition may be understood as male guilt and anxiety (due to lust) having been projected onto the bodies of women who were constructed as an exotic, ontological Other. Or, as Huntington observes in relation to sex between foxes and men in the *Liaozhai zhiyi*, "it is sexual indulgence, not the relationship with a fox, that is dangerous. See Rania Huntington, *Alien Kind: Foxes and Late Imperial Chinese Narrative* (Cambridge, MA: Harvard University Asia Center, 2003), 182.

29. Li Jianguo also notes the heroine's human-like portrayal. See Li Jianguo, *Tang Wudai zhiguai chuanqi xulu* (Beijing: Zhonghua, 2017), 275.

30. *Taiping guangji*, vol. 4, 452.340–45. The translation throughout is Stephen Owen's from *An Anthology of Chinese Literature: Beginnings to 1911* (New York: Norton, 1996), 518–26.

31. Jing Wang also notes the location's significance. See *Courtesan Culture in the* Beili zhi (Records of the Northern Quarter) *in the Context of Tang Tales and Poems* (PhD dissertation, University of Wisconsin, Madison, Wisconsin, 2009), 97.

32. Shortly before the An Lushan Rebellion, a monk bought a pair of Lady Yang's stockings when the imperial couple were selling personal effects to raise money for flood relief. Long after the rebellion, they were (supposedly) bought by the statesman Li Yuan (graduated 831). See "The Precious Consort's Stockings" (*Guifei washi*), in Liu Fu, *Qingsuo gaoyi*, 413–15.

33. See Owen's translation from *An Anthology of Chinese Literature*, 525.

34. *Taiping guangji*, vol. 4, 484.538.

35. Although no description of the protagonists' physical appearance is offered, we may infer important psychological aspects of the male articulating subject. Wei's joke implying that Zheng was not handsome reveals anxiety in regard to physical attributes. Zheng himself furthermore fears that Miss Ren might betray him. When he meets her again in the clothing store and professes indifference to her Otherness, he asks, "Would you betray me?" She replies, "How could I bear betray you? I only fear that your lordship will find me repulsive."

Zheng, it seems, represents a man of needy financial means who must demean himself to relatives despite his apparent high status—one of average looks who fears rejection by women. His anxiety over physical attributes and possible betrayal are projected onto the female protagonist. As we shall see, similar anxiety occurs in other stories of the period.

36. On the concept of "interpellation," see Louis Althusser, "Ideology and Ideological State Apparatuses (Notes toward an Investigation)," in Ben Brewster, trans., *Lenin and Philosophy and Other Essays* (London: Monthly Review Press, 1971), 174–77.

37. Hsieh, *Love and Women in Early Chinese Fiction*, 26.

38. Besides "Miss Ren's Story," Shen is known for his "World inside a Pillow" (Zhenzhong ji). For a concise biography in English, see Donald Gjertson, "Shen Chi-chi," in *The Indiana Companion to Traditional Chinese Literature*, 674–75.

39. See the *Xin Tang shu*, cited in Li Jianguo, *Tang Wudi zhiguai chuanqi xulu*, 275.

40. See Hong Yue, "The Discourse of Romantic Love in Ninth Century China," 22.

41. Arthur Waley, *One Hundred and Twenty Chinese Poems* (London: Constable, 1918, rpt 1945), 4.

42. The translation is Rouzer's from *Articulated Ladies*, 216.

43. Rouzer, *Articulated Ladies*, 202. Rouzer understands Miss Liu as an "accessible reward for talent." Ibid., 217.

44. Owen, *The End of the Chinese Middle Ages*, 103.

45. *Taiping guangji*, vol. 4, 485.541–42.

46. For a brief discussion with examples of patronage, see Luo, *Literati Storytelling in Late Medieval China*, 103.

47. Linda Feng Rui, *Youthful Displacement: City, Travel and Narrative Formation in Tang Tales* (PhD dissertation, Columbia University, New York, 2008).

48. Li Jianguo, *Tang Wudai zhiguai chuanqi xilu*, 960.

49. *Taiping guangji*, vol. 4, 491.573–76.

50. The translation is that of Luo, *Literati Storytelling in Late Medieval China*, 123–24.

51. Green Pearl is first mentioned in the *Shishuo xinyu*, although her alleged suicide is traced to later commentators. See Liu Yiqing, *Shishuo xinyu* (Taipei: Pingping, 1975), 692. For a brief summary of the story and its basis, see Bossler, *Courtesans, Concubines and the Cult of Female Fidelity*, 86–87.

52. Luo, *Literati Storytelling in Late Medieval China*, 125.

53. Ibid., 125.

54. Ibid., 125.

55. *Taiping guangji*, vol. 4, 485.542.

56. Feng Menglong, *Qingshi leilüe* (Taipei: Guangwen, 1982), 2.2b–3a.

57. Parlor maids and the like who served in the palace were, however, generally married once their term of service elapsed or during times of retrenchment. This was not so for consorts who had slept with the emperor.

58. Hsieh, *Love and Women in Early Chinese Fiction*, 49.

59. For a concise summary of this idea, see Luo, *Literati Storytelling in Late Medieval China*, 138–46.

60. *Taiping guangji*, vol. 2, 160.78.

61. Ibid., vol. 3, 276.66. Also see Meng Qi, *Ben shi shi* (Shanghai: Shanghai guji, 1991), 8.

62. The translation is that of Alister Inglis, *The Drunken Man's Talk*, 26.

63. Why this hereditary position was awarded so long after his father's supposed death is curious and perhaps points to a corrupt text.

64. *Taiping guangji*, vol. 2, 159.70–71.

65. Luo, *Literati Storytelling in Late Medieval China*, 146.

66. *Taiping guangji*, vol. 3, 386.329–30.

67. During the Yuan dynasty, the story was adapted for a southern opera (*chuanqi*) of the same title by Bai Shouzhi. In the Ming, it provided the story for Lu Cai's "Record of the Gleaming Pearl," while Cui Yingjie in the Qing period adapted it for his "Record of Two Immortals." The earliest version is found in chapter 486 of the *Taiping guangji*. It was later included in the *Liqing ji*, chapter 16 of the *Fenmen gujin leishi*, the first section of the *Lüchuang xinhua*, chapter 120 of the *Shuofu*, chapter 5 of the *Yuchu zhi*, chapter 23 of the *Yanyi bian*, chapter 1 of the *Wenyuan zhaji*, chapter 4 of the *Xiugu chunrong*, and chapter 2 of the *Hushi*.

68. *Taiping guangji*, vol. 2, 486.546–49. The translation, which I have slightly modified, is that of Dale Johnson, "Wu-shuang the Peerless," in *Traditional Chinese Stories: Themes and Variations*, ed. Y. W. Ma and Joseph Lau (Boston: Cheng and Tsui, 1986, rpt. 2011), 52–57.

69. *Taiping guangji*, vol. 4, 484.533–38. The translated summary is that of Glen Dudbridge, *The Tale of Li Wa* (London: Ithaca, 1983), 105–85 *passim*.

70. For a discussion of the dating problem in English, see Dudbridge, *The Tale of Li Wa*, 14–37; for the same in Chinese, see Cheng Yizhong, *Tangdai xiaoshuo shi* (Beijing: Renmin wenxue, 2003), 131; Liu Kairong, *Tangdai xiaoshuo yanjiu*, 68–71.

71. The translation is that of Dudbridge, *The Tale of Li Wa*, 183.

72. Hu Yingling, *Shaoshi shanfang bicong*, 41.567. Cited in Luo, *Literati Storytelling in Late Medieval China*, 111–12.

73. Feng Menglong, *Qingshi*, 16.3a. Cited in Luo, *Literati Storytelling in Late Medieval China*, 112.

74. Liu Kairong also makes this point. See *Tangdai xiaoshuo yanjiu*, 67.

75. Dudbridge, *The Tale of Li Wa*, 77.

76. Ibid., 39. See also Cheng Yizhong, *Tangdai xiaoshuo shi*, 131.

77. Dudbridge, *The Tale of Li Wa*, 41.
78. Owen, *The End of the Chinese "Middle Ages,"* 131–32.
79. Sima Qian, *Shiji*, in *Ershiwu shi*, vols. 1–2, 81. For an English translation, see *The Grand Scribe's Records*, vol. 1, ed. William Nienhauser Jr. (Bloomington: Indiana University Press, 1994), 74.
80. What appears to be the earliest surviving use of the term *youwu* is found in the *Zuozhuan*, vol. 2 (Changsha: Xinjiang renmin, 2002), 649.
81. See, for example, Chen Yinke, "Du Yingying zhuan," in *Chen Yinke xiansheng wenshi lunji* (Hong Kong: Wenwen, 1973), 397–406; James Hightower, "Yuan Chen and the 'Story of Ying-ying,'" *Harvard Journal of Asiatic Studies* 33 (1973): 90–123; Uchiyama Chinari, "Ōō den no kōzō to shudai ni tsuite," *Nihon Chūgoku gakkai hō* 42 (1990): 156–68.
82. "Hongniang" means "red lady." The term "red," besides constituting the traditional wedding color, is often found in the personal names of heroine's maids.
83. The translation here and above is Owen's from *The End of the Chinese Middle Ages*, 197
84. *Taiping guangji*, 488.555–59. The translated portions are Owen's from *The End of the Chinese Middle Ages*, 193.
85. Owen, *The End of the Chinese Middle Ages*, 193.
86. Ibid., 203.
87. Manling Luo also understands Yingying's character in this light. See her *Literati Storytelling in Medieval China*, 130.
88. Ibid., 200.
89. Ibid., 200.
90. Ibid., 149–50.
91. Ibid., 149–50. See also Luo, *Literati Storytelling in Late Medieval China*, 132.
92. *Taiping guangji*, vol. 3, 274.68–69.
93. Su Hua, "Ouyang Zhan," in *Zhongguo wenxue da cidian* (Taipei: Baichuan, 1994), 7567.
94. Luo, *Literati Storytelling in Late Medieval China*, 101.
95. Ibid., 101.
96. Li Jianguo, *Tang Wudai zhiguai chuanqi xilu*, 554.
97. The reference to "husband" indicates Xiaoyu's status as a concubine or secondary wife.
98. *Taiping guangji*, vol. 4, 487, 550–55. The translated excerpts are from Owen, *An Anthology of Chinese Literature*, 531–40.
99. Liu Shu, *Jiu Tang shu*, in *Ershiwu shi*, vol. 23, 137.1876–77. Liu Kairong also quotes this passage in her discussion of "Huo Xiaoyu's Story," although she erroneously cites the *Xin Tang shu* as the source. See Liu Kairong, *Tangdai xiaoshuo yanjiu*, 86.

100. These are outlined in Li Jianguo, *Tang Wudai zhiguai chuanqi xilu*, 550.

101. On the cult of the Queen Mother, particularly during the Tang period, see Suzanne Cahill, *Transcendence and Divine Passion: The Queen Mother of the West in Medieval China* (Stanford, CA: Stanford University Press, 1993).

102. Scholars generally accept Zhang Zhuo (660-732) as author, although this has been challenged. See Wang Chung-han, "The Authorship of the *Yu-hsien k'u*," *Harvard Journal of Asiatic Studies* 11 (1948): 153-62. If Zhang Zhuo is, indeed, the author or recorder, it places the story around a hundred years earlier than what is generally considered the culture of romance's formative period.

103. Rouzer, *Articulated Ladies*, 70-71.

104. Li Fang et al., *Taiping guangji*, 1.341. Translated snippets are those of Inglis, *The Drunken Man's Talk*, 85-87.

105. Owen, *The End of the Chinese Middle Ages*, 130.

106. Luo, *Literati Storytelling in Late Medieval China*, 101.

107. Stephen Owen, "What Did Liu Zhi Hear? The 'Yan Terrace Poems' and the Culture of Romance," *T'ang Studies* 13 (1995): 1-118; Rouzer, *Articulated Ladies*, 249-83. The influence of urban examination culture on the rise of the *chuanqi* short story is also well recognized. See, for example, Liu Kairong, *Tangdai xiaoshuo yanjiu*, 16-19; Sarah Yim, *Structure, Theme and Narrator in T'ang "ch'uan-ch,'"* 3.

108. On this, see Owen, *The End of the Chinese Middle Ages*, 130-48.

109. Ibid., 131-32. Based on Owen's idea, Linda Rui Feng explores the gulf between the romantic ideal and realities of the *demimonde* in "Unmasking *Fengliu* in Urban Chang'an: Rereading *Beili zhi* (Anecdotes from the Northern Ward)," 1-21 *passim*.

110. Owen, 133.

111. Ibid., 135.

112. Liu Fu, *Qingsuo gaoyi*, 442-43.

113. *Taiping guangji*, vol. 4, 491.573.

114. See Owen's translation in *An Anthology of Chinese Literature*, 528.

115. Lee Yu-hwa also makes the point about wish fulfillment. Throughout her monograph, she approaches Tang-period love stories as fantasies measured by what was socially and legally sanctioned. For her idea about wish fulfillment, see Lee Yu-hwa, *Fantasy and Realism in Chinese Fiction* (San Francisco: Chinese Materials Center Publication, 1984), 54.

Chapter 2

1. For an overview of early Song dynasty political history, see Paul Jakov Smith, "The Sung Dynasty and Its Precursors," in *The Cambridge History of China*, vol. 5, ed. Dennis Twitchett and Paul Jakov Smith (Cambridge: Cambridge University Press, 2009), 1-37.

2. Zhuge Yibing, "Songdai shidafude jingyu yu shidafu jingshen," *Renmin daxue xuebao* (2001): 107–8.

3. Other scholars have also noted this trend. See Ihara Hiroshi, "Sōdai Minshū ni okeru kanko no konnin kankei," in *Chūō daigaku daigakuin kenkyū nenpō* 1 (1972): 157–68; Robert Hymes, *Statesmen and Gentlemen: The Elite of Fu-chou, Chiang-hsi, in Northern and Southern Song* (Cambridge: Cambridge University Press, 1986); Beverly Bossler, "Powerful Relations and Relations of Power: Family and Society in Sung China 960–1279" (PhD dissertation, University of California, Berkeley, 1991); Patricia Ebrey, *The Inner Quarters: Marriage and the Lives of Women in the Sung Period* (Berkeley: California University Press, 1993), 65.

4. Lau Yap-Yin, "Founding and Consolidation of the Sung Dynasty Under T'ai-tsu (960–976), T'ai-tsung (976–997), and Chen-tsung (997–1022)," in *The Cambridge History of China*, vol. 5, ed. Dennis Twitchett and Paul Jakov Smith, 238.

5. My understanding of Song social and demographic change is largely informed by Robert Hartwell. See his "Demographic, Political and Social Transformations in China, 750–1550," *Harvard Journal of Asiatic Studies* 42 (1982): 365–442, particularly 405–20.

6. Ibid., 420.

7. Ibid., 412, 419, 420.

8. Cong Ellen Zhang, "Writing on Illicit Sex in Song China (960–1279)," *Journal of the History of Sexuality* 22, no. 2 (2013): 259.

9. Bossler, *Courtesans, Concubines and the Cult of Female Fidelity*, 164.

10. James Hargett, *Jade Mountains and Cinnabar Pools: The History of Travel Literature in Imperial China* (Seattle: University of Washington Press, 2018), 177.

11. See Hong Mai, *Yijian zhi*, vol. 2 (Taipei: Mingwen, 1994), 944.

12. This reference to a shrewish wife was rare for Song dynasty stories, yet such would become a major theme during the Ming and Qing periods. On this theme, see Keith McMahon, *Misers, Shrews and Polygamists: Sexuality and Male–Female Relations in Eighteenth Century Chinese Fiction* (Durham, NC: Duke University Press, 1995).

13. Liu Fu, *Qingsuo gaoyi*, 383–85.

14. Bettine Birge, *Women, Property and Confucian Reaction in Sung and Yüan China (960–1368)* (Cambridge: Cambridge University Press, 2002), 76–78.

15. Patricia Ebrey, "Women, Marriage and the Family in Chinese History," in *The Heritage of China*, ed. Paul Ropp (Berkeley: University of California Press, 1990), 209–10.

16. On this, see Ebrey, "Women, Marriage and the Family in Chinese History," 208.

17. Martin Huang, *Desire and Fictional Narrative in Late Imperial China* (Cambridge, MA: Harvard University Asia Center, 2001), 223.

18. Anon., *Guidong*, in *Songdai biji xiaoshuo daguan*, vol. 24, ed. Zhou Guangpei (Shijiazhuang: Hebei jiaoyu, 1995), 246–47.

19. Luo Ye, *Xinbian zuiweng tanlu*, 12–13.
20. Assuming that Luo Ye is also author of the chapter in question.
21. Luo Ye, *Xinbian zuiweng tanlu*.
22. Although this seems callous to modern readers, as it may have for contemporary readers, a wife's contracting a "nasty" disease was a grounds for divorce in Song China.
23. Zhang Qixian, *Luoyang jinshen jiuwen ji* (Shanghai: Gushu liutong, 1921), 3.7a–8b. When Feng Menglong included this story in his *History of Love*, he did so under the category of "conjugal predestiny." See *Qingshi leilüe* (Liben tang), 2.4b–5b.
24. Hong Mai, *Yijian zhi*, vol. 3, 1041–42.
25. Bossler, *Courtesans, Concubines and the Cult of Female Fidelity*, 22.
26. Given that the narrative concludes in the early 1050s and some thirty or so years must have elapsed before Tan's son could have passed the examinations, Li Jianguo dates the story to the Yuanfeng reign period (1078–1986). See *Songdai zhiguai chuanqi xulu*, 164. The story was later anthologized in Zeng Zao's (fl. 1131–1163) *Leishuo*.
27. For a description of the six stages of the traditional marriage ritual, see Christian de Pee, *The Writing of Weddings in Middle-Period China* (Albany, NY: SUNY Press, 2007), 27–30.
28. Liu Fu, *Qingsuo gaoyi*, 543–48. A summarized version is included in the *New Stories from a Green Lattice Window*. Another, similar in diction to the *New Stories'* version, found in both the *Qingshi* and the *Qingni lianhua ji*, concludes with Tan's death. It is unclear if the recorder deliberately changed the conclusion or if the wife's death was mistaken for that of Tan's. Nonetheless, the *Qingshi* version resembles the betrayal prototype. For the *New Stories'* version, see Huangdu Fengyue Zhuren, *Lüchuang xinhua* (Shanghai: Shanghai guji, 1991), 140. Also see Feng Menglong, *Qingshi leilüe* (Liben tang), 13.16b–17a.
29. Bossler, *Courtesans, Concubines and the Cult of Female Fidelity*, 53 and passim.
30. Ibid., 75.
31. Liu Fu, *Qingsuo gaoyi*, 544.
32. For a discussion of the idea that writing embodied the Way (*wen zai Dao*), see Peter Bol, *This Culture of Ours: Intellectual Transitions in T'ang and Sung China* (Stanford, CA: Stanford University Press, 1992), 23, 83–84, 94–97, 118–22.
33. Ibid.
34. Wolfram Eberhard, *A Dictionary of Chinese Symbols*, trans. G. L. Campbell (New York: Routledge and Kegan Paul, 1986, rpt. 2001), 132–33.
35. Poem 23 in chapter 14 of *Ouyang Xiu ji*, "*Ji zaoren xing shu zeng Zilü xueshi*." Accessed online: https://zh.wikisource.org/zh-hans/%E6%AD%90%E9%99%BD%E4%BF%AE%E9%9B%86/%E5%8D%B7014.
36. The first poem in the *Shijing*, "Guanju" (Fish-hawks), according to the influential Mao commentary, is an allegory pointing to the lack of jealousy

exhibited by King Wen of Zhou's queen; the King's offspring were numerous because of this. See *Shijing quanshi*, ed. Qu Wanli (Taipei: Lianjing, 1983, rpt. 2002), 4–5. For a discussion of the poem's exegesis and imagery, see Pauline Yu, *The Reading of Imagery in the Chinese Poetic Tradition* (Princeton, NJ: Princeton University Press, 1987), 44–53.

37. This somewhat unusual turn-of-phrase may indicate a corrupt text, especially given the second reference to "the breeze."

38. Zhao Wei also notes this characteristic. See Zhao Wei, "Mingdai liqing chuanqi xiaoshuo yanjiu," 61.

39. He Xinling also make this point. See He Xinling, "Songdai chuanqi xiaoshuo nüxing xingxiangde yanbian," *Sha'anxi ligong xueyuan xuebao* (*shehui kexue*) 27, no. 3 (2009): 68.

40. In imperial times, it was customary for brides to wear an opaque, red veil that husbands removed on their wedding night.

41. In Chinese mythology, Nong Yu was the daughter of King Mu of Qin (Qin Mu Gong), who married the immortal Xiao Shi. The couple was thought to have ascended into the heavens astride a phoenix. As an early example of a loving couple, allusions to them frequently appear in both love stories and poetry. For an early reference, see Liu Xiang, *Liexian zhuan* (Beijing: Zhonghua, 2001), 80.

42. Li Xianmin, *Yunzhai guanglu* (Beijing: Zhonghua, 1997), 32–33. Li Xianmin catalogued it in his *liqing* section.

43. This also stands in contrast to poetry featuring the abandoned woman motif, pioneered during the Tang dynasty, according to which it was the woman who lamented an absent husband. "Record of Three Dreams" tells of an absent husband who saw his wife carousing with strange men in a dream. See *Shuofu*, comp. Tao Zongyi (Taipei: Shangwu, 1972), 5.23b–24a. For an analysis in English, see Allen, *Shifting Stories*, 55–65.

44. In the *Zhengde Jianchangfu zhi* (15/8 *xia*), 1115 is given as the year in which one Zhou Mo passed the *jinshi* examination. Since the *Qingsuo gaoyi* must have been completed by 1113, the known year of the compiler's death, either this is the wrong Zhou Mo or else the story was interpolated into the collection by a later hand. See *Songren zhuanji ziliao suoyin bubian*, ed. Li Guoling (Chengdu: Sichuan daxue, 1994), 635.

45. The use of the word "drink" (*yin*) suggests that the two women might have drunk alcohol. Unfortunately, what they drink is not specified as little is known about women's drinking habits during the Song dynasty. For a rare study on this topic using material found in Hong Mai's *Yijian zhi*, see Shio Takugo "*Ikenshi* kara mita Sōdai jyosei no inshoku seikatsu," in *Ikenshi no sekai: Nansō no kakureta besuto serā*, ed. Ihara Hiroshi and Shizunaga Takeshi (Tokyo: Bensei, 2015), 112–20.

46. Liu Fu, *Qingsuo gaoyi*, 416–19.

47. For an excellent book-length, English language study on sex and the law in imperial China, see Matthew Sommer, *Sex, Law and Society in Late Imperial China* (Stanford, CA: Stanford University Press, 2000).

48. One notable exception is "Journey to the Immortal's Grotto" (*You xianku*) whose brief direct description of a sexual act is accompanied by a lengthy build-up replete with comparatively transparent, erotic double-entendres. Such elliptic treatment of a sexual encounter contrasts starkly with the more explicit depiction found in erotic novels and stories of the late-imperial period. On this, see Patrick Hanan, "Sources of the *Chin P'ing Mei*," *Asia Major* 10 (1963): 46.

49. As Li Jianguo observes, the phrase "newly expanded" (*xinzeng*) follows the story title in some editions of *High Minded Conversations*. This strongly suggests that this story was not originally included in this collection. Furthermore, it is not included among the summarized items copied from *High Minded Conversations* by Zeng Zao (fl. 1131–1163) in his *Leishuo* (*Topicalized Stories*). Li Jianguo considers it of late Northern Song provenance given (1) its inclusion in *New Stories from a Green Lattice Window*, and (2) his judgment that *New Stories* was compiled during the early Southern Song. See Li Jianguo, *Songdai zhiguai chuanqi xulu*, 165.

50. *Daguan yuan*. I use David's Hawke's translation of the term. See Cao Xueqin, *Story of the Stone*, vol. 1, trans. David Hawkes (London: Penguin, 1973).

51. Both parties would have lost face in the event of a broken engagement.

52. Liu Fu, *Qingsuo gaoyi*, 555–57.

53. Qu You, *Jiandeng Xinhua* (Taipei: Shijie shuju, 2010), 29.

54. Thomas Hardy, *Tess of the d'Urbervilles*, 143.

55. See Huangdu Fengyue Zhuren, *Lüchuang xinhua*, 60.

56. Vladimir Nabokov, *Lolita* (London: Weildenfeld and Nicolson, 1955), *passim*.

57. Chen Tung-yüan also notes Song-period men's preference for virgins and virginity in regard to marriage. See Chen Tung-yüan, *Zhongguo funü shenghuo shi* (Taipei: Shangwu, 1970), 146.

58. He Xinling also make this point. See He Xinling, "Songdai chuanqi xiaoshuo nüxing xingxiangde yanbian," *Shaanxi ligong xueyuan xuebao* (*shehui kexue*) 27, no. 3 (2009): 70.

59. Ebrey, *The Inner Quarters*, 47.

60. Luo Ye, for example, reserves an entire chapter for wittily crafted legal judgments. See part 2 of the *geng* chapter in the *Xinbian zuiweng tanlu*. Modern scholars, however, may well question whether this genre was not so much intended for formal legal documents than a parody of such.

61. For an extensive introduction to Gong'an stories in English, see Y. W. Ma, "Kung-An Fiction: A Historical and Critical Introduction," *T'oung-Pao* 65 (1979): 200–59.

62. On this, see Ronald Egan, *The Problem of Beauty: Aesthetic Thought and Pursuits in Northern Song Dynasty China* (Cambridge, MA: Harvard University Press, 2006), 150.

63. The Prince of Zhao refers to Sima Lun (249–301), an Eastern Jin dynasty (265–316) prince involved in the Rebellion of the Eight Princes.

64. Li Xianmin, *Yunzhai guanglu*, 38–40.

65. In one of Luo Ye's stories, a ditty circulates about an upper-class man who supposedly sleeps with both his wife and concubine simultaneously under an extra-large quilt. See *Xinbian zuiweng tanlu* (1957), 13–14.

66. Li Xianmin, *Yunzhai guanglu*, 35–37.

67. See, for example, "Wu xiao yuanwai" in Hong Mai, *Yijian zhi*, vol. 1, 29–30. For a discussion of ambiguity in Song period narrative works, see Alister Inglis, "Narratological Ambiguity in Hong Mai's (1123–1202) *Yijian zhi*," *Transactions of the International Conference of Eastern Studies* 59 (2014): 24–46.

68. Liu Fu, *Qingsuo gaoyi*, 397–98.

69. Zhu Xi, *Zhuzi yulei* (Beijing, Zhonghua, 1986), 106.2644. For an English translation of the passage, see Patricia Ebrey, "Confucianism," in *Sex, Marriage and Family in World Religions*, ed. Don Browning et al. (New York: Columbia University Press, 2006), 423.

70. Cited in Bossler, *Courtesans, Concubines and the Cult of Female Fidelity*, 150–51.

71. By "scholarly elite," I refer to literate men who may or may not have held office. During a period of low literacy, the very ability to read, let alone compose narratives, was sufficient to distinguish one from regular townsfolk, regardless of lasting fame.

72. The number of Chinese scholars to have noticed this trend are too many to cite. See, for example, Li Jianguo, *Songdai zhiguai chuanqi xulu*, 8–9; Xiao Xiangkai, *Song Yuan xiaoshuo shi*, 7–9; Zhang Zhenjun and Wang Jing trans., *Song Dynasty Tales: A Guided Reader* (New Jersey: World Scientific, 2017), 7–10.

73. In the poem "Mt. Hua and Environs" (*Huashan ji*), a young man dies after swallowing an apron sent by his lover as a keepsake. As his funeral cortege passes her door, she sings to him to open his coffin and, when he does, she jumps in. In a second poem, the "Clerk from Lujiang" (*Lujiang xiaoli*), the heroine is forced to remarry after her mother-in-law drives her away. She then commits suicide so as to remain loyal to her husband. The original husband follows suit. In a short story eponymously titled "Xue Yiliao," the male protagonist leaves his courtesan-lover to take up an official posting. He dies in office soon after. When the coffin is returned to his native place, the courtesan comes to see it. Inexplicably, she touches it and immediately dies. See *Yuefu shiji*, ed. Guo Maoqian (Beijing: Zhonghua, 1979), 46.546–47; Lu Xing, *Yutai xinyong jian zhu* (Beijing: Zhonghua, 1985), 1.42–54; *Taiping guangji*, vol. 3, 274.69, respectively.

74. *Li ji* in *Shisanjing zhushu* (Taipei: Yiwen, 1981), 26.19a. Cited in *Li Chi, Book of Rites*, trans. James Legge (Oxford: Oxford University Press, 1885), 1.439.

75. Zhang Jiucheng, *Huang Pu xiansheng wenji* (facsimile edition of a Ming reprint, 1925), 20: 18a; Qin Guan, *Huai hai ji* (Taipei: Shangwu, 1990), 36: 247–48; both cited in Ebrey, *The Inner Quarters*, 207.

76. Xiong Huizhong, *Xinbian tingyong qizha jiejiang gang* (Song edition in the Seikadō Library, no date given), 205, cited in Ebrey, *The Inner Quarters*, 205.

77. Ebrey, *The Inner Quarters*, 194–200.

78. Cheng Hao and Chang Yi, *Er Cheng ji* (Beijing: Zhonghua, 1981), 22b.301, cited in Ebrey, *The Inner Quarters*, 199.

79. Ibid., 213.

80. Li Jianguo, *Songdai zhiguai chuanqi xulu*, 66.

81. Xu Ji, *Jiexiao ji*, in *Wenyuange siku quanshu*, vol. 1101 (Taipei: Shangwu, 1983), 856. The poem may also be found in Zhao Lingzhi, *Houjing lu* (Beijing: Zhonghua, 2002), 66.

82. Tao Zongyi, *Nancun chuogeng lu* (Beijing, Zhonghua, 1959, rpt. 1997), 15.180.

83. For the summarized version, see also Zhang Bangji, *Shi'er xiaoming lu shiyi* (Shanghai: Shangwu, 1937), 3b–4a.

84. Xu Ji, *Jiexiao ji*, 856.

85. Ibid., 856.

86. Li Jianguo, *Songdai zhiguai chuanqi xulu*, 66.

87. Chapters 270–74 of *Taiping guangji*, vol. 3, 39–64.

88. Zhang Zhuo, "Deng Lian's Wife," in *Taiping guangji*, vol. 3, 271.46–47.

89. "Gezhe fu," in *Taiping guangji*, vol. 3, 270.44.

90. He Xinling also notes this. See He Xinling, "Songdai chuanqi xiaoshuo," 68.

91. Bossler, *Courtesans, Concubines and the Cult of Female Fidelity*, 199–200.

92. Bossler, *Courtesans, Concubines and the Cult of Female Fidelity*, 53 and passim.

93. Liu Fu, *Qingsuo gaoyi*, 478–79.

94. Bossler, *Courtesans, Concubines and the Cult of Female Fidelity*, 76.

95. Bossler, *Courtesans, Concubines and the Cult of Female Fidelity*, 53 and passim.

96. Like many famous short stories of the Tang era, this was circulated in both narrative and ballad form. Only the latter dates to the eleventh century. The most detailed and extant version of the narrative is found in Luo Ye's *Drunken Man's Talk*. It is, however, unclear whether the *Drunken Man's Talk* was compiled in the late twelfth, thirteenth, or fourteenth century; it is certainly later than the original story. Nevertheless, as its main points correlate with the eleventh-century ballad, we may be confident of the narrative's essential "fidelity" regardless of any

minor embellishments. Alternatively, Luo Ye may have faithfully copied an early written version. For the ballad version, see Li Xianmin, *Yunzhai guanglu*, 41–43.

97. A full account may be found in Luo Ye, *Xinbian zuiweng tanlu*, 96–103. A poem titled "Ballad of Wang Kui" appears in Li Xianmin, *Yunzhai guanglu*, 41–43. A summarized version of the story may also be found in other Song-period texts, notably Zeng Zao's *Leishuo*, vol. 5 (Beijing: Wenxure guji, 1955), 37–39. The selected translation presented here is that of Alister Inglis, *The Drunken Man's Talk*, 115–20.

98. For He Xinling, "Story of Wang Kui" clearly exhibits the influence of "Huo Xiaoyu's Story." See He Xinling, "Songdai chuanqi xiaoshuo," 68.

99. These dates are based on Chu Yushi's account.

100. Cited in chapter 6 of Zhou Mi, *Qidong yeyu*, in *Songdai biji xiaoshuo daguan*, vol. 11, 58.

101. Zhang Shizheng, *Kuo yi zhi*, chapter 3, *Songdai biji xiaoshuo daguan*, vol. 11, 555–56.

102. *Minggong shupan qingming ji* (Beijing: Zhonghua, 1987), 9.344. The translation is Bossler's. See *Courtesans, Concubines and the Cult of Female Fidelity*, 200.

103. Cited in Zhou Mi, *Qidong yeyu*, op cit.

104. Li Xianmin, *Yunzhai guanglu*, 41.

105. Li Jianguo, *Songdai zhiguai chuanqi xulu*, 107–112. Li reproduces and eruditely analyzes excerpts from Zhou Mi, Li Xianmin, and Zhang Shizheng relevant to the story's circulation.

106. Feng Menglong, *Qingshi leilüe* (Liben tang), 2.4b–5b; *Wudai shi bu*, in *Congshu jicheng xubian* (Shanghai: Shanghai shudian, 1994?), vol. 23, 5.209–10.

107. *Taiping guangji*, vol. 2, 463.

Chapter 3

1. For further information in English on this period, see chapters 8 to 12 of Twitchett and Smith, ed., *The Cambridge History of China*, vol. 5.

2. Hartwell, "Demographic, Political and Social Transformations in China, 750–1550," 422.

3. Paul Jakov Smith, "Problematizing the Song-Yuan-Ming Transition," in *The Song-Yuan-Ming Transition in Chinese History*, ed. Paul Jakov Smith and Richard von Glahn (Cambridge, MA: Harvard University Press, 2003), 23.

4. Smith, "Problematizing the Song-Yuan-Ming Transition," 21; Peter Bol, "Government, Society and State: On the Political Visions of Ssu-ma Kuang and Wang Anshi," in *Ordering the World: Approached to State and Society in Sung Dynasty China*, ed. Robert Hymes and Conrad Shirokauer (Berkeley: University of California Press, 1993).

5. Wang Mingqing's compiler-authorship has been questioned. See Li Jianguo, *Song Yuan xiaoshuo xulu*, 330. Chang Bide considers it of early Southern Song provenance. See Chang Bide, *Shuofu kao* (Taipei: Wenshizhe, 1979), 247.

6. For an overview, see Li Jianguo, *Song Yuan xiaoshuo xulu*, 331.

7. Marriage between cousins was allowed providing the two bore different surnames. The idea of two or more marriages between families was appealing throughout the Song era and there was an historical precedent in the marriages between the states of Qin and Jin during the Warring States period. These factors, together with the males being slightly older than the female, strongly suggests that contemporary readers would have read this story as one of marital predestiny, as I will discuss below. On interfamilial marriage, see Ebrey, *The Inner Quarters*, 66–71.

8. Wang Mingqing, *Zhiqing zashuo*, in Tao Zongyu, ed., *Shuofu*, 18*xia*: 12a–17a, https://ctext.org/library.pl?if=gb&file=66325&page=25&remap=gb. Concluding details about a couple's offspring and their career success would have been read as evidence of marital predestiny.

9. It was legally permissible for the groom's family to break off an engagement, but not so for the bride's; were the bride's father to break an engagement, he may have been subject to judicial punishment. On this, see Ebrey, *The Inner Quarters*, 88.

10. On the betrothal of young children, see Ebrey, *The Inner Quarters*, 63–64.

11. Hartwell, "Demographic, Political and Social Transformations in China, 750–1550," 406.

12. Wang Mingqing, *Zhiqing zashuo*, in *Shuofu*, 18*xia*: 8b–18b. The story was extremely popular in later periods. Feng Menglong rewrote it as the vernacular short story "Fan Qiu'er's Twin Mirror Reunion" in his *Comprehensive Words to Awaken the World (Jingshi tongyan)* and included it in the "chaste women" section of his *History of Affection*. It was rewritten as "Feng Yumei's Reunion" in Hong Bian's *Qingpingshan tang Vernacular Stories (Qingpingshan tang huaben)*. The Ming dynasty playwright Mu Chengzhang adapted the plot for his opera, "Twin Mirror Reunion." For a full list, see Li Jianguo, *Song Yuan xiaoshuo xulu*, 330–31.

13. Feng Menglong, *Qingshi*, 1.1. The subcategory's translation is based on that of Hua-yuan Li Mowry trans., *Chinese Love Stories from* Ch'ing shih, 38.

14. On the perceived dispensability of concubines during the Song dynasty, see Ebrey, *The Inner Quarters*, 217–34.

15. Hong Mai, *Yijian zhi*, vol. 1, 11–12. The translation is that of Inglis, *Hong Mai's Record of the Listener and Its Song Dynasty Context*, 13–16.

16. Keith McMahon, *Misers, Shrews and Polygamists*, 55–81.

17. Hong Mai, *Yijian zhi*, vol. 1, 143.

18. Li Changling, *Le shan lu* (Taipei: Shangwu, 1971), 6.12b–13a, cited in Ebrey, *The Inner Quarters*, 214. I have slightly modified Ebrey's translation.

19. Cheng Hao and Chang Yi, *Er Cheng ji*, cited in Ebrey, *The Inner Quarters*, 213.

20. Cited in Bossler, *Courtesans, Concubines and the Cult of Female Fidelity*, 234.

21. Ibid., 235.

22. Hong Mai, *Yijian zhi*, vol. 1, 608–9. The translation is that of Inglis, *Hong Mai's Record of the Listener and Its Song Dynasty Context*, 251–57.

23. Hong Mai, *Yijian zhi*, vol. 3, 1192. For an English translation, see Inglis, *Hong Mai's Record of the Listener and Its Song Dynasty Context*, 98–99.

24. Zhou Zizhi, *Tai cang ti mi ji*, in *Siku quanshu*, vol. 1141, 49.4b–6a, https://ctext.org/library.pl?if=gb&file=3622&page=110. For an English translation and discussion, see Bossler, *Courtesans, Concubines and the Cult of Female Fidelity*, 258.

25. Ibid.

26. Hong Mai, *Yijian zhi*, vol. 4, 1332–33.

27. "Tao Pei shuang yi," in Zhou Mi, *Guixin zashi*, bieji juan shang, cited in Kim Wŏnhŭi, Qing shi *gushi yuanliu kaoshu*, 234–35. The suicide that Zhou records is also the subject of a lyric poem, to the tune of *Shuangtian xiaojiao* (A Frosty Morning), found in Huang Sheng, *Zhongxing yilai juemiao cixuan* (*Anthology of Marvelous Lyric poems Since the Zhongxing Reign Period*, Sibu congkan edition), 4.4b. On this poem, also see Cheng Yizhong, "Jiao Hong ji zai xiaoshuo yishu fazhan zhong de lishi jiazhi," *Journal of Xuchang Teachers College* 2 (social science edition; 1990): 16.

28. Dating *New Stories* is problematic. Li Jianguo argues that it was completed between 1148 and 1162. See his *Song Yuan xiaoshuo xulu*, 294. Tsiperovitch, however, asserts a mid-thirteenth-century completion date. See her note titled "Lü-ch'uang hsin-hua," in *A Sung Bibliography*, ed. Etienne Balazs and Yves Hervouet (Hong Kong: The Chinese University Press, 1978), 346.

29. Huangdu Fengyue Zhuren, *Lüchuang Xinhua* (Shanghai: Shanghai guji, 1991), 116–17. The story is not included in the received text of the *Nanchu xinwen*.

30. Ibid., 172.

31. As Cheng Yizhong observes, romantic tragedies became increasingly popular throughout the Song period. See Cheng Yizhong, "Jiao Hong ji zai xiaoshuo yishu fazhan zhong de lishi jiazhi," 16.

32. Luo Ye, *Xinbian zuiweng tanlu*, 99. The translation is that of Inglis, *The Drunken Man's Talk*, 125.

33. For an erudite analysis of this complex area, see Cheng Hsiao-wen, *Traveling Stories and Untold Desires: Female Sexuality in Song China 10th–13th Centuries* (PhD dissertation, University of Washington, Seattle, Washington, 2012), 83–104.

34. Liu Fu, *Qingsuo gaoyi*, 440.

35. Feng Menglong, *Qingshi leilüe*, 3.26–27. The source is the thirteenth- or fourteenth-century *Stories from the Green Window* (Lüchuang jishi). Although no longer extant, several surviving texts both cite and preserve its stories. It also appears in tbook collectors, Chao Li and Chao Dongwu's (1532–1554) Baowentang

catalogue. For an evaluation and summary of its contents, see Cheng Yizhong, *Song Yuan xiaoshuo yanjiu*, 215–16.

36. This myth is first recorded in Liu Xiang, *Lie xian zhuan*, 80.
37. Huangdu Fengyu Zhuren, *Lüchuang Xinhua*, 110.
38. Chapter 168 of *Taiping guangji*, vol. 2, 124.
39. See chapter/*juan* 49 of Zeng Zao, *Lei shuo*, vol. 5, 26.
40. Hong Mai, *Yijian zhi*, vol. 2, 902–3. The translation is that of Alister Inglis, *Selections from* Record of the Listener (Beijing: Foreign Language Press, 2009), 329–32.
41. Belief that a human soul comprised three heavenly and seven earthly souls (*sanhun qipo*) was widespread throughout ancient and imperial China. On the duality/plurality of the soul, see J.J.M. de Groot, *The Religious System of China*, vol. 4 (Taipei: Southern Materials Center, 1982), 5; Howard Smith, "Chinese Concepts of the Soul," *Numen* 5, vol. 3 (1958): 165–79.
42. Hong Mai, *Yijian zhi*, vol. 1, 564–65. For a translation slightly modified here, see Inglis, *Selections from* Record of the Listener, 228–29.
43. The translation is that of Wilt Idema, "An Eighteenth Century Version of 'Liang Shanbo and Zhu Yingtai' from Suzhou," in *The Columbia Anthology of Chinese Folk and Popular Literature*, ed. Victor Mair and Mark Bender (New York: Columbia University Press, 2011), 503.
44. Wilt Idema also doubts its authenticity. See ibid., 503.
45. Cited in ibid., 503.
46. Shi Nengzhi, *Xianchun piling zhi*, in *Song Yuan difang zhi congshu* (Taipei: Dahua shuju, 1987), 27.10a–b, cited in Altenburger, "Is It Clothes that Make the Man?," 178.
47. Ibid., 196n24.
48. Hong Mai, *Yijian zhi*, vol. 4, 1701–2.
49. Luo Ye, *Xinbian zuiweng tanlu*, 26. The translation is that of Inglis, *The Drunken Man's Talk*, 35–36.
50. See "The Kunshan Townsman," in Feng Menglong, *Qingshi*, 2.3b–4a. On the story's anthologizing in Ming and Qing collections, see Jin Yuanxi, Qingshi *gushi yuanliu kaoshu* (Nanjing: Fenghuang, 2011), 211.
51. Luo Ye, *Xinbian zuiweng tanlu*, 55. The translated excerpts are taken from Inglis, *The Drunken Man's Talk*, 71–72.
52. It quotes, almost verbatim, the "Wanzhang shang" chapter of the *Mengzi*. See *Sishu duben* (Taipei: Mingshan, no date given), 490.
53. See section 3 of the "Xiushen" chapter of the *Yangzi fayan*, ed. Dong Zhian and Zhang Zhongwang (Shandong: Shandong youyi, 2000), 39.
54. See the "Third Year of Duke Ai" section of the *Zuozhuan*, 715. On Bai Juyi's poem titled "Zhu Chen cun," see *Quan Tang shi*, ed. Peng Dingqiu (Zhengzhou: Zhengzhou guju, 2008), 433: 1. For a brief explanation of this poem and its allusions in English, see Ebrey, *The Inner Quarters*, 71.

296 | Notes to Chapter 4

55. Luo Ye, *Xinbian zuiweng tanlu*, 6–11. The translated excerpts are taken from Inglis, *The Drunken Man's Talk*, 10–17.
56. On exchange of wedding gifts, see de Pee, *Writing of Weddings in Middle-Period China*, 64–66 and *passim*.
57. *Zhouli dingyi*, ed. Wu Yuzhi, *Siku quanshu* edition, 14.13b. Such is the importance of this aged-old tradition that many engaged couples in present-day Taiwan still hire professional matchmakers despite having freely chosen each other.
58. Pomegranates symbolized fertility. In this context, their auspicious value is clear.
59. Feng Menglong, *Qingshi leilüe*, 3.1–4.
60. Ibid., 4.
61. Ibid., 3.4.
62. Brian McKnight and James Liu trans., *The Enlightened Judgements*, 15–16.
63. Ebrey, *The Inner Quarters*, 64.
64. On the completion of Hong Mai's *Record of the Listener*, see Alister Inglis, "A Textual History of Hong Mai's *Yijian zhi*," *T'oung Pao* 93 (2007): 323–24.
65. Hong Mai, *Yijian zhi*, vol. 1, 59–60 and vol. 2, 787, respectively. Both versions are so similar that unknown Yuan dynasty editors used the second to complete missing portions of the first. The translation is that of Inglis, *Selections from* Record of the Listener, 59–61.
66. Liu Fu, *Qingsuo gaoyi*, 557–61. Based on details in its attached poem, Li Jianguo believes that the storyteller fabricated his account. See Li Jianguo, *Songdai zhiguai chuanqi xulu*, 60–62.

Chapter 4

1. On the fall of the Southern Song, see Richard L. Davis, *Wind against the Mountain: the Crisis of Politics and Culture in Thirteenth-Century China* (Cambridge, MA: Harvard University Press, 1996); Richard L. Davis, "The Reign of Tu-tsung (1264–1274) and His Successors to 1279," in *The Cambridge History of China*, vol. 5, ed. Denis Twitchett and Paul Jacov Smith (Cambridge: Cambridge University Press, 2009), 913–61.
2. Kong Qi, *Zhizheng zhi ji* (Shanghai: Shanghai guji, 1987), 13–14. Cited in Smith, "Impressions of the Song-Yuan-Ming Transition," 82.
3. Smith, "Impressions of the Song-Yuan-Ming Transition," in Smith and von Glahn eds., *The Song-Yuan-Ming Transition in Chinese History*, 90–91.
4. On the rise of the dramatic arts during this period, see Wilt Idema and Stephen West, *Chinese Theater 1100–1400, A Source Book* (Wiesbaden: Franz Steiner Verlag, 1982).
5. On Mongol marriage customs, see Bettine Birge, *Women, Property and Confucian Reaction in Sung and Yüan China*, 200–30; Bettine Birge, "Women

and Confucianism from Song to Ming: The Institutionalization of Patrilinity"; Jennifer Holmgren, "Observations on Marriage and Inheritance Practices in Early Mongol and Yuan Society," *Journal of Asian History* 20 (1986): 127–97; Jennifer Holmgren, *Marriage, Kinship and Power in Northern China* (Aldershot, Great Britain: Variorum, 1995), 180–90.

 6. See, for example, Xiao Xiangkai, *Song Yuan xiaoshuo shi*, 360.

 7. Indeed, Hoyt Tillman has argued that many members of the educated elite turned to writing and other cultural activities as a form of catharsis from the deep psychological trauma wrought by the turbulent Song-Yuan transition. There is little reason to believe that storytelling would be exceptional in this regard. See Hoyt Tillman, "Disorder (*luan*) as Trauma: A Case Study of Reactions to the Mongol Conquest," unpublished paper, 2002, cited in Bossler, *Courtesans, Concubines and the Cult of Female Fidelity*, 377.

 8. Lucille Chia, *Printing for Profit: The Commercial Publishers of Jianyang, Fujian (11th–17th Centuries)* (Cambridge, MA: Harvard University Asia Center, 2002), 67.

 9. Y. M. Ma, "Tao Tsung-i" in William Nienhauser ed., *The Indiana Companion to Traditional Chinese Literature*, 768.

 10. Ibid.

 11. I borrow Cyril Birch's translation of the title. See Meng Chengshun, Cyril Birch ed. and trans. *Mistress and Maid* (New York: Columbia University Press, 2001).

 12. For a discussion of dating and authorship, see Itō Sōhei, *Kyo ko ki*, 470–72; Chen Yiyuan, *Yuan Ming zhongpian chuanqi xiaoshuo yanjiu* (Hong Kong: Xuefeng wenhua, 1997), 20–27. Also see, Song Yuan, *Jiao Hong ji*, in Zheng Zhenduo ed., *Shijie wenku*, vol. 3 (Shanghai: Shenghuo shudian, 1935), 27.

 13. Itō Sōhei, in his painstaking analysis of the historical background, concludes that details are historically faithful based on our current knowledge of the early twelfth century. See Itō Sōhei, *Kyo ko ki* in *Chūgoku koten bungaku taikei*, vol. 38 (Tokyo: Heibonsha, 1973), 472–78.

 14. An opera based on the short story, whose preface dates 1435, identifies Song as the original author-compiler. Nevertheless, the famous poet and prose author, Yu Ji (1272–1348), is named as author on an imprint dated 1548. The May Fourth period literary historian Zheng Zhenduo, however, rejects this as a printer's attempt to profit from Yu's reputation. Itō Sōhei concurs with Zheng's view. Regardless of whether Song or Yu was the actual author, both were alive during the Yuan dynasty so dating the work to this period is unproblematic.

 15. Itō Sōhei, *Kyo ko ki*, 483.

 16. Song Yuan, *Jiao Hong ji*, 3.

 17. Sun Kaidi coined the term *shiwen xiaoshuo* (verse-prose narrative) to characterize short stories and longer narrative that combine copious poems and narrative technique. Although the inclusion of poetry in narrative was a feature

of Chinese narrative since the Tang dynasty, from the Yuan and Ming period onward poetry was included in significantly larger quantities. See Sun Kaidi, *Riben Dongjing suo jian xiaoshuo shumu* (Beijing: Renmin wenxue, 1958), 126–27. Also see Cheng Yizhong, *Ming dai xiaoshuo conggao* (Beijing: Renmin wenxue, 2008), 20: Chen Dakang, *Ming dai xiaoshuo shi* (Shanghai: Shanghai wenyi, 2000), 318–19; André Lévy, *Le Conte en Langue Vulgaire du XVIIe siècle* (Paris: Presses Universitaires de France, 1981), 22, 113.

18. Little Cold (*xiaohan*) was one of the twenty-four solar nodes that fell around the fifth, sixth, or seventh day of January according to the solar calendar.

19. During this period, women's small, bound feet were not only the height of fashion and a status symbol but were also considered an erotic zone, hence the smaller the better.

20. In this context, swallows denote a happy couple while geese were considered messengers between loved ones.

21. Song Yuan, *Jiao Hong ji*, 1–27; Song Yuan, *Jiao Hong shuangmei* in Xiansou Shigong ed., *Huazhen qiyan* (Taipei: publisher not identified, 1987?).

22. This is Mao number 73. The translation is that of James Legge, *The She King or the Book of Poetry* (Taipei: SMC, 1991, rpt. 2000), 121. For the original, see Qu Wanli ed., *Shijing quanyi*, 131.

23. Meng Chengshun, *Jieyi yuanyang zhong Jiao Hong ji* (Shanghai: Guben xiqu congkan, 1955), 1, cited in Richard Wang, "The Cult of *Qing*: Romanticism in the Late Ming Period and the Novel 'Jiaohong ji,'" *Ming Studies* 1 (1994): 27.

24. Richard Wang, "The Cult of *Qing*, 18.

25. Xiao Xiangkai also notes this. See Xiao Xiangkai, *Song Yuan xiaoshuo shi*, 365.

26. The story may well have been written during this early period when no examinations were held. If so, this might explain why the author sets his story during the late Northern Song instead of his own life and times, as was the norm.

27. On the significance of heroes valuing love over career as a distinctive literary theme throughout the Ming, see Zhao Wei, "Mingdai liqing chuanqi xiaoshuo yanjiu," 19.

28. Richard Wang, "The Cult of *Qing*," 19; Cheng Yizhong, "*Jiao Hong ji* zai xiaoshuo yishu fazhangzhongde lishi jiazhi," 17. Furthermore, for Cyril Birch, *Bella and Scarlett* likely provided a model for *Dream of Red Mansions*. See Birch, *Mistress and Maid*, xv. For an extensive comparison of the two works, see Lin Ying, "*Hong loumeng* yu Yuan Ming zhongpian wenyan chuanqi yuanyuan bulun," *Hong Lou Meng xuekan* 6 (2019): 185–205.

29. Xiao Chi, *The Chinese Garden as Lyric Enclave: a Generic Study of Story of the Stone* (Ann Arbor: University of Michigan Press, 2001), 111.

30. Itō Sōhei, *Kyo ko ki*, 482; Cheng Yizhong, "Jiao Hong ji zai xiaoshuo yishu fazhan zhong de lishi jiazhi," 15.

31. "Mengzi," in *Sishu duben*, 420.

32. Song Yuan, *Jiao Hong ji*, in Zheng Zhenduo ed. *Shijie wenku chatu ben*, vol. 3, 27.
33. Itō Sōhei, "Kyō kō ki kaisetsu," 484.
34. Birch, *Mistress and Maid*, xvii.
35. Qu You, *Jiandeng Xinhua* in An Pingqiu ed., *Guben xiaoshuo jicheng* (Shanghai: Shanghai guji, 1990-), vol. 82, 166–85.
36. Qu You, *Jiandeng Xinhua*, 237–44.
37. On this phenomenon, see, for example, Emily Ahern, *The Cult of the Dead in a Chinese Village* (Stanford, CA: Stanford University Press, 1973); Majorie Topley, "Ghost Marriages among the Singapore Chinese," *Man* 55 (1955): 29–30; Maurice Freedman, *Family and Kinship in Chinese Society* (Stanford, CA: Stanford University Press, 1970), 165.
38. Cheng Yizhong, *Song Yuan xiaoshuo yanjiu*, 212, 214.
39. The translation is that of Christian de Pee, "Words of Seduction, Lines of Resistance: Writing and Gender in Zheng Xi's *Dream of Spring* (1318)," *Nan Nü* 9 (2007): 251–52.
40. Sun Qi, *Beili zhi*, in Lu Ji, ed., *Gujin shuohai* (Shanghai: Shanghai wenyi, 1989), 6.
41. de Pee, "Words of Seduction, Lines of Resistance," 274.
42. Ibid., 257.
43. Ibid., 258.
44. Slightly modified from Ibid., 256.
45. Ibid., 250.
46. Liu Fu, *Qingsuo gaoyi*, 439–43.
47. de Pee, "Words of Seduction, Lines of Resistance," 268.
48. Ibid., 276–77.
49. Cheng Yizhong, *Song Yuan xiaoshuo yanjiu*, 213.
50. de Pee, "Words of Seduction, Lines of Resistance," 274.
51. Ibid., 264.
52. Ibid., 269.
53. Ibid., 261.
54. Qu You, *Jiandeng Xinhua*, 150–66.
55. Li Changling, *Le shan lu*, 6.12b–13a, cited in Ebrey, *The Inner Quarters*, 214.
56. Bossler, *Courtesans, Concubines and the Cult of Female Fidelity*, 234.
57. Tao Zongyi, *Chuo geng lu* (Taipei: Shijie shuju, 1971), 12.185–86.
58. Feng Menglong, *Qingshi*, 1: 4b–5b.
59. Tao Zongyi, for example, records a story about two former Song palace women, Ladies Chen and Zhu, who, together with two serving girls, committed suicide rather than serve the conquering Mongols. They were posthumously beheaded as a punishment and deterrent to others. Tao Zongyi includes many such stories in his anecdotal collection. See his *Chuo geng lu*, 3.57.

60. This story has many versions. See, for example, Tao Zongyi, *Chuogeng lu* (Taipei: Shijie, 1971), 3.57; Li Xiaoguang, *Wu feng ji* in *Siku quanshu*, vol. 1215, 1.19a–20b and 8.13b. For a summary in English, see Beverly Bossler, *Courtesans, Concubines and the Cult of Female Fidelity*, 373–74. In another of Tao Zongyi's stories, "Faithful Wife Lin," the heroine similarly writes a suicide poem in blood after biting her finger. See Tao Zongyi, *Chuogeng lu*, 27.421.

61. That is, a woman must have been widowed before the age of thirty. She must have undertaken a vow of chastity and refrained from remarrying until the age of fifty. See *Da Yuan shengzheng guochao dianzhang* (Taipei: Gugong bowuguan, 1976), 33.13a–b, cited in Bettine Birge, "Women and Confucianism from Song to Ming: The Institutionalization of Patrilineality," in Paul Jakov Smith and Richard von Glahn, eds., *The Song-Yuan-Ming Transition in Chinese History* (Cambridge, MA: Harvard University Asia Center, 2003), 235. Also see Beverly Bossler, *Courtesans, Concubines and the Cult of Female Fidelity*, 371–72.

62. On widow chastity and the status of women during the Song-Yuan-Ming transition, see Bettine Birge, *Women, Property and Confucian Reaction in Sung and Yüan China (960–1368)*; Birge, "Women and Confucianism from Song to Ming," 212–40.

63. Qu You, *Jiandeng Xinhua*, 48–61.

64. See "Lady of Green Youth," in Li Fang et al., eds., *Taiping guangji*, vol. 1, 68.327–29.

65. Martin Huang, *Desire and Fictional Narrative*, 85.

Conclusion

1. Since such stories offer no new insights on thematic development, I have not included examples in this study.

2. "Mengzi" in *Sishu duben*, 420.

3. For a discussion of the Qingli reforms, see Michael McGrath, "The Reigns of Jen-tsung (1022–1063) and Ying-tsung (1063–1067)," in *The Cambridge History of China*, vol. 5, ed. Dennis Twitchett and Paul Jakov Smith, 316–27. For Wang Anshi's New Policies, see Paul Jakov Smith in ibid., 347–83.

4. Bossler, *Courtesans, Concubines and the Cult of Female Fidelity*, 417.

5. Zhuge Yibing, "Songdai shidafude jingyu yu shidafu jingshen," 107–8.

6. Bossler, *Courtesans, Concubines and the Cult of Female Fidelity*, 159.

7. Wang Yi-pei, "Songdai wenyan xiaoshuozhong nüxing qunxiangzhi tanjiu" (PhD dissertation, Taiwan National University, 2006), 32.

8. Paul Rouzer, *Articulated Ladies*, 201.

9. Ibid.

10. Song Yuan, *Jiao Hong ji*, in Zheng Zhenduo, ed., *Shijie wenku chatu ben*, vol. 3, 27.

11. Ibid., 26.

12. The scholarship on this is too bountiful to mention. For major studies in English, see Kang-I Sun Chang, *The Late Ming Poet Ch'en Tzu-lung: Crises of Love and Loyalism* (New Haven, CT: Yale University Press1991); Wai-yee Li, *Enchantment and Disenchantment: Love and Illusion in Chinese Literature* (Princeton, NJ: Princeton University Press, 1993); Dorothy Ko, *Teachers of the Inner Chambers: Women and Culture in Seventeenth Century China* (Stanford, CA: Stanford University Press, 1994); Ellen Widmer and Kang-I Sun Chang eds., *Writing and Women in Late Imperial China* (Stanford, CA: Stanford University Press, 1997); and Martin Huang, *Desire and Fictional Narrative in Late Imperial China* (Cambridge, MA: Harvard University Press, 2001).

13. Hsieh, *Love and Women in Early Chinese Fiction*, 3.

14. Hong Mai, *Yijian zhi*, vol. 1, 537.

15. See note 69, chapter 2.

16. Hu Yinglin, *Shaoshi shanfang bicong*, 36.474.

Chinese Character Glossary

beifang zhi youzhe 北方之尤者
benshi shi 本事詩
bu 捕
bugan yi shisu ernü tai, yao jun ju si ye 不敢以世俗兒女態要君俱死也
cainü 才女
Changhen ge zhuan 長恨歌傳
Changhen ge 長恨歌
chuanqi 傳奇
chuse 出色
ci 詞
congliang 從良
dai 黛
dangsan 蕩散
Daoxue 道學
donggua 冬瓜
Ducheng jisheng 都城記勝
Dule yuan 獨樂園
en'ai 恩愛
enqing 恩情
faji 發跡
fei ouran 非偶然
fen 粉
fumu zhi ming 父母之命
fuxin 負心
fuyue 負約
gong'an 公案
guai 怪

Guo Huaqing gong 過華清宮
Guozi jian 國子監
hejian 合姦
hongzao 紅棗
huaibao 懷抱
huoni 惑溺
hutao 胡桃
jian qi shi, yi dong er zu 見其詩，一慟而卒
jian 姦
Jiang Shaoyu 江少虞
jianmin 賤民
jianmin 賤民
jiaren caizi 佳人才子
jiayou 嘉祐
jieyi 節義
jinhu bixia 金虎碧霞
jinshi 進士
jiong yuan chensu 迥远尘俗
juan 卷
juexing er fu 崛興而富
li 里
Li xianming 李獻民
liangmin 良民
Lin'an 臨安
liqing xinshuo 麗情新說
longhu bang 龍虎幫
lou 樓
luan 亂
Luo ye 羅燁
Mengliang lu 夢粱錄
mingfu 命婦
minghun 冥婚
mingjian 明鑒
minjia 民家
mofang 模仿
Mu Chengzhang 穆成章
muzhi 墓誌
Nai deweng 耐德翁
qi 奇

qi 氣
qi nüzi 奇女子
qing 情
qinggan 情感
qingli 慶歷
Qingming 清明
Qingshi 情史
qiyi 氣義
san zhen 三貞
san'gang 三綱
sanhun qipo 三魂七魄
se yi guan zhong 色亦冠眾
Shangsi 上巳
shi dafu 士大夫
shimin 市民
Shishi leiyuan 事實類苑
shisu ernü 世俗兒女
Shuangtao ji 雙桃記
sihe xiang 四合香
siwen 斯文
sui 歲
Taiping guangji 太平廣記
Taixue 太學
tanhua lang 探花郎
tian zuo zhi he 天作之合
tianbao 天寶
tonglie 同列
tongsu xiaoshuo 通俗小說
wenjian 聞見
wen zai Dao 文載道
Wu Zimu 吳自牧
Xiangguo si 相國寺
xiangsi bing 相思病
xiangsi zi 相思子
xiaoshuo 小說
xiaoshuo kaipi 小說開闢
Xinbian zuiweng tanlu 新編醉翁談錄
xiumei 秀美
xuanhe 宣和

yanfen 煙粉
yang 陽
yanhua daifen 煙花黛粉
yanyou 延祐
yaoxin 妖釁
yi wei xiaoshuo zhe 意為小說者
yi you zu 以憂卒
yin privilege 陰
yinghuo 熒惑
yinyuan 姻緣
Yizhi 宜之
you qing zhe 有情者
you qing 有情
youming zhi shu 幽明之殊
yu shili yu nianshao xiaxie bei 欲市利於年少狎邪輩
yuanfu 元符
Yuanyan ji 遠煙記
Yunchao bian 雲巢編
Yunzhai guanglu 雲齋廣錄
za 雜
zalu 雜錄
zao 棗
zazhuan 雜傳
Zhang junfang 張君房
zhangfu 丈夫
zhenfu 貞婦
zhenlie 貞烈
zhiguai 志怪
zhizheng 至政
zhongpian chuanqi xiaoshuo 中篇傳奇小說
zhu 主

Works Cited

Primary Sources

Anonymous. *Da Yuan shengzheng guochao dianzhang*. Taipei: Gugong bowuguan, 1976.
Anonymous. *Ershiwu shi*. Taipei: Yiwen, rpt. Wuying dian edition, no date given.
Anonymous. *Guidong*. In *Songdai biji xiaoshuo daguan*, vol. 24, edited by Zhou Guangpei. Shijiazhuang: Hebei jiaoyu, 1995.
Anonymous. *Li ji* in *Shisanjing zhushu*. Taipei: Yiwen, 1981.
Anonymous. *Minggong shupan qingming ji*. Beijing: Zhonghua, 1987.
Anonymous. *Mu Tianzi zhuan xizheng jiangshu*. Edited by Gu Shi. Shanghai, Shangwu, 1934.
Anonymous. *Shijing quanshi*. Edited by Qu Wanli. Taipei: Lianjing, 1983, rpt. 2002.
Anonymous. *Zhouli dingyi*. Edited by Wu Yuzhi. *Siku quanshu* edition,
Anonymous. *Zuo zhuan*. Changsha: Xinjiang renmin, 2002.
An Pingqiu, ed. *Guben xiaoshuo jicheng*, vol. 82. Shanghai: Shanghai guji, 1990.
Bai Juyi. *Bai Juyi ji*. Beijing: Zhonghua, 1979.
Chao Gongwu. *Junzhai dushu zhi*. Taipei: Shangwu, 1978.
Chen Zhensun. *Zhizhai shuli jieti*. Taipei: Shangwu, 1978.
Cheng Hao and Chang Yi. *Er Cheng ji*. Beijing: Zhonghua, 1981.
Feng Menglong. *Qingshi leilüe*. Jinling: Jiezi yuan, Liben tang edition, between 1622 and 1722.
Feng Menglong. *Qingshi leilüe*. Taipei: Guangwen, 1982.
Gan Bao. *Soushen ji*, edited by Huang Diming. Taipei: Guji, no date given.
Hong Mai. *Yijian zhi*. Taipei: Mingwen, 1994.
Hu Yinglin. *Shanshi shaofang bicong*. Beijing, Zhonghua, 1958.
Huang Sheng. *Zhongxing yilai juemiao cixuan*. Sibu congkan edition, accessed via Ctext, 6.11.2020.
Huangdu Fengyue Zhuren. *Lüchuang Xinhua*. Shanghai: Shanghai guji, 1991.

Kong Qi. *Zhizheng zhi ji*. Shanghai: Shanghai guji, 1987.
Li Changling. *Le shan lu*. Taipei: Shangwu, 1971.
Li Changqi. *Jiandeng yuhua*. In Qu You, *Jiandeng Xinhua*. Taipei: Shijie, 2010.
Li Fang et al., eds. *Taiping guangji*. Shanghai: Shanghai guji, 1990.
Li Xianmin. *Yunzhai guanglu*. Beijing: Zhonghua, 1997.
Liu Fu. *Qingsuo gaoyi*. In *Songdai biji xiaoshuo daguan*, vol. 24, edited by Zhou Guangpei. Shijiazhuang: Hebei jiaoyu, 1995.
Liu Xiang. *Liexian zhuan*. Beijing: Zhonghua, 2001.
Liu Yiqing. *Shishuo xinyu*. Edited by Yang Yong. Taipei: Pingping, 1975.
Liu Zongyuan. *Liu Hedong ji*. Hong Kong: Zhonghua, 1972.
Lu Xing. *Yutai xinyong jian zhu*. Beijing: Zhonghua, 1985.
Luo Ye. *Xinbian zuiweng tanlu*. Shanghai: Shanghai gudian wenxue, 1957.
Luo Ye. *Xinbian Zuiweng tanlu*, edited by Zhou Xiaowei. Shenyang: Liaoning jiaoyu, 1998.
Meng Chengshun. *Jieyi yuanyang zhong Jiao Hong ji*. Shanghai: Guben xiqu congkan, 1955.
Meng Qi. *Benshi shi*. Shanghai: Shanghai guji, 1991.
Meng Yuanlao. *Dongjing menghua lu*. Beijing: Wenhua yishu, 1998.
Ouyang Xiu. *Xin Tang shu*. In *Ershiwu shi*, vol. 26. Taipei: Yiwen.
Peng Dingqiu, ed. *Quan Tang shi*. Zhengzhou: Zhengzhou guji, 2008.
Qin Guan. *Huai hai ji*. Taipei: Shangwu, 1990.
Qu You. *Jiandeng Xinhua*. Taipei: Shijie, 2010.
Qu You. *Jiandeng Xinhua*. In *Guben xiaoshuo jicheng*, vol. 82, edited by An Pingqiu. Shanghai: Shanghai guji, 1990), 166–85.
Shi Nengzhi. *Xianchun piling zhi*. In *Song Yuan difang zhi congshu*. Taipei: Dahua shuju, 1987.
Sima Qian. *Shiji*, vols. 1–2. In *Ershiwu shi*. Taipei: Yiwen, rpt. Wuying dian edition, no date given.
Song Yuan. *Jiao Hong shuangmei*. In *Huazhen qiyan*, edited by Xiansou Shigong. Taipei: publisher not identified, 1987?
Song Yuan. *Jiao Hong ji*. In *Shijie wenku* vol. 3, edited by Zheng Zhenduo, 1–27. Shanghai: Shenghuo shudian, 1935.
Sun Qi. *Beili zhi* in *Jiaofang ji, Beili zhi, Qinglou ji*. Beijing: Zhonghua, 1959.
Sun Qi. *Beili zhi* in *Gujin shuohai*. Edited by Lu Ji. Shanghai: Shanghai wenyi, 1989.
Tao Zongyi. *Nancun chuogeng lu*. Beijing, Zhonghua, 1959, rpt. 1997.
Tao Zongyi. *Chuo geng lu*. Taipei: Shijie shuju, 1971.
Tao Zongyi. *Shuofu kao*. Edited by Chang Bide. Taipei: Wenshizhe, 1979.
Wang Shizhen and Wang Yunwu, eds. *Quan Tangshi*. Taipei: Shangwu, 1966.
Wu Zhen. *Wudai shi bu*. In *Congshu jicheng xubian*, vol. 23. Shanghai: Shanghai shudian, 1994?
Xiansou Shigong, ed. *Huazhen qiyan*. Taipei: publisher not identified, 1987?
Xiao Tong. *Wen Xuan*. Beijing: Zhonghua, 1977.

Xiong Huizhong. *Xinbian tingyong qizha jiejiang gang*. 新編通用啟劄截江綱 Song edition in the Seikadō Library, no date given.
Xu Ji. *Jiexiao ji*. In *Wenyuange siku quanshu*, vol. 1101. Taipei: Shangwu, 1983.
Yang Xiong. *Yangzi fayan*. Edited by Dong Zhi'an and Zhang Zhongwang. Shandong: Shandong youyi, 2000.
Yu Ji. *Daoyuan xuegu lu*. Taipei: Shangwu, 1968.
Zeng Zao. *Lei shuo*. Beijing: Wenxue guji, 1955.
Zhang Bangji. *Shi'er xiaoming lu shiyi*. Shanghai: Shangwu, 1937.
Zhang Jiucheng. *Huang pu xiansheng wenji*. facsimile edition of a Ming reprint, 1925.
Zhang Qixian. *Luoyang jinshen jiuwen ji*. Shanghai: Gushu liutong, 1921.
Zhang Shizheng. *Kuo yi zhi*. In *Songdai biji xiaoshuo daguan*, vol. 11, edited by Zhou Guangpei. Shijiazhuang: Hebei jiaoyu, 1995.
Zhao Lingzhi. *Houjing lu*. Beijing: Zhonghua, 2002.
Zhou Mi. *Qidong yeyu*. In *Songdai biji xiaoshuo daguan*, vol. 11, edited by Zhou Guangpei. Shijiazhuang: Hebei jiaoyu, 1995.
Zhu Xi, *Zhuzi yulei*. Beijing, Zhonghua, 1986.
Zhuang Chuo. *Jilei bian*. Beijing: Zhonghua shuju, 1983.
Zuo Qiuming. *Zuozhuan*. Changsha: Xinjiang renmin, 2002.

Secondary Sources

Ahern, Emily. *The Cult of the Dead in a Chinese Village*. Stanford, CA: Stanford University Press, 1973.
Allen, Sarah M. *Shifting Stories: History, Gossip and Lore in Narratives from Tang Dynasty China*. Cambridge, MA: Harvard University Asia Center, 2014.
Altenburger, Roland. "Is it Clothes that Make the Man? Cross-Dressing, Gender and Sex in Pre-Twentieth Century Zhu Yingtai Lore." *Asian Folklore Studies* 64, no. 2 (2005): 165–205.
Althusser, Louis. "Ideology and Ideological State Apparatuses (Notes Toward an Investigation)." In *Lenin and Philosophy and Other Essays*, translated by Ben Brewster. London: Monthly Review Press, 1971.
Balazs, Etienne, and Yves Hervouet, eds. *A Sung Bibliography*. Hong Kong: The Chinese University Press, 1978.
Birch, Cyril, trans. *Mistress and Maid*. New York: Columbia University Press, 2001.
Birge, Bettine. *Women, Property and Confucian Reaction in Sung and Yüan China (960–1368)*. Cambridge: Cambridge University Press, 2002.
Birge, Bettine. "Women and Confucianism from Song to Ming: The Institutionalization of Patrilineality." In *The Song-Yuan-Ming Transition in Chinese History*, edited by Paul Jakov Smith and Richard von Glahn, 212–40. Cambridge, MA: Harvard University Asia Center, 2003.

Bodde, Dirk trans. Fung Yu-lan, *A History of Chinese Philosophy*, vol. 2. Princeton, NJ: Princeton University Press, 1953.

Bol, Peter. "Government, Society and State: On the Political Visions of Ssu-ma Kuang and Wang Anshi." In *Ordering the World: Approached to State and Society in Sung Dynasty China*, edited by Robert Hymes and Conrad Shirokauer, 128–92. Berkeley: University of California Press, 1993.

Bol, Peter. *This Culture of Ours: Intellectual Transitions in T'ang and Sung China*. Stanford, CA: Stanford University Press, 1992.

Bossler, Beverly. "Powerful Relations and Relations of Power: Family and Society in Sung China 960–1279. PhD dissertation, University of California, Berkeley, California, 1991.

Bossler, Beverly. *Courtesans, Concubines and the Cult of Female Fidelity*. Cambridge, MA: Harvard Asia Center, 2013.

Cahill, Suzanne. *Transcendence and Divine Passion: The Queen Mother of the West in Medieval China*. Stanford, CA: Stanford University Press, 1993.

Campany, Robert Ford. *Strange Writing: Anomaly Accounts in Early Medieval China*. Albany, NY: SUNY Press, 1996.

Chan, Leo Tak-hung. *The Discourse on Foxes and Ghosts: Ji Yun and Eighteenth Century Literati Storytelling*. Hong Kong: Chinese University of Hong Kong Press, 1998.

Chang, Kang-I Sun. *The Late Ming Poet Ch'en Tzu-lung: Crises of Love and Loyalism*. New Haven, CT: Yale University Press, 1991.

Chang, Kang-I Sun, and Ellen Widmer, eds. *Writing and Women in Late Imperial China*. Stanford, CA: Stanford University Press, 1997.

Chen Dakang. *Ming dai xiaoshuo shi*. Shanghai: Shanghai wenyi, 2000.

Chen Jue. "A Supplement to Jiang Zong's Biography of a White Ape." *Renditions* (Spring 1998): 74–85.

Chen Ruheng. *Shuoshu shihua*, 说书史话 Beijing: Zuojia, 1958.

Chen Su, ed. *Song chuanqi xiaoshuo xuan*. Taipei: Sanmin, 2010.

Chen Tung-yüan. *Zhongguo funü shenghuo shi*. Taipei: Shangwu, 1970.

Chen Yinke. *Chen Yinke xiansheng wenshi lunji*. Hong Kong: Wenwen, 1972.

Chen Yiyuan. *Yuan Ming zhongpian chuanqi xiaoshuo yanjiu*. Hong Kong: Xuefeng wenhua, 1997.

Cheng Hsiao-wen. *Traveling Stories and Untold Desires: Female Sexuality in Song China 10th–13th Centuries*. PhD dissertation, University of Washington, Seattle, Washington, 2012.

Cheng Yizhong. "Jiao Hong ji zai xiaoshuo yishu fazhan zhong de lishi jiazhi." *Journal of Xuchang Teachers College* 2 (social science edition; 1990): 15–19.

Cheng Yizhong. "Songdaide chuanqi xiaoshuo." *Wenshi zhishi* 2 (1990): 10–16.

Cheng Yizhong. *Song Yuan xiaoshuo yanjiu*. Nanjing: Jiangsu guji, 1998.

Cheng Yizhong. *Tangdai xiaoshuo shi*. Beijing: Renmin wenxue, 2003.

Cheng Yizhong. *Ming dai xiaoshuo conggao*. Beijing: Renmin wenxue, 2008.

Chia, Lucille. *Printing for Profit: The Commercial Publishers of Jianyang, Fujian (11th-17th Centuries.* Cambridge, MA: Harvard University Asia Center, 2002.

Davis, Richard L. *Wind against the Mountain: the Crisis of Politics and Culture in Thirteenth-Century China.* Cambridge, MA: Harvard University Press, 1996).

Davis, Richard L. "The Reign of Tu-tsung (1264-1274) and His Successors to 1279." In *The Cambridge History of China*, vol. 5, edited by Denis Twitchett and Paul Jacov Smith, 913-61. Cambridge: Cambridge University Press, 2009.

de Geest, Dirk, and Hendrik van Gorp. "Literary Genres from a Systemic-Functionalist Perspective." *European Journal of English Studies* 3, no. 1 (1999): 33-50.

de Groot, J.J.M. *The Religious System of China: Its Ancient Forms, Evolution, History and Present Aspect, Manners, Customs and Social Institutions Connected Therewith*, vol. 4. Taipei: Southern Materials Center, 1982.

de Pee, Christian. *The Writing of Weddings in Middle-Period China.* Albany, NY: State University of New York Press, 2007.

de Pee, Christian. "Words of Seduction, Lines of Resistance: Writing and Gender in Zheng Xi's *Dream of Spring* (1318)." *Nan Nü* 9 (2007): 251-52.

Dong Guoyan. *Dangzi, Rouqing, Tongxin: Mingdai xiaoshuo sichao.* Taiyuan: Beiyue wenyi, 1992.

Dudbridge, Glen. *Books, Tales and Vernacular Culture: Selected Papers on China.* Leiden: Brill, 2005.

Dudbridge, Glen, trans. *The Tale of Li Wa.* London: Ithaca, 1983.

Eberhard, Wolfram. *A Dictionary of Chinese Symbols.* New York: Routledge and Kegan Paul, 2001.

Ebrey, Patricia Buckley. *The Inner Quarters: Marriage and the Lives of Women in the Sung Period.* Berkeley, CA: California University Press, 1993.

Ebrey, Patricia Buckley. "Women, Marriage and the Family in Chinese History." In *The Heritage of China*, edited by Paul Ropp, 197-223. Berkeley: University of California Press, 1990.

Ebrey, Patricia Buckley. "Confucianism." In Don Browning et al., eds. *Sex, Marriage and Family in World Religions.* New York: Columbia University Press, 2006.

Egan, Ronald. *The Problem of Beauty: Aesthetic Thought and Pursuits in Northern Song Dynasty China.* Cambridge, MA: Harvard University Press, 2006.

Feng, Linda Rui. *Youthful Displacement: City, Travel and Narrative Formation in Tang Tales.* PhD dissertation, Columbia University, New York, 2008.

Fitzgerald, C. P. "The Consequences of the Rebellion of An Lu-shan upon the Population of the T'ang Dynasty." *Philobiblon* 2 (1947): 4-11.

Fu Xihua. *Mingdai chuanqi quanmu.* Beijing: Renming wenxue, 1959.

Fusek, Lois. "The K'ao-t'ang fu." *Monumenta Serica* 30 (1972-73): 392-425.

Freedman, Maurice. *Family and Kinship in Chinese Society.* Stanford, CA: Stanford University Press, 1970.

Gjertson, Donald. "Shen Chi-chi." In *The Indiana Companion to Traditional Chinese Literature*, edited by William Nienhauser et al., 674-75.

Grant, Beata, and Wilt Idema. *The Red Brush: Writing Women of Imperial China*. Cambridge, MA: Harvard University Asian Center, 2004.

Gu, Ming Dong. *Chinese Theories of Fiction: A non-Western Narrative System*. Albany, NY: SUNY Press, 2006.

Guo Maoqian, ed. *Yuefu shiji*. Beijing: Zhonghua, 1979.

Hanan, Patrick. "Sources of the *Chin P'ing Mei*." *Asia Major* 10 (1963): 23–67.

Hardy, Thomas. *Tess of the d'Urbervilles*. London: The Folio Society, 1988.

Harper, Donald. "The Sexual Arts of Ancient China as Described in a Manuscript of the Second Century B.C." *Harvard Journal of Asiatic Studies* 47.2 (1987): 539–93.

Hartwell, Robert. "Demographic, Political and Social Transformations in China, 750–1550." *Harvard Journal of Asiatic Studies* 42 (1982): 365–442.

Hawkes, David, trans. *Story of the Stone*, vol. 1. London: Penguin, 1973.

He Xinling. "Songdai chuanqi xiaoshuo nüxing xingxiangde yanbian." *Shaanxi ligong xueyuan xuebao (shehui kexue)* 27, no. 3 (2009): 66–70.

Hervouet, Yves, and Etienne Balazs, eds. *A Sung Bibliography*. Hong Kong: The Chinese University Press, 1978.

Hightower, James. "Yuan Chen and the 'Story of Ying-ying.'" *Harvard Journal of Asiatic Studies* 33 (1973): 106–19.

Hightower, James. "Yuan Chen and the 'Story of Ying-ying.'" *Harvard Journal of Asiatic Studies* 33 (1973): 90–123.

Holmgren, Jennifer. *Marriage, Kinship and Power in Northern China*. Aldershot, Great Britain: Variorum, 1995.

Holmgren, Jennifer. "Observations on Marriage and Inheritance Practices in Early Mongol and Yuan Society." *Journal of Asian History* 20 (1986): 127–97.

Hong Yue. *The Discourse of Romantic Love in Ninth Century China*. PhD dissertation, Harvard University, Cambridge, Massachusetts, 2010.

Hong Yue. "Romantic identity in the Funerary Inscriptions (muzhi) of Tang China." *Asia Major* 21, vol. 1 (2012): 33–62.

Huang K'uan-chung, and Lau Nap-Yin. "Founding and Consolidation of the Sung Dynasty Under T'ai-tsu (960–976), T'ai-tsung (976–997), and Chen-tsung (997–1022)." In *The Cambridge History of China*, vol. 5, edited by Dennis Twitchett and Paul Jakov Smith, 206–78.

Huang, Martin. *Desire and Fictional Narrative in Late Imperial China*. Cambridge, MA: Harvard University Asia Center, 2001.

Hucker, Charles. *A Dictionary of Official Titles in Imperial China*. Stanford, CA: Stanford University Press, 1985.

Huntington, Rania. *Alien Kind: Foxes and Late Imperial Chinese Narrative*. Cambridge, MA: Harvard University Asia Center, 2003.

Hsia, C. T. *Zhongguo gudian xiaoshuo*. New York: Columbia University Press, 1968.

Hsieh, Daniel. *Love and Women in Early Chinese Fiction*. Hong Kong: The Chinese University Press, 2008.

Hymes, Robert. *Statesmen and Gentlemen: The Elite of Fu-chou, Chiang-his, in Northern and Southern Song*. Cambridge: Cambridge University Press, 1986.
Hymes, Robert, and Conrad Shirokauer, eds. *Ordering the World: Approached to State and Society in Sung Dynasty China*. Berkeley: University of California Press, 1993.
Idema, Wilt. "An Eighteenth Century Version of 'Liang Shanbo and Zhu Yingtai' from Suzhou." In *The Columbia Anthology of Chinese Folk and Popular Literature*, edited by Victor Mair and Mark Bender, 503–51. New York: Columbia University Press, 2011.
Idema, Wilt. "The Story of Ssu-ma Hsiang-ju and Cho Wen-chün in Vernacular Literature of the Yuan and Early Ming Dynasties." *T'oung Pao* 70 (1984): 60–109.
Idema, Wilt, and Stephen West. *Chinese Theater 1100–1400, A Source Book*. Wiesbaden: Franz Steiner Verlag, 1982.
Idema, Wilt, and Beata Grant. *The Red Brush: Writing Women of Imperial China*. Cambridge, MA: Harvard University Asian Center, 2004.
Ihara, Hiroshi. "Sōdai Minshū ni okeru kanko no konnin kanke." In *Chūō daigaku daigakuin kenkyū nenpō* 1: 157–68;
Ihara, Hiroshi and Shizunaga Takeshi, eds. Ikenshi *no sekai: Nansō no kakureta besutoserā*. Tokyo: Bensei, 2015.
Inglis, Alister. "Hong Mai's Informants for the *Yijian zhi*." *Journal of Song-Yuan Studies* 32 (2002): 83–125.
Inglis, Alister. *Hong Mai's* Record of the Listener *and Its Song Dynasty Context*. Albany, NY: SUNY Press, 2006.
Inglis, Alister, trans. *Selections from* Record of the Listener. Beijing: Foreign Language Press, 2009.
Inglis, Alister. "Narratological Ambiguity in Hong Mai's (1123–1202) *Yijian zhi*." *Transactions of the International Conference of Eastern Studies* 59 (2014): 24–46.
Inglis, Alister. "Luo Ye's *Zuiweng tanlu* and the Culture of Romance." *Chinese Literature: Essays, Articles Reviews* 35 (2013): 99–104.
Inglis, Alister, trans. *The Drunken Man's Talk*. Seattle: University of Washington Press, 2015.
Itō Sōhei. *Kyo ko ki*. In *Chūgoku koten bungaku taikei*, vol. 38. Tokyo: Heibonsha, 1973, 462–90.
Johnson, Dale. "Wu-shuang the Peerless." In *Traditional Chinese Stories: Themes and Variations*, edited by Y. W. Ma and Joseph Lau, 52–57. Boston: Cheng and Tsui, 1986, rpt. 2011.
Kim Wŏnhŭi. Qingshi *gushi yuanliu kaoshu*. Nanjing: Fenghuang, 2011.
Ko, Dorothy. *Teachers of the Inner Chambers: Women and Culture in Seventeenth Century China*. Stanford, CA: Stanford University Press, 1994.
Kroll, Paul. "The Flight from the Capital and the Death of Precious Consort Yang." *Tang Studies* 3 (1985): 25–53.

Lau Nap-Yin, and Huang K'uan-chung. "Founding and Consolidation of the Sung Dynasty Under T'ai-tsu (960–976), T'ai-tsung (976–997), and Chen-tsung (997–1022)." In *The Cambridge History of China*, vol. 5, edited by Dennis Twitchett and Paul Jakov Smith, 206–78.
Lee Yu-hwa. *Fantasy and Realism in Chinese Fiction*. San Francisco: Chinese Materials Center Publications, 1984.
Legge, James, trans. *Li Chi, Book of Rites*. Oxford: Oxford University Press, 1885.
Legge, James, trans. *The She King or the Book of Poetry*. Tai pei: SMC, 1991, rpt. 2000.
Lévy, André. *Le Conte en Langue Vulgaire du XVIIe siècle*. Paris: Collège de France: Bibliothèque de l'institut des hautes études Chinoises, 1981.
Levy, Howard. "Love Themes in T'ang Literature." *Orient/West* 7, vol. 1 (1962): 67–79.
Li Guoling. *Songren zhuanji ziliao suoyin bubian*. Chengdu: Sichuan daxue, 1994.
Li Jianguo. *Songdai zhiguai chuanqi xulu*. Tianjin: Nankai daxue, 1997.
Li Jianguo et al., eds. *Zhongguo xiaoshuo tongshi*. Beijing: Gaodeng jiaoyu, 2007.
Li Jianguo. *Tang Wudi zhiguai chuanqi xulu*. Beijing: Zhonghua, 2017.
Li Jianguo. *Gu baidou shaolu*. Tianjin: Nankai dauxue, 2004.
Li Mowry, Hua-yuan, trans. Feng Menglong, *Chinese Love Stories from "Ch'ing-shih."* Hamden, CT: Archon Book, 1983.
Li Shiren. "Songdai lishi wenhua yu wenyan duanpian xiaoshuo de liubian." *Qiushi xuekan*, 38, no. 2 (2011): 125–27.
Li, Wai-yee. *Enchantment and Disenchantment: Love and Illusion in Chinese Literature*. Princeton, NJ: Princeton University Press, 1993.
Li Xiaolong. "*Qingsuo gaoyi* banben yuanliu kao." *Wenxian* 1 (2008): 115–24.
Li Zongwei. *Tangren chuanqi*. Beijing: Zhonghua, 2003.
Lin Ying. "*Hong loumeng* yu Yuan Ming zhongpian wenyan chuanqi yuanyuan bulun." *Hong Lou Meng xuekan* 6 (2019): 185–205.
Liu Kairong. *Tangdai xiaoshuo yanjiu*. Taipei: Shangwu, 1966, rpt. 2005.
Liu Ying. *Tangdai chuanqi yanjiu*. Taipei: Zhengzhong, 1982.
Lu Xun. "Zhongguo xiaoshuode lishi yanbian." In *Lu Xun xuanji*, vol. 9. Beijing: Renmin wenxue, 2005.
Lu Xun. "Zhongguo xiaoshuo shilüe." In *Lu Xun xuanji*, vol. 9. Beijing: Renmin wenxue, 2005.
Luo, Manling. *Literati Storytelling in Late Medieval China*. Seattle: University of Washington Press, 2017.
Luo, Manling. "Remembering Kaiyuan and Tianbao: The Construction of Mosaic Memory in Medieval History Miscellanies." *T'oung Pao* 97 (2011): 263–300.
Ma, Y. W. "Kung-an Fiction: A Historical and Critical Introduction." *T'oung Pao* 65 (1979): 200–59.
Ma, Y. W., and Joseph Lau. *Traditional Chinese Stories: Themes and Variations*. Boston: Cheng and Tsui, 1986, rpt. 2011.
Ma, Y. W. "Tao Tsung-i." In *The Indiana Companion to Traditional Chinese Literature*, edited by William Nienhauser Jr. Taipei: SMC Publishing, 1986.

Mair, Victor, and Mark Bender, eds. *The Columbia Anthology of Chinese Folk and Popular Literature*. New York: Columbia University Press, 2011.

McGrath, Michael. "The Reigns of Jen-tsung (1022–1063) and Ying-tsung (1063–1067)." In *The Cambridge History of China*, vol. 5, edited by Dennis Twitchett and Paul Jakov Smith, 279–346. Cambridge: Cambridge University Press, 2009.

McKnight, Brian, and James Liu, trans. *The Enlightened Judgements*: Ch'ing-ming Chi. Albany, NY: SUNY Press, 1999.

McLaren, Anne. *Chinese Popular Culture and Ming Cantefables*. Leiden: Brill, 1998.

McMahon, Keith. *Misers, Shrews and Polygamists: Sexuality and Male-Female Relations in Eighteenth Century Chinese Fiction*. Durham: Duke University Press, 1995.

Nabokov, Vladimir. *Lolita*. London: Weildenfeld and Nicolson, 1955.

Nagasawa Kikuya, and Usui Kyōichi, eds. "Shimpen Zuiō danroku ni tsuite." *Shoshi gaku* 15, no. 4 (1940): 6–12.

Nienhauser, William, ed. *The Indiana Companion to Traditional Chinese Literature*. Taipei: SMC Publishing, 1986

Owen, Stephen. *End of the Chinese Middle-Ages: Essays in Mid-Tang Literary Culture*. Stanford, CA: Stanford University Press, 1996.

Owen, Stephen. "What Did Liu Zhi Hear? The 'Yan Terrace Poems' and the Culture of Romance." *T'ang Studies* 13 (1995): 1–118.

Owen, Stephen. *An Anthology of Chinese* Literature: *Beginnings to 1911*. New York: Norton, 1996.

Pan, Lynn. *When True Love Came to China*. Hong Kong: University of Hong Kong Press, 2015.

Plaks, Andrew. *Archetype and Allegory in* Dream of the Red Chamber. Princeton, NJ: Princeton University Press, 1977.

Plaks, Andrew. *The Four Masterworks of the Ming Novel*. Princeton, NJ: Princeton University Press, 1987.

Pritchard, Earl. "Thoughts on the Historical Development of the Population of China." *The Journal of Asian Studies* 23, vol. 1 (1963): 3–20.

Pullyblank, Edwin G. *Background of the Rebellion of An Lu-shan*. London: Oxford University Press, 1955.

Ropp, Paul, ed. *The Heritage of China*. Berkeley: University of California Press, 1990.

Rosch, Eleanor, and B. B. Loyd, eds. *Cognition and Categorization*. Hillsdale, NJ: Lawrence Erlbaum, 1978.

Rosch, Eleanor. "Human Categorization." In *Studies in Cross-Cultural Psychology 1*, edited by N. Warren, 1–49. London: & New York: Academic Press, 1977.

Rosch, Eleanor. "Principles of Categorization." In *Cognition and Categorization*, edited by Eleanor Rosch and B. B. Loyd, 22–48. Hillsdale, NJ: Lawrence Erlbaum, 1978.

Rouzer, Paul. *Articulated Ladies: Gender and the Male Community in Early Chinese Texts*. Cambridge, MA: Harvard University Asia Center, 2001.

Roy, David Tod, trans. *The Plum in the Golden Vase*, vol. 1. Princeton, NJ: Princeton University Press, 1993.
Shio Takugo. "Ikenshi kara mita Sōdai jyosei no inshoku seikatsu." In Ikenshi *no sekai: Nansō no kakureta besuto serā*, edited by Ihara Hiroshi and Shizunaga Takeshi, 112–20. Tokyo: Bensei, 2015.
Shirokauer, Conrad, and Robert Hymes, eds. *Ordering the World: Approached to State and Society in Sung Dynasty China*. Berkeley: University of California Press, 1993.
Shizunaga Takeshi, and Ihara Hiroshi, eds. Ikenshi *no sekai: Nansō no kakureta besuto serā*. Tokyo: Bensei, 2015.
Sima Qian. *The Grand Scribe's Records*, vol. 1. Translated and edited by William Nienhauser Jr. Bloomington: Indiana University Press, 1994.
Smith, Howard. "Chinese Concepts of the Soul." *Numen* 5, no. 3 (1958): 165–79.
Smith, Paul Jakov, and Denis Twitchett, eds. *The Cambridge History of China*, vol. 5, Part 1. Cambridge: Cambridge University Press, 2009.
Smith, Paul Jakov. "The Sung Dynasty and Its Precursors." In *The Cambridge History of China*, vol. 5, edited by Dennis Twitchett and Paul Jakov Smith, 1–37. Cambridge: Cambridge University Press, 2009.
Smith, Paul Jakov. "Shen-tsung's Reign and the New Policies of Wang An-shih, 1067–1085." In *The Cambridge History of China*, vol. 5, edited by Dennis Twitchett and Paul Jakov Smith, 1–37. Cambridge: Cambridge University Press, 2009.
Smith, Paul Jakov. "Impressions of the Song-Yuan-Ming Transition." In *The Song-Yuan-Ming Transition in Chinese History*, edited by Paul Jakov Smith and Richard von Glahn, 1–34. Cambridge, MA: Harvard University Press, 2003.
Smith, Paul Jakov. "Problematizing the Song-Yuan-Ming Transition." In *The Song-Yuan-Ming Transition in Chinese History*, edited by Paul Jakov Smith and Richard von Glahn, 1–34. Cambridge, MA: Harvard University Press, 2003.
Smith, Paul Jakov, and Richard von Glahn, eds. *The Song-Yuan-Ming Transition in Chinese History*. Cambridge, MA: Harvard University Press, 2003.
Sommer, Matthew. *Sex, Law and Society in Late Imperial China*. Stanford, CA: Stanford University Press, 2000.
Su Hua. "Ouyang Zhan." In *Zhongguo wenxue da cidian*. Taipei: Baichuan, 1994, 7567.
Sun Kaidi. *Riben Dongjing suo jian xiaoshuo shumu*. Beijing: Renmin wenxue, 1958.
Sun Xun, and Zhao Weiguo. "Chuanqi ti xiaoshuo de yanbian zhi bianzhe." *Shanghai shifan daxue xuebao (shehui kexue ban)* 30.1 (2001): 84–94.
Tan Zhengbi. *Huaben yu guju*. Shanghai: Shanghai gudian wenxue, 1956.
Tillman, Hoyt. "Disorder (*luan*) as Trauma: A Case Study of Reactions to the Mongol Conquest." Unpublished paper, 2002.
Ting Ch'uan-ching. *Songren yishi huibian*. Beijing: Zhonghua.

Topley, Majorie. "Ghost Marriages among the Singapore Chinese." *Man* 55 (1955): 29–30.
Tsiperovitch, Isolda. "Lü-ch'uang hsin-hua." In *A Sung Bibliography*, edited by Etienne Balazs and Yves Hervouet, 346–47. Hong Kong: The Chinese University Press, 1978.
Twitchett, Denis. *The Birth of the Chinese Meritocracy: Bureaucrats and Examinations in T'ang China*. London: China Society, 1976.
Twitchett, Denis. "The Composition of the T'ang Ruling Class: New Evidence from Tunhuang." In *Perspectives on the Tang*, edited by Arthur Wright and Denis Twitchett, 47–86. New Haven, CT: Yale University Press, 1973.
Twitchett, Denis, and John K. Fairbank. *The Cambridge History of China*, vol. 3. Cambridge: Cambridge University Press, 1978.
Twitchett, Denis, and Paul Jakov Smith, eds. *The Cambridge History of China*, vol. 5, Part 1. Cambridge: Cambridge University Press, 2009.
Uchiyama Chinari. "Ōō den no kōzō to shudai ni tsuite." *Nihon Chūgoku gakkai hō* 42 (1990): 156–68.
Usui Kyōichi, and Nagasawa Kikuya, eds. "Shimpen Zuiō danroku ni tsuite." *Shoshi gaku* 15, no. 4 (1940): 6–12.
van Gulik, Robert. *Sexual Life in Ancient China: A Preliminary Survey of Chinese Sex and Society from ca. 1500 B.C. until 1644 A.D.* Leiden: Brill, 1974.
von Glahn, Richard, and Paul Jakov Smith, eds. *The Song-Yuan-Ming Transition in Chinese History*. Cambridge, MA: Harvard University Press, 2003.
Waley, Arthur. *One Hundred and Twenty Chinese Poems*. London: Constable, 1918, rpt. 1945.
Wang Chung-han, "The Authorship of the *Yu-hsien k'u*," *Harvard Journal of Asiatic Studies* 11 (1948): 153–62.
Wang Jing. *Courtesan Culture in the* Beili zhi *(Records of the Northern Quarter) in the Context of Tang Tales and Poems*. PhD dissertation, University of Wisconsin, Madison, Wisconsin, 2009.
Wang Jing, and Zhang Zhenjun, trans. *Song Dynasty Tales: A Guided Reader*. New Jersey: World Scientific, 2017.
Wang, Richard. "The Cult of *Qing*: Romanticism in the Late Ming Period and the Novel *Jiao Hong Ji*." *Ming Studies* 33 (1994): 12–55.
Wang, Richard. "Liu Tsung-yüan's 'Tale of Ho-chien.'" *Tang Studies* 14 (1996): 21–48.
Wang, Richard. *Ming Erotic Novellas: Genre, Consumption and Religiosity in Cultural Practice*. Hong Kong: The Chinese University Press, 2011.
Wang Yi-pei. *Songdai wenyan xiaoshuozhong nüxing qunxiangzhi tanjiu*. PhD dissertation, Taiwan National University, 2006.
Warren, N., ed. *Studies in Cross-Cultural Psychology 1*. London: & New York: Academic Press, 1977.
Widmer, Ellen, and Kang-I Sun Chang, eds. *Writing and Women in Late Imperial China*. Stanford, CA: Stanford University Press, 1997.

Wikipedia. "Butterfly Lovers." https://en.wikipedia.org/wiki/Butterfly_Lovers
Wittgenstien, Ludwig. *Philosophical Investigations*. Oxford: Blackwell, 1978.
Wu, Laura Hua. "From *Xiaoshuo* to Fiction: Hu Yinglin's Genre Study of *Xiaoshuo*." *Harvard Journal of Asiatic Studies* 55, no. 2 (1995): 339–71.
Wu Zhida. *Tangren chuanqi*. Shanghai: Shanghai guji, 1983.
Xiao Chi. *The Chinese Garden as Lyric Enclave: a Generic Study of* Story of the Stone. Ann Arbor: University of Michigan Press, 2001.
Xiao Xiangkai. *Song Yuan xiaoshuo shi*. Zhejiang: Zhejiang guji, 1997.
Yan Dunyi. *Shuihuzhuan de yanbian*. Taipei: Liren, 1996.
Yang Bo. *Chang'an de chuntian: Tangdai keju yu jinshi shenghuo*. Beijing: Zhonghua, 2007.
Yang Shuhui, and Yang Yunqin trans. *Stories Old and New*. Seattle: University of Washington Press, 2000.
Ye Dejun. "Xiqu xiaoshuo congkao." In *Xiaoshuo suotan*. Beijing: Zhonghua, 1979.
Yim, Sarah. "Chuanqi." In *The Indiana Companion to Traditional Chinese Literature*, edited by William Nienhauser et al., 356–60. Taipei: SMC Publishing, 1986.
Yim, Sarah. *Structure, Theme and Narrator in T'ang "ch'uan-ch'i."* PhD dissertation, Yale University, New Haven, Connecticut, 1979.
Yu, Pauline. *The Reading of Imagery in the Chinese Poetic Tradition*. Princeton, NJ: Princeton University Press, 1987.
Yu Shiu-yun. *Songdai chuanqi xiaoshuo yanjiu*. Taipei: Huamulan wenhua, 2007.
Zadeh, L. A. "Fuzzy Sets." *Information and Control* 8 (1965): 338–53.
Zeitlin, Judith. *Historian of the Strange: Pu Songling and the Chinese Classical Tale*. Stanford, CA: Stanford University Press, 1993.
Zhang, Cong Ellen. "Writing on Illicit Sex in Song China (960–1279)." *Journal of the History of Sexuality* 22.2 (2013): 253–80.
Zhang Zhenjun, and Wang Jing, trans. *Song Dynasty Tales: A Guided Reader*. New Jersey: World Scientific, 2017.
Zhao Jingshen. "Yin *Zuiweng tanlu* de faxian." In *Zhongguo xiaoshuo congkao*. Jinan: Jilu shushe, 1980.
Zhao Wei. *Mingdai liqing chuanqi xiaoshuo yanjiu*. MA dissertation, Heibei Normal University, 2006.
Zhao Weiguo, and Sun Xun. "Chuanqi ti xiaoshuo de yanbian zhi bianzhe." *Shanghai shifan daxue xuebao* (*shehui kexue ban*) 30.1 (2001): 84–94.
Zhao Weiguo. "Lun *Liqing ji* yu Songdai liqing xiaoshuo chuangzuo." *Henan daxue xuebao* (*shehui kexue ban*) 43.1 (2003): 57–62.
Zheng Zhenduo. *Chatuben Zhongguo wenxue shi*. Taipei: Zhuangyan, 1991.
Zheng Zhenduo, ed. *Shijie wenku*, vol. 3. Shanghai: shenghuo, 1935.
Zheng Zhimin. *Xishuo Tang ji*. Taipei: Wenjin, 1997.
Zhuang Yifu. *Gudian xiqu cunmu huikao*. Shanghai: Shanghai guji, 1982.
Zhuge Yibing. "Songdai shidafude jingyu yu shidafu jingshen." *Renmin daxue xuebao* (2001): 107–12.

Index

"A Husband and Wife Honor Their Old Pledge" (*Fuqi fu jiuyue*), 163–68, 254
"Account of the Ballad of Eternal Sorrow" (*Changhen ge zhuan*), 36–38, 150
advanced degree. See *jinshi*
Allen, Sarah M., 15
An Lushan rebellion, 35–36, 38–39
Analects of Confucius, 99, 163, 166
Anne McLaren, 18
Ao Taoshun, 173
aristocrats, 29–30, 95; as characters in love stories, 87; intermarriage of, 11, 30, 69
authorship, 17. See also storytelling
Ayurbarwada Buyantu khan, 210

Bai Juyi, 36, 51, 194
Bai Minzhong, 51
Bai Xingjian, 43, 51, 65, 66
"Ballad of Eternal Sorrow" (*Changhen ge*), 36–38
Bamboo-Dwelling Maverick's Collection (*Zhuyin jishi ji*), 143
banqueting, 33
Baosi. See Lady Bao of Si
Beili zhi. See *Record of the Northern Quarter*

Bella and Scarlett (*Jiao Hong ji*), 13, 213–30, 234, 266–67
benshi shi (poems based on stories): as a literary category, 116, 184, 236–37
Bilian lu. See *Trousseaus Recorded with a Brush*
Birch, Cyril, 229
Birge, Bettine, 262
Boccaccio, Giovanni, 45
Book of Documents, 163, 166, 230
Book of Mencius, 99, 163, 166, 193, 227, 258
Book of Rites, 145
Book of Songs, 166
Bossler, Beverly, 106, 110, 152, 174, 177, 248, 262
bride price, 30, 103, 211
broken promises: as a literary subcategory, 24, 76, 81, 176
"Bu Feiyan," 51–53, 91–93 *passim*, 122, 135, 240
bureaucracy: during the Tang dynasty, 30–31; during the Yuan dynasty, 210; faction fighting among the, 259
butterflies: as a literary motif, 3, 189, 190, 191, 224, 228, 243
"Butterfly Lovers," 1–3, 189–91

Campany, Robert Ford, 26
Canterbury Tales, The, 45
Cao Zhi (192–232), 9, 83
Changhen dian. See *Palace of Everlasting Youth*
Changhen ge. See "Ballad of Eternal Sorrow"
Chao Gongwu, 21
Chaucer, Geoffrey, 44
Chen Han, 12
Chen Hong, 37
"Chen Shuwen," 151–54
Cheng Hao, 98
Cheng Yi, 98, 145–46, 171
Cheng Yizhong, 6, 7, 66, 227, 237, 242
Chu Cheng, 181
Chu Cheng's Posthumous Work, 181
Chu Huaiwang. See Huai, King of Chu
Chu Yushi, 157–59 passim
Chuanqi: as a book-title. See *Transmitting the Remarkable*
chuanqi: as a literary genre, 13–14, 21–23 passim, 149
Chun meng lu. See *Dream of Spring*
Chuogeng lu. See *Records after Ploughing*
ci. See lyric poetry
clandestine love and legal cases: as a literary sub-category, 24
Clarissa, 237
Classic of Poetry, 112, 163, 224, 230
"Clerk Liu's Daughter," 57–59
Cloud Nest Compilation (Yunchao bian), 16
Collected Love Stories (Liqing ji), 12, 20, 26, 51, 59, 62, 68, 185
Collection of Strange Tales Heard (Yiwen ji), 12
Collection of the Filial and Chaste (Jiexiao ji), 147
Commentary on the Spring and Autumn Annals, 118

Comprehensive Record of the Cloud Studio (Yunzhai guanglu), 12, 21, 116, 150, 159
concubines, 103, 139, 171, 179, 265
Confucius, 14, 98, 112
Conversations beside Cloud Creek (Yunxi youyi), 12
courtesans: and banqueting during the Tang dynasty, 33; liaisons with scholar-officials, 34–35, 83, 100, 110–11, 151, 153, 156, 241, 247; and pecuniary interests, 88–89; and performing arts during the Yuan dynasty, 211; and poetry, 111, 166; proliferation during the Song dynasty, 99; regulation of during the Tang dynasty, 34. See also marriage, scholar-officials
cross-dressing, 191
Cui Lingqin, 33

Dai Fu, 12, 117
Dalliance in the Immortal's Den (You xian ku), 82–83, 237, 254
Daoxue. See Neo-Confucianism
de Geest, Dirk, 25
de Pee, Christian, 238, 240
debased people (*jianmin*), 29
Decameron, The, 45
desire: male sexual, 71; of males to sexually possess another's woman, 50–51, 53, 55
Doctrine of the Mean, 99
dominance: in Russian formalist literary criticism, 24
Dong Zhongshu, 38
dowries, 103, 145, 211, 265
Dream of Liang (Mengliang lu), 22
Dream of Red Mansions (Honglou meng), 124, 131, 215, 225, 229, 236, 268
Dream of Spring (Chun meng lu), 236–44

Drunken Man's Talk (Xinbian zuiweng tanlu), 12, 21, 51, 59, 62, 68, 76, 191, 192, 195, 264, 278n64
Ducheng jishi. See *Recording the Splendor of the Capital*
Dudbridge, Glen, 25, 66
Dule yuan. See *Garden of Solitary Joy*
Dumas, Alexander, 93

Ebrey, Patricia Buckley, 103, 145, 203
Empress Wu of the Tang dynasty, 80
Empress Zhen, 83
"Encouragement for Goodness," 18
Enlightened Judgements of Famous Magistrates (Minggong shupan Qingming ji), 158, 202
Entertainment Bureau, 210
erotic threesomes: as a literary theme, 252, 254
erotic triangle: as a plot device, 45–49 passim, 52, 61–62, 91, 122, 127–28, 203–4, 233, 263
examinations: as a bureaucratic recruitment mechanism, 30–33, 97–98, 162; and judicial privilege, 202; as a means of social mobility, 97–98, 106, 122, 143–44, 153, 203; as a plot device, 88; suspension of during the Yuan dynasty, 210
Exemplary Sayings of Master Yang (Yangzi fayan), 193–94
Extensive Collection of the Marvels (Guangyi ji), 12, 57, 117
Extensive Records from the Era of Supreme Peace (Taiping guangji), 20, 29, 74, 185, 186, 190, 213

faithful hearts: as a literary subcategory, 24
faji: as a literary prototype, 105, 107, 159
family organization, 38
Famous Gardens of Luoyang, 131

Fan Ruwei, 168
Fan Shu, 12
"Fan Xizhou," 168–71, 172, 174, 176, 225–26
Fan Zhongyan, 262
female Gaze, 50, 74, 90, 181, 182, 184, 252
femme fatale, 50, 67, 68, 71–72, 73–75, 92, 135, 159, 167, 173, 186
Feng Menglong, 6, 22, 54, 65–66, 201
Feng, Linda Rui, 51
fiction, 14–15, 88–89
"Fifth Brother Sun," 180, 187–88, 226, 234
filial piety, 118, 142–43, 149, 170–71, 196, 231–32, 236, 247, 262
founding elite of the Song dynasty, 96
"Four-Fold Blended Incense," 137–41, 204
fox-fairies, 39, 281n28
Fuqi fu jiuyue. See "A Husband and Wife Honor Their Old Pledge"
fuzzy sets: as a mathematical theory, 25

Gaozong, Tang dynasty emperor, 30
Garden of Solitary Joy, 131
gardens: as a setting for love stories, 130, 228–29, 258
gentry, 97, 162
Gleanings from the Tang Dynasty (Tang zhiyan), 32
Goddess of the Luo River (Luo shen), 9, 82, 83
Goddess of Witch's Mountain (Wushan shen), 9, 274n20
goddesses of the Xiao and Xiang rivers, 145
gong'an: as a literary genre. See legal cases
gossip: as a basis for short stories, 12, 14, 17–19, 38, 66, 75, 80, 81, 113, 136, 153–54, 157–58, 261

Great Learning, 99
Green Pearl, 133, 135
Gu Ming Dong, 15
Guangyi ji. See *Extensive Collection of the Strange*
"Guo Han," 84–86
Guo Huaqing gong. See "Passing Floral Purity"

Han Ping, 37
Han Shou, 10
Han Xizai, 16
Han Yu, 73
Hardy, Thomas, 127
Hargett, James, 99
Hartwell, Robert, 95–98 *passim*, 106, 143, 162
High-Minded Conversations behind the Green Lattice Window (*Qingsuo gaoyi*), 12, 107, 114, 206
Historical Changes in Chinese Fiction (*Zhongguo xiaoshuode lishi yanbian*), 5
History of Affection (*Qingshi*), 22, 54, 58, 171, 250
Hong Mai, 15, 17–18, 105, 172, 173, 176, 178, 187–89 *passim*, 191, 205, 206, 270
Hong Yue, 11, 45
Honglou meng. See *Dream of Red Mansions*
"Hou Xutu," 55
household registration: during the Yuan dynasty, 210
Hsieh, Daniel, 4, 29, 35, 54, 268
Hu Yinglin, 17, 23, 65, 75, 270
Huai, King of Chu (Chu Huaiwang), 9, 274n20
Huang Chao rebellion, 33
Huang, Martin, 104, 166, 239, 255
Huangdu fengyue zhuren (Romance Master of the Imperial Capital), 12
Huangfu Mei, 51

humorous tales: as a literary subcategory, 24, 192
"Huo Xiaoyu's Story," 76–81, 87, 89, 93

Idema, Wilt, 17
immortal women: literary constructions of, 140; of Mount Tiantai, 82, 83; romantic affairs of, 81–86, 91, 254
immortality: the quest for, 81
immortals: as a literary category, 21
"Inn of Betrothal," 55–57
Investigation into the Spirit World (*Jishen lu*), 17
island-woman stories, 205–7
Itō Sōhei, 227, 229

jealousy: as a literary theme, 105, 228
Jia Baoyu, 225, 229, 236
Jia Sidao, 235
Jia Wu, 10
Jiandeng xinhua. See *New Stories Told while Trimming the Lampwick*
jianmin. See debased people
Jiao Hong ji. See *Bella and Scarlett*
Jiao Hong zhuan. See *Bella and Scarlett*
Jiaofang ji. See *Record of the Entertainment Bureau*
jiaofang. See Music Bureau
Jiexiao ji. See *Collection of the Filial and Chaste*
jinshi (advanced or presented scholar degree), 31, 97
Jishen lu. See *Investigation into the Spirit World*
Jurchen, 95, 161, 162, 176, 204, 264

Kang, Prince of the State of Song, 37
"Kingdom of Black Apparel" (*Wuyi guo*), 206
knight-errant tales, 61

Kong Qi, 209
Kublai khan, 210

La Dame aux Camélias, 93
Lady Bao of Si (Baosi), 68
"Lady in Green, The," 235–36
Lady Yu, concubine of Xiangyu, 42
Lai Zhishao, 152
Lau Yap-yin, 97
leaves: as a literary motif, 55
legal cases (*gong'an*): as a literary genre, 21, 130; and love stories, 130, 153, 196, 201
Levy, Howard, 11, 14
Li Bo, 79
Li Changling, 173, 176, 248, 266
Li Gefei, 131
Li Gongzuo, 68
Li He, 79
Li Jianguo, 7, 51, 76, 107, 147, 149, 159
Li Kezhuang, 173
Li Shiren, 6
"Li Wa's Story," 43, 54, 62–68, 75, 89, 91, 93, 112, 114, 115, 151
Li Xianmin, 12, 21, 25, 116, 159
Li Yi, 79–81
Li Yue, 36
"Li Zhangwu's Story," 89
Li Zhi, 268
Liang Shanbo, 1–3, 189–191, 235, 267
"Liang Yiniang," 192–95, 204, 255
Liaozhai zhiyi. See *Liaozhai's Records of the Strange*
Liaozhai's Records of the Strange (*Liaozhai zhiyi*), 6
Lin Daiyu, 225
Ling Mengchu, 6
Liqing ji. See *Collected Love Stories*
liqing xiaoshuo. See love stories
"Little Ghost Wife, The" (*Gui xiao niang*), 191
Liu Fu, 12, 107, 113, 114, 154
Liu Kairong, 69

Liu shi zhuan. See "Miss Liu's Story"
Liu Zai, 173
Liu, James T. C., 202
"Love between Zhang Dao and Liang Chu, The," 178
love stories (*liqing xiaoshuo*): ambiguity in, 139–41; bibliographic classification of, 13, 20–26; circulation of, 12–13, 113, 149–50, 158–59, 186, 189–90, 241; constructed settings found in, 85, 88, 115, 117, 150, 205, 258; emplotment of, 87, 262–63; historical development of, 11–12, 263–64, 269–70; as a literary corpus, 8; and moral orthodoxy, 111–12, 121–22, 136, 149–50, 234, 242, 248, 250, 255, 257, 261–62, 266–67, 269; and social critique, 247–48; social status of, 19; suspicion as a theme in, 228; and symbolism, 217, 229, 240, 243; tragic conclusions of, 93, 144, 178, 188, 202, 225–27, 233, 241, 242–43, 255, 265–68
Love. See romance
loyalty: as a literary theme, 38, 42–43, 80, 92, 134, 142, 171, 177, 248, 257, 258. See also women
Lu Jiuyuan, 174
Lu Jun, 173
Lu shi zashuo. See *Mr. Lu's Miscellaneous Records*
Lu Xun. See Zhou Shuren
Lüchuang jishi. See *Stories from a Green Lattice Window*
Lüchuang Xinhua. See *New Stories from a Green Lattice Window*
Luo Manling, 52, 75, 87
Luo shen. See *Goddess of the Luo River*
Luo Ye, 12, 21, 81, 105, 179, 191, 192, 195, 202, 264, 278n64

Luoyang mingyuan ji. See *Famous Gardens of Luoyang*
lyric poetry (*ci*), 100

Ma Zhou, 159
"Madam Sun's Story," 119–22
"Madam Zheng," 172–74
magistrates: as arbiters of romantic happiness, 130, 198, 201–2, 258
Mai fen er. See "The Powder Seller"
"Maiden of Huyin, The," 176
male: anxiety about female chastity and fidelity, 45–49, 62, 70, 72, 79–80; castration anxiety, 173; conjugal fidelity, 171–73, 175–76, 226, 236, 243–44, 250, 255, 260, 264–65; fantasies about women, 57; Gaze, 75, 90, 239, 248, 263; lovesickness, 180–81, 184, 192, 207, 225, 265; moralistic attitude of vis-à-vis women's sexuality and fidelity, 52–53; patronage, 48; protagonists dying for a lover, 144, 179, 185, 186, 188, 189, 224, 226, 233, 234, 243–44; sexual competition, 45–49, 53, 61, 90, 122, 244; sexual desire, 71; social bonding, 45–46, 62, 81, 201–2, 233; sympathy for women's sexuality and fidelity, 53
Manchus, 161
Maps and Facts of Siming in the Qiandao Reign (*Qiandao siming tujing*), 190
marriage, 54, 61, 91, 114–15, 119, 126, 257–61; arranged, 67, 92, 117, 196, 244, 258, 264; arranged versus freely-chosen, 42, 93, 258–59; of courtesans, 111–12, 166, 167, 247; of cousins, 61, 98, 168, 293n7; and financial considerations, 103, 230, 260–61; freedom of choice in, 61, 73, 109, 128, 192, 194, 198, 200, 204, 258, 260, 264, 269; gender equality in, 173–74, 207, 255, 265, 266; between ghosts and humans, 235–36, 257; inter-class, 67–68, 114, 168, 202–3, 247, 260; inter-ethnic, 209, 212; levirate, 211; predestiny in, 54–57, 58, 109, 168, 192, 194, 196–98, 201, 204, 258–59, 264; sanctity of, 141, 157, 166, 171–72, 196, 198, 204, 260; as a means of social mobility, 98; as a means to neutralize the subversive nature of love and sex, 114, 123, 127, 149, 192, 194, 200–1, 204, 255, 257, 264; successive-generational, 168, 194, 197
"Martyr's Grave, The," 248–51
"Master Wang and Miss Pei both Hang Themselves," 178
"Master Yang Accompanies Xiunu on a Journey," 178
matchmakers, 196
May Fourth period intellectuals, 5, 13
McKnight, Brian, 202
McMahon, Keith, 173
medium-length short stories (*zhongpian chuanqi xiaoshuo*), 213–14, 255, 270
Mencius, 98
Meng Chengshun, 224
Meng Jian, 74, 75
Mengliang lu. See *Dream of Liang*
merchants: as protagonists in love stories, 87, 143–44, 244, 270
Minggong shupan Qingming ji. See *Enlightened Judgements of Famous Magistrates*
Minor Documents from Sanshui (*Sanshui xiaodu*), 51
Miscellaneous Stories from the Green (*Zhiqing zashuo*), 13, 163

"Miss Fu Jiulin," 178
"Miss Liu's Story," 46–50, 86, 90–91, 233
"Miss Ren She's Story," 16
"Miss Zhang Elopes with Star Brother at Night," 195–98, 204, 239
Mongols, 95, 162, 209; marriage customs of, 211, 251
Mr. Lu's Miscellaneous Records (*Lu shi zashuo*), 186
Mu, King of Qin (Qin Muwang), 9, 184
Mudan ting. See *Peony Pavilion*
Music Bureau, 33, 34

Nabokov, Vladimir, 129
Nai Deweng, 22
Nanchu xinwen, 178
Neo-Confucianism, 98–99, 112, 135, 143, 146, 160, 162, 166, 173, 198, 261–62
New Stories from a Green Lattice Window (*Lüchuang Xinhua*), 12, 128, 147, 178, 185, 186, 193, 198
New Stories Told while Trimming the Lampwick (*Jiandeng xinhua*), 13, 212, 213, 267
Nongyu, 184–85, 288n41
"Nun from West Lake Convent," 186–87

Ouyang Bin, 159
Ouyang Xiu, 111, 262
"Ouyang Zhan," 73–75, 186, 265
Oxherd and Weaver Maid: the legend of, 9–10, 84, 86, 197

Palace of Everlasting Youth (*Changhen dian*), 268
"Palace of Twin Fragrance," 252–55
"Pan Yongzheng," 181–85

parents: as arbiters of romantic happiness, 61, 117, 184, 258; as obstacles to romantic happiness, 227
"Passing Floral Purity" (*Guo Huaqing gong*), 36–37
patriotic literature, 176
Peach Blossom Fan (*Taohua shan*), 268
Pei Xing, 12, 13
Peony Pavilion (*Mudan ting*), 243, 268
performing arts, 210–11
Plum in a Golden Vase, 131, 213, 229, 268
poetry: social function and status of, 111
"Powder Seller, The" (*Mai fen er*), 275n32
Precious consort Yang, 36–38 *passim*, 68, 84; and stockings, 42
predestined meetings: as a literary sub-category, 24
"Preface to the Ballad of Ai'ai," 147–50, 266
presented scholar degree. See *jinshi*
Prince Huo, 80
professional elite of the Song dynasty, 95–96, 162
promises kept: as a literary sub-category, 24
prototype theory, 25–26

Qiandao siming tujing. See *Maps and Facts of Siming in the Qiandao Reign*
Qin Chun, 107, 113
Qin Gui, 161, 176, 177
Qin Muwang. See Mu, King of the Kingdom of Qin
qing, 22–23, 114; cult of, 104, 268–69

qinggan: transformation brought about through qing, 20, 21, 23, 58, 186
Qingshi. See History of Affection
Qingsuo gaoyi. See High-Minded Conversations behind the Green Lattice Window
Qu You, 212, 230, 235, 244, 252
Queen Mother of the West (Xi Wangmu), 9, 10, 82

rare liaisons with immortal women: as a literary sub-category, 24
Record of the Entertainment Bureau (Jiaofang ji), 33
Record of the Listener (Yijian zhi), 15, 18, 270
Record of the Northern Quarter (Beili zhi), 33–34, 151, 238
Recorded Stories from a Green Lattice Window (Lüchuang jishi), 198–99
Recording the Splendor of the Capital (Ducheng jishi), 22
Records after Ploughing (Chuogeng lu), 213, 266
records from the red-light district: as a literary sub-category, 24
Records of the Heated Room (Xuanshi zhi), 189
Records of the Hidden and Visible Worlds (Youming lu), 275n32
Redacted Records of Housemaids (Shi'er xiaoming lu shiyi), 147
Reflection of Things at Hand, 146
remarriage, 98, 122, 145, 171, 173, 176, 221, 236, 248, 250, 251
"Ren's Story" (Ren shi zhuan), 39–46, 86, 92, 112, 135, 235–36
Renzong, Song dynasty emperor, 101
retribution: as a literary prototype, 154, 156, 176

reunion: emplotment of, 87, 232; examples of, 46, 59, 163, 168–70, 174, 232; as a literary prototype, 24, 67, 76, 162–63, 177, 232–34, 264, 267
Revenge. See retribution
Richardson, Samuel, 237
Romance Master of the Imperial Capital. See Huangdu fengyue zhuren
romance, 233, 234, 257; culture of, 11, 67, 73, 88, 114, 128, 156, 158, 184, 207, 255, 258, 264, 265, 268; destiny in, 236; freedom of choice in, 58, 61, 81, 86, 87, 91–92, 206; and scholastic/bureaucratic success, 118, 225; as a short story category, 21. See also marriage, women
Rouzer, Paul, 8–9, 11, 35–36, 46, 263
"Ruiqing," 159

san gang. See three cardinal relationships
Sanshui xiaodu. See Minor Documents from Sanshui
scholar-beauty romances: as a literary genre, 3, 198, 255, 270
scholar-officials (shi dafu), 29, 97; and interaction with courtesans, 34–35, 74, 80, 81, 83, 88, 99–100, 150–51, 156, 167–68; as protagonists in love stories, 87, 225; social status of, 153, 203, 230, 244, 259
seafaring: as a literary theme, 204–7
"Second Sister Zhang," 105–6
separation of lovers: as a literary theme, 232–33, 243, 267–77. See also Oxherd and Weaver Maid
sexual hygiene techniques, 81
sexual intercourse, 123, 140, 257; among debased people, 44; with

immortal women, 85–86; subversive nature of, 58, 67, 81, 91–93, 127, 134–35, 200–1, 255; sympathetic treatment of, 113, 124, 126–27, 134, 136
sexuality, 257. See also sexual intercourse
Shanghan jiushi lun. See Treatise of Ninety Manifestations of Cold Damage
Shen Jiji, 39
Shen Liao, 16
"Shen Zhenzhen Marries Liu Huaigu," 185–86
Shenzong, Song dynasty emperor, 102
shi dafu. See scholar-officials
Shi'er xiaoming lu shiyi. See Redacted Records of Housemaids
Shimin. See townspeople
Short History of Chinese Fiction (Zhongguo xiaoshuo shilüe), 5
short stories: bibliographic categorization of, 13–14, 20; perceived authenticity of, 14–18, 75, 136, 144; reception of, 75, 87, 180, 194, 232 33, 241–42; of the Song dynasty, 5, 6–7, 269–70; of the Tang dynasty, 4, 5; transmission of, 14, 19, 45, 68, 75, 212. See also love stories
Shouxin, Yin dynasty king, 71
Shun, legendary king, 145, 198
Shuofu. See Unverifiable Stories
Sima Guang, 131
Sima Xiangru, 10, 144, 184–85
social mobility, 257, 269; and class boundaries, 106, 166, 202–3, 259; and the examination system, 98, 106, 143–44, 153; and lower-class women, 106, 109–10, 166, 247; and upper-class women, 101, 103, 120, 122, 166, 170, 230

Song Meidong. See Song Yuan
Song Yuan, 213
sorcery: as a literary prototype, 21
stave-wielding: as a literary prototype, 21
Stephen Owen, 11, 47, 73, 86, 88, 89, 260
Stories from a Green Lattice Window (Lüchuang jishi), 13
"Story of Aiqing," 244–48
"Story of Courtesan Yang," 89
"Story of Cuicui," 230–35, 267
"Story of Distant Mist," 141–44, 177, 227
"Story of the Western Chamber," 68
"Story of Twin Peaches," 131–37, 204, 239–40, 266
"Story of Wang Kui," 76, 154–59
"Story of Yingying," 16, 68–73, 76, 91, 92, 128–29, 135, 215, 242, 258
storytellers, 8, 21, 87, 99, 259, 260–61, 269, 274n13
storytelling, 12, 14–15, 21–22, 44–45, 234: and gender, 8–9; popular versus elite, 18, 144
Su Shi, 16
Su Shunqing, 147
suicide: as a demonstration of male romantic devotion, 224, 246–48, 250; pacts, 177–80, 226, 234, 265; in response to the Mongol invasion, 209, 245, 251; as a means of salvaging sexual immorality, 134–35, 202, 204, 224, 251, 266
Sun Qi, 33, 34–35
Sun Xun, 278n64
swordsmen: as a literary prototype, 21

Taiping guangji. See Extensive Records from the Era of Supreme Peace
Taizong, Tang dynasty emperor, 159

"Tale of the White Ape," 15
"Tan Yige," 107–15, 123, 127, 149, 269
Tan Zhangbi, 22
Tang Poems and Their Narrative Context (*Tang shi jishi*), 186
Tang shi jishi. See *Tang Poems and Their Narrative Context*
Tang Xianzu, 243
Tang zhiyan. See *Gleanings from the Tang Dynasty*
Tao Gu, 16
Tao Zongyi, 213, 248, 266
Taohua shan. See *Peach Blossom Fan*
Tess of the d'Urbervilles, 127
"The Woman who Sold Hammers," 159
"They Became a Couple Thanks to their Brother and Sister," 191–92
three cardinal relationships, the (*san gang*), 38
Tian Xi, 262
townspeople (*shimin*), 144
trade: during the Southern Song dynasty, 204
Transmitting the Remarkable (*Chuanqi*), 12
Treatise of Ninety Manifestations of Cold Damage (*Shanghan jiushi lun*), 181
Trousseaus Recorded with a Brush (*Bilian lu*), 13
"Tryst of Crimson Silk," 76, 139

union stories: emplotment of, 87; examples of, 55, 59, 109, 115, 139, 148; as a literary prototype, 24, 76, 139, 148, 239, 260, 267
Unverifiable Stories (*Shuofu*), 213

van Gorp, Hendrik, 25
"Vice-Censor Zheng," 53–54, 55

"Villagers Kill Barbarian Horsemen," 176

Wang Anguo, 102, 103
Wang Anshi, 102, 259
Wang Dingbao, 32
Wang Mingqing, 13, 163, 168
"Wang Qiongnu," 101–105, 114, 122
"Wang Xie," 206
Wang Yangming, 268
Wang Yi-pei, 263
"Wang Youyu," 89, 159, 181, 241
Wang Yuran, 262
Wang Zhi, 16
Wang, Richard, 4, 224
Wei Chishu, 178
widow: chastity, 150, 251, 257; fidelity, 145–48, 244, 255. *See also* women
wish-fulfillment: as a literary theme, 44, 50, 54, 88, 89, 119, 166, 234, 261, 264, 267. *See also* male fantasies
women: as accomplished poets; 110–11, 117, 239; agency of in love stories, 85, 91, 115; arranging marriages, 196–97; and chastity, 112, 121, 127, 134, 136, 142–43, 150, 171, 227–28, 244, 247, 257; as cross-dressers, 191; dying for a lover, 52, 93, 144, 202, 225, 233, 234, 238, 240, 241, 257; as faithful wives, 244, 246–47, 251, 260; fidelity of to one man, 44, 72, 80, 244, 250, 255; as foils for androcentric values, 50, 62, 91, 128, 137, 166–67, 263; and immorality, 66, 72; inheritance rights of, 102–3; languishing in adversity, 104, 110, 111, 148, 166, 170, 239; and lovesickness, 181, 184, 188, 265; martyrs, 251, 266; portrayal of in love stories, 75, 90, 102, 107, 119,

Index | 329

125, 129, 131, 140, 163–64, 184, 206, 230; resisting alien invaders, 176–77, 266, 299n59; as a reward to men, 46–47, 93, 115, 117, 122, 171, 203; and romantic fidelity, 52, 80, 255, 260, 262, 266; as romantic heroines, 72, 80, 180; violence against, 103–4, 233; as virtuous paragons, 43–44, 65–67 *passim*, 111–12, 121, 134, 149, 176, 224, 247, 262–63. See also *femme fatale*, courtesans, concubines, dowries, suicide
Wu Zimu, 22
Wu, emperor of the Southern Qi dynasty, 190
Wushan shen. See Goddess of Witch's Mountain
"Wushuang's Story," 59–62, 67, 90, 91, 93
Wuyi guo. See "Kingdom of Black Apparel"

Xi Wangmu. See Queen Mother of the West
Xia E, 159
Xiangyu, king of the State of Chu, 42
Xiao Chi, 225
Xiao Shi, 184–85
xiaoshuo: as a literary genre, 14, 20; as a popular literary form, 270–71; status of, 18–19. See also love story
Xie An, 190
Ximen Qing, 229
Xinbian zuiweng tanlu. See *Drunken Man's Talk*
Xu Ji, 147–50 *passim*
Xu Shuwei, 181
Xu Xuan, 17
Xuanshi zhi. See *Records of the Heated Room*

Xuanzong, Tang dynasty emperor, 33, 36–38 *passim*, 83
Xue Diao, 59

Yan Lingbin, 238, 242
yanfen: as a short story category, 21–22
Yang Guifei. See Precious Consort Yang
Yang Guozhong, 36
Yang Shi, 173
Yang Su, 232
Yangzi fayan. See *Exemplary Sayings of Master Yang*
yanhua: as a literary category, 22
Yao, legendary king, 198
Yijian zhi. See *Record of the Listener*
"Yiniang of Taiyuan," 174–77
Yiwen ji. See *Collection of Strange Tales Heard*
You xian ku. See *Dalliance in the Immortal's Den*
You, Western Zhou king, 68, 71
Youming lu. See *Records of the Hidden and Visible Worlds*
"Young Mr. Ding's Pleasant Dream," 115–19
youwu, 68, 71. See also *femme fatale*
Yu Ji, 13
Yu Shiu-yun, 7
Yuan Cai, 158
Yuan Xie, 174
Yuan Zhen, 16, 68
Yunchao bian. See *Cloud Nest Compilation*
Yunxi youyi. See *Conversations beside Cloud Creek*
Yunzhai guanglu. See *Comprehensive Record of the Cloud Studio*

Zadeh, 25

zalu: as a literary genre, 23
zazhuan: as a literary genre, 20
"Zhang Cong'en's wife," 105, 122
Zhang Du, 189
Zhang Fu, 173
"Zhang Hao," 124–31, 204, 261
Zhang Ji, 16
Zhang Jin, 190
Zhang Jun, 173
Zhang Junfang, 12, 15, 20, 25, 185
Zhang Shicheng, 230
Zhang Shizhen, 157–58
"Zhang Youqian," 191, 198–204
Zhang Zai, 98, 146, 171, 173, 225
Zhang Zhuo, 150
Zhao Dingchen, 143
Zhao Gou, Song dynasty emperor, 95, 161
Zhao Guangyin, Song dynasty emperor, 95, 96
Zhao Mengfu, 210
Zhao Shixian, 152
Zhao Weiguo, 278n64
Zhen Zishu, 242
"Zheng Huaigu," 185–86
"Zheng Jun's Wife," 173
Zheng Xi, 236
Zheng Zhenduo, 5
Zheng Zhizhen, 18

zhiguai: accounts of the paranormal, 12, 274–75n24; as a literary genre, 10, 14, 21–23 *passim*; and the love story, 26–27 *passim*, 45, 57–58, 61, 91, 153, 156, 188, 225–26, 267; narrative conventions of, 139–40, 144, 235
Zhiqing zashuo. See *Miscellaneous Stories from the Green*
Zhongguo xiaoshuo shilüe. See *Short History of Chinese Fiction*
Zhongguo xiaoshuode lishi yanbian. See *Historical Changes in Chinese Fiction*
Zhou Dunyi, 98
Zhou Mi, 157, 178, 179
Zhou Shuren (Lu Xun), 5, 7, 87, 99, 269
Zhou Zizhi, 176
Zhu Xi School of Learning, 162
Zhu Xi, 98, 99, 121, 143, 145–46, 162, 166, 173, 193, 261
Zhu Yingtai, 1–3, 189–91, 234–35, 267
Zhu Yuanzhang, 230
Zhuge Yibing, 262
Zhuo Wenjun, 10, 144, 184–85
Zhuyin jishi ji. See *Bamboo-Dwelling Maverick's Collection*
Zuozhuan, 194

www.ingramcontent.com/pod-product-compliance
Lightning Source LLC
Chambersburg PA
CBHW031434230426
43668CB00007B/528